To D

From

Grandma Walker

*The Woman You Want to Be*

# THE WOMAN YOU WANT TO BE

MARGERY WILSON'S

COMPLETE BOOK

*of*

CHARM

J. B. LIPPINCOTT COMPANY

PHILADELPHIA AND NEW YORK

Library of Congress catalog card number 42-13943

PRINTED IN THE UNITED STATES OF AMERICA

# AUTHOR'S NOTE

It has always been a conviction of mine that a service which grows from a need has a substance and integrity, and therefore lasting value. The three courses in this book grew from the questions, the problems and the needs of actual women. Almost every word in it was originally written to some real person in answer to her specific need. Years were required to knit them into a pattern of development.

There are truth and proved effect, living results back of its every sentence. Does it fill a need? Does it work? This has been my only test of an idea, an exercise or suggestion. Nothing has been included just because it was pretty or was thought to be a good idea. And when experience has proved some fresh approach to be better in any instance, the change has been made.

So this is a living book, not a compilation of static ideas. It is a pulse of the modern woman's progress in personal achievement. PART ONE of this book, the First Course, was written as a general tonic covering all phases of personality. Enthusiastic clients asked for more— so the Advanced Course—PART TWO—was given them in time. Then on the request of many students for a course devoted entirely to Conversation, the course which is PART THREE of this book was created— all from the practices and ideas that had proved their worth many times over.

The work has spread to the far places of the earth. Still, as a living service in keeping with the times, publication in book form seemed the best way to meet the demands of today—to remove any stumbling block of price.

The hope of any nation lies in the personal qualities of its individual members. In dealing with essentials that make for personal strength and healthy minds these courses become more important than ever as our way of life is challenged.

To refresh, to encourage, to inspire, to build from within—this is the service offered in this book—to you—and to our country.

# CONTENTS

## PART ONE

## *The Cultivation of Charm*

7

PART TWO

*Refinements of Charm*

# PART THREE

## *Effective Conversation*

# CONTENTS

## Postscript

*The Woman You Want to Be*

# *Introduction*

Dean Swift once suggested that a nation could raise a great deal of money by taxing beauty. He suggested that the amount would be triple if women should be allowed to rate their own charms and pay accordingly. He said also that the tax would be cheerfully paid. I wonder.

Certainly women today would have every reason to rate their beauty high. Almost every woman is—or can be—lovely-looking. And having conquered her problem of appearance, she seeks other fields. The prettiest and the smartest women aren't the happiest, she notes. Nor do they always snatch the matrimonial prizes.

Actually beauty is becoming so common that a homely woman, if she has a degree of charm, enjoys a great distinction and therefore a kind of advantage. Hardly one of the most successful women is beautiful by old standards. *Pleasing to see.* Haven't you, for instance, heard someone remark of a homely woman, "She's not good-looking but after you get to know her, you regard her with such affection that she seems very pleasant to see. She has a kind of beauty after you know her." Which reminds me of a truism of Ouida's—"Familiarity is a magician that is kind to ugliness, but cruel to beauty." Charm is kind to both.

Fashions in personalities change as surely as do hair-arrangements—each era bringing to the fore those qualities and effects that seem most admirable under the circumstances. Yet the breath of charm, that warmth and flowing quality in her presence is always needed, always appreciated—and always possible. For charm is timeless and will lend that quality to any woman who has it.

In this book is the effort of a lifetime, three separate courses, the gleanings of long and earnest effort through experience, observation and the trial-and-error method to find just those ways by which women—and men too—though the book is addressed to women—may develop and express that "perfume of the soul"—their own charm.

Age cannot wither nor custom stale its infinite variety. Catch phrases and publicized glamour blow away like a mist and leave charm, classical and enduring, a challenging citadel for us to climb. Shall we start?

*Part One*

THE CULTIVATION OF CHARM

# CHAPTER ONE

## *First Essentials*

### 1. BELIEVE IN YOURSELF

How do you do? May I come in? Into your mind and heart and life—for several weeks? No, it doesn't take that long to find and use many points that will add to your pleasure and effectiveness—however great it may be right now.

In this first chapter are suggestions, usable immediately, that you will enjoy putting into practice. It will amuse you, at least interest you, to see the response you will get.

But if you will give the whole work your careful attention, you and I can accomplish almost a miracle—mental and social ease, the miracle of inner peace and outer attractiveness that can mold your world nearer to your desires.

No, you need not believe in me. This is not a "faith" cure. But, *it is necessary for you to believe in yourself*—not the little self you see in the mirror, with eyes and nose and elbows—but your inner self, that is part of, and in contact with, the forces and purposes that put you here. Of such belief are modesty, poise and un-self-consciousness born. Little by little you find this strength.

*CHARM LIES IN COMPLETE FORGETFULNESS OF SELF.* Yet, I defy anyone to forget herself when she knows she is inadequate. Without a heroic effort, a woman can no more send her thoughts away from herself and be un-self-conscious when she is unequal to a situation than she can forget a blister on her heel when it is smarting.

Tetrazzini, the great opera star, was a working girl, elevated to a glittering career through her great voice. She shook with fright at the thought of facing a bejeweled audience of wise and worldly people

On one occasion she paced up and down backstage in an agony of shyness. The stage manager, the prompter and the conductor had all tried to quiet and console her, to no effect. Finally her maid, a woman of firm character, said to her sharply, "It is not you, Madam, but your voice that has brought these people here. It is rude and vulgar of you to introduce yourself into the matter in this childish way. If you will just give them your voice and not your ideas of social distinctions this evening I'm sure they'll all be grateful—not to mention your poor company." Tetrazzini flushed with embarrassment over the stinging truth, but lifted her head, squared her shoulders and started toward the center of the stage. She sang magnificently, and tumultuous applause rewarded her.

Once back in her dressing-room, her maid, with happy tears in her eyes, said, "Ah, Madam, you were superb. And weren't you frightened at all? Not even a little?"

"Yes," said the great soprano, "I was—and once it almost overwhelmed me. It was all so quick, though. I couldn't remember what you had said to me before I made my entrance. But I knew that if I didn't think of something else at once that I should run from the stage."

"And could you think of something else at a time like that?" pressed the anxious maid.

"Yes, I did," the star explained, "I couldn't cope with the scene before me, so I switched my mind entirely—and just when I sang that last highest cadenza I made myself believe that I was basting a leg of mutton in the kitchen oven. I felt right at home again and those notes came out so easily." Then she and her maid had a good laugh over how the distinguished audience would have felt had they known that their august presence, their gowns and jewels had suddenly changed into a kitchen for Tetrazzini.

*A MENTAL TRICK.* That is a little mental trick that all of us can use almost as soon as we get the hang of it. To put yourself at ease, in moments of panic for any reason—make believe that the scene before you is a familiar one—and that the seemingly formidable person or people before you are just kindly neighbors with whom you are as comfortable as you are in your old slippers.

We want genuine poise and real control—but since these require a little time to build within ourselves, we shall find a few little defenses convenient—a sort of first aid.

*DON'T WORRY TOO MUCH ABOUT SELF-CONSCIOUS-NESS.* Even self-consciousness can be charming at times, especially if it shows as a kind of becoming modesty. Some women pretend it when they don't feel it, because they know that a little of it brings a rush of sympathetic feeling and chivalry from men.

*DON'T STRUGGLE SO HARD.* A girl I know, when she feels self-consciousness stealing over her, makes no effort to stem it. Not for her a public struggle. She just admits it with a deprecating (and quite graceful) shrug and says something like, "It's because you're all so impressive"—or "My job is too big for me, I guess."

This girl has, consciously or unconsciously, come upon one of the greatest secrets of poise—nonresistance—*just the knack of letting the waves of life wash over one.*

But the worst of self-consciousness is that when its grip is a real one, we may lose our sense of perspective and go to extremes, either of vivacity or austerity, to compensate for it. It causes us, from sheer tension, to trip into tactlessness, or extravagance, or loud laughter. And sometimes it makes us too eager to please.

*YES, WE CAN BE TOO EAGER TO PLEASE,* so eager that we become diffident. Let's dispose of this attitude, which is so damaging, with one fell swoop, with a truth that is like a lodestone.

Drop the idea of trying to turn in a perfect performance yourself, for should you achieve it you would excite only envy. Give rapt attention and appreciation to other people. Rivet your attention on them and it will not matter greatly what else you do. But there is a joker about that truth.

*IF YOU TURN YOUR MIND FROM YOURSELF BECAUSE YOU DO NOT LIKE THAT SELF YOUR PERSONALITY WILL BE WEAKENED.* In other words, your move away from yourself will be an escape with all the elements of cowardice. But if you rivet your attention and appreciation on other people and their affairs because you like them and are honestly interested in them—

then you truly enlarge your powers through the breadth of your interests.

*SELF-RESPECT OR -CONCEIT*. Here we come head-on into the difference between self-respect and self-conceit. We do not want to be like the young naval officer, who in Lincoln's presence kept watching himself in a mirror and postured this way and that. Lincoln remarked, "You must be a very happy man."

"How is that?" said the officer, without taking his eyes from his reflection.

"Why, because," replied the President, "you are in love with yourself and you haven't a rival in the whole world."

*MAKE PEACE WITH YOURSELF*. The estimate of the self is an important point to be settled before much progress can be made in self-development. The ideal is to make your peace with yourself—and then turn away, at least with a comfortable acceptance of yourself, to the other matters of living.

"I doan' aim to do no quarrelin' wid mahse'f. De good Lawd knows mah rights and mah wrongs. I'm gonna 'tend to mahse'f, but I ain't gonna do no hatin'." Such was the wise and philosophic remark of my colored nurse when I once asked her if she liked herself.

The matter is not so easily turned aside. Glib phrases do not satisfy our wonder about ourselves, nor our craving to fit ourselves comfortably into a mental niche. We want an attitude toward ourselves that will help us in our everyday life—provide us with aplomb enough and modesty enough to keep us on an even keel.

*PRETEND POISE, THEN GET IT*. Many women have acquired the manner of poise and inner self-acceptance but they may be just as sufferingly uncertain as the most inexperienced girl. Outer gestures help—but only inner solution is certain. We shall have both.

*A DEFINITE METHOD*. So, it is clear that we have a definite program to follow, a planned structure to build. Originally these chapters were called lessons and were sent to clients one at a time, a week apart. For, while certain gestures can be acquired at once, it is in the week by week building and coaxing and unifying of all the different parts of your personality into a well-coördinated whole that you will have the most telling result.

## 2. MAKE PEOPLE LIKE YOU

*START TODAY TO MAKE PEOPLE LIKE YOU MOF*
ideas you can use at once are given you first, not just to sh
how easy it is to heighten your effectiveness, but also to begin to build
the suggestion of success deep within you. We may learn a bitter lesson from our failures—and profit by avoiding those same mistakes—
but our confidence feeds upon our successes.

*A CHARMING COMPLIMENT.* The gracious woman never says,
"You look lovely in that hat!"—which gives the hat a lot of credit.
With charming tact and greater truth, if the hat is becoming, she says,
"That hat looks lovely on you," which implies that the wearer makes
the hat effective. From this remark alone you can govern hundreds of
expressions in your daily conversation that will add to your pleasing
effect on others, who in turn will call you charming. Will it be flattery? I do not think so. Do you know that every human being feels a
sense of failure at some point? Thus, no matter what glittering circumstances surround the individual she struggles secretly or openly
with a sense of inferiority. When you lift this feeling from her, even
temporarily, you help her back to self-approval—you help her back to
full possession of her powers. This is a noble thing to do.

*CALL OUT THE BEST IN OTHERS.* To call out the best in
people by speaking only to and of that best draws them up to your
standard. The most successful hostess knows how to draw out her
guests until they become superlative expressions of themselves. Such a
woman quickly gains the reputation of being charming. Her guests go
home in a glow of happiness and sing her praises thereafter. *The same
elements of personal appeal that attract socially will influence others
to seek you in business or at any other point in life!*

*EASY THINGS FIRST.* So begin to gather small successes and
note the effect upon your poise.

*Today,* make more people smile at you by your interest in them. By
night you should have at least a dozen small triumphs in your collection. Add your own ideas to the following suggestions:

1. Keep your voice soft, lilting and uncomplaining.
2. Neither think nor speak one single criticism.
3. Write a gay little note to someone. Perhaps a soldier?
4. Let not one sigh rise from your heart.
5. Spend five minutes looking at some beautiful scene. Realize that you do not have to buy beauty to possess it.
6. Sing! While the water runs if you want to drown the sound of it—but sing for your soul's sake and your charm's sake.
7. Pour a strong mental germicide on any lurking self-pity—realize that you are privileged to live in momentous times and must be worthy of them.
8. Love something—if it's only a rag doll.

In other words, get a more pleasant "rise" out of everyone *and yourself*. Just this alone will make life sweeter, more responsive, more helpful and noble.

*REALLY BE A WOMAN.* Get about the business of *being a woman,* encouraging, nourishing, healing, even in gay little ways. And you'll find that men will find you! And so will other people!

Just having a kind heart and possessing many virtues are not enough for successful living. Even you are not pleased with yourself, if you have not fitted your virtues into a becoming frame of gracious and agreeable actions. On the other hand, the mere gestures of charm will wear thin and collapse.

*ENERGY FEEDS CHARM.* On the rock-bottom practical side the first requisite for successful living is *energy*—physical energy, mental energy, spiritual energy. Today there is little excuse for ill-health for the average person.

Vitality plays a large part in being pleasing. Even one's glance has a striking quality if there is energy behind it. Besides if one has only energy enough for oneself there is no strength left to be gracious and unselfish. Weakness breeds selfishness, not intentionally, but surely.

*A MIRACLE IN HEALTH.* After an absence of several years from California I returned and in the lobby of the Ambassador Hotel there stood a woman I used to know as a whiny, always-under-par person. But here she was now, straight, vital and sparkling. After our greetings I asked her about the wonderful change in herself and her answer was—"I just made up my mind to be healthy—and started doing all the things that would make me so. It wasn't easy at first, because I'm naturally lazy and always putting things off. But I got my determination going, and the rest was easier. It certainly was worth the effort. I feel like a million dollars." She looked it.

*SO, HAVE A CHECK WITH YOUR DOCTOR AND DENTIST.* Read health magazines, if you can keep a normal, middle-of-the-road attitude toward them. A well-balanced diet rather than trick ones is preferable.

*GET A GOAL.* To add to that vital look take up a *cause* that brings the light of enthusiasm to your eye and animation to your whole being. In other words, get a direction. Almost all listless, negative people just trickle around through the days without any particular direction or reason. *You must have a goal*—whether it is a husband, the learning of a language, a civilian defense job, or public service. A cause in which you firmly believe will do more to strengthen and *unself* your personality than all the pretty gestures ever taught.

But for truth's sake it must be added that the pretty gestures used wisely will help you further your cause. The better the combination of genuine worth and feminine wisdom, the greater are one's chances of success. And write this on your heart—

*NO CYNICAL WOMAN IS HAPPY—OR ATTRACTIVE.* In spite of all the so-called realists, the materialists and those who attribute all attraction to sex alone, history keeps recording beautiful romances and splendid devotions. Why shouldn't we strive toward the ideal in romance?

In our own times, we see eyes soften whenever we think of General Pershing's devotion to Mrs. Pershing during her life and afterward to her memory. Her gentleness and bright spirit he held in his strong hand like a flower—and never forgot its perfume. And golden weddings are not rarer than they used to be.

*CERTAIN PERSONAL QUALITIES WIN DEVOTION.* I know many more happily married couples than the other kind. I'm sure they do not live in constant ecstasy or even in constant harmony —but there is a strong cord of beauty between these people, too strong to snap under ordinary strains—which holds them to the best of them-selves. Mrs. James Polk, Mrs. Zachary Taylor, Mrs. Dwight Morrow are just a few among many prominent women whose marriages have been devotionally romantic. These splendid women all had more than worth—they had charm.

*EXPRESS THE JOY OF LIFE.* History does not record the worth of Cleopatra, but it does tell of the devotion she enjoyed, especially that of Marc Antony. Her flair for the dramatic and the voluptuous, while wholly out of key for modern women, still expressed an intensity and a joy of living that we should express in our own way.

None of us can go sailing toward the man of our choice with purple, perfumed panoplies, golden oars and enchanting song. But most modern men, not having much use for a perfumed sail, would prefer what we can produce, (1) a refreshing, faint odor of spicy cologne, (2) a soft throaty laugh, (3) sparkling eyes and (4) some pleasant, not too exhausting, talk. *With these for a start, any woman can make a bit of history for herself.*

*ACT AS THOUGH YOU HAD A GUEST.* Do not get into a strain of self-consciousness over trying too hard to be charming at once. Try, instead, to imagine that a very welcome and helpful guest is visiting you for these weeks. Keep yourself, your house and your mental attitude just what you would have it if you were entertaining a charming guest for that time. Of course, you would not try to be somebody else. You would be your own best self. You would not subject a guest to an embarrassing exhibition of family quarrels, would you? Then, quarrel with no one, not even yourself, for ten weeks. You would not let a charming guest see soiled garments, hair that needs a shampoo or neglected fingernails, would you? Then attend to these matters religiously.

You would try to provide entertainment for a charming guest, wouldn't you? Improve your conversation by bringing up subjects that draw out others. Choose the most tongue-tied member of the family and find ways to make him talk. This is wonderful practice. If you can stimulate the interest of a thirteen-year-old boy who is reluctant to express himself, you have the "makings" of a charming conversationalist—one who might be able to draw out a silent partner at a formal dinner, or a picnic.

Later I take you through a large tea-party from arrival to departure, smoothing personal and social difficulties. The casual and unpiloted contacts at a tea present the problems of meetings and conversation like those of our everyday experiences.

## 3. WOMEN MUST PRESERVE CIVILIZATION

In the coming years we shall need all the charm, aplomb and philosophy we can get. It will be the task of women to keep the world from despond, to keep the prettier gestures of good living going with meager materials. Women will not, for many a year, perhaps never, descend again to the status of toys.

Under the most trivial, be-curled, made-up and high-heeled female, there burns a desire to be needed. All the talk of our softness and laziness will fall meaningless, blunted on the fact that close under the surface of the average woman is more strength of purpose (when it isn't needed, it's called stubbornness), fierce loyalty (no lioness can equal it), and capacity for comradeship than the modern man even suspects.

In commending Clara Barton, one-time clerk in the Patent Office, who started the American Red Cross, Lincoln said of women in general, "If all that the poets have ever said or sung, were gathered together to describe the women of America during the war, it could not do them justice."

*WE WILL NOT FAIL IN ANY CRISIS TO COME.* To the extent of our ability we will keep the torch of civilized home-life burning. We will create beauty with whatever materials are at hand. We will fan the embers of kindness in a brute-stricken world. We will hold high the gains of learning, decency. We will heal and hold to our hearts the wounded, the young, the needy. It is a great privilege to be a woman today.

That we may do it better than ever before, with less waste and pain and time, I humbly offer the method given in this book, a method that has helped many women to find themselves, to heighten their general effect, to bring them content and usefulness.

And now that you have begun with me this study of yourself, we are already well into it, for, as Horace says, "What's well begun is half done!" "The beginnings of all things are small," says Cicero—so let's go on and see what fine discoveries and skills lie ahead for you.

*Every exercise or instruction given you accomplishes more than one object. Each of them starts a whole train of better effects. You may not always be aware of just why you are asked to do some certain exercise, but you will understand the result!*

## 4. REALIZE YOUR BEST SELF

The expressions of charm are endless. One sees it sometimes in a vivacious girl who can keep a crowd in roars of laughter. But wouldn't you say that the quiet girl who walks off with the season's brightest beau has charm too? We must conclude that charm cannot be confined in any rule or particular set of actions. Charm lies in being yourself—*your best self*. Charm lies in complete naturalness. But no woman *can* be natural when she is bound up in self-consciousness and other inferiority notions or confusions.

*THE REAL YOU* may be a person you have never met. How do you know what your *nature* is until you relax your tensions and let that *real self* out? Until you give that self a chance to express through the worthy instrument of a graceful body—and a mind sufficiently at peace with itself to concentrate on other people? Even though you are a thoroughly sophisticated woman it will do you good to inspect your foundations.

Let's find out about *you*. Do you really know much about yourself —that inner, deeper self? This is the self that must be liberated if you would have the attractions of charm. You are an independent entity— choosing how you will think, how you will react to anything that happens to you. You are on a journey of self-realization with no apparent limit to your possibilities. This is not meant to be merely cheerful or vague encouragement. The Bible states, "It does not yet appear what ye shall be." So infinite is the possibility that lies ahead of you!

But whoever or whatever you are, you have your own set of obstacles to overcome, either inner, or outer, or both. Your strength of personality is enhanced by the way you carry your special burden. It may be something small or something great. The size of it is not as important as the opinion you have of yourself because of it.

Unruly hair can wreck the lives of some women because they have come to believe that if they only had obedient lovely hair the world would be theirs. Now, naturally we want to solve as many of our problems as we can, ignore a portion of the rest—and carry the balance with poise and courage.

DEFY YOUR DIFFICULTIES. Why don't you turn the table on your troubles? They have been challenging you, threatening you with defeat. Why not try challenging them? Go on in spite of a handicap. Never say "I cannot be a charming person because of this or that."

Once at a party I met and talked to a plain-looking woman who enchanted me by her wit and warm presence. I gave her my card and asked her to write her name and address on a card so that I could get in touch with her again. She pushed my pen away gently saying, "Will you please write it? You see, I am blind."

You and I with our supposedly great obstacles should sink to our knees in reverence and awe before the sublimity of the courage of those really handicapped.

And always know that though life seems to challenge us harshly at times, to make us eat bitter bread with the sweet, nevertheless, if we will stop wailing and look we will see a sustaining arm across our shoulders, the arm of infinite love—and if we listen we can hear a voice whispering, "Deep within you is the strength to bear anything, the nobility to be willing to do so, and the intelligence to create magnificently and beautifully, come what may."

EVERY OBSTACLE AN OPPORTUNITY. Wasn't it St. Francis who tried to help an emperor moth after watching it struggle to free itself of its cocoon? The moth thus spared its terrific effort, instead of spreading his gloriously colored wings and flying away, drooped and died. His wing muscles were not developed and thus he could not fulfil his inherent beauty and his destiny. Through application and effort and constant trying we develop the control and the ability to fulfil the beauty inherent in our pattern.

*DON'T BE MERELY SWEET.* There is a great affinity between strength and beauty. It is mere prettiness that is perishable and fragile. Women who are merely sweet remind one of that spun-sugar candy sold at carnivals. It looks like something, and it has a whiff of sweetness in it, but the minute you try to eat it, it all goes to nothing in your mouth. And such is the fate of the too-sugary compliment.

## 5. UNIFY YOUR ENERGY

Lillian Russell was very clever at arranging her life so that she had a minimum of harassing confusion and discord. When asked how she could keep her face so smooth in spite of all the problems of her life that she was unable to push aside she replied, "I have learned to draw down a blind that shuts out distracting sights and sounds, and I have put a sign on my mental door that reads—'Only the serene and the lovely can enter here.' A thousand voices call me away from my resolve but I have trained myself not to hear them. I hold myself together, not by straining against the winds of life, but by always sitting calmly in the center of the storm where there is no wind." In this way she gathered and held her forces.

You and I are very complex people. We share the heritage of the race in tangled backgrounds, transplanted emotions, and the battle of the higher and lower tendencies. The pressure of the demands made upon us by ourselves, life and other people tends to add to our confusion. And it is this inner and outer chaos that scatters our forces and weakens our personalities.

*DON'T THROW YOURSELF AWAY.* We are diffused. Part of our energy is going off in one direction and other desires or inner conflicts are wrenching parts of it away on other lines. Not that I am interested in having you save your energy! But I do want you to get it all together—see what it is composed of—and then use it for some fine purpose or accomplishment.

Those of us who are unnoticed, ineffective—and even those of us who should accomplish a great deal more than we do—fall below par because we permit the strength of our personalities to "leak away" in unguarded *waste!*

You will stop these leaks and direct your unified energies into charming expression that is telling and effective.

## 6. LEARN HOW TO RELAX

To clear the decks for better judgment in all matters, we take our first step toward poise by learning to relax.

Whatever may be the real self trying to express through flesh, fears, mental tangles, mannerisms and odd notions that make up the average human personality, our best approach to it is first through relaxation. Let go!

Relax so that your energies can flow together harmoniously. Relax so that your forces of mind and spirit can bring you your natural vitality—so that your body may become supple and graceful—and renewed by a free-flowing bloodstream. Relax so that the pattern of your real self can begin to be revealed. Relax so you may get a new mental picture of whatever is weighing on your mind, and poise will gradually replace confusion and tension.

*LAUGH AWAY AWKWARDNESS.* Things go a bit awkwardly at first—naturally one must become accustomed to thinking and planning in certain ways. But after a *few repetitions* your actions become automatic, which is what we really mean when we say "natural." And you really can have a great deal of fun. When you are awkward, laugh at yourself. Few of us laugh enough. Let's not go after charm grimly, with determination. Think how funny you'd look with a set expression on your face while you said something intended to be tossed off airily. We should relax and just "go with the wind" for a few days and see what happens. Make a high adventure of the conquest of charm.

*OF COURSE YOU CAN RELAX!* You can relax if you will just remember a few things. *First*—no one can take away from you anything that is rightfully yours, and anything that isn't really yours can't be kept anyway. So relax. *Second*—you are an important part of a vast, wonderful universe and were put here to express, else you wouldn't be here! *Third*—there is no need for you to explain, justify, or argue, even with yourself, about your importance. Just take it for granted—as you do the air and sun. Stop trying to make yourself important in artificial ways. Real importance is quiet and the force of its presence is felt by everyone. You do not have to try to *make* yourself important. *You already are!* The thing that *you really are* is grander by far than what you are trying to be. So relax and just *be* for a while. It can't hurt—and no one knows what lovely and interesting pattern of your real personality may flow out into expression.

*DON'T PUNISH YOURSELF BY COMPARISONS.* Never mind comparisons! Never mind environment! What does it matter if Susy's second finger nail is longer than yours, or that your hair is straight, or that your Mother is rich and spoiled—or poor and petulant? Never mind anything except the fact that *you are going to exercise your divine right of choice* and become the kind of woman who can rise above every seeming obstacle and be delightfully charming.

Let every external consideration fade from your mind while you take your relaxing exercise. Let Johnny and Mary and Annie and those ungrateful people across the street, and all of the world be pushed aside for a time.

*EXERCISE 1.* At least once a day—oftener if you can arrange it—take the following relaxing exercise. First drink a full glass of water. Then lie down on the floor where the hard surface compels your back into a straight line. A smart figure and an aura of importance are part of the reward of a good posture. This exercise helps your posture and accomplishes a number of other things as well. After you are sure that your entire framework has been straightened out on the floor—usually after a couple of minutes—get up and lie on your bed or couch without a pillow. Beginning with your feet, mentally tell your muscles to relax, your insteps, your ankles, your calves, your knees, your thighs, your hips.

Now start to lift (toward your head) the muscles of your entire body. Lift your lower abdomen—think on up your body slowly lifting—your stomach, your heart, your lungs—the whole chest cavity—

stretch your neck out and push your head as high as it will go. Take three deep breaths, inhaling and exhaling slowly—then relax with your body and head in this lifted position, and breathe naturally. Mentally inspect every muscle of your body to be sure they are all relaxed—even your ears and your eyelids, your throat and your little finger.

*SHUT OUT THE WORLD FOR A FEW MINUTES.* Now that you are fully relaxed *let your mind wander to some pleasant spot,* preferably where there is a little brook or stream. Let yourself realize that the stream of consciousness flows through you bringing refreshment, healing, new ideas, fresh inspiration, bubbling humor and a cleansing, revivifying point of view. How smoothly and gracefully water flows! See it in your mind's eye.

From now on your own movements will be more smooth and flowing and rhythmic. *See how the water meets an obstacle.* That gay, ceaselessly flowing little stream glides around the rock in its path. When it falls into a depression, it quietly fills up, then flows over the top and is on its resistless way again. It doesn't strive and struggle. It moves by the law of its own being—quietly and ceaselessly, without resistance—but nothing can stop it—for long!

Of course, one does not have to think about a brook. I tell you about it because I like to when I take this exercise. There is a great lesson in it—one we should try to learn for *smoothness of thinking and moving.* When we have attained inner peace and smoothness we shall find it expressing outwardly to our own and our friends' delight.

*A VICTORY IN SELF-MANAGEMENT.* After you have tried it several times, you will be able to lie completely relaxed for ten or fifteen minutes—not moving a single muscle. This will be a victory in your new program of self-management. Your body will obey you more perfectly. Your mind will become better disciplined. If you already have an obedient, perfectly postured body and a trained mind, it will do you good to take the exercise anyway just to make assurance doubly sure.

Do not be impatient. In a very short while you will feel yourself to be in control of your own forces and it will tend to build your confidence. The French have a proverb, "Petit au petit, l'oiseau fait son nid," meaning, "Little by little the bird builds his nest." I wish there were some magic words I could say over you, but there is no abraca-dabra charm I can give you. But I can promise you that you will be delighted with swift improvement from the very start if you will be faithful in doing what I ask you to do. Remember that there is no magic in any one exercise, thought or sentence. It is the accumulation of fine reactions that builds *charm* within us.

*EXERCISE 2.* While you are relaxed is a splendid time to take another important exercise. It is a great help in "getting acquainted with yourself." Please put aside temporarily your own opinion of it and DO IT. That is all I ask.

*CALL YOUR OWN NAME ALOUD.* Go somewhere alone every day, at the same time, if possible. Sit down and be quiet. Now repeat your own name over and over again—aloud. It is truly an odd experience, but a valuable one. It will seem at first as though you are talking to a stranger. Gradually your name will seem really to belong to you—but you will have a different attitude toward it.

(If you are married, or if there is any question in your mind as to what name you should use, choose the one that seems to identify you most clearly to yourself. This may be just your first name—or it may be all your names. Only you can choose.)

Your name belongs to that inner you we have been discussing as well as to the outer physical self. As you speak to your complete self, you will realize that deep within you *there is a point of contact be-tween your individuality and the source from which you come*—you will see that you derive from it the stream of your consciousness and that it feeds and nourishes you when your contact is kept cleared.

*YOUR SOURCE.* You are not alone in the world. You are, in the depths of your nature, connected with *all there is.* Your name is the designation of your point of consciousness in the *whole* of life. Thus, you have access to your source. You share in *everything.*

You perceive how important it is to be an individual expression of such immensity. Why should you ever again be afraid of anything or anybody? You are needed, or you wouldn't be here. You are delegated as an independent individual to experience life and to realize *all of it* you can possibly encompass. When you call your name, you define that important individuality. You contact the *source* that pours itself into the person of that name. You sense the importance—*the importance of life in you.* Your head goes up proudly. Your eyes become clear, steady and unafraid. *You* are *you!* And that is a wonderful thing to be.

*THIS PRIDE AVOIDS CONCEIT.* As a part of a mighty and wonderful *life* you are not the author of yourself and therefore the credit is not yours. While you are pleased and proud to be thus honored you nevertheless feel humble before the majesty of the force in which you share. You are grateful, modest in your grasp, and hope to use well the opportunities and the blessings before you. You are not you as a separate, self-proud little tempest in a tea-pot. You are proud of being a vessel, a listening and obedient vessel of *life.* Therefore all that you can claim for yourself is but a compliment to the Allness that produced you and nourishes you.

*PRIDE IN "BEING" GIVES NATURAL DIGNITY.* When we do not have this deep, basic pride of self, we try to make up for it by external bragging, defenses, and super-sensitiveness that are unbecoming. But when we have a true, justified, natural pride in *being,* there is no urge to be conceited and unbecomingly self-assertive. A fine and natural dignity blossoms in our personality and we begin to be an impressive person—one whom people listen to.

## 7. THE IMPORTANCE OF SPEECH AND VOICE

*HOW ABOUT YOUR SPEECH?* Your voice and the way you talk can, when they are pleasing, cause your hearer to think you are attractive. Many of the so-called "tricks" of charm, known and used by continental women, are but clever uses of the voice and conversation. One of them is this:

*DO NOT DROP YOUR VOICE AT THE END OF A SENTENCE.* It spoils that delightful feeling of continuity that keeps talk running on its own momentum. It seems to stop talk abruptly unless your vis-à-vis has a great impulse to talk anyway! But shy or uninterested people simply will not cope with the finality of a dropped voice.

If you happen to find it hard to have sustained conversations, try keeping your voice up at the end of a sentence. There is a charming graciousness in doing so, for it seems to say that you do not think *your* remarks are the last words to be said on the subject. It prevents you from seeming opinionated. How men dislike an opinionated woman! No one really likes her! To keep your voice up sounds as though you are interested in other people's ideas. The subject is still open!

*BE CAREFUL OF VOICING OPINIONS. Speaking of opinions, the charming woman does not air hers very freely.* The crude woman is eager to let you know what she thinks of every matter, person or object that bobs up. She comments on every passing item—even in public, as you may have noticed. Not only is it bad taste for her to be so desperately interested in her own reactions and opinions—but she throws away the precious aura of reserve and mystery that makes a woman attractive.

The great value of "small talk" is that it furnishes a protective barrage over the *sanctum of our inner thinking*. Not that one is to misrepresent her opinions—but merely to withhold her private convictions somewhat from the public gaze. Her mind should not be a shop window for every passerby to gaze into. Her opinions should be as private as her toothbrush—unless there is a very good reason to state them.

*ONLY TWO OPINIONS AN EVENING.* A clever woman I know says that she allows herself only *two stated opinions* during an evening—just so that people won't think she is weak-minded and hasn't any! The rest of the time she refuses to be pushed crudely into a corner where she must needlessly pass as a critic or a master mind.

Under direct questioning she says, "Mr. Jones put it so well when he said . . . ," or "Well, it certainly seems that the opposition is in a difficult spot but, on the other hand, don't you think that . . . ?" And she never says *all* she thinks about anything. She finishes most of her own remarks with either a question, the words "—and yet" or "—on the other hand." Needless to say, conversation around her is spirited and usually lasts hours and hours. People love to go to her house. She is regarded as an "intellectual" but she really doesn't know much about anything except human nature!

CONCLUSIONS END CONVERSATION. Remember that *delightful conversation does not consist of conclusions* but is an interested and interesting or amusing examination of a subject, whether it is a puppy or a political issue.

If you are the shy type of woman who *never* states an opinion, make it a rule to force yourself to express two during an evening. We do not strive to become expert at evasion—we merely wish to have a certain mental decency that shrinks from too much crude exposure. We do not want to be "hard to know." But we do want to appear always to have *something withheld* that makes the other person willing to dig to find it. Hold yourself and, at least, some of your opinions as precious and you will find other people will approach you with more delicacy. The moment this happens *you take on a greater value* in their eyes.

This is as good a time as any to warn you about being too delicate, however, and too nice. A woman who thinks too much about her own niceness is enjoying a one-man show in which no one else can possibly be interested for long. To have the thoughts circling affectionately around the self is just as bad for the personality as self-blame and criticism. One of the main objects of this book is *to free you from the necessity of either praise or blame*. Only then can true poise come to dwell within you.

SPEAK CLEARLY. The too-nice voice, that is widgy-widgy with affectation, is a sure sign of self-consciousness and lack of faith in oneself! Above all you do, speak in a forthright, downright manner and voice. A compliment given with brief, direct downrightness of voice and facial expression will sound sincere, while the same words spoken through a smirk in self-conscious affectation, that seems to hope too desperately to please, is almost offensive with the impression of insincerity—and therefore fails to give pleasure. I'm sure you have often noticed that the person with a blatant speech is preferred to the one who speaks mincingly, almost in a "refined" whisper. This person is simply not tolerated in this modern world of increasing directness. However, *the cultured woman has a relaxed, musical voice only if she has assurance.* As you build your inner strength you will find your voice improving automatically, for the voice is one of the best barometers of mental attitudes and emotions.

*MAKE YOUR VOICE FLEXIBLE.* The beauty of the natural voice cannot be heard when the throat has been squeezed, throwing its sound into a nasal twang. To restore the free, mellow quality to your voice, relax the throat muscles by yawning. Then push the lips out as far as possible (no, it isn't pretty) and say "oo-oo-oo." Do this exercise ten times twice a day. Yes, you're right. If you do it properly you'll sound like a fog-horn off the coast at night. But what's the difference if you're going to get your voice down into a lovely tone, into a relaxed elasticity that enables you to express many shades of emotions and ideas with it.

When we are sure that your voice is a controlled and flexible instrument, I shall show you how *to make it do wonders for you* in expression. Until your next lesson, however, do take the yawning exercise and let your head roll from side to side with your throat completely relaxed—just let go of it!

*VALUE WORDS.* When you speak this week, try not to attack words so abruptly as most of us usually do. Words are beautiful, meaningful things and should not be jumped on with both feet. Think how dreadful it would be if we had no words! Realize their great value to happiness and culture—then approach them more gently. An appreciation of words will lend more force to your own speech, for oddly enough people put the same interpretation on you that you put on yourself.

The person whose speech is all but meaningless, tiresome and ineffective is the one who throws words around with no regard for their sound or meaning. Even a comedian must weigh his words for their every value. With just a little study we can learn a few uses of speech that will bring surprising results. The right word at the right time always "accomplishes that unto which it was sent."

While I seem to be giving you a great deal to do in this first chapter, you will find that a *few minutes* devoted to each exercise is sufficient. I certainly do not want you to go about all the time watching yourself and listening to yourself. As soon as your conscious mind takes up the definite direction of your whole personality and expression, your subconscious mind carries the work on even though you may not be thinking of it.

## 8. THE IMPORTANCE OF PHYSICAL PRESENCE

*LOOK AS WELL AS YOU CAN.* Here we've been talking about your inner self, your importance in the universe, and we've gone over suggestions for easier and more effective conversation that you can use immediately. But we must not imagine that your appearance has nothing to do with your personality. While it is true that personality can overcome any deficiency in beauty, it is also true that we can make our bodies help our personalities greatly. And *we should use every attribute we possess* to build up our best effect. We should use everything we have!

As a rule, people see us before they even hear us—and their first impression of us is greatly influenced by what they see. Certain positions of the body definitely indicate to the beholder our state of mind, health and character. Throughout the book there is a profitable study of these attitudes that is interesting and amusing. It is possible to bring forth a response in other people without speaking a word. *It is possible to sit silently and gradually have everyone who is talking address his remarks to you!* Such is the significance of posture and movement. This I give you in CHAPTER TWO.

*AVOID JERKY MOVEMENTS.* A controlled body and graceful movements are necessary if you would keep from interrupting the flow of thought and personality that makes you effective. When your movements are jerky, abrupt and uncoördinated they snip the flow of charm in graceful action just as though you had wantonly cut a silken cord with a butcher knife. Staccato movements offend the senses. It is as though your personality were trying to speak above a steel riveter. We do not seek the exaggerated grace of a dancer, but that of the "lady of the manor."

Grace, as you can readily see, is not the adding of flourishes. It is really *economy of movement*. To secure this, we have numerous ways by which we defend ourselves against the possibility of awkwardness.

One of these is the "trick" of pausing in a doorway for an instant on entering a room anywhere, any time. It gives you an opportunity to show yourself as a framed picture if you have dressed for the occasion. But, more important, you use that brief instant to locate your hostess, to see who is there and to determine which way you will go. Sophisticated men and women say, "Let me see a woman enter a room and I will tell you what she is."

So few women walk well or seat themselves gracefully. (Do you?) All too often they amble loosely up to a chair and waddle around unbecomingly like ducks before they plop down. And one ridiculous move can dispel the most carefully built-up illusion of grace. All women trained for public appearances have been taught the proper way to be seated and how to walk.

*HOW TO WALK. Have you a full-length mirror?* Good! Place a chair a few feet in front of it so that you can watch yourself sit down. Your friends must look at you every day. You should be willing to watch yourself a few times. Start with your back against the mirror and go toward the chair, walking on one line—not on two like a streetcar! Your heel should touch this imaginary line at each step, the toes pointed slightly outward.

*HOW TO TURN AND SIT.* When your forward foot is right at the chair (the back foot must be a normal step straight behind the front foot) turn completely around *on the balls of your feet* without moving out of your tracks. If your left foot is forward, turn to the *right.* If your right foot is forward, turn to the *left.*

This movement will place your back to the chair and you can see in the mirror that your feet are in a graceful position. Without moving your feet, rest your weight on your back leg and let yourself down into the chair. Isn't that simple and lovely?

All you need do now is to pull the forward foot a little nearer after you are seated—and there you are, graceful and poised. *Never be seated when your feet are side by side.* It gives a squarish impression. *Always keep one slightly in advance of the other.*

Now, as you try it over again, do not divide it into three movements—getting to the chair, turning around, then sitting. *Put these three actions all together in one smooth continuous movement.* You perceive that you have eliminated about five usual movements in being seated.

*YOUR FEET WHEN SEATED.* As you sit before the mirror, try your feet in different positions, just to avoid monotony. After being seated a few minutes, suppose you cross your ankles. Then, if your left ankle is the underneath one, move your feet over to the right. You will observe that the line of your legs is elongated and that the line of your whole body ends in a point—the toe of your right shoe. (Or the whole movement can be to the left if the right foot is the underneath one.)

It's such a satisfaction to *know what you're going to do with your body—what you're going to do with your feet!* Now it's settled once and for all, and you know you'll always look well when you sit down, that you will not be awkward or conspicuously graceful. Your mind is more free for other things and other people. All uncertainty as to just how you will move and how you will look when you do is gone forever! You will always *know* that you look like a lady when you sit down.

*YES, YOU MAY CROSS YOUR LEGS.* Of course *it's quite all right to cross your legs,* but we shouldn't be uniformly dependent upon it for comfort—like monkeys who must grasp at something. You have never seen a queen cross her legs. Wouldn't she look funny sitting on a throne with crossed legs? All of which proves that simple and powerful dignity lies in a *balanced poise* of the body.

*SIMPLICITY—NOT FANCINESS—IS FORCEFUL AND DRAMATIC*—in speech, in manner, in dress and in movement. Against the background of strong simplicity the accents of your own individuality show forth to advantage. But if I must try to get at *you* buried in confused colors, too many veils, ruffles, gadgets and broken lines, I'm not going to have a very strong impression of *you.*

As these chapters progress we will seek for you a supple, willowy straightness—not a ramrod stiffness. You will be fascinated and surprised as you learn more of this. It is really *very easy* to be pleasingly effective.

*FORGET YOUR BODY.* The little work we do with the body is really to dispose of it nicely in order for your personality to be tran-

scendent. *This is as important for a young girl as for an older woman.*
When you accomplish this purpose, you will be surprised to note that
you make friends more readily—and *keep them.* You will have appealed to them mentally and subconsciously and your friendship will
not be based on obvious, physical things.

## 9. THE IMPORTANCE OF BREATHING

*BREATHING AS A MAJOR AID.* There is another point to discuss now—and that is the matter of *breathing.* We do not want to be
mysterious about it—but the fact remains that a great deal of importance attaches to breath. Since breath is the most necessary item on the
physical plane, we feel justified in assuming that it is the symbol of
vital spiritual force. Certainly breath is life—and our control of our
breathing represents, to a great extent, our control of our own lives.
Truly!

Our emotions and our attitudes are easily read in the way we
breathe. It is common knowledge that the breath is short and gasping
when we are under the strain of hurry, anger, fear or uncertainty.
Thus it is easy to understand that at all times we breathe according
to our inmost thoughts and feelings.

*FAITH BUILDS CONFIDENCE.* Until we have some faith in
life and ourselves, our breathing is necessarily shallow and uncertain,
making us seem unimportant and insignificant to other people. There
are those who say that personality has an "odor" apart from that of
the physical breath. A novelist has written of the "peculiar odor of
failure" about a character in her story. It is not necessary to go to such
extremes in order to realize that all of us give off *certain* emanations
of various kinds that, in the aggregate, determine our effect on other
people. The impression others gain from the way we breathe is extremely important. Since proper breathing is healthful and adds greatly
to the sum total of personality as well, let's spend more than a few
minutes daily in making ours what it should be.

Keep the shoulders down and relaxed. Breathe deeply, evenly and
rhythmically. As a radio receives only what it is tuned into—let us see

that we breathe in from the atmosphere what we wish to have from it. It is a good mental exercise to think, while you breathe, that you are attracting splendid things from the universe—faith, love, friendship— and above all, the opportunity for service.

*CHEST UP FOR MAGNETISM.* We must have plenty of room in our chests for the extra air we are going to need to vitalize our bodies and personalities. We must have more oxygen—and we must have somewhere to put it—so—*raise your chest!* Almost all wall-flowers have low chests and breathe shallowly! Watch it yourself and you will see that this is true. Now, please understand that there is no magic in a raised chest—its value lies in the train of feelings, thoughts and reactions that it engenders both in you and the beholder.

*WALL-FLOWER OR WINNER?* It is not only the wall-flower who has a low chest—but also a great majority of those people who think that life has not played fair with them—who seem to be victims of circumstances—and often "enjoy" ill-health. There is no doubt that the low-chest posture is the position of emptiness, of defeat and failure.

*SO RAISE YOUR CHEST!* People are not interested for long in a person with "defeat posture." The world rightly gives its applause and interest to the person who seems to be gallantly and expectantly facing life. A raised chest indicates both these attitudes.

In moments of confusion—when panic may overtake you—when you want to gather your forces for concentration on a piece of work —when you need a moment in which to become poised—stop—smile quietly—raise your head and your chest and take one or two long deep breaths. The difficulty will unravel almost at once!

*A HINT IN BEGINNING TO TALK.* Before addressing an audience, if you will take a moment to look pleasantly over your audience while you breathe deeply to catch the rhythm of the assembly, they will receive you better. Before asking for a job—before you must face someone you dread or want especially to please—at the entrance to a room—at any time when you want more quiet force than you seem to have at the moment—breathe deeply with raised chest and chin—and you will at least appear poised—usually, you actually will be poised.

## 10. CONCLUSION

We have covered in these pages a handful of the simpler, more obvious forms of charm. Necessarily, this chapter is of an introductory nature, to prepare your mind for my treatment of the subject. Later chapters are more definitely concerned with the specific, practical applications of the principles involved. There are many things that contribute to the impression you make—how you walk across a room, how you stand, what you do with your hands, how you accept and make introductions, how you listen, how you laugh, your choice of words, the modulation of your voice, how you take leave of your hostess, how you apply for a position, and so on ad infinitum. These and hundreds of other points are blended into their proper place in the book where they are needed for your rounded development. Most important is the radiation of *yourself, from within.*

*GIVE YOURSELF TIME.* A few weeks is a very short time in which to bring your personality to a splendid fulfilment. While you are using the immediately applicable ideas I give you, other development is taking place within you. And this time is really necessary for its fruition.

For this reason, I want you to resolve with me here and now that you are going to go straight ahead with each chapter until the Courses are completed. It is unfair to look at a mason's scaffolding and imagine that the house, when completed, will look like that. Some of the things you will do are but scaffolding that enables you to reach the higher points of charm—scaffolding which must be removed before the finished product is ready.

You must take every suggestion just as it is designed to be taken or you will have an uneven result. But if you proceed from week to week in the way they are scientifically arranged for your benefit, you will reap their every value—and when you have finished you will understand *why* I asked you to do it this way.

In this chapter we have merely opened the door and I have given you some interesting ideas that you can put to use at once, so that you will not be impatient. I must not give you enough to confuse or tire you—and yet I want to press you a little—I am so eager for you to have the benefit of these teachings at the earliest possible moment. But don't forget that—*this is only the beginning.*

*PUT FIRST THINGS FIRST.* It is a dangerous thing to put personal power into hands that are not prepared to handle it. This is why I strengthen your poise, lead you out of that clammy sense of inadequacy that shrivels your personality and consumes your magnetism—why I seek to kill every vestige of your inferiority complex—before giving you the ornaments and "tricks" of Charm. Then your relation to others and their reactions to you are *under your own control.*

*ALL THE CHAPTERS TEACH WHAT TO DO AND WHAT NOT TO DO ACCORDING TO THE CONCEPTS OF THE CULTURED, SOPHISTICATED WORLD.* They contain the technique of graciousness and tact in conversation. Graciousness is the glowing fire of charm that draws everyone to its warmth.

Great actresses and other prominent women have, through these teachings, added a finishing touch to their already delightful personalities. Others have come like ugly ducklings to be transformed into poised, charming individuals. No matter at what point you now stand in personal development, I congratulate you on your decision to improve yourself.

Few people are *born* with the ability to project themselves into the hearts of others—to inspire love and loyalty. But many of them have *learned,* just as they have learned to walk—and just as easily!

A clever friend showed me that the very letters of the word "charm" tell the mystical story of its power in the individual's life. Thus:

*Arm* against *harm* with *charm!*

This is more than just a play on a word. It holds a deep truth that strikes home with a vital message.

Today the world needs and wants charming women more than ever before. Humanity is heart-hungry for the grace and beauty of Charm. They will pay for it eagerly in money, honor and affection. So, here and now, you and I, seriously, yet joyfully, dedicate ourselves to the delightful task of placing your personality where it expresses the beauty and loveliness of the Charm you want—and *can have!*

# CHAPTER TWO

## *Like a Few Strokes of Magic*

### 1. CREATE THE ILLUSION OF BEAUTY

Dean Hole loved his garden, especially the fine roses he grew. Every visitor was urged to "come out into the garden and see my roses." One day a lovely woman was brought to call, a woman whose beauty of mind and heart gave glamour to her face and body. The Dean looked at her a few moments and then said, "Come out into the garden. I want my roses to see you." What young woman wouldn't give her head to have that said of her!

Perfection in a human being includes the inner and the outer. But the effect is felt from the free and simple coördination between the two. Often a lovely mind expressed in easy, natural movement will give an impression of great physical beauty, whether or not it actually exists.

The famous coach of Pavlowa, Madame Hatlanek, herself once a great dancer in Russia, grew to be enormously fat in middle life. Seated in a chair, her plump hand grasping a cane, she would roar her encouragement or her insults to the dancers she coached. One rainy afternoon in Chicago, she was devoting herself to Pavlowa, but the great dancer was unable to please her. No one but a great star would have taken the drubbing she was getting. Finally she threw her hands up in despair and cried, "But, Madame, I am doing my best! What is the matter?" The tyrant Hatlanek spat back at her. "You are lying! You do not do your best. You have been reading the newspapers about the great Pavlowa and you have got yourself separated from the spirit of the dance. You are thinking of Pavlowa. Now get out there and think only of the spirit of motion and beauty and meaning,

Let it pour through you until every part of you flows into the other part. It is only the spirit of beauty flowing through the earth and you as a tiny part of it that is great!" She pounded her cane and roared. "Take fire again, Pavlowa, with expressiveness that burns away your self. Now dance!" And Pavlowa danced, slowly, then faster, then madly. Tears crept over the fat old cheeks of Hatlanek as Pavlowa sank finally at her knees, exhausted. "That is what it means to be Pavlowa," the teacher whispered. "To lose yourself in what you do!" Pavlowa was not a beautiful woman, but so perfect was her liquid grace and the perfection of that all-important *coördination* that she created beauty while one looked.

If form alone enthralled, crowds would gather before the mannequins in store windows. We want all the beauty of form we can get, but knowing all the while that living animation and expression of movement, voice, and ideas are the deciding factors. Sculptures are interesting only as they express ideas.

It takes strength and muscle to support beauty in the human body—just as it does in character. What is more beautiful than a perfect pole-vault? What more graceful than the slow-motion view of some of our hardier sports? A man's or a woman's body, at the peak of efficiency—all of it coördinating to some one idea—is a thing of beauty. Grace is efficiency of movement.

Children and athletes are the most graceful of people. The natural coördination of the athlete, the natural movement of joy and health as expressed by a child, all point the way to us who would make the most of our own bodies.

Every man and woman has some outstanding feature which can make him or her pleasant to look at. Just as one attribute can make people say, "Isn't she or he charming?"—so can one physical perfection delight the eye. You needn't be a Venus or an Adonis to be considered good to look at. If you are well-groomed, move with efficient grace, and have one better-than-ordinary feature, you can be handsome in the beholder's eye.

Never mind what you *haven't* in the way of beauty. What *have you?* No one is so bereft that there isn't something to start building on.

Then build up your good features to overshadow the bad or the indifferent ones.

Is your chin weak? Then play up your eyes and your hand-clasp to convey the strength of your personality.

Are you too short? Then carry your chin up so that as you look at taller people you will not seem to be appealing to them. The eyes looking up when the chin is down seem supplicating. Few of us have just what we would like in the way of physical equipment.

The eyes of Alexander the Great did not match—one was black and the other green. One of Lord Byron's eyes was larger than the other, and he was lame besides. Charles Lamb had one hazel eye and one grey-speckled eye. Yet these gentlemen seem to have left quite an impression of their charms as well as of their abilities.

Napoleon was in the habit of saying, "When I require a man for head work, I always take one with a long nose, if I can find one who has the necessary qualifications. He breathes boldly and freely, and his brain, heart and lungs, are cold and clear. In my study of human nature, I have almost invariably found that a long nose and a good head are inseparable."

Suppose you have good hands or nice hair—or *could* have them. Almost anyone can acquire these two good points. Good teeth, good skin or a fine forehead—any one of these alone can constitute a reputation. Perfection is quite uninteresting.

With good posture and good voice we can minimize our physical deficiencies so that they will fade from our own and other people's awareness. When fear of our wants threatens our new resolves we can remember the system of Orpheus, god of poetry and music. Remember the island of sirens that lured men to their death, those same sirens against whom Ulysses had his men fill their ears with wax and tie him to the ship's mast so they might sail by in safety? Orpheus, instead, decided that he would drown the sound of their voices by making sweeter music on his ship. So with us, when other voices would blur our good efforts, we must just redouble the song of our own chosen way.

## 2. BE YOURSELF

To have strong personalities each of us should make this agreement with himself—

1. I am *willing to be myself*. (The Divine pattern is surely worthy.)

When J. P. McEvoy was preparing an article about Walter Winchell, he asked the famous columnist: "What do you want to do next, Walter? What do you want to be?" "Why," said Winchell, "I want to be a columnist—like Walter Winchell." This is not necessarily conceit. It is a fine acceptance of his appointed place and talents.

2. I am *willing to be wrong*. (No living person turns in a perfect performance. If I stumble in trying to advance I am within my right. I shall stare down anyone who challenges that right.)

To withhold trying, lest one be ridiculous or awkward, is to be so conceited that one thinks he must be perfect at all times. Shrug off your failures or inaccuracies and go serenely ahead!

*DEFEND YOURSELF FROM YOURSELF ONLY*. But don't make the mistake of making too much fun of yourself while you stumble, or fall short of the mark. This point is one of the most important we shall ever know. Your words fall upon the ears of others, somewhat analyzed by their minds *at the time,* so they may laugh with you when you make fun of yourself.

But no one's subconscious mind is equipped with analysis and logic. This great mental stomach takes whatever is dropped into it, *minus* the explanations, and works that into the fabric of thought. So, over a period of time, the impression gathers, owing to your own words, that you are a light and inaccurate, somewhat ridiculous creature.

If you feel that you simply *must* say something amusingly derogatory about yourself, then add, just as amusingly, something of a good quality. If the mood is light, one will be as appropriate as the other.

For instance, if you should insist, though I hope you won't, that you are a "perfect fright," then add, "but I'm a marvelous cook (or dancer)." Such compensating remarks will tend to keep a balance in that unanalytical subconscious that, in the end, will pass judgment upon you. Naturally, all of this talk is smiling and gay.

In brief encounters, the derogatory remark may be the only impressive one. Then, if you were sufficiently airy and beautiful, or helpful or entertaining in some way, it might be considered a virtue—but this realm of suggestion is dangerous ground.

*CAN YOU TAKE IT?* However, should you be the butt of a joke or placed by circumstances in an unfavorable light, it is not necessary to defend yourself. These quick, cheap little self-defenses often keep us from the larger, more casual elegance of "being able to take it." If you have trained yourself not to mind being wrong from your own point of view, you can stand up under other people's unfavorable estimate and often disabuse their minds by your own relaxed attitude of ignoring it and letting it roll off your back. When you are under fire, your attitude is noted, admired or condemned.

Don't let circumstances or wily enemies trip you into an unbecoming attitude of being over-disturbed, thrown off base, pressed in a corner where you must strike out. Whenever you feel such an emotion gripping you, just don't say anything, if you can catch yourself in time and just look pleasantly curious and silent, as though expecting your critic to give more interesting opinions and information. You may, if you can do it without sarcasm, invite him to express himself further—ask a question about a fine point.

## 3. LEARN HOW TO MANAGE YOURSELF

If you can control yourself, you have just opened the door to controlling others. Always remember that nothing, no issue, however burning, is as important as your inner serenity. True, many charming people have been hot-headed, but it was seldom in self-defense that they raged.

"Better conquest never canst thou make than arm thy constant and thy nobler parts against giddy, loose suggestions," wrote Shakespeare.

But to try to aggrandize oneself in argument is one way to defeat one's purpose.

*QUEEN VICTORIA'S TEMPER.* When Queen Victoria was little more than the bride of her beloved Albert, there were the usual quarrels and struggles for supremacy, but made more acute by her authority. Once Albert left the scene of discord and locked himself in his chamber. Infuriated, Victoria threw herself on the door, pounding and commanding. Albert answered calmly, "Who is there?" She answered imperiously, "The Queen of England! Open this door!" Silence. Then once again she ordered him to obey. Silence. After some minutes of this fruitless performance she went away in tears. Then being unable to stand the discord longer she crept humbly back to the door and knocked gently. "Who is there?" inquired Albert politely. In a meek little tearful voice, she replied, "It's your wife, Albert. Please let me in." The door was opened and she flew into the arms of her husband.

Almost everyone is loving and forgiving. So, it pays us to admit a fault at once—but never grovel! Never place yourself for too long where the thoughtless person can cease to value you because you do not value yourself.

*APOLOGIZE EASILY—CASUALLY.* When you are wrong, say so, casually, easily and at once. "Sorry, Dear, I'm wrong," should be easy to say without a blush or a qualm to grown-up or child. In fact courteous children who adjust easily to life nearly always have an example of courtesy before them. *Ease* in courtesy is almost as important as the courtesy itself. As the old Scotsman says, "When a man maketh a muckle of his manners, they fit him ill."

It's so hard for some of us to apologize. But the person with the charming mind does not have to struggle with himself before he can grudgingly admit a fault. He believes that having the right to live, to experience, to grope and to discover, a certain number of errors are naturally going to be made, and by the law of averages he will make his share. So what of it, he thinks, as casually as a kitten who went to sleep too close to the edge of the cushion and fell off.

The charming person lives in a kind of halcyon mental state that does not harbor its own or anyone else's faults for long. It is a searcher for beauty. And whatever we search for—is what we find!

*LET QUARRELS BLOW OVER.* It is the irritations and the little scratches and envies of life that shrivel our charm, our bodies. Let them blow over. "What!" a woman said to me once. "Just let people walk over me!" Well, it pays in the end to do just that, if that is the only way peace can be held. (I'm speaking of individuals, not countries.) One of the bitterest experiences I ever had was with people in my own house, some years ago. I worked out this little formula for my own attitude. "It is possible that I am at fault, for it is hard to see one's own irritating qualities. If they are at fault, they will discover that some day—and if I have added fuel to the flame it may destroy any future friendliness, which, regardless of what I think of them now, is always desirable." So I bit my tongue—almost off—to keep from making pointed remarks. I still do not admire these people, but I am glad I did not allow them to upset my emotions further.

We must decide what is important and what is unimportant to deal with in the frictions of our lives. It is said that Voltaire praised his contemporary, Dr. Haller, a great deal. Dr. Haller criticized Voltaire. When told of Haller's remarks, Voltaire thought a moment and then said, "Possibly we are both mistaken."

Here is where we make most of our mistakes, mistakes that trip us into ugliness of all kinds—and when we lose the touchstone of beauty we have lost *all*. Fortunately it can be regained, through non-resistance.

Of course, it is wise to remove oneself as painlessly as possible from definitely incompatible surroundings or people. But there are wiser ways of doing even that than most of us use. Don't burn bridges, "tell people off," "cast out forever" or indulge in other East Lynne melodramatics.

## 4. YOUR SEARCH FOR THE BEAUTIFUL

Do you want to be lovely quickly? Do you want to regain some lost quality that has slipped away somehow?

1. Then cultivate the acquaintance of some deep and lovely mind— some woman whom you admire, some man whose life has been

full and rich and mellow, some graceful and charming girl. It may be the neighbor's daughter grown now to a natural, uncanny poise, instinctively being a high type regardless of environment. It may be a child, a teacher, a minister or some new friend.

2. Have no traffic with pessimists. Remember a pessimist never built a bridge—he knew all the reasons why it couldn't be done!

3. Dislike no one—even someone who has injured you—or whom you have injured!

4. Don't think too much of your own failures. Every bright person has at least one eating frustration, one agony of unfulfilment. This state of affairs cannot be prevented. I shouldn't like to be so dull that my mind did not race ahead of my performance.

5. Drink in beauty and charm and loveliness from every possible source.

You will be astonished when you watch your days and see how little you have guarded beauty in your life. If someone very close to you neglected your interests as you disregard yourself, I wonder if you would call that person "friend."

Write down a list of 100 people and things you like. Begin collecting "satisfactions." If you like the feel of clean sheets, write that down. Start agreeing with life and watch how it will agree with you.

## 5. SETTLE THE MATTER OF DISLIKES

Unlovely ideas leap at us continually in life—and we usually accept them with a sigh or challenge them with an unlovely resistance. I am not referring to world affairs but to your own inner daily frictions when I say *meet the unlovely things of life with non-resistance* —ignore them—and they will melt into the veriest nothing. Two things cannot occupy the same place at the same time. Fill yourself to the brim with loveliness—every expression of it! Do not permit yourself to be hurt by people. Their tactlessness or desire to aggrandize themselves must leave you serene and unmoved.

I want you to examine your thinking for an hour or so and see if you have been wasting much energy in resistance and criticism. It can be very subtle—and it is truly very hard sometimes to be honest with oneself in these matters. But, if you find that you have been going about the world—even as you pass in the street—criticizing someone's hat—disapproving of someone's manner—condemning a color combination in a window display—permitting yourself to feel disdain for some uncouthness—resisting the thousand and one little things that jar on your senses—you are wasting precious force that you must learn to conserve for better purposes.

## 6. KEEP FRESH AND YOUNG MENTALLY

If you want to remain young and keep your face fresh and luminous learn to let the rest of the world wear, do and think what it pleases. The cultured globe-trotter to whom the world is a passing show is no more critical of what he sees people do than if they were animals in a zoo. They are simply interesting phenomena and he is seeing the world as it is, with no thought whatever of resisting it.

Resistance to what is disliked is a problem that took me years to settle, so I am familiar in my personal experience with all its ramifications. The friction set up by these countless little irritations we permit ourselves to feel can wear away our happiness—and in extreme cases even our sanity. Whenever you feel yourself tensing under resistance to some idea—just stop it abruptly—and say to yourself, "I am willing to let other people find their way without hindrance from me —even my thoughts."

*STOP BEING SO AWARE OF WHAT YOU DON'T LIKE.* A resistance is a hindrance, isn't it? When, through lack of self-discipline, we permit a careless accumulation of resistances in our daily thinking we have quite a large amount of force labeled "hindrance" in our subconscious minds. Since your "habit mind" cannot select what you give it but must work on whatever you dump into it, there is no discrimination there between resistance generated by you toward somebody else or toward yourself! Your subconscious mind is building the idea of resistance and hindrance into *you!*

When things come to you that are undesirable and unlovely, do not tense yourself for battle, even mildly. Remain relaxed and refuse it in your mind as casually as you might say to a waiter, "Bring me fruit instead of pie."

## 7. DEVELOP TRUE AND DEEP JUDGMENT

This procedure will not conflict with discriminations or selectivity. As a matter of fact, it will make you more highly keyed to excellence —for you will recognize only the best in people. As for the worst— see it merely as a place or opportunity for beauty and loveliness to be also! This is the only way you can protect yourself from ugliness and preserve your own fineness at the same time.

If you must turn definitely away from someone or something, do it without condemnation or bitterness. Do it simply in the interest of order—of having things and people where they belong. Learn to send your earnest good wishes whenever you are tempted to condemn. You will be amazed how much force you will feel accumulating within you. You will build up a reserve of constructive power that will aid you in all you undertake. Any automobile mechanic will tell you that *when you cut out resistance and friction you cut out wear and tear*. In the human mind and soul, a great deal more than this is accomplished!

## 8. DO NOT FEEL SUPERIOR

As you become more and more sensitive to beauty, beware of acquiring a critical attitude toward people who have not yet begun to expand along lines of harmony. *It is childish to enjoy feeling superior to someone else*. Watch yourself for this feeling! It is a slow leak that lets out the charm you have acquired in other ways.

*DON'T COMPETE! JUST BE YOURSELF!* Enjoy your charm for the sake of its own beauty—not because someone else has less. A beautiful rose seems to be exulting in its power to express beauty from its own lovely heart—for the sheer joy of being beautiful. There is no room in its fullness for less than beauty. Certainly there is no beauty in being glad that someone else has less.

In other words, vanity is death to charm—while self-respect and a feeling of natural power are your just birthright—a part of your very *being*.

And no matter how low or ugly another person has become, it is not your place to criticize—but it is your duty to your own *charm* to remember that that person has within himself the same power to express beauty that you have within yourself. Charm will remember this. Kindness will remind him of his power—if not in words, by example.

Never get the idea that you want to be charming in sharp contrast to those around you. Charming people help you to be charming. Clever people help you to be clever. A good actress surrounds herself with the best talent, the finest cast available. It is a fact that in the company of clever people, you will often astonish yourself by your own cleverness. Like begets like.

*RECOGNIZE OTHERS' CHARM.* Remember that charm is simply your effect on other people—your value to them—what you have to give them. If you remember at all times that other people have inherently as much charm as you have, you will open the way for more of your own to come forth. A clever hostess brings her guests out to their best. That is charm!

## 9. BE A POWER FOR GOOD

*BE REFRESHING.* Remember that it is woman's place in the world to be refreshing. The whole world, young and old—the tired husband—and groping child—all unconsciously look to the mother or sister or some other woman to give new inspiration. So you must, at every point, express the clean, fresh source, like a stream of clear, clean water, that soothes and refreshes.

Every woman can be refreshing in appearance and personality, no matter what else she may be—and if she truly is, charm brings its gifts. She may be the youngest, gayest person in her set and still be refreshing. She may be the most serious madonna type and yet have this quality that draws the weary world to her. All human beings have a sense of disappointment in themselves, a feeling of frustrated ambition. Therefore, the woman who can refresh their eyes, their minds and their spirits is a popular woman!

*ALMOST EVERY STEP IN OUR CULTIVATION OF CHARM IS A PREPARATION TO MAKE US SO SURE OF OURSELVES THAT WE CAN PUT OUR MINDS COMPLETELY ON OTHER PEOPLE!* In apparent contradiction is the woman who demands everything and gives nothing—and seems to "get away with it." Analyze this woman. If her demands make other people think of their own abilities instead of her selfishness, she is still working on the principle just outlined. Whatever makes a man aware of his own power pleases him. When a tired man or a world-weary soul is refreshed, he has a new sense of power. A woman can be a miraculous power for good in the world even while she is arranging her life to get the most out of it.

*PROTECT YOURSELF.* But don't get the idea that you are to go around the slums reminding people of their innate power. That is a profession in itself and a very worthy one. You cannot raise people—you can only inspire them and *provide opportunities for them.* They must work their own way up. Many a promising woman has thrown her life away by a mistaken idea of impractical kindness.

The average unprotected woman had best remember that men and women of her own type need her just as much as any other kind. Their hearts are just as heavy and their spirits sag just as low as those of the people who would simply drag her down. Give your support to plans that provide *equal opportunities for all*—then give your overflow of human kindness to children and old people. Let able-bodied men and women find their own strength of character and do for themselves if it is possible for them to do so. Don't let people weaken themselves and you by leaning on you overmuch and sapping your strength. It is a thankless job, for you can never do enough or give enough to suit them. Help people to get on their feet—not yours—then they will think you are charming. Every woman worthy of the name is eager to help humanity.

It is important for you to realize that unless your own brightness lights the path for others, your personal efforts will avail little. What you do can never be "just your own business," for you are a responsible member of society. The higher you lift your own light, the wider its radiance shines. This fact has much to do with charm. It is necessary to serve our fellow men wisely, else better not do it at all. If you ruin your own reputation, scatter your forces to the wind, what have you to give the world the rest of your life? And *giving* is *charm!* Give the world only your blossoms—not your roots!

## 10. VOICE CULTURE

*PUT HEART-WARMTH IN YOUR VOICE.* Your voice reflects emotions as surely as a mirror gives back the image of what is placed before it. No amount of vocal exercises will put "soul" into a voice. The magnetic, warm overtones that can make a homely woman seem charming are the definite results of sweetness, generosity and love of humanity. There is no way to imitate this warmth in the voice. It must come from within. Throughout these lessons we bring out certain qualities of mind and character that give this entrancing timbre to the voice.

However, many of our noblest people pitch their voices so badly that the natural sweetness is choked out. It behooves everyone to place the speaking voice correctly and to modulate it musically. Here is an exercise that will take the shrillness and nasal quality out of any voice and lend it a lovely mellowness:

EXERCISE: Yawn. Hold your throat open and repeat the word "mood" very distinctly three times, pitched as low as you can without growling or producing a false tone. Imagine that the "oo" sound comes from your chest. This vowel opens your throat. Now with your throat in the position it took to say "mood" repeat the word "ice" three times. Again "mood" three times—then with the throat in the "oo" position say "ice" three times. Do this ten times. Now say "mood" three times; with the throat in the "oo" position say "early"—then substitute the words "regular," "Mary," "pie," "fancy" and "three." Always say "mood" first and be sure to pronounce distinctly. This exercise will take the shrillness and nasal quality out of any voice and give it a lovely mellowness. Do this regularly and whenever possible and as long as you can without tiring unused muscles. Practice using the principle of contrast in conversation.

*THE VOICE A BADGE OF CULTURE.* A bird is known by its note—a human being by his voice. The importance of a pleasing voice cannot be overestimated. A stranger must judge only by what he sees and what he hears. Experience has taught him that certain kinds of people speak in certain ways. Listen carefully to your own voice and see what sort of person a stranger would consider you to be. A cultured tone of voice is recognized the world over as a mark of distinction just as the Masonic emblem indicates that brotherhood. Guard against the slightest tinge of affectation in tone or word, but do pronounce distinctly and don't swallow the last syllables of words.

Needless to say, you should never substitute a mere sound for a word, such as "I told um," meaning "him" or "them." If the broad Bostonian or English "a" does not come naturally to you, don't use it, but do get that letter down out of your nose (if it is there) and pronounce it as in "at." This sound is always soft and lovely. Drop localisms and provincialisms. Speak a cosmopolitan English. But the *tone and quality* of your voice stamp you more finally than anything you can say. Voice production will be explained fully in PART THREE.

In this chapter I simply want to start you using your voice for the most charming effect and to start you on your "Search for the Beautiful," which will give *emotional reality* to all things you will learn to do. There is a beautiful side to everything. It is a pleasant and profitable task to find it and make it part of yourself. Then it will shine out from your face, vibrate from your body, give rhythm, color and harmony to your whole personality. Try it.

## 11. HOW TO LISTEN GRACEFULLY

*A TRICK IN TALK.* Instead of waiting to get to the chapters on conversation, you may as well be trying out an interesting and amusing trick of listening.

Here is a simple way to become part of—or even the center!—of a conversation without saying a word. Listen for the name of a familiar place or person in the speaker's talk and move your hands from one position to another as though a chord of your mind had been struck. Suppose one of your hands is in your lap and the other on the arm of your chair. The speaker is directing his remarks to others, ignoring you. He mentions Quebec. You lean forward responsively and put your other hand up on the arm of the chair.

He will probably glance at you. Then, if you move your hands to still another position as though you were very responsive to any mention of Quebec, he will very likely turn to you with a side remark of intimacy about this lovely old city.

After this bond is established, he will look to you for approval in any extravagant remarks he may make. Then move your hands less and less in response to what he says,—that is, unless it is beneath your womanly integrity to use such a trick to make a man work for your approval.

Then give him your enthusiastic response again, *briefly,* just before you leave, or he leaves. But move your hands only when a point or name impresses you. Make your hands accent your thought and responses. Too much movement at the wrong time confuses both you and the speaker.

It will amuse you to experiment with this odd and interesting law of attention following responsive movement. Not only is it valid with men and women, but with children—and even dogs. It is valid only because it is what you really do when you are genuinely interested. Any workable technique is founded on fundamental facts.

*HAND POSITIONS.* The average woman has only two habitual positions for her hands. She should have five or ten.

Exercise: Sit down in front of a full-length mirror and invent five different positions in which to place your hands.

I hesitate to dictate these positions. It would be better if they were an expression of your spontaneity. I don't want all my pupils to be doing the same things. Nevertheless, you might start with these five positions and gradually find others of your own.

1. Palms down, right hand on middle of left leg—left hand laid lightly over right wrist.

2. Right hand in same position—left hand slides up right arm and rests near elbow.

3. Left hand in center of lap, palm down—right hand on seat of chair, half-way between knee and thigh or more toward knee (lean slightly forward).

4. Palms down, one hand on top of the other, resting on knees. (Leaning forward.)

5. One hand in your lap—the other on arm of chair.

You need not change your hands in the same routine over and over. Alternate the positions occasionally. Also, there is no special magic in having five positions for your hands. You may have four or nine. But, you should have, at least, four hand positions, so as to be sure that you will never look set or monotonously phlegmatic.

*DON'T SIT WITH CLASPED HANDS.* These exact positions might never be used, but it is very comforting to feel that you know what you're going to do with your hands, come what may! At any rate, the woman so prepared will be less likely to fall into the dreadful clasped-hand habit. Never sit hour after hour and day after day with your hands clasped meekly in your lap. To you it may mean complacency and contentment. To others it merely looks dull, as though you had finished with vital living and were just sitting around waiting for the end.

A child's hands are never together. Study the young if you want to prevent, in yourself, those mannerisms that accompany an aging, slower pulse, and an edgeless mind. The too-vivacious woman needs to calm her hands. It is not good taste to accompany every remark with violent gestures. There is a desirable middle path. Movement of the hands must not interrupt thought or take the eye from the face too much. Voice and facial expression should be aided but not over-whelmed by the hands.

If you sit with your hands clasped inertly, people will pass you by. But if your hands are separated, even though they may be *still* (as I hope they are most of the time) they look as though they had just finished some activity or anticipate some action. Life is action!

Yet—and this is the hardest point to teach—it is only through repose that action has meaning. Movement is exactly like the trimming on a woman's costume. Too much of it confuses the eye and we call the result bad taste. But a little is accent—gives meaning to the harmony of the whole.

## 12. HOW TO CONVERSE GRACEFULLY

While the charming, cultured woman has a smoothness in talk that the novice cannot achieve and but dimly recognizes, anyone may attract interest by making what I shall call a "flank attack" on conversation. That is to create at once in the hearer's mind a stimulation that starts the talk rolling spiritedly. There are two major ways of doing this. The first way is to use astonishing frankness and the second is to use the trick of immediate contrast. Neither of these should go beyond the boundary of tact and good taste. Often they work together very well.

Have you ever been drifting along in a dull conversation of banalities (perhaps about lawn-sprinklers) wondering just why one of the fairly intelligent persons pursuing it could not or did not enliven it? And then like a refreshing breeze another woman arrives. She is introduced to three or four people and then turned loose. Usually she is drawn into the existing talk.

But if no one tells her what has been under discussion, she has recourse to two ways of entering the talk. One, most frequently used, is to say animatedly, "What are you talking about?" Someone may say, "We were just discussing the relative merits of sprinkling methods." She responds quickly with "Gardening or religious?"

One woman I know never fails to make people laugh by saying things she could not possibly say after she has thorough knowledge of what was going on before she arrived. These few moments after arrival which are the dread of most of us, she turns to account in this amusing way. If she does not at once strike a note of response by taking up the threads of an existing conversation, she wastes no time in making a new one which always relieves any strain there may have been. She invariably touches on something entirely removed from personalities.

She quickly glances about the room for some outstanding object upon which to comment. A vase of flowers suffices. She says, "Oh, those divine tulips! That's the reddest red I've ever seen. Are these meant to be violent or merely gay?" An animated conversation inevitably follows for all immediately think of the most brilliant red they've ever seen before and in a few moments the talk may have switched to Spain, dye-stuffs, Germany, Hitler, national colors, Chinese red lacquer, politics, "the noble experiment"—red noses, red cheeks, health, health resorts—then the talk darts around the globe again.

Whenever conversation seems to be growing dull this woman throws the idea of contrast into the talk, which acts like yeast in dough. Often this habit will gain for a woman the reputation of a wit. For it usually brings a laugh to have the exact opposite of anything brought forth as a sharp contrast. It also relieves the unpleasantness when someone insists upon telling brutally horrid things. A short comment such as "Playful people, aren't they?" will usually break the tension with a laugh. These are, of course, the most simple illustrations of the principles involved. In actual practice the ramifications can be endless and limitlessly interesting or amusing.

*SAY WHAT YOU THINK.* Often the odd little thoughts that we censor and crowd back from our tongues are just the things we should say. People with imaginations sufficiently facile to bring forth these contrasts quickly become the most entertaining talkers. It really isn't difficult and will prove useful in many kinds of situations. The best rule for genuine, spirited conversation is—*say what you want to say* without wondering too much about it. This is a dangerous rule unless one is at heart kind and is interested in the happiness of others. But I give it, for I am assuming that only this sort of woman is interested in being charming. This advice is addressed to those who are seeking a real and lasting *charm.*

*WHEN YOU ARE TALKING,* it is well to bear in mind that *suggestion is the most powerful force in the world.* The suggestion of your phrases and words is often more potent than the meaning of your statement. We've all laughed at the story of the mother who left her children alone with the admonition not to put beans in their ears. So of course they promptly tried it as soon as her back was turned. All of us are guilty of the same backward use of principles, unless we train ourselves to their effective use.

*DON'T PUT "NO" IN THE OTHER PERSON'S MIND.* How many times have you heard someone say, "I don't suppose you could do so and so." Such a negative approach to anyone will usually net absolutely no results. We should never assume that someone else has either the energy or the interest to reason out the meaning of every-thing we say. The casual attention we get from other people leaves them very susceptible to the suggestion of what we say.

## 13. CULTIVATE MENTAL ALERTNESS FOR CONVERSATIONAL EASE

*HAVE SOMETHING INTERESTING ON YOUR MIND.* It behooves every woman to have a mental hobby. A deep interest always lends a fascinating expression to the eyes—and a relief and protection from the bad taste of being too personal. The prettiest woman in the world has an empty face that cannot hold attention unless she has an *active continuity of interest in her mind*. Otherwise her beauty has the same fleeting appeal as that of a doll. Quick to gain admiration. Quick to lose attention.

So you must have at least two interests which apparently take your mind altogether off yourself. One must be—*other people*. The second can be anything from aviation to collecting postage stamps. This point is applicable to every living human being.

If you are one of these spasmodically self-conscious people who has thought about her shortcomings until it has become a painful habit, why, you simply must train yourself into another habit—the more charming one of keeping your mind on something else. I am going to give you now an exercise that is more important than anything so far in the book except the exercise in CHAPTER ONE of calling your own name aloud, which I hope you are practicing regularly and faith-fully.

*MAKE YOUR THOUGHTS STAY WHERE YOU PUT THEM.* Practice holding a thought or an object in mind to the exclusion of everything else—just one thought or one object (one that has nothing to do with you). See how long by the clock you can think exclusively about—well, your neighbor's canary bird, for instance. Don't think anything *about* the bird—just hold it in your mind as an object as long as possible. The average is thirty seconds the first time! You can't do it for very long, can you? For your habit of thinking is centered around yourself. Well, then you are just that far from real charm.

When your mind finally slips uncontrollably back to yourself, then begin to think things *about* the canary bird. Think of his song. This will suggest perhaps other singing—the church choir, radio crooners, opera singers and singing. Think of the canary bird's color—yellow, like the sun which is so life-giving that we have sun lamps for health. Yellow is the color of gold. Gold suggests far places, romance, stock-selling swindles, wedding-rings, etc. Think of every possible point about the bird and see how many kindred ideas each thought brings in its train. *This is marvelous exercise for conversation.* I can't imagine anyone's being stuck for something to say. The world is full of millions of things to talk about. Of course you can't think about them quickly and easily until you have trained your mind to go *out from yourself* and get them.

When you have exhausted the canary bird for conversational possibilities, choose the nearest object at random and try holding that in mind. You can do this going to and from town, whenever you are alone and before you go to sleep at night. When you discover for yourself the inexhaustible sources of conversation, you will have more poise. The way is really easy.

# CHAPTER THREE

# *Your Body Talks All the Time—the "Tattle Tale"!*

## 1. CLEANLINESS AND GOOD GROOMING

When my great-grandfather was courting my great-grandmother, he was very attentive and devoted. He would say goodbye to her in the hall and then tell her that she must be the one to go—that so long as he could see her he was rooted to the spot. So it developed that she walked up the stairs, waved a kiss and disappeared before he made his exit. Some time after their marriage she had the courage to say something that had long been in her mind. "Why did you always keep your eyes on my ankles when I was going up the stairs?" she queried. "I almost refused to marry you because of your boldness."

"And why didn't you?" he teased, secure in having her.

"Because, if I had sent you packing, I never could have asked you so bold a question."

"Well," he returned, "you may have married me to ask me a question. But I married you because of what I saw as you went upstairs."

"Oh, you villain," she said. "Avowedly immodest! 'Tis almost more than a good woman can bear!"

"Calm yourself, my dear. Your ankles were pretty enough to turn any man's head—but that is not what I mean."

"Then speak, Sir, and turn the conversation to decency."

"Dear Heart," he replied, "you always seemed like an angel to me, leaving me upward, away and upward—leaving my view, ascending. But for all the grace of you and the proud lift of your head and the slimness of your waist, there was yet another charm. Darling, with each swish of your skirts, as you lifted the front of them for the steps, there was a cascade of petticoat—and always, always, the ruffles were

white, snowy white and dainty. They were never soiled. I thought
to myself, there is no fault within her covered by pretense. She's dainty
throughout."

Such is the story that is repeated, just so, to each generation. So
pretty a scene bears reconstructing often.

Addison says, "Beauty commonly produces love, but cleanliness preserves it. Age itself is not unamiable while it is preserved clean and
unsullied, like a piece of metal constantly kept smooth and bright."

And what poet sings of a dead, lost love who comes back as a
fragrant presence to keep his mind from the living? In the sparkling
hush of the starlight, his love would return to him, announcing her
tryst and devotion with the odor of mignonette. If I should ever make
up my mind to be a ghost I should love to make my presence known
"with the odor of mignonette." "Like a silken scarf left on the garden
bench with only its perfume to tell of what manner of lady that wore
it."

But we need not wait to be sentimental ghosts to leave an impression of exquisiteness. We can be daintily fragrant while we are alive
and give much pleasure and evoke much sentiment. Though certainly
too much dependence upon perfume or cologne is likely to mar our
effect, make it coarse instead of ethereal. "Jes doan give no advance
notice of yo' approach," counseled a wise Mammy years ago.

Exquisitely clean skin, and clothes that have laid in lavender, leave
a far more intriguing waft than a last-minute dousing from a bottle.
Though of course, every woman and many men like a perfume about,
to be used with discretion and restraint. Napoleon's bill for cologne
was so large it was hotly protested by his advisers.

But in this well-groomed America, every woman knows that perfume is made for flesh, not fabric. And both Mr. and Mrs. America
are daily bath addicts. Also they are well-informed on the subjects
of halitosis, gingivitis, falling hair and B.O. All to the good if heeded.
Next to her powder puff, the wise woman respects and uses deodor-
ants, at least two!

It is in all our little physical habits that our strength of personality
gathers or leaks away. Your opinion of yourself which is important
to your poise, is based to a remarkable extent on your care of your

body. To keep up your courage, keep up your grooming. Nothing aids morale so much as a feeling of physical freshness—and nothing damages it so much as little neglects.

Keeping right up with coiffure and style in your grooming makes you want to keep in the forefront of life. Don't let yourself fall back. As General Sherman used to say—"Up front on the firing line all is hope and optimism. It is when we drop back where we see the wounded, the stragglers and deserters that the task seems hopeless."

So, it is not from the standpoint of neatness or hygiene that I discuss any of them. It is from the standpoint of morale.

We have so many trappings for our grooming. Yet many feminine travelers, from Margaret Bourke-White, who photographed Russia at work, to Osa Johnson of jungle lore, have lived away from conveniences and learned how to keep their routine of personal daintiness just the same.

And there is the story of Marie Antoinette, the exquisite, whose last dark years were lived in prison. Stripped at last of all her elegant trappings, no bottles, no scents, no lotions and vapors, she asked only for soap. And to the end, with only the crudest conveniences, she kept herself spotlessly clean. Not for her the tousled head and unkempt body of most of her prison mates. And when the tumbril called for her to take her to the guillotine, she asked only for the time to put on a clean shift. So the daughter of the Empress of Austria, the matriarch, Maria Theresa, rode in a rude cart to her death. But she rode like a queen, head up, unafraid and immaculately clean.

We may have to revert to the woodland and garden herbs for our beauty ingredients, and if we do we shall have some pleasant surprises. We may miss the crystal bottles but we can have very satisfactory cosmetics that way, if we must. We are a resilient people who can do whatever we *must* do—and do it with zeal and thoroughness. Just give our nervous energies a direction and all kinds of results are achieved.

Indeed, so close is the relation between a pervading sense of beauty, so necessary to good personality, and personal daintiness, that they are all but inseparable. Possibly because one must feel exquisite before that impression can be given.

*EXPRESS BEAUTY EVERY DAY.* For this reason I urge you to take conscious pleasure in your routine of cleanliness. Heretofore you may have taken it for granted, thought about something else, or considered it a dull and uninteresting routine.

But please enjoy your bath, revel in it—be grateful for your body and care for it. Become a bath-tub singer. Be joyous about it. Be æsthetic and poetic about it. I am convinced that those things we do in dull duty have only a quarter of the effect of those we do in high spirits and conscious pleasure in them.

Enjoy your soap and water. Enjoy whatever scent you provide for it, whether in soap or salts. Under any and all conditions never be without at least one accessory in which you find pleasure and a sense of grateful luxury. It may be your soap, a caressing powder, a pungent lotion, or a single rose in a bud vase. But you must have something in the rite of personal grooming that is delightful to you, that you may absorb and glow with it! Did you ever try brushing your body with a dry brush before your bath—or any time, for that matter? It is very revivifying and makes your skin satiny. Did you ever try resting on the hard floor for two minutes for a quick "come-back"?

A dainty body and underthings are generous contributors to feminine charm. Little personal luxuries can be afforded by practically everybody. And if any farm girl is unable to attain them for any reason, tell her to give her hair a mint rinse—or a jimson-weed rinse, or to sleep with a little cap of rose petals on her hair—or pine needles —or lavender, or cedar bark. Don't smile, you may be doing it! If that time ever comes you'll be saving your nasturtiums and honeysuckle and forty other things.

You'll be brushing your teeth with salt and soda, and wondering why you didn't do it before. Maybe with a brush of elm bark twisted, dried and cut in lengths, such as the mountaineers have always used. You'll be soaking oat-meal to get a softening wash for your face—and using corn oil on your scalp and discovering that there's nothing better. Remember the body can absorb vegetable oils, but not a single drop of mineral oil such as vaseline.

You'll be saving rain-water for your shampoos. You'll make your own facial packs with clay and witch-hazel—in fact you might make your own witch-hazel. And you'll be able to get free recipes for all kinds of herbal concoctions. That day may never come, but if it does, we shall be equal to it. One thing is certain, the American woman will never let up on her grooming. She knows its value too well.

So far as her health is concerned, she'll continue to make a fetish of it—and it may be easier to keep her figure molded to the desired proportions when she must be very active.

*FOR YOUTH AND STRENGTH.* She knows her youth and strength depend on water, vegetables, fruit, exercise and a high heart and mind. With mood dragging in the dust how can she be healthy, charming or youthful? So she lifts her thoughts Up, Up, UP!

Will Rogers once said that age is indeed no coward. It walks right up to a woman's face and socks her under the chin. If this seems to be happening to you, give it thought.

The best beauty treatment is serene nerves and good nature. As we get past twenty-five, and sometimes before, it is well to be sure that we haven't depleted our store of volatile minerals, glandular substances and vitamins. Calcium and vitamins can be put back into the body, thus pushing off age surprisingly. Get them in special foods or have your doctor prescribe the proper way for you to take them. They work wonders! Calcium may save your teeth. And it has a thousand benefits. Carrots raw or cooked to keep your eyes bright, raw turnips and cabbage for their refreshing properties. And the only way to improve on the "apple a day" is two apples a day or a pound of grapes.

Didn't it amuse you to read that modern football coaches insist on their teams taking daily doses of vitamin $B_1$ (called facetiously, "Courage in a test tube").

One thing is certain. It is only the energy "left over" from our own needs that we can give other people. And only that surplus energy trickles into our caring about other people and making them happy, which they in turn call "charming."

## 2. A ROUTINE FOR HEALTH AND BEAUTY TREATMENT

*REMAIN FEMININE IN BUSINESS.* The American woman is too clever to let herself get grim about the duties and responsibilities before her. She can toss off a fine accomplishment without looking like a musical-comedy admiral about it. She knows that it's smart to make big deals in a feminine way. She recalls how Katharine Hepburn sold her producers a story for $100,000.00. No, a grim look has no place in feminine accomplishment, however serious the matter before us seems.

But seriously, deeply, she has learned that merely good ideas and good intentions are not going to do any job. She has learned, with blushes, that she isn't likely to stay at the task of exercise or facial treatments—unless she makes a hard and fast program—a daily program for herself,—and lives up to it, even though she gets so tired of it that she'd rather be dead than continue. But if she sticks to it for *three* weeks, it's habit after that!

*PAGES FOR YOUR PROGRAM ARE IN BACK OF BOOK.* Choose a routine that you think you can live up to—and turning to the back of this book, you will find two pages, left for your convenience, to set down the program, hour by hour, that you choose for yourself. Method is the only way to success!

Set aside a time for the care of your face, nails, hair, scalp, clothes, answering your mail, a little daily informative reading. Learn to dovetail the jobs of grooming, bathing and exercise. It is possible to get considerable exercise in the act of bathing and drying oneself if the movements are all exaggerated. If creams are put on the face before the bath, they will have all that time to stay on and do their work. A little stretching exercise and a moment of scalp massage can be had before a foot is put on the floor each morning. *And don't forget your doctor and your dentist.* See them twice a year.

## 3. NEATNESS OF CLOTHES AND FIGURE

Try in every way to eliminate confusion. Orderly belongings and clothes that will stay neat-looking on one's body are a step in the right direction. For instance, wear plain, well-cut dresses that take only a moment to press. Depend upon jewelry for relief or accent— jewelry or little collars and cuffs that come off for cleaning. Don't wear pleated skirts unless you have time to keep them right.

Remember that knitted or lace dresses travel better than most. (Use tissue paper at folds when packing.) For your further peace of mind have tiny cloth straps sewed in the shoulders of all your dresses, straps with a snap at the end, to keep all your underwear straps from slipping off your shoulder. Most custom-made dresses have these straps when you buy them.

*IDEAS TO IMPROVE YOUR FIGURE.* Remember that heavily boned corsets will never make you look slimmer. Wear only a light, restraining garment—and if there is something really the matter with your figure go to a gymnasium or have someone massage you at home into a better shape. With your body in a vise, no matter how shapely a prison it is, it renders you immobile and incapable of graceful, expressive movement. I'd rather look fat! The most famous of the old French corsetières often used no bones at all. The strength of Nylon may inspire some American designers to create better corsets.

Large hips call for flared skirts, no matter what the current style.

Narrow shoulders call for epaulets of some kind.

Be willing to be your height, whatever it is. Play up your type and make it an asset.

Flat chest calls for better posture primarily, deep breathing—and soft surplice draperies across the bosom, large collars, fichus, jabots or blouses gathered into a yoke and belt.

A large bosom should be let alone and no attempt made to hide it. The best you can do to hide a large bosom is worse than the original effect, which isn't bad at all. It's fashionable to look like a woman, so hold up your head, your chest, and let nature take its course. At least, you'll look womanly, queenly, and you'll probably have a lot of magnetism.

*THE CORRECT POSTURE FOR ALL TYPES* is chest up as though it were suspended from the ceiling. Your back will be flattened and your stomach pulled in by this single gesture. Under no conditions put your shoulders back. Leave them loose and down. Now tuck the hips under just a trifle with a slightly spanked movement. Now draw your knees together. That is the perfect posture. If you feel strained—just persevere in exercising for that position and you will win in a surprisingly short time.

When we watch a charming, finished, delightful woman of savoir-faire, we receive an impression of her perfection. We may not be aware of the means by which she achieves her effects that are apparently so natural. Nevertheless, behind her performance is her knowledge of the meaning of posture and gesture, the technique of voice, expression, timing. Every detail of her dress is designed to express something definite. Nothing is left to chance.

The impression we all make on others is based on these same principles. What a privilege it is to be a woman! Yet most of us take no advantage of the technique of expressing what we are and what we mean. The average woman is so pitiably thoughtless of how she handles her body.

*KEEP YOUR FEET NEAR EACH OTHER.* The mystics say that the feet are actually the symbol for understanding. If knowledge is power—and power gives poise—we realize the necessity of having firm support for our bodies as well as for our ideas and ideals. Smart people do not lean on furniture, walls or one another. They are not stiff—they are poised on their feet.

To give the impression of true feminine beauty by preserving the artistic lines of the body in repose, *the feet should always be close together* when you are standing or sitting—*but not side by side.* The ankles may be gracefully crossed. Even when one foot is slightly in advance of the other, the front view should show no separation (or very little) at the ankle line.

*THE FEET IN ART.* In the Metropolitan Museum in New York there is a sketch (by Rodin) which shows that the flowing, beautiful lines of the Grecian urn were suggested by the feminine figure—the smallest breadth at the ankles giving grace to the body as the lines curve gently up. This line is broken when the ankles are widely separated.

The most strenuous, athletic dancer, in repose, has her feet together. The greatest complaint of artists against the modern girl is that she has lost so much of the compelling beauty of her woman's form by standing with her feet apart—which throws her whole body into aggressive awkwardness. A heavy woman looks still heavier with her feet apart—such a posture adds grossness to her appearance.

In every picture of a lovely woman you will find her feet daintily together. Every actress who is successful has learned how to preserve the grace of her bodily lines by keeping her feet together.

Sometimes the hoydenish type or the small, "cute" girl can be amusing by striking a boyish attitude with a wide stride—but one must have a great many other virtues to get away with it. The "cute" girls have never changed history very much. Femininity is the keynote of those none-too-beautiful women who have left their names on the scrolls of the past.

The business woman of today sacrifices none of her femininity to her job. Soft-voiced, gentle-mannered, feminine girls and women are to be found in high executive positions at large salaries. To see one of them rise and walk across her luxurious office is to see a poise and a grace not to be excelled in any drawing-room.

Study the pictures of successful actresses—invariably the feet are drawn together. Study the pictures of the truly patrician types of society women—the feet are together. The thoroughbred, the aristocrat, the purest examples of femininity never stand with the feet apart.

The legs should look like the stem of a flower. Who ever heard of a flower with two stems?

I have often looked at a crowd of women, well dressed and eager to make a pleasant impression—but—almost without exception they stood so badly that nothing of their true worth and innate beauty could reach the beholder. I have longed to shout at them a sort of military command that would make them instantly put their feet together.

At first you may not be able to find perfect balance in this position. No? Then do this. Take a small step—put your weight on your forward foot and use the other foot as a balance slightly behind it. I want you to practice this exercise and practice it until you could do it in your sleep, for this is one of the most important postures in the world.

*MAKE YOUR BODY LOOK ALERT.* This is the position of poise and alertness. If you should ever have occasion to speak before a group of people, you must stand in this position while you are speaking, in order to make a favorable impression. You may change your weight to the other foot, of course, but it must be on the forward foot, especially at the beginning and at the end of your talk. I remember, as a child, I saw a very old picture of the correct posture for public speaking. It showed a man standing with his weight on the back foot, the forward knee bent loosely and nonchalantly. Today such a speaker could not keep his audience awake. In this modern day there are so many claims on the attention that we stop to listen only to the speaker who has sufficient alertness to make us feel that he, himself, is interested in his message. Certainly a man who believes passionately in what he is saying would not, *could not* stand with his weight on his back foot. He may, however, have the weight equally divided at times by standing solidly on both feet.

You cannot interest people unless you have something for them. Now the physical attitude of *giving* is a forward movement toward the person you wish to receive your gift (of whatever nature). Certainly you could never present a gift by backing away from the recipient. By standing with the weight on your forward foot—even though you are not moving—you give the impression of having something to *give,* for you are in the attitude of giving.

As almost everybody wants (consciously or unconsciously) to *get,* they react to the promise of your attitude and are interested in you. Why? Because you look as though you have something for them! A hostess with her weight on her back foot looks inhospitable and inadequate—if not actually tired and bored. The average woman must depend upon a certain vitality in her personality to put herself forth attractively. There are other kinds of charm but this kind wears better and fits into all the demands of life.

*THE LANGUID WOMAN'S APPEAL.* Almost diametrically opposed to the alert attitude is that of the languorous, graceful woman who can draw a circle of admirers into the most secluded corner.

She always seems to be thinking of something that is better not put into words, but which seems to her well worth thinking about. (Not herself, of course. To appear to be thinking about one's self is the greatest sin against charm in any kind of personality!) She is quiet because her forces appear to be taken up by this inner concentration. She excites curiosity, for people are always curious about someone who appears to be interested in something. And curiosity is a form of interest—a most intense, but not the most lasting, form of interest.

When you have finished this book I want you to have not only the delightful social graces and what the world calls "tricks" of attraction, I want you to be on such firm footing, so poised, that life cannot sway you and swing you this way and that at the mercy of circumstances. I want you to be able to face the most important people and the greatest occasions with a gracious ease and a clear mind.

*ANYONE CAN LEARN POISE.* People who have poise know they have it. It is their best friend in society—a marvelous asset in business. The greatest enemy of poise is self-consciousness which creeps insidiously from any feeling of inferiority. At any time it may attack anyone who is not prepared. People who lack poise are continually reminding themselves that they haven't it and suffer accordingly. I have seen men and women in an absolute agony of uncertainty. Poise would have smoothed out the confusion.

Poise gives us the strength and balance that enables us to see and grasp the fleeting opportunities. In this swift-moving age, competition is so sharp, education so general, decisions made so quickly, that we rarely have a second chance at anything.

Self-confidence is the only way to perfect poise. Both are more quickly attained through understanding your really limitless possibilities. You *must* believe in yourself, and understand your relation to others. I believe that if we really knew what we are and who we are and our place in the large, universal scheme of things, we would be so happy about it that we could never know fear, or that shrinking feeling of inferiority.

To be alive is sufficient evidence that we are needed in the world. Otherwise we wouldn't be here. Just for a moment let go mentally of every limitation—forget for an instant all the reasons why you think you cannot achieve and express the best and the highest things in the world. Why, with just an instant's release, that soaring, natural spirit of yours can lift your mood so high that you can see over the top of all things that seem to hinder you. Then, why put the lid back on? Keep it off!

## 4. CULTIVATE FREEDOM OF BODY MOVEMENTS

*YOUR BODY RESPONDS TO YOUR MIND.* Let your mind go up and out—up and out until you have a sense of freedom that causes your body to respond with an easy grace. While you are in this mood, I want you to take a physical exercise that demonstrates the point perfectly. I want to teach you to use your arms and hands gracefully.

The average person's arms never get much farther away from his self than do his thoughts. The gestures are cramped, little, awkward, self-conscious thrusts. I want you to be able to stretch your arms out in a full-length gesture without feeling in the least self-conscious about it.

Most people are afraid of their arms—afraid to let their hands get very far away, as though fearful that they may not be able to get them back again.

In order to have a casual grace in the ordinary uses of the hands and arms, you must be *able* to do still more things with them. It is always *reserve* power that makes for grace and poise. No one is ever effective if he makes us feel that he has stretched himself to the limit— that he has nothing left.

*NEVER MOVE IN A STRAIGHT LINE.* You must be perfectly comfortable making large gestures if you wish to make small ones well. In order to stretch as far as possible, stand on tiptoe and reach as far as you can in all directions. Make circular movements—never move your arms with a straight thrust. It is abrupt, crude and instantly dispels the illusion of grace. Every movement must be a curve, be it ever so slight a curve.

When you are handing an article to someone, see that the gesture is a slight curve—not an affected flourish—just not a straight line.

Usually your hands should not be in a straight line with your arms; they should bend one way or the other. In moving the arms let the wrists lead the hands so they follow the wrists like pieces of chiffon. The wrists should lead the hands in every movement. This action is exaggerated in dancing for a more spectacular grace—but in modified form it insures grace in the daily walks of life.

*WHAT TO DO WITH YOUR HANDS.* If you are puzzled as to "what to do with your hands" watch the gestures of women whose grace you admire. You will discover that they do very little with their hands. This point is worth your study.

Now raise your arms in front of you. Let your hands droop (the wrist is leading the hand, you see). Now lower your arms and raise your hands as the arms descend (the wrist is leading again).

Charm in movement is an illusion of harmony that straight lines and jerky movements yank instantly into oblivion.

Walk about the room on tiptoe making large circles with the arms, crossing your body with them, never forgetting to let the wrists lead the hands. Sway from side to side with a circular movement. Get your whole body accustomed to moving in curves. Say to yourself, or aloud if it gives you more inspiration, "I would like to travel around the world!" making a wide circular gesture that describes the world.

I want you to get accustomed to the feel of your hands at arm's length from your body. Loosen up. Stand in front of your mirror and make your gestures as gracefully as you can. I want you to be as graceful as grace itself, both mentally and physically. I want you to enjoy being lovely.

*DON'T WALK ON TWO LINES.* Now walk freely across the room, not striding, not stiff. Be dainty without taking silly, little, mincing steps. Be free without being military *and see that you are walking on one line!* As walking is a series of falls, it is economy of motion to catch each fall directly in the center of your weight. Practice this when you are coming downstairs and you will understand and more easily master *walking on one line.* Never walk on two lines. Make your steps of natural length—and don't forget that each heel touches an imaginary line—your toes pointed out at a comfortable angle.

*HOLD YOUR HEAD UP.* Almost all women walk with their heads down. It is very damaging to them. It looks sad from the front and decapitated from the rear. Raise your chest, not with pride and arrogance, but for the sheer joy of living alertly. I want you to feel free of every mental and physical restriction. Practice this walk religiously. So few women walk well. Most of them walk as if something hurt them and they were trying to hold things together until they get home. Or else they wobble from side to side as the result of walking on two lines.

Practice until your walk is smooth and free and floating, so that you may enter a room as though you were already a part of that room instead of something that was bounced in by the wind. A graceful walk gives the impression of physical and mental harmony.

*IN BEING SEATED,* when you must approach a chair from the side—if your right side is next to the chair, see that your left foot is slightly ahead of the right one—then sit down sideways in the chair— and your feet will be in a graceful position. Your left foot will be flat on the floor and your right foot will be arched with only the ball or toe on the floor. You are now facing the person on the right of your chair. If you approach the chair from the other side simply reverse this procedure. You can then turn the body to the front or opposite side as your comfort requires.

*TO RISE GRACEFULLY.* Get to the edge of the chair without jerky lunges or thrusts. Don't lower your head to butt your way up. Put your right leg under you and make it do the most of the work as a lever—let your left leg and foot be a graceful balance, slightly behind it. There is no reason for rising on the right leg except that you want your greatest strength under you so you will not wobble and falter as you rise. Any exercise that strengthens the legs will help you gain grace in sitting and rising.

## 5. CONCLUSION

There is no one living who does not prefer to be a channel for— and an instrument of—the principle of beauty. Yet, it is one of life's tragedies that we can be utterly filled with beauty, so sensitive to it that we tremble with emotion in its presence—and still lack the ability to give it utterance in our personalities. On the other hand, we may have glib tongues, graceful bodies, pretty faces and correct manners, yet still lack that living spark of animating, motivating feeling for beauty that would blend our assets into the unit of personality called *charm.* The cultivation and the harmonizing of the outer and the inner is the basis of my work.

The exercises given are the most telling ways of impressing your subconscious mind deeply so that the ideas become at once a part of you; hence, their expressions are natural. This is your protection from artificiality and affectation. Always bear in mind that being over-sweet and over-polite is not charming. So, one should always be careful not to overdo. There is a danger of becoming simpering and artificial.

*LEARN TO BE EFFORTLESS.* In a beautiful house among brilliant people where good manners and perfect service smooth the social path, Charm shines forth as *effortlessness.* This is truly "The Smart Point of View." To be effortless—to be casual in your correctness, your brilliance and your grace—is actually *the art of hiding art.* A woman skilled and perfect in social contacts has *learned a technique,* just as any other artist must if he be truly effective. This technique is effective in business also.

Every woman has Charm within her but how is she to express it unless she learns the *laws of its expression?* She must feed her sense of the beautiful and *learn to articulate it* in speech and act. This flowing harmony throughout her person and personality attracts, delights and soothes others. People respond to such a woman as pleasantly as they start swaying to the lilt of a waltz tune. Therefore, the charming woman *creates her own environment!* She causes others to respond to her in her own tempo. For others fall in line with rhythm in a personality just as they begin to tap their feet to music! This is not only a psychological phenomenon, but it smooths and simplifies life for you, enabling you to remain serene and happy.

Try out the ideas in these chapters slowly—don't expect smoothness and perfection at once—and you will be surprised and delighted to note how quickly you will make them *your own* in everyday reactions.

## INSTRUCTIONS

1. Practice walking on tip-toe for balance, lightness and grace—also the standing "position of giving"—weight on the forward foot, chest raised, head up.

2. *A must!* Practice holding in your mind an object which has nothing to do with you. See how long you can hold it in your mind without letting anything else slip in. *Nothing in all your life is more important.*

3. Set aside a regular time to take the mental exercise described on Page 54, Section 6. A good time is immediately following the exercise of calling your own name, which you should continue.

4. Perform the arm and hand exercises outlined in this chapter. They aid so much in developing confidence. Grace is an additional reward. Also practice walking.

5. Write in longhand with a pen or pencil, "I am interested in other people and other things" five hundred times—one hundred a day for five days.

6. Watch your talk and refrain from saying uncomplimentary things about yourself or anyone else.

7. Taking the words "music," "bulb," and "science," make a list of words they suggest in association of ideas. This is a test of imagination and information for conversation to show you how you may start with any subject and go in talk around the world, ending on something totally different from the beginning word. If you will write this exercise *frequently* it will make conversation easier and richer for you.

# CHAPTER FOUR

# *You Are Society*

## (Fitting In with People)

### 1. HOSPITALITY

One of Alexander the Great's fantastic and luxurious celebrations of his victory over the Persian Darius was a mass wedding-feast. Hundreds of his men took Persian wives, some of them carelessly forgetting that they had wives at home—indeed Alexander, himself, had a wife at home, but he married the daughter (some say the wife) of Darius, whose later devotion to him was phenomenal.

But having captured the harem of Darius, he became more and more attracted by Oriental ideas. The splendors, extravagances and worship of rulers seemed made just for him. So he strutted and postured as an Oriental monarch.

He had the idea of welding the East and West by wedding them and set the style by his mass-marriage in one of the most extravagant pageants of pomp in history. Dancers by the thousand, music and flowers to drug the senses, meats and wines and fruits brought by a steady stream of servers—hundreds of runners bringing snow from the mountains to chill the sun-sweet grapes. White doves drawing tiny jeweled chariots down the banquet tables, carrying love messages. Melody, poetry, romance and wit—provided for the guests.

Hospitality, the most civilized gesture on earth, is just as well served in modest ways. In Merrie Old England, there was a time when the villagers would gather in the castle courtyard and dance to the music they could hear from within. So pretty were the girls and such fine dancers were the young working men that the royal party often decided that there was more fun outside than inside and for a lark joined the peasants in the courtyard.

The act of sharing what one has, to offer a bit of rest and a "spot of tea" to anyone, is just as heart-warming as a great invitation. Today, so swiftly is the world, in spite of wars, moving into a unit of friendship and understanding, that it would be wise for all of us to begin widening our minds to think hospitably of all people.

*THERE IS NO BETTER WAY TO ENLARGE PERSONALITY THAN TO ENTERTAIN.* In war or peace, in poverty or riches, we can share hospitably whatever we have, and invest the occasion with warm companionship and an air of festivity. And no matter how charming an individual may be, he never reaches the height of his powers until he begins to reach others, to serve them in some way—to include them in his thinking. Common sense should be used, of course,—as to getting one's affairs in order, and one's first duties. One says, "I must pay my bills before I start giving parties."

Yet, it is not wholesome to stay too long away from the pleasantries of social activities, be they ever so slight or ever so modest. When the mind dwells too deeply and too long on the self, it shrivels those tendrils of the heart that reach out from the warm and inclusive human being.

As in anything else, only practice keeps a talent bright and shining. You can't sleep for twenty years or twenty months or twenty days and find the world the same.

You may think you can neglect people and still keep your way with them—but you can't. You should do at least enough to keep your hand in, as the saying goes.

*YOU NEED NOT BE A MASTER OF CEREMONIES.* A modest hostess has great charm. Timidity is not the menace to personality that inertia and inexperience are.

Few of us have the opportunities that Dolly Madison, for instance, had. She was head of the White House for sixteen years—hostess for Thomas Jefferson for eight years and mistress during her own husband's two terms.

But from all such brilliant records the truth still emerges that however large the crowd, you succeed with one person at a time—so experience can be gained every day by improving your relations with people.

*TREAT OTHER PEOPLE AS THOUGH YOU WERE RE-SPONSIBLE FOR THEIR HAPPINESS.* In a bombed village of France with chaos and ruin and deprivation all around, several children crawled under a pile of debris for mutual comfort. They were separated from their parents and huddled pitifully together. Presently the oldest one, about twelve, decided that they would only be more miserable by huddling and howling, so she suggested that they pretend they were having a party. They began with more determination than gaiety—spread their lunches that had been hastily wrapped in newspaper, and before long they were thoroughly in the festive spirit of the thing. Several hours later they were found and rescued by a searching party that included the fathers of the children. The older child, in her father's arms, said, "Papa, we used our imaginations to please ourselves instead of listening to the bombs."

The spirit of festivity can at all times rule out much that is dark. When the atmosphere gets taut at home or at the office—turn the strain into some festive channel, however small it may be. Suggest a movie, a game, some refreshment, a trick of home magic. A sense of entertainment clears the air, relaxes everyone.

*START WHERE YOU ARE AND WITH WHAT YOU HAVE.* The ancients believed that all kinds of blessings were attached to hospitality. The Hindu woman left her own food untouched sometimes until afternoon, lest some wayfarer ask for it. There is more than one idea to be gained from the miracle of the loaves and the fishes—from the old stories of entertaining angels unaware.

And remember that strangest of statements in the Bible—"To him that hath shall be given—and from him that hath not shall be taken away even that which he hath." This is a warning to use what we have—to plant the seed of our endeavors else there will be no harvest.

You'll be surprised how quickly your skill will grow.

*RICH AND POOR ALIKE NEED EXPERIENCE.* None of us is free from the necessity of learning graciousness by being gracious. To buy one's service at a hotel may be a convenience—but the hostess must still breathe warmth and unity into her party.

Though it is possible for a charming woman to live in one room, never entertain, and yet occupy an enviable social position, there are very few such people. Ordinarily, the easiest and the happiest social life ensues when we do at least a little of the entertaining. Besides, the woman in one room, if her bed can be made to look like a couch, may entertain as many people as the space will contain, standing up.

*THE CASUAL MANNER IS IDEAL.* All too many people regard a party as a great undertaking. But if one's house is always kept shining and well-ordered, the actual party preparations amount to very little. I am urging you to entertain more often—but do learn to do it more easily, more casually. If a party is a great work to you, school yourself to think otherwise about it. No matter if you live in a palace or a hovel—give a party and see how casual and relaxed you can be about it.

Give a late afternoon or evening party, since more men will be available at those times. For an afternoon party, city or country, indoors or out, you can do with a punchbowl and some tiny sandwiches and canapés. You may have fine flowers for decoration or a stone jar full of wild yarrow or Queen Anne's lace. It is becoming smart to use nature's flowers as often as the cultivated varieties. Besides these material things, which are simple in the extreme, all you need is something to talk about, a happy face and a gracious manner.

Your invitations can be telephoned—or a mere sentence written on your note paper: "Dear Mrs. Allison, A number of friends are coming in Tuesday from five to seven to tea. Please come too. Alice Jones." Or, on your visiting card, write in the lower left corner, "Tuesday, June 8, five to seven, Tea."

Your evening party is a matter of your own inventive mind and the type of guests you will invite. For friends you know very well it would be amusing to take them to a movie and then home again for a buffet supper.

*SIMPLE DELICIOUS FOOD IS PREFERABLE.* Food, for such occasions, may be simple if it is delicious. The main dish in many smart houses is Italian spaghetti, with a hot tomato and meat sauce. Or it may be baked beans if they are exceptionally good. Corned beef is enjoyed for a change. Or a Chinese dish. Salads in large wooden or other bowls may be the simplest apple and celery mixture, or the most expensive frozen concoctions, or maybe avocados, halved and filled with French dressing. Coffee and cake are sufficient dessert. A buffet usually has both cold and hot dishes on a table arranged as attractively as possible.

Of course, if you prefer to have elaborate parties, go right ahead. But you'll find your social contacts easier if you'll learn the knack of getting up spontaneous little parties (or large ones either) that do not require much preparation. At any party a large wooden or other bowl of popcorn or potato chips is welcome indeed. Also, people seem to enjoy nibbling crisp little slivers of raw vegetables taken with the fingers from a bowl of crushed ice. Celery, carrot, and turnip are delicious served this way. I'm not attempting to suggest menus, but merely to point out the great simplicity of smart, modern entertaining. Learn to entertain effortlessly. Plan now for a simple, joyous party.

*KEEP A CARD FILE OF PEOPLE'S NAMES.* About your guests —do you keep a list of friends and acquaintances? Everyone should do so! Many more parties would be given if it weren't such a task to look up the full names and addresses of those whom we wish to invite. Oh, do learn to keep in touch with people! A girl should never let herself sink into the uninspired groove of being in touch with people only at their parties or when she entertains them.

*The successful man or woman keeps himself in the minds of other people. This ability is a great asset in either business or private life. CHAPTER FIVE discusses ways and means to keep yourself before your friends—tells you how to stay in active contact with people.*

## 2. HOW TO BE SOCIALLY AT EASE

Now suppose we make a practical application of what we have learned so far. Let us imagine that you are invited to a lovely party where you will meet strangers as well as people you know. I have decided to make this a tea, as the uncharted casual contacts of a tea-party most nearly parallel those of everyday experience.

*PLACE YOURSELF MENTALLY BEFORE YOU GO.* Before we go to the party it will be well to study your attitude on your relation to other people generally. Right here your inferiority complex—everybody has one of sorts—begins to stir like a waking beast, doesn't it? So our first task is to put him to sleep again until we can get rid of him permanently.

You can't have a good time at a party or be charming unless you feel on an equal footing with everyone present. Of course, it would be absurd and stupid to compare yourself with your hostess or host and each guest to see if you are an equal. So we must rid ourselves of these surface comparisons. They are unprofitable and odious.

If a great singer is present you can't honestly feel that your voice is as good as hers. If the richest woman in the community is there, gorgeously gowned, how could you feel that you are as well-dressed as she? Unless you are a striking beauty you can't honestly feel that you are as good-looking as the prettiest woman there. Unless you have a dynamic personality and are a witty conversationalist you can't even imagine that you are as entertaining as the cleverest woman present. The most popular and beloved woman may be none of these —but she is *charming*. So why bother with such comparisons!

There is another more important and deeper equality that you *can* feel which will enable you to mingle easily and enjoy yourself with people above you and below you on the social ladder. It is impossible to keep your social contacts on an even keel. If you lived in a palace and had six secretaries to protect your exclusiveness you would still meet a number of undesirable people. So you must reach a point in poise and charm where you remain the same regardless of what or whom you contact!

For this type of poise we must have a little philosophy that supports our conviction of equality. There is a danger here that in striving too hard for a sense of equality with the highest types of people one may be a little belligerent and say with a chip on the shoulder, "I am as good as anybody in the world." The crudeness and bad taste that would prompt such a statement in that mood are sufficient proof that one is not!

*FEEL A BASIC KINSHIP WITH EVERYONE.* But what we do want to realize deeply is that all of us are of one fundamental essence. We are all traveling the same path. The only difference in people is that each has arrived at a different place on that same path—but we all have the same feelings and the same reactions somewhere along the way.

So no matter how shy and small you feel, you may know that everyone present has experienced that same thing. If they have overcome it and seem assured, that should only prove to you that you, also, can conquer your self-consciousness. Try to understand that the other fellow has his problems of inferiority, perhaps not just the same as yours, but, nevertheless, just as real to him.

When you are meeting a new person, try to think of the stranger's problem of instantly adjusting to you—try to help him find familiar ground where he can be at ease. This will accomplish two things. It will take your mind off yourself, eliminating for the moment any possibility of your self-consciousness. (You know you can't be self-conscious unless you are thinking about yourself!) Then, too, your interest in the new-comer will make him think you are charming. Never be afraid to go more than half-way to establish social ease. Don't be afraid to walk up to people at a reception or party or tea to say or do something that will make them happier. A wall-flower is usually self-elected. She slips through the door and slides into a side seat on the edge of the room as though she were clinging to the edge of a whirling disk and might be thrown off any minute.

*NEVER TAKE THE FIRST CHAIR IN A ROOM*—walk calmly well inside and take the most inviting chair that is vacant! Step aside and relinquish it only to a much older woman—never to a man.

Pause before you enter the room, see where people are, locate your hostess or whoever is in charge of the affair. Go to her and shake hands. She will introduce you to those standing in her immediate group. A man never extends his hand first to a woman. Women are shaking hands less and less—a cordial bow and a "How do you do" suffice. But never refuse a proffered hand. If you are enthusiastically glad to see someone, extend your hand warmly.

A charming hostess will never let people dangle after she introduces them—she will give them some basis for conversation, if nothing more than, "Miss Smith has just returned from Chicago," or "Mr. Smith was kind enough to pull himself from his beloved garden to come

over today." If the words "Chicago" or "garden" don't start an ava-
lanche of conversation it is because the guests have lock-jaw. There
is always *something* that a hostess can say that may serve as a conversational springboard. But I am getting ahead of myself. This is not
a lesson on conversation. Much of that follows in the book. Perhaps
lessons on conversation are the ones we need and enjoy most, but we
are not quite ready for them yet.

*ROUND-THE-ROOM INTRODUCTIONS.* In a small room, if
everyone stops talking and looks up at a new-comer, then and only
then should there be a round-the-room introduction. Don't start hand-
shaking in this case. It takes too long. Men always stand when women
are standing *anywhere,* and when being introduced to men or women.
If the party has broken up into several conversational groups, introduce the new arrival only to those nearest. A clever hostess will break
up these groups before they get "frozen" and let others reassemble.
She may walk deliberately up to a group and take out a man or
woman whom she leads to another group for some special purpose
or sometimes for no reason at all. Guests under one roof may con-
verse without specific introductions. (This is not true of public parties.)
They may give their names to each other if they wish.

No matter how austere or important any person may be, you may
know that just below the polished surface he is a quivering mass of
sensitiveness, finding protection behind good manners, aloofness or,
sometimes, like a cactus, putting out stickers to fend off intruders.

Never let such a person throw you off your base. Sympathize with
him! Always know that the sharper the barbs, the tenderer the mar-
row! *No one but the woman (or man) with a tremendous inferiority
complex would find it necessary to bolster up her own confidence by
rudeness.*

The woman who is sure of herself is inclusive in a gentle way—
not as a side-show barker is inclusive. Perhaps one of the greatest
secrets of charm is to give those near you the feeling that they are
included in your thoughts, your conversation. Make them realize that
you are aware of their presence and are concerned, a little, about their
happiness and comfort.

*A LITTLE SMILE DOES A BIG JOB.* A gracious woman I know can smile in such a way at a timid girl sitting across the room that the girl is instantly at ease. Her smile seems to say, "You and I understand something together, don't we?" Now the only difference between the timid girl and the gracious, charming woman who is poised enough to be able to put her mind on others *completely* is this —the charming woman has so broadened her mind and her sympathies that she finds other things and other people *actually* more interesting than her own affairs.

This same woman, standing once in a mixed group in a fashionable ballroom, felt her little pink, silk panties drop to her ankles. She calmly stepped out of them and without hurry stooped to pick them up and, folding them into a little bundle, stood holding them while she finished a conversation. Then she walked calmly and naturally from the room and put them on again. Even losing such an intimate garment could not bring her mind to herself sufficiently to cause her to be awkwardly embarrassed. The other guests discreetly paid no attention except one girl who tittered—no one noticed her and she was the only one who was embarrassed.

This is another proof that people put the same interpretation on us that we put on ourselves. They take their cue from us! We cannot control the smoothness of life from without—but we *can* control it from within—we *can* control our reactions to anything that happens to us. This is poise!

*NEVER DO ANYTHING THAT IS AWKWARD AND GROTESQUE JUST FOR THE SAKE OF A LAUGH.* When you feel tempted to turn clown, lock yourself in your room and turn somersaults until you get over it. When the laugh is over people seek beauty and charm for permanent associations. You can be funny, "side-splittingly" funny without doing anything actually unlovely. A laugh may have so much disillusion in it that it costs you too much in the end. If you can't be funny without being ugly—then *don't*. Take your friends to the theatre or circus or buy them an amusing book.

How often have you heard a woman say, "Poor Jane, she's had such a sad life and she used to be such a 'cute' girl—the life of the party!"

Don't think that I mean you must bury humor in order to be lastingly charming. By all means be light and gay. A long face is not charming. But your fun, no matter how gay, must never go beyond the bounds of good taste and *femininity!* Even Marie Dressler's appeal was based really on her universal kinship with humanity and her golden, womanly heart.

*DON'T BE AFRAID TO ADMIRE AND INQUIRE.* While at a party, or at any time, never be afraid to admire some object or aspect of any room you may be in. All people like to have their acquisitions appreciated. The inexperienced, self-conscious girl is ashamed of not knowing about things. The cultured girl is eager to learn what is new and never hesitates to say she doesn't know either a new or an old fact. Of course she doesn't say or act "I don't know much" in a silly, diffident way. Rather she takes the attitude that everyone *should* tell her something she doesn't know—just by way of entertaining her if nothing more.

*CULTURED PEOPLE ASK QUESTIONS.* If you do not know what fork or knife to use and feel that it makes any difference (usually it doesn't) ask casually of your dinner partner or your host, "Just which of these is intended for this course?" No one will think twice about it, for silver does vary in size, shape and purpose in different houses. But if you act confused and get tightened up over what you suppose to be an exhibition of your ignorance, everyone will notice you. Again—people put the same valuation on your acts that you put on them.

Social form is not nearly as rigid as some people would like to have us believe. The only real faux pas (social error) is unkindness. A delightful Englishwoman dining once at my house asked for a spoon to replace the cocktail fork. Her reason was that my cocktail sauce was so delicious and she could not get it all with a fork. While it was a daring thing to do, her reason made it a compliment. The dinner immediately became very informal and everyone had a delightful time. The point is—make your silver serve you—don't be a slave to it. I'm sure the most formal hostess would eventually forgive a guest who stood on her head better to appreciate a decorated ceiling! The unforgivable thing is little, tight, stiff, fearful unresponsiveness.

*NEVER BE OBVIOUSLY COCK-SURE.* Perfect freedom of thought, movement and speech contributes to charm. Never lose your humanness! Never let it be sapped away from you by the false weight of formality. "Formal" refers to dress and service—and not to personality. If you feel that you must dress up your personality when going to a formal function you may know that you are less than you should be in your daily living. When I said "perfect freedom," I meant, of course, within the bounds of good-taste and kindness. So don't be afraid of making mistakes. The only important mistake you *can* make that will condemn you in good society is to pretend to be something you are not—to know something you do not know. *Never* be "cock-sure." This manner is a challenge and calls for a perfect performance from you. Appearing just a little uncertain enhances your feminine appeal and enables you to fall short without your shortcomings being noticed.

## 3. THE PERSON YOU REALLY ARE

*WHEN WE REALIZE THAT THERE IS A STEADFAST, DIVINE PERSONALITY WITHIN US THAT IS BIGGER AND FINER THAN ANYTHING THAT CAN HAPPEN TO IT, WE HAVE JUST BEGUN TO LIVE!* This is when we get up on two feet from the all-fours of animalism and bewildered ignorance and realize that we have souls. *The experience passes but the experiencer remains* to have other experiences.

When you realize the importance of this "experiencer" within you, then you are in a position to develop unshakable poise. This is not a religious conception—it is an unalterable fact of life. *The person that you really are is so basically a part of the harmony of the universe—so established in the world of reality—that you can afford to take your importance for granted and put your mind on others.*

When you understand this *basic truth* you will become socially un-selfed and immersed in sociability. Just to refrain from talking about yourself, not to be patting your hair and clothes and not to patch your make-up in public—these do not guarantee charm. These are but the first baby steps toward charm in being socially unselfed. Charm demands that you be *genuinely* interested in your companions—you can't fake it!

*YOU MUST SHOW GENUINE INTEREST.* You must be so interested in other people that you understand their humanness, stand ready to smile at their arrogance, to fix up their failures, to admire their accomplishments and to ignore their errors. People are fascinating—the most fascinating study in the world!

While I wouldn't for anything let you get a morbid attitude toward other people's problems, nevertheless, *if you can always feel a little sorry for humanity in general, you will find it easier to keep your poise among people who may be your social or intellectual superiors. In other words, if you can give humanity a mental handclasp of sympathy and at the same time a wink of tolerance, no king nor queen can throw you off poise!*

Just relax before you enter a room full of people, no matter who is in it, and say to yourself, "Well, bless their hearts, we're all in the same boat even if we have tried to paste different labels on ourselves and parade in different costumes." (Someone objected to this as a mixed metaphor but I contend that we can paste and parade if we want to.)

Now, let us think of you as a musician with a divine inspiration—the very spirit of melody in his veins, eager to pour his message out to soothe and heal the world with the perfect beauty of his music. He cannot sway the hearts of people unless he is thus fired from within. But—neither can he be effective if his instrument is inferior. Your personality is your instrument!

On the other hand, imagine a musician with a fine instrument, who has faithfully applied himself to the mastering of a difficult technique. Hours upon hours, years upon years, he has devoted to finger exercises, to the execution of an exacting craft. But if he has not the fire of inspiration back of his playing, its cold perfection will leave his audiences unmoved and ready to criticize any fault.

An audience will love the one who interprets inner beauty by the fire of his personal passion to do so and will forgive and ignore his mistakes.

*"THE GODS DEPART ON FEET OF WOOL."* This old Chinese proverb means that enchantment, power and full inspiration leave us quietly, slowly. We do not hear them go.

Have you ever watched the sudden success of people whose accord with universal power (inspiration) was so absolute that they simply swept the world before them? Have you ever wondered what had happened to them in later years when success faded from their grasp? Nine out of ten times it was simply that the adulation they received gradually convinced them that they were great—independent of anything else. They slowly lost touch with the great universal power of beauty—thought it was contained in their own persons—and their inspiration diminished as it was cut off from its source until it became too small to continue to interest the public.

*YOU MUST NEVER LOSE TOUCH WITH YOUR SOURCE.* I am telling you this because I want you to realize that charm cannot be confined to the merely personal things—never lose the feel of humanity in its largest and strongest sense. If you *will* hold that power you will have an electrical presence. When you enter a room everyone in it will know that "somebody" has arrived.

*No matter how perfectly groomed, how smooth, how poised, and correct you may be, you are still a corpse, a very mockery of charm unless you radiate this inner and universal fire of beauty!*

It tends to keep your mind off yourself, thus helping to conquer self-consciousness. It frees your energies for others. How much easier it is to drink from the eternal stream of power than to try to generate it all yourself!

Keep your vision high and know that your soul can grow and grow and keep on growing through eternity—that there is no end to the beauty and charm that you can absorb and express—that the world needs the highest of you—the best of you, at its most charming freedom, to lead on by sheer fascination to a glimpse of the glory in its own soul.

This sort of charm has real power—draws the best things of life to you. This is the sort of charm that draws delightful people and happenings like a dynamic magnet. Why? Because you are in touch with the source of all beauty, the rhythm of life itself. You are bringing to people the very magnetism that holds the world in its place and swings the stars.

*KEEP CLOSE TO THIS FEELING OF ONENESS WITH THE WORLD.* Drink deep of the loveliness of the harmony and rhythm that sway the tides back and forth—that speak through the measures of music—and the meter of poetry—and the beat of your own heart. Do you not see that it is really the heart of the universe pulsing in your own body?

What king or queen can have more? Put your head up—your shoulders back. Lift your eyes and never let them shift or waver uncertainly again, no matter what or whom they behold. For the real nature of you is divine and is itself all the graces the mind can possibly conceive. So sweep out all in your thoughts that tends to restrict or bind or limit the flow of this natural charm in and through you.

### INSTRUCTIONS

1. Practice pausing an instant at the door of a room.
2. Continue the exercises of CHAPTER THREE, especially the mental ones and those concerned with finding conversation material.
3. Continue the "getting acquainted with yourself" exercise, as well as the exercises given for graceful walking.

# CHAPTER FIVE

## *The Party Begins*

### 1. WE ARE GOING TO THE PARTY

Now we're going to have need of our "small talk"—for we are going to the party.

Let us suppose that you are now standing ready to ring the doorbell of a large, fashionable house where the party is being given. Your hostess is a woman you meet very seldom. Invitations to her affairs are coveted by everyone who knows her. This particular day she is giving a tea in honor of a novelist who lived in your town before she became famous. You wonder if the novelist will remember you. You wonder just how intimate your greeting of her should be. You wonder as you press the bell if the hostess really likes you. You wonder what impression you will make on the guests or if you will be so awful or negative that you will not be invited again. You wonder what you will say to the servant or to whomever opens the door. Too late now! You should have decided all these points before you put your hat on. What are you going to say? What are you going to do? As we go through this occasion you may see yourself as hostess, assisting friend or as the guest. The same principles that apply here are equally valuable in all human contacts whether social or business.

### 2. WHAT WILL YOU WEAR?

So much depends upon where you live—and what the customs are of those about you. In New York we wear quite plain clothes during the day—and do our blossoming in the evening. With the exception of middle-aged women who make quite a function of lunch in fash-

ionable places, and who invariably wear delicious millinery concoctions and some jewels, the rest of New York is likely to be tailored.

In New York, we do not wear long-skirted dresses to afternoon
functions. But in many places the ladies *do* wear long dresses in the
afternoon. One comes finally to admire the woman who wears what
she pleases at any time—clothes that are suitable to what she is doing,
how she is living, her purse, and her picture of herself.

It is just common sense for most of us to get through the morning
in a sort of practical neutral outfit—to add to it for afternoon, if we
don't or can't change, a flower, a veil, nicer gloves or our best furs.
Or a small flowered or otherwise decorated hat will sometimes look
well with a simple dress or suit for afternoon. Certainly flowered
flounces and consciously trimmed dresses have no place except at
home or calling in one's immediate neighborhood.

Instead of getting all dressed up, most women would look better
if they had a smart hair-do and fresh make-up, a shoe-shine and a
lingerie jabot. Hats are usually worn to lunch in public and private—
but there is no law to prevent a woman at home from taking off her
hat and inviting her guests to do likewise.

At dinner, one is hatless, if there is any attempt at all to dress for
dinner. There are some women with such a flair for chic that they
can put on just one outstanding accent and look smarter than smart.

If money or time means anything, the average woman had better
let exotic clothes alone. That hat that looks so arresting in the magazine is likely to draw a gallery of small boys in one's home town.
Unless there is a maid available, she had best shun all ruffles and all
pleats. The smartest busy women I know depend upon color and accents of removable decorations.

But having dressed, inconspicuously, we hope, but becomingly,
you now put everything about yourself firmly out of your mind—completely out of your mind—and go forward to see and enjoy *other
people*. Your mind has been so well-trained (to stay on one subject
to the exclusion of all else) that it will stay off yourself—and not stray
back to wonder if the nice-looking man in the corner is thinking that
you look nice. You will not do that back-and-forth agonizing about
how you are registering in any way with anybody.

You are going to see how other people register with you! You are genuinely interested in them—like them. You enjoy their color, movement, companionship and conversation. Every bit of your mind is free for them. You are going to help them put on their show. You haven't any show to put on, no tricks—nothing up your sleeve. You're just an amiable, relaxed, appreciative *audience*.

## 3. THE "NOT-AT-HOME" ETIQUETTE

People eager to get to the masters of the house sometimes do not realize the rudeness of pelting with questions the person who answers the door. The Negro maid mentioned previously was a past mistress at evasion if she did not wish to give out any information about the family. "I tells 'em whut I wants 'em to know," she said firmly, "but when dey starts signifyin' I doan tell 'em nuthin', no, ma'am, not nuthin'." How nice it would be if small brothers or little sisters could be trained into the same non-communicativeness.

But all too often a fifth column could not divulge family weaknesses better than one of its own members. One little girl I know said to an insistent caller, "Father's not at home. He's upstairs deciding what bills to pay this month—mother is taking a nap with her frown plasters and her chin strap on—and I've got to run next door and see if we can't keep their ladder another week, so there's nobody at home."

Which reminds us of the note a French housekeeper pinned on the front door when she went to do an errand. She had been trained in the school of courtesy that gives reasons for all restrictions or refusals —a school of thought still alive today. The note read, "Please do not ring the bell. Monsieur is shaving, Madame is in a rage, Mademoiselle is courting—and me, I have gone to market."

A kind fate has finally fixed things so that it is not lying to send word that one is not "at home." Neither is it an affront—it might well spare the caller under some circumstances.

## 4. WHAT DO YOU BRING TO THE PARTY?

A child will look squarely in your eyes and say frankly, "What did you bring me?" Grown-ups do not say it but they think it and think it constantly. And by the way, what do you bring? Anything anyone will want? Do you bring poise, beauty, cheer, freshness, a clipping, a story, some harmless gossip or a compliment? Do you bring appreciation, admiration, good-looks, affection or a box of candy?

Surely you brought something. If you didn't why did you come? Oh, you came to get some sympathy and admiration! Then, if you don't overdo it, you did bring something of value—the compliment of assuming that your friend can and will help you.

One of the most beloved couples in our town was to some extent also one of our greatest nuisances. But in all truth it must be admitted that everybody liked them. They were always included! While some people criticized them, it was like criticizing a member of one's family—an art many tongues should acquire.

Personally, I'd rather be considered a pest than to be ignored altogether. As our maid once expressed it, "It sho' is the truf, ma'am, dat de pests is allus at de parties! Dey sho' keeps theyse'f in mind. Dey sweet-talks ev'ybody into doin' sumpin' fer 'em. But dey sho' is nice and thoughtful."

Anything is better than a negative, aloof, detached, independent, cold, unresponsive attitude that says, "Well, here I am at your party. I don't know why you invited me—or why in the world I came—but I'm here now—what are you going to do about it?" These are the people one simply can't remember the next time, though they're nice enough, whatever that means. However, a certain type of waiting, not pushing, is always better for new people. A woman alone had better be very careful about pushing or over-enthusiasm. She is easily misunderstood. She should understand that she is a social menace anyway (of which more later) and conduct herself accordingly.

## 5. THE IMPORTANCE OF LIKING PEOPLE

*YOU MUST HONESTLY LIKE PEOPLE.* Theodore Roosevelt was once talking to Judge John Carver Rose. He was telling the judge of having talked with McKinley for two hours.

He said, "Do you know, I believe Mr. McKinley likes me."

The judge smiled and said, "You and Mr. McKinley both have a way of making any man you talk to for five minutes believe that you like him." Roosevelt thought this over and then said, "The truth is, I never talk to a man for five minutes without liking him."

It is so with all people who have great extensive influence. Only a genuine caring carries the warm vibrations of the heart out to warm the hearts of others. Wasn't Lincoln's greatest hold over people the fact that he loved them?—so much that he perfected the art of words so that he might more sensitively communicate with them.

Most of the people who really succeed on the stage or the screen have or develop great hearts—have deep capacity for understanding and pity—and most of them do far more charity work than is ever reported by their publicity people.

Many years ago I was deeply impressed by the extremes to which Mary Pickford would go in her tenderness and kindness. I was driving through the crowded narrow streets of Venice, California, when an old lady stumbled and fell in front of my car. We picked her up and helped her into our car and took her home. She gave us the name of Mrs. Moore—and we dismissed the incident from our minds. The next morning, the telephone rang and the voice of Miss Pickford, not her secretary, thanked me for my kindness to her erstwhile mother-in-law. I listened with amazement as I swiftly counted the years since Owen Moore had been in Mary Pickford's life—but she never gave up being kind and generous to the elderly Mrs. Moore.

The college girl or boy who is popular is usually discovered to be sincerely interested in his fellows.

Most of us *do* like other people. But, we may fear them a little—fear their ridicule, fear that they will usurp the advantages we want for ourselves, or the affections of someone we care about. All this fear is based on a sense of inferiority which a certain amount of training in correct thinking and acting will dissolve. In the realm of personality we can truly quote President Franklin D. Roosevelt in the time of national uncertainty, "The greatest thing we have to fear, is fear itself!"

## 6. YOUR SOCIAL LIFE

Before we go further with our party, let's talk a minute about your own social plans. World conditions, no doubt, alter them—but no matter what we do or how we serve, we shall be in contact with others. Our effect on them can aid us in any duty or career. Let's review your habits and equipment for making a success of those plans. When I speak of social success I do not confine my meaning to parties but refer to society in the larger sense which includes all of humanity. Let's bear in mind that the ability to meet people well, smoothly and effectively is as important in business as it is in a drawing-room. Because one's living may depend upon it in business, it is probably more important.

*MANNER IN SOCIETY AND BUSINESS THE SAME.* Yet it is hard to tell just where social life stops and business life begins. I suppose that depends on the business one may be in. Our need of using an effective technique in dealing with other people is seen in every walk of life—at home where our influence should be great in molding the characters of our children and in gaining good service from tradespeople; in an office, whether as telephone operator, confidential secretary or executive; in social life both as guest and hostess— *the same qualities and abilities are needed.*

Sometimes a woman says that my work is keyed to society and asks for something directed to a simple housewife. I write to her and explain that the *same principles apply* to all social intercourse. She must meet human beings—and there is a *best way* to meet them, a way to have more satisfactory relations with everyone with whom she comes in contact. So do not be blinded by the setting of a party in our little drama, but picture in your mind how you can use each point in other situations in your own life.

In this way you can make the lessons useful to you at every turn every day. The advice given here simply points out the best way to have happy relations with people. To get the most out of anything we must approach it with some idea of organized efficiency—not enough to strangle inspiration and spontaneity, but enough to get dependable results. So let's apply one or two ideas of efficiency to social life and see if, by comparing your own habits with them, you can improve your own life.

*YOU CAN'T BE INDEPENDENT.* To begin with—people are necessary to our success. No matter how much we think we want to be absolutely independent, it is impossible. We are definitely dependent upon others for happiness, for business, for consolation, for companionship and for appreciation. Just to carry out our little analogy we'll call the people in your life your "stock in trade." Now, a business cannot succeed unless an accurate record is kept of its stock—otherwise it would not know where it stood. As a store carries an inventory of its stock, so should you carry an inventory of every acquaintance you are fortunate enough to have.

*HAVE YOU STARTED YOUR FILE OF ADDRESSES?* No doubt you have a list of friends to whom you send Christmas cards and a list tucked away somewhere of young people who were invited to your sister's graduation party or your daughter's debut. But, have you a systematic filing system where you cherish the names *and addresses and telephone numbers* of all the people you meet who make more than a slight impression upon you? If you are going to keep in touch with people as you should, you need a well-kept list. Otherwise it is such a great effort to get all their names together every time you want them that you simply don't make the effort. Part of effortless party giving is in a neat list. If you must call up Mary Jones to find out what her cousin's new married name is, you may do it once, or even twice—but there you stop.

For your own sake, for your children's sakes and for your friends' sakes, start today—if you haven't already done so—to keep a file-card list of your acquaintances. I cannot urge you too strongly to do this. Its value may not be apparent at this moment but, if you have it in good shape, you'll *use it*—though you may not think so now.

You can, of course, have an expensive and elaborate little file box. But you can get quite decent-looking ones at the five-and-ten-cent store, an alphabet and cards for another twenty cents—and you have started a sensible way of keeping your most valuable possession for an investment of thirty cents. The card system is vastly superior to a little book too easily lost and with no space for corrections.

If you have only two friends—start with those names. Almost automatically you'll add to them rapidly, once you become alive to the interest in them. A woman in the most modest circumstances, even living in one room, should know at least fifty people whom she could get in touch with quickly. I have tracked down the reasons for social failures—it is my business to do so—and I am convinced that a common cause is the lax- or no- list failing. We should make it easy for ourselves to make certain gestures of friendliness—else they remain unmade. So we sit at home by the open window looking out wistfully, wondering how on earth one keeps in touch with the surging life out there in the world.

*ONE FRIEND LEADS TO ANOTHER.* "But," you say, "I want to be discriminating and I know only two or three people of my own kind—and if I can't go with the best I'll just stay at home." Not a very courageous point of view! Water seeks its own level anyway. Each of those "undesirable" people you are shunning knows two or three "desirable" ones. And it's odd how the "undesirable" ones have the impudence to blossom out almost overnight, make brilliant marriages, take up an interesting career or begin to assume positions of importance in the community through service to it. Everybody can teach you something. Learn to gather to yourself bits of knowledge from them.

Start right where you are to make a wider social life for yourself. Social talents are developed, as a rule, and you may as well practice on the material at hand. If you develop your social talent and have a warm, loving attitude toward all humanity, you'll be drafted for more important duties some day in the social scheme. And even though you may feel (wrongly) that you have nothing to gain from certain people, you will gain a great deal by being of service to them. To think of yourself all the time is the best way to kill your charm completely. Make yourself active with every decent, self-respecting person who comes within reach of your smiling friendliness.

But while we are being of service to these people we should never let them suspect that we are condescending to boss their lives for them.

A good way to be cordially hated is to be obviously superior. We should tactfully and not hurriedly or too firmly introduce our ideas into other people's lives. Gratuitous advice should be given in the spirit that only a very little thing is needed to make the "advisee" quite perfect. And even then, only if you're asked!

*PROMPT REPLIES ARE CHARMING.* But we must examine your social habits with an eye to improving them. Do you answer your mail more or less promptly? Do you reply to every invitation? Etiquette doesn't demand that visiting-card invitations be answered unless an answer is requested but charm says every thought of you should be thoughtfully answered. To a friend, reply on your own card, crossing out "Miss" and your last name. Write any little message from "Delighted to come, Wed. 17th," to "Indeed I'll be there," or "Wild horses couldn't hold me next Wednesday," or "Sweet of you to think of me. I'm certainly coming," or anything else you want to say.

A note of regret would be worded in the same person as the invitation. A formal regret would read—"Mr. and Mrs. Invited regret that owing to a previous engagement they cannot accept Mrs. Inviter's kind invitation to dinner at . . . on . . ."

A telephoned invitation can be accepted or regretted likewise by telephone. "Mary? We just got in and found your message. How sweet of you to ask us over—but unfortunately we won't be able to come. Fred's brother has arranged the whole day and evening for us—and I know we wouldn't be back in time. I'm so sorry to miss being with you."

Or if an informal note is dropped, it, too, should give a reason why the invitation cannot be accepted. "Dear Alice, If we'd only known about your party sooner! But here we are with plans and arrangements made quite a while ago to take the children to a concert—tickets bought and youthful hopes high. We'll be thinking of you and hoping that we will be more fortunate next time."

No ordinary mortal can indulge in the witty rudeness attributed to a Hollywood star who is supposed to have answered an unwelcome telephoned invitation with—"I shan't be able to come. I have a previous engagement which I shall make as soon as I hang up."

Little notes are the smart response these days. Women of chic who are active write an incredible number of notes. There is no better way of keeping in touch with a number of people. Have a good supply of good-looking note paper, a good pen, ink, stamps and a good light —then write short little notes to two people every day of your life. A note may have but two lines in it. There need be no further excuse for it than the fact that you thought of the person to whom it is addressed. Enclose a newspaper clipping, perhaps, and say, "What do you make of this?" or "This is in line with our discussion. Wondered if you saw it." Or "Here's an opposite point of view that certainly vanquishes me. I'm yielding the palm. Why not come and get it next Wednesday?"

*WRITE SHORT NOTES.* It isn't necessary to weary yourself and exhaust your topic by a long letter, unless there is a real reason for writing one. Form the habit of jotting down brief little thoughts that show an interest in the welfare and amusement of the people you know. But with men it is best to be absolutely impersonal. Don't enclose sentimental verses in letters to them—though something that is beautifully worded would do very nicely. Make your note stimulating, ignite the fire of thought with it. But make it short. Don't hold the match until you burn your fingers with it.

*LET OTHERS HELP YOU LIVE.* Mrs. Franklin Roosevelt says that the reason she can accomplish so much is that she gets everybody to help her. To be closer to numbers of people, let them help you live. I do not refer to financial assistance, of course. But get your friends to do little things for you. Ask them for information. There is nothing "personal" in calling up a man to ask him for help with a puzzle if you are casual and gay about it. Ask him something if it's only how to spell "cat." Don't get the conversation off the point—be brief— thank him for his help and hang up. At least let any other topic come from him.

If some man thinks that you are pursuing him, call him up sweetly and casually ask him to bring another girl to your house, either to a party or for an evening. This leaves you free to approach him whenever you want to. Call up women of all ages when some little message occurs to you that would interest them—not at meal time!

The point is—*keep in touch with people* if you have to organize a hiking club or a front-porch choir.

*BE A BOOK BORROWER*—if you are equally punctilious about returning them. Books furnish one with an impersonal approach to their owners. But the interest in the subjects must be genuine. A discussion of the characters or ideas in a book is always stimulating. One can always say, "Would you have done what this man did under the strange circumstances of the story?" or "Does that seem consistent to you?"

*BE WILLING TO GO MORE THAN HALF-WAY* in keeping in contact with your friends. Don't count calls or invitations. Learn to live on the plane of spontaneous interest. Don't wonder self-consciously what the person you approach is going to think—just proceed with an open mind and heart and let nothing crush your enthusiasm.

*LEARN TO MAKE LITTLE CASUAL CONTACTS WITH PEOPLE.* Then you will be in their minds much more often than if you merely wait to be seen at your or their parties. Invent your own ways of keeping in touch with your friends. Don't let lethargy, or lack of a list, or improper writing facilities keep you from being more in touch with people. *People make life. The more people—the more life.* From among numbers there will grow up close to you a group that will belong to you—people you would not have had, had you not kept yourself in circulation. Don't think that it takes smart clothes and money. They help, of course, but accomplish very little in themselves. Cultivate a casual, inclusive manner. Snobs are distinctly out of style—passé! Go ahead and give parties—with much or little equipment. Practice hospitality, answer your mail, write notes— lots of them. *Keep in touch with people. And keep a list of acquaintances.* This suggestion has unusual significance in your life.

In the preceding four chapters we have discussed the fundamentals of fitting yourself for public contacts. But please do not abandon them now that we are in the more-interesting-to-you discussions that concern others as well as yourself. The first four chapters will bear re-reading and re-studying. Please continue the exercises throughout the book. Even if you have grasped all the teachings mentally, that does not mean that you can use the principles involved without practice.

Read them over for their inspirational value too. They are rather crowded with ideas and points, perhaps too many for easy digestion, but I feel that I am dealing with eager, intelligent women who are serious about getting the maximum benefit from this book.

*LET ME SUGGEST THAT YOU REVIEW THE FIRST FOUR CHAPTERS BEFORE YOUR MIND BECOMES TOO FILLED WITH YOUR EFFECT ON OTHERS.* You will find the gaining of effects much easier if you are thoroughly prepared for them.

## 7. AT THE PARTY

The party begins! You have pressed your hostess's bell. The door is opened by a perfect servant to whom you give your name, calling yourself "Miss" or "Mrs." as the case may be. She (or he) will probably ask, "What name, please?" if you hesitate more than a moment. You can depend upon the fact that well-trained servants are a discerning clan and judge accurately your nature and your position in life by your treatment of them. Just be casually pleasant. One is neither haughty nor over-familiar. If the servant is known, through past contact or favors exchanged between friendly neighbors, it is not only correct, but very natural, to greet the servant in a kindly and interested way, but briefly. You may have time to ask one short, personal question of the servant—about her health or some little fact you may know about her. Don't linger.

*BE PLEASANT, BUT BRIEF* and go where she directs you. She will show you or direct you to a room or place where you may remove your things. Perhaps she is the only servant in sight. In that case it is thoughtless to hand her your things and go straight into the drawing-room, for then she must leave her post to dispose of your effects. It is customary to remove your outer coat and keep your hat on at a tea—unless the local custom is to the contrary. Always try to do what is usually done in the place where you are.

*THE HOSTESS WILL BE NEAR THE DOOR* so as to greet her arriving guests conveniently. The host does not stand with her in line, but nearby. She will probably be standing, especially in the early part of the affair. Later she will sit down, to enjoy her guests more and to keep the men near her from standing too long. (No man sits down as long as any woman remains standing in his presence.)

She will be far enough away from the door so that your entrance and the disposal of your coat need not be an *arrival*. You arrive so far as she is concerned when you enter the room where she is. However, I have enjoyed many a small tea where the hostess answered her own bell and seemed to be everywhere at once.

If the servant does not announce you as you enter, and your hostess plainly does not place you, though she is, by her attitude of welcome and the expression of her face, trying to be gracious as she extends her hand to you, you should say clearly, "I am Elizabeth Brown," or if you are married, "I am Mrs. John Brown." If it seems advisable, add a short qualifying sentence, such as "your new neighbor" or "Mrs. Philip Brown's daughter" or something of the sort.

*DON'T PLAY GUESSING GAMES WITH YOUR NAME.* It is very provincial to stand with a self-conscious smile and dare anyone to remember you. I've seen people do this, causing much embarrassment to the hostess, and then tease her with little suggestions, clues, by which she might remember them. It is only the socially inexperienced person who will call on the telephone and say, "Guess who this is." The hostess may have five hundred other guests and may not remember her own name if things are not going right in the back of the house. Good form demands that you do everything possible to make social intercourse as easy and smooth as possible for others.

The hostess says, "How do you do? I remember your mother well. How is she? It is nice to have you living so near. I hope we get to know each other well." To which you reply, "Oh, thank you, I hope so." As you should not take up time in a doorway when other people are trying to claim the hostess, she will probably turn to Mrs. Smith, who is at her elbow to help her receive, and say, "Mrs. Smith, Mrs. Brown, our new neighbor." Mrs. Smith extends her hand because she is on the receiving line. You both say, "How-do-you-do?" which is the official and constant greeting of good society.

*GETTING STARTED.* Mrs. Smith will then lead you away from the door if you look as though you may stand there and talk. She, wishing to make you feel at home, will probably say something amusing, such as, "Well, I don't know whether to sympathize with you or congratulate you on moving among us. Suppose we go over there to the table and get you some tea so you can look us over at your comfortable leisure. We're really not a bad lot—just a little peculiar."

And you would probably say, "I'm so glad to hear you say that—because you look simply too perfect from the outside." On the way over to the tea-table (which is also a coffee table and has tiny, dainty sandwiches as well as small cakes piled attractively on platters of silver or china or glass) Mrs. Smith may introduce to you several guests, each time taking you away after the introduction so that you may quickly meet a number of people who may come up to you later, thereby making the crowd mingle better and giving you a more sociable time. Mrs. Smith may say, "You can't have her now, though I know you're dying to know her. We're going to get a cup of tea and talk about you."

At the tea-table you are presented to the hostess's special friend or friends who are "pouring" for her. Here again do not block the way too long—but don't appear hurried in getting your tea and exchanging pleasantries. Mrs. Smith will leave you there and go back to help the hostess again.

*NOW YOU MUST SINK OR SWIM!* So far you've been led; now you must go alone. You glance about. In spite of the hostess's cordiality and Mrs. Smith's hominess, many of the guests seem to have an aloofness that makes you realize that you are not making any impression—good or bad—you just don't exist! The little group you met at the tea-table has gradually melted away—drifted to other parts of the room. Oh, to be able to drift gracefully in a crowd of people! How is it done?

Well, don't stand there staring wistfully at people's backs. Find an object of art to examine and admire. Sip your tea casually and devote your attention to that painting of misty trees above the mantel—or perhaps a modernistic sculpture.

You wish some man would come over and talk to you as attentively as that one is talking to the girl in the corner. Take your time. Relax. You have at least an hour, perhaps more, in which to make friends.

Here comes a man! No, he's taking an empty cup back to the tea-table. As he starts back you turn around and look squarely at him—not flirtatiously—but eagerly, as though he might be someone you know and want to welcome.

*LOOK EXPECTANT—NEVER HOPEFUL.* Look at him openly—expectantly. This one little word, "expectancy," holds a great big secret of Charm. Do not confuse it with "hopefully." *Never* look at a man hopefully. He hates it—dodges it. But to look at everybody with an eager, almost childlike *expectancy* in your face causes them to respond to you. Expectancy gives the face a freshness, an animation and an interest that stop most people in their tracks.

Then too, it makes a subtle demand on the person who receives your look of expectancy—and everyone likes to come up to demands made on them—it flatters them. The charming woman has an expectant expression always, more or less, that seems to say, "You are the sort of person who always does or says something interesting or pleasant. What is it now?"

So, ten to one, your young man (or old man) will stop to talk to you. He may look at you quizzically and if he is not sure whether he has met you he will start at once to talk about other things, leaving you free to ask his name and give yours if you wish—or not, if there doesn't seem to be any particular impulse to do so.

*ASK HIM SOMETHING OR DEFER TO HIS JUDGMENT* in some way (this goes for women, too), such as, "I was just wondering if you could tell me who painted this picture—could it be a 'Keith'?" Now your man may be able to go into a long and pleasing-to-himself explanation about the picture and pictures in general and all you need to do is to prod him now and then to keep him going until you are tired of it.

But, on the other hand, he may stammer and say, "I don't know a darned thing about painting, but I like them when they're pretty—in fact, I like everything that's pretty," paying you a compliment with a mere glance. Now, don't smile and simper, the compliment was too indirect to take to yourself. Don't even appear to have noticed it!

*SHUN THE PERSONAL.* Go on talking impersonally. "Well, you don't have to know 'art' to admire the ruggedness of modern sculpture. Don't you like the arm on that figure there—looks as if it could do things." He will probably straighten up and say, "Oh, so you like people who do things."

*MEN EXPECT YOU TO FLIRT—SO DON'T.* Now don't let such a remark trip you into saying something flirtatious, for that would be one way to lose the man very quickly. Men all *expect* women to corner them as soon as possible and will hang around for some time wondering when the hooks will be put out. Well, just fool this one—don't put any out. He will want to see you again out of curiosity. Flirting is a cheap, dangerous shortcut to get something you can't hold after you get it.

However, if your young man is forcing you, by a very personal smile, to think of him, you can turn humorous instead of serious and say, "Yes, I admire big, strong men who can carry cups back to the table without spilling them." Be sure there is no sarcasm in your voice—just casual gaiety. "There is art for you. I've practiced that for years," he may say. Always be ready to turn from a serious discussion to light banter, especially if in the light banter there is still a background of your knowledge of the subject in hand.

*NEITHER TOO SERIOUS NOR TOO LIGHT.* Few people, especially men, care to spend a long time discussing the serious aspects of art, politics, drama, or literature, but neither do they like to feel that they are talking to empty heads. So you should be absolutely "up" on the news of the day, at least know enough about it to know how to get *him* to tell you the rest. Just say, "I've read enough about this to be confused. Could you straighten me out on the such-and-such matter?"

Smart people never feel that it is necessary to show off how much actual information they have. *This is very second rate.* They do seem to strive, however, to find the humorous, human side of the most serious questions. Smart women are able to make "small talk" about big matters. Even if you have a reputation as intellectual, don't let anyone force you into boring people with a "heavy" discussion of your pet subject.

*DON'T AIR YOUR PREJUDICES OR FIRM CONVICTIONS SOCIALLY.* A tea is not a debating hall and you owe it to your hostess not to offend anyone who is enjoying her hospitality with you.

*DON'T CLING.* Now you don't want your young man to feel that you are clinging to him desperately as any old port in a storm. It is only kind of you to set him loose so that he can go to talk to others, if he wishes. However, you can't say, "Don't you want to go and talk to somebody else?" for then he would have to swear that he had rather talk to you than to go to heaven. So if you can't think of anything else, you might say, "Well, being a stubborn sort of person, I'm determined to find out who painted the picture, so I'm going to desert you and go ask Mrs. Smith." He may trail right along with you or he may do his duty to his hostess and "circulate." You should be neither flattered nor offended by what he does. You are being correct and true to the occasion—and *charming*. Never forget that *unfinished conversations* bring men back again—women and children, too. This is an important point in being popular at a party.

In the next chapter we shall hurdle other conversational difficulties in mixing with our tea crowd.

## INSTRUCTIONS

1. Practice your look of expectancy on everyone you meet. When you greet people—when you're shopping—when your husband or friends come home—and see what happens. Raise your chin slightly, lean forward a little—and look expectantly at everybody— and at yourself and at life in general. They will all respond!

2. Study the situations in this chapter, think of your own remarks to suit each occasion and write them down. If you will force yourself to write out your remarks it will help you to crystallize your thoughts into words. While you may never use the expressions you write for practice they will give you greater facility in "small talk" and more ease generally. I want you to study and thoroughly digest the many points in this chapter before we proceed. Please study and apply these suggestions regularly.

# CHAPTER SIX

## *Points That Please in Talk*

### 1. DELICACY IN CONVERSATION

At the time of his coronation no one had ever loved pomp and show more than Napoleon. At a great court function, Madame de Chevreuse appeared wearing a dazzling display of diamonds. Napoleon was pleased by all the glitter. His curiosity overcoming his manners in this case, he asked, "Are they genuine, Madame?" The lady tossed her head and laughed with that impudence admired in women and said, "Mon Dieu, I do not know for certain. They are the gift of my husband. But even if they are make-believe, is it not appropriate that I wear them here?"

Personal questions deserve such a retort—but few of us have the courage to give it.

*RESPECT OTHER PEOPLE'S PRIVACY.* It is in the little delicate observances of life that love and friendly loyalty, through undemanded respect, blossom most beautifully. James Lane Allen, that master of the delicate and leisurely aspects of human relations, wrote a beautiful scene in "Aftermath." The slender, lovely girl with a never-spoken-of injury to one leg finally marries her neighbor, whose years of devotion to her prove his great love. The scene is a summer, moonlit night. The heat of the day has not entirely drifted off. She is asleep beside him, but he lies awake, thinking tenderly of her as she sleeps. He has never seen the injured leg. He has never asked her about it and she has never told him—as though such matters had no place in the high perfection of their love. The moonlight moves slowly across the room. She stirs in her sleep and her movement causes the sheet to slip off her body. Her thin gown is raised by one knee and the injured leg is exposed. He sits up eagerly to see it at last. In one more instant the moonlight will fall full upon it—and he will know. But, a sigh from her wakes his mind to the fact that he does not want to know what she does not tell him of her own free will. Just as the clear moonlight moves to bare the injury he turns his head away. No passage in any love story could be more tenderly moving, more delicate, more fine.

Probably nothing gives such personal dignity as the recognition of other people's rights. But faced with questions one does not wish to answer it is better to ignore them than to flick the questioner. One can always go right on with something like, "They are pretty, aren't they? They say the gem market is greatly affected by present conditions . . ." *Just simply ignore a question you do not wish to answer.* Do not get fussed or confused or show anger.

*DON'T TRY TO BE IMPORTANT.* Ease of manner will establish your presence better than insignia or gestures of importance. A calm modesty and self-possession can bear lack of recognition all evening if necessary. Chauncey Depew told the story of a young man, the son of a great bishop, who called on him. Mr. Depew was busy and asked the young man to have a chair and wait. The young man thought his importance was not being sufficiently recognized, and he stammered uncomfortably, "But, Mr. Depew, my father is Bishop ——." Mr. Depew quickly said, "Oh, then, have two chairs!"

*DON'T BE SUSPICIOUS OF PEOPLE.* Then, too, I've always loved the tale about Daniel Webster's being the lone passenger in a stagecoach with a rough-looking driver. They were passing through dark woods. Fears crept into Webster's mind. Suppose this driver were a thug and would attack him for the valuables in his baggage. Suddenly the driver stopped and, turning, questioned him. "Who are you?" he asked. "Where are you going?" "I'm going to the Capitol, I'm a Senator," said Webster, nervously. "Phew!" said the driver, "I'm shore glad to hear it. I thought shore you wuz the same man that held up my coach last year—and I shore wuz nervous."

*BE SURE THE OBJECT OF YOUR CRITICISM ISN'T PRESENT.* Some years ago in New York I went to a very crowded cocktail tea. It was a veritable subway crush. Practically mashed together.

another woman and I tried to talk. Perhaps our physical discomfort made us captious. But we were trying to discuss the pleasures of reading versus radio. She said, "I usually prefer to read when I can get something worthwhile—but I'd rather listen to anything than to try to read W——'s latest book. I can't find anything important in it." At that very instant a hand pulled her around and a voice said, "Mrs. ——, I want you to know Miss W——." I was the only one who had heard the whole thing—we hoped.

But taking no lesson from this, I said a few minutes later, "I simply can't get interested in the radio. The programs are such drivel, I never listen." A hand pulled at my shoulder and I turned while my hostess introduced to me the man whose shoulders had been literally pushing my own. "Miss Wilson," her voice came, "may I present Major Bowes."

The truth was I had listened to several programs and enjoyed them —but I foolishly made this sweeping remark, which the Major resented—and I don't blame him. He said, "Well, it's no compliment to your intelligence."

Having placed myself in this unfair position I could certainly blame no one but myself. But I rallied somehow and said, "Well, I really do listen to two programs, Major—yours—and—I don't remember what the other one is." He smiled in spite of himself, but he didn't believe me.

I believe most men and women can say with me that the most uncomfortable moments and social losses ever suffered come from making critical remarks—no matter how well-intended they may be.

Wholesale condemnations of races and creeds are vulgar and retrograde. They are practically primitive. To fear what is not like ourselves smacks of the animal kingdom. Civilized people who know the world have inclusive minds. Alexander Woollcott's remark about Paul Robeson, the Negro singer, is a case in point. "I am proud to belong to his race," Mr. Woollcott said, *"the human race."*

Wholesale condemnations of points of view and political issues can have some embarrassing echoes in history too. The same brilliant Daniel Webster is on record with a vitriolic speech denouncing the development of the West. "Never," he said, shouting in the legislative hall, "never will I vote one penny to be spent west of the Mississippi

River. It is a desolate, unresponsive country, a waste, fit only for cacti and rattlesnakes."

In like manner, the airplane, the steamboat, the telephone, the submarine and the radio have been ridiculed by those who go in for sweeping denunciations. The thoughtful man or woman stills words that strike stupidly and blindly at *the unknown*. Such striking is the blind fear and dislike that prompts the snake when the *unknown* and the *unfamiliar* are presented to him suddenly.

Since it never pays and is always unattractive (even when true) let us, as civilized people, rule out condemnation. But since the human mind does not stay put—and is likely to take up again, through insidious suggestion, those things it has laid aside, it pays to clean out our mental houses regularly. It takes more than good intentions to *keep* our minds and tongues clean of sweeping criticisms.

Certainly in world issues we must condemn destructive practices—but we can do even that without viciousness and the lust of destruction.

In Shaw's "Cæsar and Cleopatra" there is a conversation between Cæsar and the young queen whom he has groomed for the Egyptian throne. He has pumped courage, manner and purpose into this energetic, fiery young pagan, but he is sometimes shocked by her violence. After a description of one of his major battles, her eyes gleam with blood-lust and she cries, "Oh, don't you just love to kill!" He recoils from her. "No," he says slowly, "no, I don't like to kill—no one does— I just hold them so they can't hurt me."

## 2. SMOOTHNESS IN CONVERSATION

Before we continue with our party there are several points of general conversation I want to cover with you. All of the situations at this tea apply to any social gathering and you are confronted by them so often that now is a good time to create little "islands" of talk (things you can be sure of) to swim to when you feel yourself getting into deep water.

*NOT CLEVER BUT SMOOTH.* A delightful conversationalist is not necessarily clever at repartee. Let us first strive for smoothness of contacts in talk. And having mastered that, you will find that it is much less trouble and even more charming to let others seem clever. "Oh," but you say, "I want to be entertaining, so that I will be popular."

*PEOPLE WILL INVITE YOU AND SEEK YOU CONSTANTLY IF YOU LEARN HOW TO GIVE THEM THE EXTREME PLEASURE OF BEING CLEVER.* People adore the one who encourages them to display their conversational wares and admires the display. Every popular woman can remember the fun she has had with some person who talked all the time and then said she was the most delightful conversationalist he had ever met. Every woman can listen well and thus be a sought-after guest, friend, sweetheart or wife.

The unpopular woman, at home and abroad, knocks the wind out of people's sails, discourages them—tells something a little more extraordinary than what has been said. The clever woman never caps anyone's climax. The French have a saying: "All generalities are false, including this one." So, no rule will fit every emergency, every case.

Nevertheless, we want smoothness first and cleverness afterward. One joyful thing about smoothness is that you are apt to discover that you need nothing else. For if you are smooth in your talk, that means that you are poised, that you have trained your mind to be absorbed in things and people beside yourself. Consequently this attitude leaves your interested, curious mind ferreting out all sorts of entertaining ideas that bubble out of you quite naturally, but *only* after you have cured yourself completely of self-consciousness by training your thoughts away from yourself!

*BE SILENT AT TIMES.* Many people plunge desperately into conversation, literally racing against a probable moment when silence will fall. This fear causes them to talk faster than ordinarily and so, of course, they come to the end of their rope more quickly than if they would just be calm and talk more easily. Nervousness paralyzes other people's tongues.

*STOP FEARING A SILENCE.* Often a moment of quiet in a room is desirable. And when you do start to talk don't rush pell-mell as though you must say something at any cost. Don't speak quickly at such a time. Keep your voice down, and speak deliberately, not hastily. This will prevent or cover up that feeling of panic because the dread moment of silence has arrived.

Sometimes two people will come to the "rescue" at the same time, both will apologize and both start to talk again or neither will start to talk—which is like two men bumping heads when they both stoop to pick up a woman's glove. It is better to ignore the silence and start talking quietly to someone near you.

TO START A GENERAL CONVERSATION FROM A DEAD SILENCE is a difficult feat. However, if it seems necessary to do so, you can always say, "Did you notice in the morning paper that . . ." mentioning something of general interest. This is usually an infallible way to start men talking. If a certain guest remains silent and yet you know he is well-informed on a certain subject you might direct the conversation to his subject. Then if he still does not join in—ask him to clear up a certain point for you—be sure you ask him for a technicality or something that would not show your obvious attempt to make him talk.

A perfect way to overcome awkward moments is just to be honest about them. I heard of a girl who had tried all the known methods to make her dinner partner talk but still could not loosen his tongue until she said, "Aren't you really interested in anything? There must be something. If I had a dictionary here I'd start with the *a*'s and go through the words until something struck you as worthy of discussion."

HONESTY IS ALWAYS DISARMING AND THEREFORE CHARMING. Just say, "I can't think of a word to say. Nothing is in my mind except Hamlet's soliloquy. Would you please look entertained while I recite it? I'd like to have those people who are watching us think that I had you charmed by my golden tongue." Honesty can be ever so amusing and awaken more interest than any amount of pretense or tricks. But, *never belittle yourself to the point where your hearer must defend you from yourself.* To do so is decidedly second rate.

In a younger set recently I heard a girl say, "Ordinarily I'm positively brilliant, but tonight is just an off night. Isn't that a break for you? Now come on, amuse me!" Honesty always dispels stiffness.

Learn to be casual at such moments. Simply refuse to let panic over-take you in conversation. Honesty will always cure it, besides being so human and amusing that everyone will relax and talk for hours.

A charming hostess giving a small dinner where table talk is general (there are more of these than any other kind) will see that each guest is brought forth in the talk. If she fails to draw a response the first or second time, she will try until her tongue-tied guest *does* talk. For she knows that he will have a better time if he has taken part in the conversation. Never let a conversation fall when your hostess calls on you. Hand the talk back to her as though it were a package, then she can pass it on to whomever she chooses.

For instance, if your hostess asks you a direct question you might say, "I know of no better authority on that than you, Mary," or "Yes, I enjoyed the trip immensely, and all the while I was reminded of your trip through Switzerland, but that's your story," or "I don't believe anyone was as much impressed by the game as your son. What did he say about it?" These are just a few sample remarks showing how you can pass the talk to someone else. If you do not wish to take the talk you should hand it to your hostess as I have described. If you just make a brief remark and run down like a clock it is hard for anyone to tell that you have finished. The ensuing silence will be at first polite and then awkward.

*KEEP TRYING.* The fine points of conversations are things we are always learning and never quite perfect, so do not be discouraged by your small failures—just keep on trying. Only constant practice gives ease.

## 3. HOW TO TREAT DISTINGUISHED GUESTS

*DON'T INVITE TOO MANY TALKERS.* One of the most amusing mistakes of my life happened when I was giving a dinner for a world-renowned artist who was also a great talker. I wanted eight people at the table and selected from my friends those I thought best qualified to appreciate this great man. I chose them for their minds, forgetting all else. I was dressing for dinner before it dawned

upon me that I had invited five inveterate talkers. I turned despair-
ingly to the young lady who was visiting me and said, "This is going
to be an evening of matched wits in a 'free for all' struggle for the
middle of the floor. I have a box seat for the performance."

My friend promised to be quiet and I became referee in a talking-
bout where the egos of a great artist, two professional lecturers, a man
at the head of one of our largest industries, and a lawyer, who had
talked the world out of several million dollars, were in mortal combat.
Phew! The artist, I believe, came out with top honors, but only because his voice was most penetrating. And I can only hope that none
of them will ever read this account of the evening.

While each of them should have politely curbed himself, yet in a
way, I felt the blame was mine, for each was accustomed to being a
dinner guest because of his talking ability. This is just to show you
how few talkers are needed in the world! Unless they are better disciplined than the average talker!

*HOW NOT TO SHOW OFF A GUEST.* For a hostess to single
out a certain distinguished guest and say, "Now, Colonel Lionhunter
is going to tell us *all* about Africa, aren't you, Colonel?" is a very
crude way of putting her guest forward. Most men who have actually
done important things resent this sort of treatment. (So do women.)
Better for the hostess to say, "Those of us who have never hunted
dangerous animals are always curious to know how you hunters
conquer your natural fear—or have you any? Just what do you do
about it?" Now the Colonel has something to take hold of which is
impersonal. He doesn't have to be embarrassed by a spot-light on perhaps unmerited heroism. He need not even mention himself! He may
say, "I can answer that best by telling you of a guide we had on a trip
through the ——. This fellow had been born into a family of guides.
Fear, to him, never came as a shock. It was an ever-present factor to
be considered . . ."

Such a conversation can draw everybody out on the question of fear,
anecdotes of danger will come to the surface readily. The talk can
drift to psychology, amusing ghost stories, childhood reminiscences,
and the hour may be late before anybody looks at a clock.

*ALWAYS GIVE THE PERSON YOU ARE DRAWING OUT AN IMPERSONAL HOLD ON THE SUBJECT YOU WANT HIM OR HER TO DISCUSS.* This eases every situation.

The rule of courtesy says, "Give the other person a chance to talk about himself." And truly your skill in leading out the other person can be measured by your experience and social discipline.

Kate Smith tells of an interview with Mrs. Roosevelt. She said she had made up her mind in advance to get Mrs. Roosevelt to tell her as much as time permitted about her life and way of getting things done. "But," said Miss Smith, "I was nearly home after the visit before I realized that I had done practically all the talking and had almost told Mrs. Roosevelt the story of my life." Which merely demonstrates the fact that Mrs. Roosevelt took first and firmest hold on the conversation.

This is not to say that it is crude or faulty to spend an entire evening answering questions. Some of our most prominent people have been great talkers—but in many instances the success must have come in spite of—and not because of—the volubility.

When the son of Abraham Lincoln was our ambassador to the Court of St. James it happened that Chauncey Depew was in London on a trip. Both of them were being entertained by Gladstone, then Prime Minister of England. Mr. Gladstone was such an inveterate talker that often during an evening no one else could even answer a question. Mr. Gladstone would answer his own questions and continue for a couple of hours or more. On this occasion the Prime Minister was meeting the American Ambassador for the first time informally. Mr. Lincoln had not had a chance to say a word—but he did enjoy the evening, for Mr. Gladstone was always interesting. After the guests had gone Mrs. Gladstone asked her husband how he liked the American. Mr. Gladstone replied, "Oh, he has a charming personality, but he certainly isn't much on conversation!"

If Mr. Lincoln had been able to ask even two or three questions to spur Mr. Gladstone on in his talk, Mr. Gladstone would probably have thought him a very brilliant conversationalist.

Almost any topic of talk is better socially than the too personal. For a distinguished visitor to hear himself taken apart must be very trying and provocative. I didn't know whether to laugh or cry when told of an occurrence in my own house lately at a charity tea. An elderly, wealthy man was present. One guest, who had somehow caught the name but did not connect it with anyone present, immediately thought of the great store of which this man was partner with his several brothers. The loose-tongued individual said, "My, but those brothers have certainly made a great success of that store—they must be worth twenty millions apiece." At which the distinguished guest is said to have leaned over and tapped the loud-speaker on the shoulder, saying, "I'm sorry, sir, but it's just five."

Discussing people's importance in whispers to other guests or questioning their importance can have just as absurd results. Many years ago I was vacationing at a California mountain resort. When I came down into the patio dining-room, I was informed in a whisper that the people at the table next were the Hawaiian royal family. There were three fine-looking, well-bred children and three grown people.

In a whisper that easily carried to their ears, someone said, "Hawaiian royalty! Is that genuine royalty?" The largest boy, a handsome lad of about fourteen, turned around and said, "May I tell you what my grandmother Queen Liliuokalani said to Queen Victoria about that? She was claiming kin with the English queen. Queen Victoria said, 'That is very interesting, what is the lineage?' My grandmother answered, trying to keep from laughing, 'Well, my grandfather ate your Captain Cook and I am of his blood.'"

Laughter went up from both tables and after that there was always an exchange of smiles whenever we met.

So, at your party you will neither seek nor give information about some unusually distinguished guest.

James Cruze, the famous director of "The Covered Wagon," used to hold open house for the great and the near great of the Coast, Hollywood in particular. Great writers and visiting celebrities thronged there on Sunday, overflowing the lovely house, filling the grounds and the swimming-pool. Here one might see H. L. Mencken talking about democracy with Beatrice Lillie, or handsome Walter Pidgeon racing at swimming with the beautiful Billie Dove, or perhaps Ina Claire.

One evening Billie Dove, with her gentle kindness, was paying sympathetic attention to a tall youth who was so serious and quiet that one wondered if he were shy or sad. It developed that he was slightly deaf, so Billie raised her voice and tried to make the youngster happy. He went to the dining-room to get her some more coffee after the buffet supper and while he was gone someone came up to her and said, "Do you know who that young man is?" "What difference does it make?" retorted Billie, disliking the celebrity fever. "That," her informant went on vulgarly, "is the rich Howard Hughes. They say he's going to invest millions in pictures." "Well, as far as I'm concerned, he's a nice boy, scarcely grown up, who is kind enough to be polite to me and to get me some more coffee which I want very much."

## 4. HAVE SOMETHING TO TALK ABOUT

Every woman should read a magazine of news such as *Time* or *Newsweek*. She should read an amusing magazine such as *The New Yorker*. Then if she will read the book reviews in a good national newspaper every week, she should have plenty of conversational material that is up-to-date. Scandal sheets and thrillers will never add much to her. They only kill time. Only one woman in ten thousand can make gossip harmless and amusing.

There is just as much stimulation and excitement in the good things. But any woman, no matter what the demands on her time, can look through *Time, Life* or *The New Yorker* and the weekly book reviews. That takes up about two hours a week and it will probably be the most profitable two hours of the week. Reading such a magazine as *Harper's Bazaar* or *Vogue* will keep her informed of fashions. In addition to these one should read a local paper every day.

A background of the classics gives a mellow, interesting point of view. If you have not read the classics, start right in on Doctor Eliot's five-foot bookshelf.

*READ TO ENJOY—NOT MEDICINALLY.* Right here, let me warn you against getting a "heavy" attitude toward reading for conversational material. The object of the game is to acquire such a richness of mind that talk is easy and spontaneous. If you are "cramming" too desperately you will destroy the very thing you want to build. "Take it easy." Read to enjoy. Read to be entertained, but never read trash! A humorous, rich, mellow, tolerant mind is the supply-house back of every splendid conversationalist.

## 5. HOW TO PUT PEOPLE AT THEIR EASE

*TO TAKE FACTS AND RELATE THEM TO THE HOMELY COMMONPLACES OF EVERYDAY* contacts is the task of the entertaining talker. To take homely facts and feelings and make them smooth out introductions and conversational openings is the task of every hostess—such as the following introduction of old friends to a new-comer.

"Mrs. Brown, Mrs. Traveler (pause a mere instant for them to bow), Mr. Traveler (pause for bow or greeting). The Travelers used to be neighbors of ours and the only time we disagreed was about the hedge." Mr. Traveler: "We've had plenty of time to regret it. If we could be back here beside you, you could put the hedge on the front porch." Now, can these people talk? If they can't they have no tongues. They have eight subjects to discuss: neighbors, new and old, property lines, hedges, front porches, tempers, temperaments, homesickness and forgiveness. All this is possible because the hostess introduced a natural and almost universal subject between neighbors. "Homey." Honest. Human.

To comparative strangers of considerable elegance, "Mrs. Brown, Mrs. Luxury, Mr. Luxury.—I have told Mrs. Brown about your adorable dog. Don't tell me you didn't bring him." Mr. Luxury says, "Tomorrow we are showing him, so he is at home resting like a prima donna before an opening."

Now these people are at ease and can talk pets and animal life, wild and domestic, until Doomsday. I have heard a new-comer make the mistake of saying to an established woman, "Oh, I saw your picture in the paper this morning!" Even though some prominent women strive to get their pictures in the papers, they like to pretend that it is distasteful to them and some of them really do not like it. But even if you are sure publicity pleases them, too marked a comment conveys the thought, "Well, you do land in the papers every now and then, don't you?" On the other hand, in speaking to an actor or anyone in public life some people manage to give the offensive impression that they have never seen the person's name in print!

If your name is a difficult one for people to catch when they first meet you, it is only kind of you to come to the rescue instantly if someone is trying to introduce you.

*TALK ABOUT THE WEATHER.* Never be afraid to talk about the weather—it is not inane—it is an always interesting subject because it is always with us and we must consider it.

*NEVER BE AFRAID TO TALK ABOUT FOOD.* The only danger here is that a compliment may clumsily imply that it is unusual to have good food at this house.

*TELL AN AMUSING STORY.* It is a good plan to remember an amusing story to tell if the opportunity presents itself. A good story goes with a crowd of any age. If you can't remember stories, then cut one out of a paper and read it or have it read.

*YOU MAY TALK ABOUT YOURSELF—A LITTLE.* There are times when you may break the rule, "Never talk about yourself." If a guest has gotten into a long rigamarole about herself and really would like to stop, but doesn't know how, it is kind to take the conversation to yourself briefly before switching to generalities.

## 6. LEARN HOW TO MAKE OTHERS TALK

A charming guest and a successful hostess learn first how to make other people talk—then they try to qualify, as time goes on, to be entertaining talkers. But *to talk well yourself is of secondary importance in charm.*

*A CLEVER HOSTESS* makes a mental note of some outstanding fact about each guest so that she will have an actual approach to easy conversation with and for each guest. She will see that no one is neglected. But she will not turn from one to another like a schoolteacher asking children to recite. She will blend the conversation from person to person. You can practice this on members of your family, your neighbors, or even children until you acquire ease in moving the talk from one person to another. It takes more attention than brains. Anyone can perfect this with a little practice.

The principle is the same whether you are entertaining children, royalty or relatives. All will *admire* you if you entertain them with clever talk—but—they will *love* you and they will think you are extremely charming if you unlock their tongues and pave the way for them to enjoy expressing themselves.

Sometimes you must put a guest at ease by talking in casual fashion until you hit upon some suggestion that loosens his tongue. Asking questions is more obvious, but better than nothing.

*WHEN YOU ARE ABSOLUTELY STUCK* for something to say, then begin to ask questions. "Is there a great difference in the climate between this place and the place where you live (or have just left)? Won't you agree with me that the air is better there than here? Is your town in the mountainous part of the State? How long does it take you to drive over here? Are the new cars equipped with clocks that don't have to be wound?" Never be afraid to discuss the physical comfort of your guests.

*IF YOU ANSWER YOUR OWN DOOR,* you can say the same things to Queen Elizabeth if she should call that you would say to your sister from another town. But on the other hand, if you fuss with guests too much they feel uncomfortable about causing you so much concern and trouble. Be casual, natural and "homey" whether you are talking to the President or your son's friend he has brought home from school. (Never help a man with his coat unless he is an invalid. Tell him where to put it.)

*THE FOUR F'S.* I once knew a woman who was going to entertain a "captain of industry" and she prepared herself to talk about great, important matters with him. In answer to each situation she brought up he gave her a short, conclusive sentence which left nothing further to be said along that line. Finally she ran out of business, political and scientific openings—still her guest was not yet involved in a real conversation that would run on its own momentum. She became panicky, got out of the room somehow and telephoned me. "For heaven's sake, what can I talk about? This is terrible!" I answered one word, "Food!" "What!" she exclaimed, "talk about food to this great man? Isn't it bad form?"

I replied, "He evidently doesn't want to talk about affairs of state, etc., etc. I think the poor man is dying to be comfortable and homelike with you. He will be quite happy if you substitute tomatoes for tariff —rheumatism for reactionaries—and well, anyway, start on food. It always works!" "Well, I don't believe you," she said, "but I am desperate enough to try anything."

She went back to her guest and began by saying it seemed odd to dine in broad daylight as one does when daylight-saving time is in effect. The great man beamed as though dining at any time was a great pleasure to him. He told her about dining at a side-walk café in Paris, related amusing incidents that this suggested to him. He spoke of odd customs of eating all over the world. He explained about the best places to go in Japan. He even confessed that he liked to go into the kitchen himself and make corned-beef hash.

Food will start an animated conversation when all else fails. Save it for emergencies! Use it for one of your little islands to swim to when your mind fails to give up any other subject. From food the conversation can drift (after about two hours) to cooking, cooks, stoves, heating plants, electricity, Edison, other great men of the age, Einstein, Millikan, Burbank, plants, flowers, vegetables, and here we are at food again!

Make little "islands" of the four F's: Food! Fear! Fire! Foolishness! Why? Because these subjects have great interest fundamentally. They are simple and common experiences of everybody. If you can get a group telling the foolish things they have done you will have a hilarious party.

*THE HUMAN TOUCH.* It is fine to talk big talk about big matters, but the main object of any entertainment of any kind is to have all your guests enjoy the occasion. If they do not click on formal, serious talk, do not be afraid to inject what I have termed a "fundamental" subject into the most formal gathering. If things are a bit "stiffish" you will earn the gratitude of hostess and guests by bringing in the more homely, "human" touch.

Oddly enough, after you have put people at their complete ease by being "human," the more intellectual side of their minds seems to find easier expression. Most people know more than they are accustomed to expressing—and if you will loosen them up and warm them into expression they are unconsciously grateful and they consider you *charming*.

## 7. THE DANGERS OF GOSSIP

A friend of Alice Roosevelt repeated some gossip to her about some· one she liked. Instead of speaking her mind in her accustomed way she quickly laughed and said it reminded her of the story of some young people playing "Gossip" at a party. To play it someone whispers a sentence to the person next to him, that person whispers to his neighbor exactly what he heard. When everyone has had a chance to hear and repeat, then the original sentence is read aloud and immediately following that, the sentence is read as it emerged from the last repetition.

In this case, the sentence that was given originally was "Moses was an austere man—and he made atonement for the sins of his people." But what came out at the end after a dozen or so repeatings was, "Moses was an oysterman, and made ointment for the shins of his people!" Which is about as accurate as most gossip!

Some of the most beloved people in the world have been great gossips—and some of the most loathed and despicable ones are also gossips. The difference lies in the malice or lack of it. A little malice can do as much harm as a great deal.

I know a woman who is always talking about how truthful and honorable and fine she is and how truthful, honorable and fine are her parents. But the moment this woman is displeased, she forgets the sterling qualities of her inherited character and repeats, just for sheer amusement, facts that have been given her in confidence. Did I say facts?—they were so embroidered by her "truthful" fancy that their own mother wouldn't have known them. Fortunately her friends know her weakness.

Displeasure does not release anyone from the obligations of keeping faith. The amusing assumption of many women that they need be loyal only so long as they are pleased is a deep commentary on feminine character. Absolutely sincere (at the time) promises never to "tell" dissolve like mist before the slightest wrath.

People who are well brought up or have otherwise developed fine sensibilities recognize the obligations of decent handling of confidences. (Confidences! the most dangerous pleasure on earth!) Others may listen avidly to disclosures of secretaries, neighbors or others who come by intimate uncomplimentary facts about someone—but having gained the gossip, the teller is instantly lowered in their estimation—not only lowered, but that person is henceforth feared!

"But suppose one doesn't wish to enter into the gossip going on, how does one avoid appearing stiff by refraining from joining in?"

Whenever that question is asked me, there always flits into my mind the image of a charming woman I knew as a child. She was liked by all factions and groups in town. And she did not bend to suit each group either. But she had developed a smiling way of coming into the talk with something she knew the others were aching to hear—some fashion, some announcement of a birth, some bit of news that would take the talk into safe channels. No, she didn't wait to think of one when in an uncomfortable situation—she had one or two always ready in her mind. She made a career of pleasant conversation. She learned several ways of changing the talk to guileless topics. She knew there were seven subjects that would win an instant audience:

1. A wedding. (Two whole pages of every Sunday paper are devoted to them.)
2. An engagement. (About a page of every Sunday paper is devoted to them.)
3. An accident.
4. Somebody's promotion.
5. An act of heroism.
6. A crime.
7. The miraculous, either ghostly or scientific.

She said to me airily when I asked her about it, "There's something cannibalistic about devouring one's friends bit by bit. I just *decided* years ago to have no part in it—so I had to invent ways of talking that *seemed* like gossip but weren't.

Yet talking about people is about the most fascinating pastime in the world—and it is absolutely impossible to cure it. I know a man who has quite a reputation as a gossip and yet if you listen closely you will see that he never tells a really damaging thing about anyone. But he has gathered a surprising fund of intimate details about everyone he has ever met—little things that make him seem positively clairvoyant. He knows, for instance, that the wife of the new professor likes twice as much salt as the professor does—that the professor is a vegetarian and that he picked up the idea while he was in India as a missionary years ago. He knows that Mrs. Mayor's youngest daughter cried because she wanted a blue party dress and her mother bought her a pink one because it was good material and a bargain—he knows that the bank president's secretary is in love with him, poetically and platonically, and that his wife is amused by it. He knows that the next door neighbor's son has decided in the middle of his law course to change to bacteriology.

How does he know so much? He keeps his eyes and ears open. *His mind is not on himself all the time*—and so, in passing, he registers little facts about people that the rest of us brush by, our brows puckered over our own selfish affairs. One thing can be said for a gossip—at least his mind isn't on himself!

## 8. A FRIENDLY VOICE

The quality of your voice has so much to do with making friends. Some people can say, "Isn't it a lovely day?" in such a way that it seems the height of sarcasm. A great many well-meaning people are in constant hot water because their voices and manner of speech are irritating to others. Some of them come to me in tears wailing that no one understands them. This is why I have begged you to listen to your own voice to try to determine how it will fall on the ears of other people and how you will be judged by it.

On the other hand, I once knew a rather profane man who by all rules should have been barred from polite society—but—his voice was so caressing and he swore so gently that staid people would simply chuckle and forgive him. One of the most valuable assets in life is a reputation for good nature—and you would be surprised how large a part your voice and manner of speech play in conveying amiability

If you establish a reputation as a critical, hard-to-please, difficult person it is probably because you snarl a trifle as you talk, clip your words out too sharply, and talk in a cold, flat tone, resounding in your nose. You may do none of these things to a marked degree and perhaps, having done them a lifetime, you can't hear them yourself. But if people "bristle" when you speak, look to your voice.

*DON'T LET YOUR VOICE DROP AT THE END OF A SEN-TENCE.* There are several tricks of voice I want you to know. First, since Charm demands that we draw out other people, we want to see how voice can aid us. Then never let your voice drop at the end of a remark as though the matter were finished and yours was the final and unquestionable opinion about it. Add to voice-dropping a quick cutting of syllables and you sound as though you were uninterested in what anyone else might say. Benjamin Franklin's advice against seeming too opinionated is still good counsel. No doubt he gained his wisdom from experience, for he was certainly an opinionated person, but clever enough to make himself liked through diplomacy.

By keeping the voice slightly up at the end of a statement it is as though you had said, "Don't you think so, too?" It sounds as though you hoped what you said was acceptable to your hearers. Franklin D. Roosevelt is a master of this inclusive manner of speech, consciously or unconsciously.

As a simple example for yourself let us suppose someone asks you to go downtown on a rainy day. You look out the window, back to the person and say, "It's raining," letting the word "raining" descend into your chest with an air of dismal finality. Your friend might never go on to say that she wanted to take you in her limousine to a lovely matinée. But if you said, "Well, it's raining," keeping your voice up with almost a touch of amusing inquiry in it, your friend will enjoy proposing her trip. Such a tone of voice *invites* a response and keeps life in any conversation anywhere.

*LET WORDS FLOW—NOT JERK.* Remember that as jerky movements dispel the visual illusion of Charm, so a jerky way of speaking dispels the emotional illusion of Charm. So let your voice linger a little over an idea, don't chop it up and throw it at people. A honeyed voice that speaks unhurriedly can charm a man even when saying smilingly, "You're such an adorable idiot." Now please do not think that I advocate my pupils' going about swearing and calling people idiots. I tell you these things to prove that it matters not half so much what you say as *how you say it.*

Remember the dramatic words that startle and jerk our senses are short, clipped little Anglo-Saxon words such as "Stop! Quick! Fire! Kill!" Use short little remarks to relieve monotony when conversation gets too soft and lifeless. Use your short ejaculations to revive a conversation at any time, anywhere.

I hope you have been doing your vocal exercise to place your voice for mellowness and pleasant pitch. Now I want you to make your voice flexible so that it conveys an emotional overtone. A woman seems more truly a woman if her voice has tones of emotion in it.

## INSTRUCTIONS

1. Take the word "love" and say it until the meaning of it trembles in your voice. Then in that same manner say "Good-morning"; "How interesting"; "Do come again soon." Let your face reflect what you have put into your voice and witness the miracle of Charm in yourself.

2. Practice making someone talk—see how long you can keep him (or her) talking. Try this on someone who does not talk readily. Write down how long you kept the conversation going and state what you talked about. A written memo of conversations will teach you many lessons.

3. If you want to improve your English and polish your speech get a copy of Woolley's "New Handbook of Composition," which you will find most helpful. (I have no personal interest in any of the things I recommend. I tell you of those books, etc., that

to my knowledge will give you the speediest results for the least effort. There are others.)

4. Practice switching the conversation from one person to another, then back again. Not only will this make you a more gracious hostess, but it will develop your own resourcefulness in talking easily.

# CHAPTER SEVEN

## *The Agreeable Guest*

### 1. BACK AT THE PARTY

Now let's see. You had left your young man under the pretext of going to ask Mrs. Smith who painted the lovely picture over the mantel. You had done this so that the young man would not think you clinging to him, also to set him free to mingle with the other guests. But you had been friendly enough with him, smiling so that he would not think you were trying to get away from him. As you catch his eye later on, smile confidentially.

*ESTABLISH LINES OF CONTACT.* When you are "paired off" with someone at a party, see to it that you later leave him, even though you come together again as the evening progresses. If you have had several encounters which were brief or interrupted, you can always go back again. You have established a line along which friendly impulses may travel.

*LEARN TO DO NOTHING—GRACEFULLY.* You find Mrs. Smith. She is occupied at the moment and here you stand waiting—nothing to keep your animation going. You feel yourself subsiding into uncomfortable dullness. There are people all around you, yet there seems to be no thread of contact you can grasp. You wonder how you can engage someone in a conversation. You think of interesting subjects but can't think of an easy way to get someone's attention to start talking. You feel foolish at the thought of stopping the woman who is brushing past to ask her if she has ever traveled in Java, or what she thinks of "swing" music. You feel that she would be gone before you could utter a whole sentence anyway—and if she did stop she would think you were crazy.

134

*HOW TO ENGAGE ATTENTION.* But all is not lost. There is a way to overcome these embarrassing moments and to draw even a hurrying fellow-guest into talk. In these emergencies resort to short ejaculations—don't bother with subjects or sentences. If the woman caught your eye and seemed even momentarily interested in you, you should smile at her (smile companionably, not wistfully!) and say something short, like—"Nice party!" or "Lovely place!" or "Beautiful garden!"

*PICK UP A WORD (OR MEANING) THAT HAS JUST BEEN USED.* The woman may say, "Mary's parties are always nice, that's why everybody comes," or "Mary's house is a real expression of herself, but then I suppose everybody's is." And you can say, "I wouldn't like to be judged by mine right now. I've been dumped, literally dumped, into the house on the corner." The woman may say, "Think what a lovely time you'll have expressing yourself in closets and bureau drawers." You can laugh and say, "Well, at least I can enjoy complaining about it." Your companion can leave the personal talk by speaking directly of your house, "Did you know that your new house is about fifty years old and has an interesting history? The story goes that . . ." Or if the place is new she can say, "The whole town has a possessive interest in your house. We've watched it grow bit by bit until we feel we own it. The hall fascinates me. I've been waiting for the chance to find it deserted so I could come in and slide down the banisters." (Any allusion to childish tendencies is very amusing to grown-ups.)

*NEVER LEAVE A "HIGHBROW" IMPRESSION.* Great statesmen cling to simple talk. Prime Minister Churchill and Mr. Roosevelt are outstanding examples of unaffected speech. They almost never use what the youngsters refer to as two-dollar words.

## 2. YOUR MANNERS IN SOCIAL CONTACTS

My object is to put you in command of an understanding of human nature that will make your contacts easy and inspire that rare quality of spontaneity in the response of others to you. This is not necessarily inelegant, low-brow or "slapstick" for you can instantly reply to the "banister" remark in this wise: "That's how I felt about the staircases at Versailles, and I had to restrain myself; but you have a standing invitation to use mine for a slide any time."

Someone may have heard a part of this amusing discussion and stopped to join in. If you create laughter and look as though you are having a good time, people will gather like flies around a sugar bowl. The various types of stairways can be discussed—noiseless ones for tiptoeing, early-American stairways, architecture in general—and from there you can go anywhere in talk. The point is that you made a brief and telling contact by starting with a short observation. Even in a store there is nothing to prevent your remarking to a woman you would like to know better, "Wonderful values, aren't they?"

*"ELEGANT" PHRASES ARE OUTMODED.* No one ever developed into a splendid conversationalist by memorizing high-sounding phrases. Yet, you can prepare yourself for various conversational emergencies by making up a number of short descriptive ejaculations, the most familiar being, "Beautiful day!" and "Frightful weather!" Now, having shown yourself pleasantly disposed by providing the opportunity for talk, go no further.

*DO NOT CONTINUE TO PRESS YOURSELF UPON ANYONE* unless you are taken up fairly quickly. Be ready to pass on in *leisurely fashion,* so that if there is no real response you can be the one to move away, but see that there is no disappointment in your face. There may be no slight intended. Most people have one-track minds and if their thoughts are otherwise occupied they may respond vaguely and pass on, hardly seeing you.

Your attitude should be one of casual good humor and remain just that. Even if you have active enemies you can often disarm them with casual good humor without waiting for or depending upon a response from them. To harbor resentment and to show it at a social gathering of any kind is a sin against both charm and good manners. At the White House functions the bitterest political enemies go through the social amenities with a graciousness that is admirable.

*BE PLEASANT EVEN TO ENEMIES. Never embarrass your host by revealing by so much as a glance that he has subjected you to an unpleasant experience by inviting people who have displeased you in the past.* Neither permit yourself to indicate that you are otherwise displeased. Your job is *always* to keep your mind and heart so full of geniality, sympathy, understanding, tolerance, forgiveness, beauty, friendship and loveliness of all sorts, kinds and descriptions—that you do not depend upon the gratitude or receptivity or responses of others.

I repeat: *Your job* is to keep yourself so saturated with *beauty* that you cannot help expressing it under *all* conditions, and continue to express it *without hope of reward*.

The practice of this does not make you saintly and "religious." It is, in the last analysis, *the sternest economy of emotion, time and happiness*. When the expression of loveliness fills you as completely as that, the reward is much greater than any return you could dare to plan or wish for.

Tune yourself, like your radio, only to those stations you wish to hear, and, if you have perfected your instrument (yourself), you will not hear the discord of life—it will not exist for you. Only those things can reach you that correspond with your own wave-length. This is as immutably true as that two and two make four.

Some years ago I had the privilege of knowing a man who had not only piloted one of America's largest corporations through stormy seas to a lasting and sensational success, but who was, himself, a great soul, a beloved man and a charming individual. This man was Colonel A. B. Chandler, Chairman of the Board of the Postal Telegraph Company, a man who blazed the trail of cooperation instead of competition between rival companies. Though the Western Union could have swallowed up the smaller company a dozen times, the Colonel's soft voice and tactful words were often instrumental in reestablishing friendliness.

I asked him to give me, from his long years of experience with human nature, business and living in general, a summing up of the most valuable truth he had learned, that I might profit by his wisdom.

He said, "I wish I could pass on to every young person in the world this warning, 'Don't have enemies!' They are the most expensive things in the world! Lower pride if necessary. Swallow injustice if need be. Bitter as this is, it is still preferable to the cancerous condition of enmity. Waste no time, no youth, in harboring ill-will or resentment. Margery, I have gone to my enemies and made peace for the sake of the stockholders of my corporation. I have thrown my dignity down to be tramped on and in the end I have been exalted and honored. With my relatives, no matter who was at fault, I have traveled miles to smooth out a misunderstanding, because I sleep sounder when I do not feel their resentful thoughts disturbing my dreams."

Sometimes it is more dignified to apologize than to stalk about with an empty head stuck up in the air. True nobility of spirit on its knees can still wear the golden crown of triumph. Go to any enemies of either sex and *ask them to help you with some problem*. Approach the haughtiest woman you know and *ask her advice* if you want to melt her. She may tell you something you already know, but you must not let her know that. Only a fool or a barbarian thinks that self-aggrandizement is the only way to success. Never forget that "the meek shall inherit the earth"! I have found this to be the soundest advice I have ever had.

*LET GO OF UGLINESS.* You can *preserve your own beauty*, charm, poise and equilibrium by throwing out of your mind every ugly or critical thought, just as you would throw soiled garments out of a drawer of dainty, perfumed lingerie. For you know that a soiled stocking can spoil the exquisiteness of *all* the lovely undies it touches— and the longer it stays among them, the more complete is the spoiling.

*DON'T TRY TO CHANGE OTHER PEOPLE DIRECTLY.* Make them—or rather *draw them* up to—your ideal of them by recognizing only their ideal side. It is amazing to watch the response. To let people know that they are displeasing you puts them on the defensive and therefore they are hard to handle. This goes for everyone from the cradle to the grave.

If threats, nagging and frowns have failed to cure your son or brother (for instance) of throwing his coat down anywhere when he comes in, don't refer directly to the coat. Just say, "John, will you pick up a little in the living-room while I telephone the drugstore to send over some ice-cream? What flavor would you like?"

You have removed the battle-of-wills idea. You have not bargained with him. You have given him a chance to do your way without sacrificing any of his individual pride (which you call stubbornness). *And* you have introduced a *pleasant subject*. He will then associate "picking up" his coat with something pleasant. Any principle that works with children will work also with grown-ups.

*PREPARE AHEAD OF TIME FOR POISE.* Again, you must continually express smoothness if you would be charming and if you would preserve yourself for future charm. You must be so full of loveliness that no discord can throw you off your course or cause your face to darken at the wrong time socially. Then you will have the poise of true graciousness, which is *charming*. This attitude is your protection as well as your greatest attraction.

*WHICH KIND OF POISE HAVE YOU?* There is a poise of indifference, of the thick-skinned person, but such a one is never charming, never magnetic, never envelops other minds and hearts in the warming atmosphere of her own beauty.

*DIVERT ATTENTION!* Whenever a conversation becomes brittle with personalities, change it to an impersonal subject as adroitly as possible. A gracious hostess and a successful guest will learn to do this in all social difficulties. Practice makes perfect along this line. Your first efforts will, of course, be obvious if not crude. But if you continue trying, you will soon be able to smooth out anything by substitution of ideas, thus solving any dilemma. This sort of practice also whets your ability to merge any subject into another. This is commonly known as tact. Here we prove that tact is not so much a matter of quick-wittedness as it is of training. A little practice will develop tactful expressions. This will be a part of our next chapter.

*RADIATE GOOD NATURE AT THE TEA-PARTY.* By this I do not mean to stand around looking overly pleased to be with distinguished people. Don't wear a dental grin—a professional, empty smile. Treat great people and little people with the same spontaneous interest. It is the in-between, half-baked, half-informed, half-experienced people who present any difficulty. Never take it upon yourself to put such persons "in their place." No cultured woman does this, though the temptation to use a sharp tongue may be almost too much. Sharp-tongued women often are witty and brilliant, but they are never beloved. The truly cultured woman goes her way serenely and uses the mighty weapons of *charm* to smooth her own path and that of everyone with whom she comes in contact. The importance of tact and how to achieve it are to be carefully considered. But first we want the poise of perpetual graciousness.

## 3. THE PARTY AGAIN

Now you have caught Mrs. Smith's eye. In approaching her you find yourself face to face with the guest of honor. Mrs. Smith says delightedly, "I have been wondering where you were. You must meet Miss Writer," or she may say, "our guest of honor."

She continues, "Amy," addressing the authoress, "you remember Elizabeth Brown, who was in your graduating class at the —— school." Under other conditions she will probably just mention your two names—"Miss Writer (with a rising inflection in her voice)—Miss Brown" (letting her voice come down as yours is the name "presented").

In either event, extend your hand warmly if there is any reason for your being particularly glad to meet the guest. You feel that you should welcome her back to your community even though you are being presented to *her*.

However, it is perfectly correct simply to look very pleased and bow without shaking hands. A good rule is not to extend your hand unless you feel a special impulse to do so. A hostess, of course, shakes hands when her guests arrive and when they leave, unless it involves some awkward reaching.

*JEALOUSY IS A WEED.* Face to face with this girl who has outstripped you in success you may feel pangs of jealousy as you start to talk to Miss Writer. But, to betray this by coldness or stiffness is unthinkable. You must at least pretend to be generous enough to be glad of her success. So you say, "Oh, Amy (or Miss Writer), we're all so proud of you! You've certainly brought honor to the old school. We feel so important basking in your reflected glory." She replies with something like this, "You're all so kind, you make me believe I've done something much more important than just adding a book to the thousands that already exist. I hope you keep on thinking so." Now you can plunge into reminiscences *if they are not humiliating to the visitor.*

In remembering the past you need all the tact you can muster. The subject is a manifold one. And if we fail in tact the rest of our Charm will not be very effective.

If Miss Writer had had a love affair or early, unfortunate marriage with one of the local men (Tom Jones), it would not be tactful to say, "Will you ever forget the dance at the country club the night you met Tom?" I once heard a woman say a similar thing. Then she realized she had brought up an unpleasant topic and tried to fix it by saying, "None of us ever understood what you saw in that man." This last remark was designed to flatter the girl but actually it was criticism of her judgment.

*LET THE DEAD PAST STAY DEAD.* All such discussions of past mistakes of whatever nature are dangerous and should be studiously avoided. No good ever came out of such talk, for there is no possible way to exonerate the person you are facing except by pointing out the error of her judgment at the time—which cannot possibly be turned to leave an impression of pleasure. If the woman has not already learned the lesson of her experience, there is nothing you can add to the situation by bringing it up, or contributing a remark to a conversation about it that has already started.

A tactful woman would, after the country club remark, perhaps say, "You must see the new club house. You would never know the old building. We had Brown and Brown do the decorating and they did a wonderful job of it. Oh, by the way, did you hear that Alice Green is studying interior decorating?" The transition from topic to topic in that sentence is so easy, so logical that Miss Writer could not be sure that you had rescued her. This is the very height of savoir-faire and tact.

## 4. GENERAL RULES FOR HOSPITALITY

*DON'T BE A BLOTTER.* Now, *you* may avoid bringing up a discussion of past mistakes (or present matrimonial or other tangles), but what about the woman who insists on telling you her past, present and future difficulties? If you are clever you will not let her do it! Nine times out of ten she is using you as an emotional outlet and later will dislike you for knowing her inmost secrets—for knowing uncomplimentary things about her or her life. *Inevitably* you will sooner or later lose her friendship! I want you to reread this, for it is one of the most important points in the book.

*Never* unburden your faults or discord on anyone except someone professionally equipped to help you—and *do not permit* people to use you as an emotional blotter which they will wish to throw into the waste-basket after the performance.

If a woman is bent on confidences, use your tact to switch her to another topic. Use any method to head her off. If she starts on a rigamarole that begins, "And that night when we got back from the theatre he started again. . ." you jump right in with a wordy discourse on any aspect of the theatre you can talk about—plays, past, present and future. Fill up the time with stories of other unfaithful husbands or whatever the talk is about *but keep her off hers*. Better that she thinks temporarily that you are inane and unsympathetic, for you can establish her good opinion of your mental stability, but you can never erase her confidences!

If it is absolutely necessary tell her gently that you do not want her to tell you things she will be sorry she told—that you think too much of her as a friend to gamble with that friendship and, if all else fails, *ask her not to tell you*.

Tell her you would not dream of advising her for you do not consider yourself expert enough to do the matter justice. Send her to her minister, priest, doctor or lawyer. But do not do this in a chiding spirit, but rather indicate that the matter is too important for you to touch. Tell her to be sure to let you know how she comes out, for you are worrying about her and will pray for her. You can be sympathetic without saying a thing or without permitting her to say anything incriminating.

*INANE CHATTER IS SOMETIMES USEFUL.* A woman once said to a man, "Your wife can talk more and say less than anybody in town." To which the husband replied, "Thank God!" While I do not advocate a continuous flow of inane chatter, it is often very useful

Busy men find it restful, amusing (flattering to their own intelligence by comparison) and always harmless. Indeed there are worse things than inane chatter. Sometimes it is an aid in helping to fend off a subject you do not wish to discuss, thereby enabling you to dodge being too personal.

The wise woman has no "too intimate" friends for she knows that they are always temporary friends. You can be so kind and friendly that you would rise from your bed in the middle of the night to do a favor, to nurse the sick or to pull a friend's car out of the ditch, yet not so intimate with anyone that you no longer have walls of reserve.

There should be places in your mind and heart where no one treads. You should be able to say to the world, "Take my purse, take my house and all that is in it. Take my heart, take my hands, but leave to me, sacred and inviolate, my inmost self. This I share with no one. For it is my Holy of Holies. Here I have my tears. Here I have my hopes, my dreams—mine alone." If you will find and guard this part of yourself, you will be benefited enormously in different ways.

*BUILD AN INVISIBLE WALL.* First, an *invisible wall* will appear in your personality which will give the air of true elegance, of self-respect that commands respect without words. You can always tell when such a person enters the room. Here is an individual! Besides the force people feel in you if you have this wall, their natural curiosity is piqued by the knowledge that you have something they cannot share. Thus glamour and mystery are added to the attraction of your femininity.

This reserve is something that must be genuine. There is no way to pretend it. Crude people have no such "wall." If you but touch their conceit they "spill all over the floor" in talk and manners. They lean on you—"maul you."

This is one reason why you should never put your hands on others —nor permit them to touch you if you can avoid it without giving offense. Your person is, or should be, sacred to you and you assume that other people feel the same way about theirs.

*REAL INTEREST PREVENTS COLDNESS.* Now, the problem is to establish this invisible "wall" without coldness and without aloofness! The only way you can do this is to have so much real interest and helpfulness in your heart that it shines out to other people and doesn't need hands to carry it.

However, there can be occasions when you should not show your distaste of an honest gesture of affection from some kind but untrained person. Only a boor would rebuke such sincerity by stiffness. A gracious woman *never* lets anyone feel that he has made an error in her presence. You have all heard the story of Dolly Madison's drinking from her finger-bowl so that her guest who had drunk from his would not be embarrassed to discover that he was alone in doing so. Today, we do not go to such extremes but we, at least, ignore other people's mistakes.

The gracious woman *never* rebukes anyone. She doesn't find it necessary. As a rule, people react to her most satisfactorily, for her personality is so delightful that everyone wishes to please her—they know not why.

It is because her charm has gradually trickled into every corner of her world and raised everybody it touched to, at least, the wish to be satisfactory and worthy of her continued recognition. But on rare occasions that might be upsetting, such as having guests late for dinner, she may find her strength tried. She will prove her mettle if, remaining gracious and understanding, she smooths over the situation as best she can and carries on pleasantly.

*WHAT TO DO ABOUT A LATE DINNER GUEST.* It is hard sometimes to understand the other fellow's problems. A great domestic upheaval might have made your guests late. They, naturally, do not wish to tell you this; so they give you some flimsy excuse that only infuriates you. But you must be the gracious, understanding hostess and eat your dried-up dinner in a spirit of gay adventure.

An alternative frequent in New York is to start dinner alone, if you must, at the hour stated, though giving a few minutes' leeway would be kinder. Then when the guests arrive, let them begin with the food on the table. Don't serve the courses they have missed! Just say sweetly, "I know you wouldn't want us all to eat cold food just because you were held up in traffic—or had a puncture—or had to wait for a long-distance call. You missed the grapefruit but it might have gotten in your eye."

If guests telephone one minute before the dinner hour and say they will be late, then you should wait a reasonable time for them and show only sympathy for their tardiness. Etiquette *demands* graciousness. Without it, charm is non-existent! You need not invite the offenders again if you do not wish to; however, do not imagine that you will ever find perfect friends.

*A FINE POINT OF HONOR.* As hostess you must not criticize a guest. As guest you must not criticize your hostess. Having "broken bread" at someone's house you must not violate the sacredness of hospitality by open criticism. If you do (even though your hearers agree with you) you stamp yourself as vulgar, unversed in the finer nuances of social obligations. If you have eaten someone's food your lips are sealed against criticism! To accept shelter, food and entertainment is to pledge your sword to the defense of that house! And, by the way, always say "house" instead of "home," wherever possible.

Unless you are paid handsomely as a critic, why give mental houseroom to the lack and discord of others? Starve your own and your friends' faults and water the virtues if you want to do something valuable and profitable with your time. If you keep your mind on your good qualities (instead of suffering over your faults) all the other elements of your person and personality will gradually fall into line. The friendly law of coördination will work for you. But, having cleaned your own house, why bring in your friends' refuse? Your house will then look just as unattractive as though the soil were your own. What difference does it make to whom the dirt belongs if it is in your house?

*DON'T BE GOODY-GOODY.* It isn't merely sanctimonious to see only good in your neighbors and yourself—it becomes an act of self-preservation if you wish to keep yourself charming. Whatever is less than lovely should at all times be ignored, diverted or changed. Of course, you *can* meet discord with flashing eye and righteous indignation and perhaps come out victorious. But what is victory worth if you are bloody, dusty, upset, panting, frowning and filled with pain and bitterness? Such tactics may win wars, but so far as charm is concerned there has been no victory.

*TACT IS A HABIT.* Tact, in the last analysis, is the ability to keep to pleasing topics in spite of opposition or chaos. If you have trained your heart to desire the pleasant, it will come more readily to your tongue. Tact is usually more a matter of heart than of brain. Poise must stand on the rock of self-respect, while tact rests heavily on kindness of heart. Tact wishes to remove the barbs and thorns and even the pinpricks that might hurt others, even slightly. Reversing the matter, you should be in such perfect control of yourself that you do not wear your heart on your sleeve. If you have built your invisible wall you will find self-control easier.

To save others embarrassment *without their being quite sure that you did so on purpose* is to be a perfect hostess, a desirable guest and the sort of charming woman before whom the world bows down. If you are proud of your tact and draw attention to it, you kill it—it is no longer tact, it is an exhibition of crudity.

You do not want to establish a reputation for tact, for that causes people to mistrust your motives whenever you open your mouth. Tact is like technique in music. You must have it, but hide it.

You want the sort of tact that will enable you to think quickly— to steer a dangerously rocky conversation into smooth waters and safe harbor. Then you leave an impression that people do not stop to analyze but which they do appreciate emotionally. They then give you credit with their hearts instead of with their heads.

*Wouldn't you rather have their unstudied affection than merely their good opinion of your mind?*

Even if you are the most intellectual woman in the community with a big, political career in front of you, you should learn the emotional values in contacts for they will get you more votes at the polls, in a drawing-room or in your love affairs. You can sum it up in this way: Be sure your motives are noble. *Use your brain* to convey that nobility to other people's *hearts*. Then you will be charming. Then *nothing* can stop you.

## INSTRUCTIONS

1. Write down a list of twenty-four short observations that would serve as opening wedges for conversation. Let them cover many subjects from babies to grand opera.

2. Write out how you would start talking if you were just introduced to the President; to a matron who is a patron of art; to your local druggist whom you have never met before; to a visiting athletic hero; to three people at a bridge table whose names you do not know. Write actual remarks, not just a description of what you would say.

3. Go to your telephone and call everyone with whom you have the slightest misunderstanding and open the way for friendly, not necessarily social, relations. The tremendous spiritual growth this will give you adds immeasurably to the magnetism of your presence. "Bigness" gives off vibrations just as "littleness" holds them in. Electrify your personality with "bigness"!

4. Every time you are tempted to use a big word substitute a little one if its meaning is the same. Say "buy" instead of "purchase." Say "go to bed" instead of "retire." Say "came in" instead of "entered." Simple talk is smart, fashionable talk. High-sounding phrases are heard only among "climbers" who are ignorant of the ways of gentle people.

# CHAPTER EIGHT

## *How to Value Yourself*

### 1. KNOW YOUR OWN VALUE

The public adoration given the late Dr. Freeman of the Pasadena Presbyterian Church was a great testimonial to the man's personal charm as well as to his fervor and abilities. His was not the smooth serene face of the usual cleric. His face was heavy with lines of combat with the world and with pain. Yet when he smiled it was as though the sun had broken through a cloudbank.

Dr. Freeman became very ill and his adoring following waited with baited breath the news of his health. He recovered from a serious operation, and the day came when he was to occupy his pulpit again. Stories flew through the town that from his dark valley of suffering he was to bring back to them some great new message. Surely some great revelation had come to him and this they would hear on that first Sunday of his return.

The day came. The church was magnificent with flowers. The organ pealed in triumph for the great minister's return. Pale, but with firm step, he took his place to preach. A hush fell over the vast congregation. Now they would hear what new revelation had come to their leader.

He smiled slowly in appreciation of their expectancy and then in simple language he told them that what he had for them was finer than if it were merely new. From the depths of pain and the jaws of death he had brought back to them renewed proof that the faith they had was a worthy thing—in the acid test of experience that faith would stand firm—would comfort the soul, satisfy the mind, and heal the body.

What finer message could be brought to us than to be told that that which we already have is worthy, has eternal and real value, that we need not be seeking the novel, the new, the mystical—but that we should value and use what we have. There is pride and strength and peace in that knowledge.

If you feel yourself to be misplaced in life—that you are a square peg in a round hole, that your personality must change its environment before it can grow—just stop such mental meandering and remind yourself sharply that you can use the *material* you now have to fashion a finer world for yourself.

You have within your grasp now, the seeds, the makings, the materials of your own salvation, whether that be mental, physical, financial or any other kind. There is something you can do, something that you are that can be put to work for you. There is no situation where any man can be entirely removed from this law that the universe is available at any point within itself. Sometimes these materials within ourselves are hard to recognize. But the integrity of the universe at every point of itself doesn't skip over you just because you don't understand it or believe it.

Delays, trials, disappointments often give us a higher use of our own particular cruse of oil—whatever it may be. There is an old legend of the desert of the Mediterranean Basin. The hero is Shapur, a vendor of salt, the commonest and cheapest commodity on earth. Once a year only can the common man enter the gates of the City of Heart's Desire by joining the caravan of traders admitted at that time. So Shapur with his camel laden with sacks of salt joins this important band to get his paltry profit from his load. His camel falls lame and cannot go forward even though Shapur throws much of his salt off its back. The caravan disappears on the horizon leaving him with broken hopes, shattered dreams, burdened with his sick camel and alone on the desert.

He feels himself to be the most cursed of men. Presently a bee buzzes around his head. It occurs to him that where there are bees there must be honey and flowers. He follows the bee and finds himself at the secret gardens of the great Alchemist Omar. The old man is kind to him and offers him work among the roses, to gather the silky petals when the moon is high. But soon this poetic task palls. The hazards of serpents and thorns make his task soon as monotonous and unpleasant as any other work—but he stays at it.

Gradually his camel is healed of his lameness, but he is still pushed out of life, an outcast even from the contest of effort. But one day Omar tells him that his patience has won a great reward—that he is going to reveal to him the secret of distilling the precious attar, so fine and precious that it will win for him fame, fortune and a special entrance into the City of Heart's Desire. Shapur, with gratitude and gladness, finds himself, through unselfish service and patience, now elevated in life as he never expected to be. And his message to men is this, "Patience! Here if thou wilt, on these arid sands that seem to engulf thee, thou mayst find thy garden of Omar—and from the daily tasks that prick thee sorest, thou mayst distil a precious attar that shall win for thee a special entrance into the City of Heart's Desire." *The very thing that seems to impede your progress can often be turned to account for you.*

*IT IS NOT "WHERE" YOU ARE BUT "WHAT" YOU ARE* that determines your personality. With dominion over all the earth, man can and does shape his environment. No one longer denies the mental laws, the sovereignty of the human will at its strongest and clearest.

## 2. SELF-FORGETFULNESS

But even so, the thought persists that happiness is seldom gained in purely personal pursuits. As destructive as war is, there are in-stances where it has saved the reason of some individuals by giving them a focus for their forces in a great cause up and away from their personal tangles. In peace time the cure, the strengthening for these people is through the same process—dedication to some absorbing cause or principle. In war or peace the strongest elements of person-ality are those that do not concern the self.

The quickest way, for instance, to forget one's own troubles is to do something for somebody else. I know of one well-known woman who, in her youth, faced the grief of having her several children all die in an epidemic. Nearly mad with sorrow, she had the good sense to go to an orphans' home and ask for children to take care of. She didn't ask for pretty, plump, attractive children as most adopting parents do. She pleaded that the sickliest and the neediest ones be given to her.

*DO YOU WANT MORE FRIENDS,* more notice for yourself? Then entertain for somebody else. Do you want to have a good time at a party? Then devote yourself to seeing that everybody else has a good time. It is sure fire. It never misses.

This is not to say that the shrinking violet is the most wise. A soul that has found itself and values itself sees no reason for shrinking— for affecting a false modesty. People mistrust a Uriah Heep as quickly as they do a braggart. When Dickens has Uriah Heep say over and over what a simple and plain and humble man he is, one knows at once he is simply trying to catch his victims off guard.

Surprising, but true, *our ability to be un-self-conscious and genu- inely interested in other people is wholly dependent on our estimate of ourselves!*

At first glance this sounds like a paradox. But it really is not a contradiction, since it is impossible to direct the mind away from the self unless it has made its peace with that self. This means that you must like yourself, that you must win your own approval—at least sufficiently to be *able* to take your mind off yourself.

If you insist upon suffering over your limitations or defects you are wasting your strength and letting the essence of your personality leak away slowly.

On the other hand, the conceited and arrogant person is just as much of a failure. The only thing in his favor is that he probably suffers less than the one who keeps his eyes on his shortcomings. To take oneself for granted casually is the ideal attitude.

When your foot hurts or any part of the body is in pain, it is hard to ignore. Yet, when all of the body is functioning well you do not think of your body at all. And so with the personality! You are not self-conscious when your adjustments are smooth and happy. You are self-conscious when *something hurts.*

That something may be a trifle or it may be a deep-seated element in your subconscious mind. One can cause as much damage as the other to your comfort and personality.

*GET RID OF MENTAL POISONS.* The pain (feeling of lack) is just as real whether it is caused by a soiled shoulder-strap or the feeling that you were born on the wrong side of the railroad track—whether you have a sense of failure because of opportunities thrown away, or because opportunity never knocked on the door.

Anything, great or small, that causes you to want to draw down the blinds, to hold your breath, as it were, lest you say the wrong thing or lest you be discovered, is extremely damaging to your peace of mind and therefore to your charm.

Aside from any moral or religious considerations, the elimination of feelings of guilt is necessary to a healthy mind and an easy, adjustable personality. But they have to be honestly dispersed. Here is where religion offers its solace and philosophy its benign reason.

The person who must struggle to be good and kind is making a noble effort toward self-control; but only when the desires are honestly sublimated into other channels is there real peace in the entire personality. Self-control is admirable—but self-direction and self-training are more ideal.

*HOW MAY ONE ELIMINATE FEELINGS OF GUILT*—either because of an unanswered letter, a neglected duty, or more serious offenses? Well, to begin, get it into your head that the universe holds nothing against you—that all the forces of nature are trying to make right any untoward happening, whether in the plant kingdom, in your body or in your mind. If you cut your finger, the wound starts to heal before the knife is through cutting. This is healing and the urge to "make things right" on the plane of your body.

*ACCEPT FORGIVENESS.* Think how quickly the forces of healing will act on the plane of the mind or the soul. Then forgive yourself. If all nature is eager to forgive you, aren't you a bit egotistical to hold to your misdemeanor in a determined effort to be dramatic about it? Truly, this is the real (but unsuspected) attitude back of most uncomfortable feelings of inferiority. There is a certain entertainment in considering oneself as "Poor, dear little me" or as the persecuted heroine of a life drama. *Nothing can do you lasting harm except as you hug it mentally and demand that it remain with you.*

Examine your feelings of inadequacy and see if you do not fling them in the face of every offered opportunity. You use them to argue down new efforts, new beginnings, and to explain your own inactivity and inertia. Most of us identify our difficulties with ourselves proudly, like the little girl who said defiantly, "I'se bad and I like it!"

*SINCE LIFE AND NATURE ARE WITH YOU* instead of against you, set your ideal of your own performance high—but do not be devastated when you fail at some point. The surest mark of the elegant person is his ability to carry on in spite of an error.

*WHERE ARE THESE PERFECT PEOPLE?* Most self-conscious people are trying to give perfect performances and therefore suffer agonies over every error. They are not good sports about life. You should be willing to be wrong occasionally. No one else is perfect, yet the self-conscious person thinks he must put on a perfect performance. A worldly, traveled, charming woman was making an introduction of a friend to a President's wife. She became mixed up and said everything in the wrong way—but instead of blushing and crawling away like a worm she laughed exasperatedly and said flat-footedly, "Well, I certainly made a hash out of *that!* Let's start all over again." The three women laughed and were closer than they could possibly have been had everything gone well at first. Be willing to be wrong sometimes. Everybody else is!

*KEEP YOUR MIND FRESH.* Relax and be yourself—clear-eyed, head up, facing life gallantly and un-self-consciously. Let your mind ride out on the smoothing, healing currents of life itself. You'll have fresh energy vitalizing your presence, because one more tension will be eliminated. Whenever you feel yourself becoming tense about anything examine yourself deeply to find the cause, and *throw it out.* Don't defend or hide your mistakes. Change them if they are truly serious. Ignore them if they are trifling, which they usually are. Do or undo whatever is necessary to cause you to approve of yourself, in order that your feelings of inadequacy may be sufficiently healed to permit you to take your mind off yourself.

### 3. TACT AND SOCIAL CHARM—THE PARTY AGAIN

*TO LOVE OTHERS AND AT THE SAME TIME TO PRO-TECT HERSELF* from them is the bewildering, paradoxical task of the cultured woman. She makes sense out of it by believing that humanity is developing slowly toward potential perfection—that we are constantly driven up by an inner urge—that in the climb we often make brilliant spurts toward the glory inherent in us; at other times we fall back miserably into discord. Now, isn't it logical to respect and love the capacity for perfection in our friends and at the same time not to be foolhardy enough to put ourselves in their power where they can hurt us when they run amuck into discord? I am telling you all this to help you keep your life free from those cross-currents that cut off the flow of charm from you to the world and from the world to you—to help you keep your life happy and free from the disappointments that will embitter and age you.

*REFER TO THE PAST TACTFULLY.* Tact comes to your rescue especially when you are speaking of the past. Miss Writer will have a pleasant impression of you if you convey appreciation for her accomplishments and draw no contrast between her success and her humble beginning. In professional circles the I-knew-them-wheners seldom get a chance to drone their reminders twice to the artists' faces. But they continue to howl it behind their backs.

When a girl in modest circumstances has made a brilliant marriage, why won't her old friends let the poverty-stricken past die! Well— they don't, somehow—and then they feel that Mary is snobbish because she does not make them a part of her new life.

An old friend once wrote to a bride saying he was so delighted that something bright had *at last* come into her life. The groom might have seen the letter and come to the conclusion that he had made a bad bargain. The bride naturally cut this well-meaning friend from her list because she was afraid his tactless remarks might spoil her happiness.

So you must think before you speak. It is selfish and tactless merely to express your own thoughts without considering the effect they might have on the circumstances of the one you are addressing.

A tactful woman wrote this same bride that she was glad the people in the groom's town had brains and sensitiveness enough to appreciate her fineness, that it is always pleasant when people of the same breadth and depth get together, etc., etc. A safe way is merely to say, "Our love and interest are always with you. The groom is a lucky man! May you both be supremely happy—always."

*HAVE YOU HEARD THIS ONE?* In listening to a story you have already heard, never spoil its telling by admitting it is familiar to you, if you can honestly keep silent.

I think Mark Twain is responsible for this "bon mot" about story telling. It seems that a speaker had just used the familiar expression "If any of you gentlemen has heard this story, stop me." Whereupon Mark Twain interrupted with, "My dear fellow, a gentleman has *never* heard a story."

However, if someone asks you directly, "Have you heard this story?" and identifies it definitely, you should say, "Yes, I have heard that one but do go on with it—it's so clever." But you should not improve upon the telling or say that you had heard the story given a funnier twist.

*IS TACT DISHONEST?* There are people who think that tact and diplomacy are forms of dishonesty, whereas they are really a means of avoiding the unpleasant; the avoiding of anything that would spoil the effect of another's effort. One need not lie.

If you are asked to express an opinion where you cannot honestly approve, such as "How do you like this hat?" when you do not like it and do not want to say that you do not, it is best in that case to calculate results. You can take one of three paths:

1. The first and easiest is to say you like it, if you can make your peace with your conscience by convincing yourself that you would only make the woman unhappy without gain to anyone if you say you do not.
2. Second is to be bluntly honest and say, "No, I don't like it," and let the hurt or disappointment come as it may.

3. But there is still another way, the way of Charm. It is to be hon-est and make the other fellow like it! It takes a little more thought, a little more tact, which after all is just civilized kind-ness. You can say, "Well, it is a nice hat, isn't it? But I can't for-get how stunning you looked in that black hat with the small velvet bow on it. It seemed to accent your distinction. This one is more hat than *your* hat. It belongs to someone with grosser features—someone who has more to hide than you have." Now the woman will be thinking much more about your saying that she has distinction, is stunning and has nice features (though you haven't thrown this at her crudely) than she will about the hat. She will accept your criticism pleasantly, benefit by it and you will have been completely honest.

*ALWAYS MAKE THE INDIVIDUAL IMPORTANT AND REGARD INANIMATE THINGS AS BACKGROUND.* Many people regard material things as more important and think of the person as incidental in the general picture. If you get the importance of the human element in your mind you have the cultured point of view. It is second-rate to be swayed too much by material things— houses, extravagant cars, jewels. Never let these warp your outlook. Keep close to the human element; then no grandeur can affect your poise. Never let the presence of an important guest cause you to neglect the least attractive one present. If the guest is really important she will see through your obvious attempt to give her your entire attention.

*IN SPEAKING TO A GUEST OF HONOR* you should remain talking until she (or he) is claimed by the hostess or someone else. Never leave a guest of honor alone. But if others are trying to get to her, you should be brief, so as not to be in the way. But never draw aside hastily like a comedian fearing a blow from the rear and say simperingly, "Oh, am I in the way?"

*TALK TO THE OLDSTERS.* Usually there are a number of older people at a tea. You are expected to go to them and make yourself agreeable and interested for a few moments, at least. You can, if you wish, save these attentions to the oldsters to fill up awkward pauses in your own contacts, but it is more charming to make a *pointed approach* to them when you have other conversational opportunities. Leave a group of fascinating, desirable people when you can do so without rudeness and introduce yourself to Grandma in the corner, "How do you do, Mrs. Andrews, I'm Elizabeth Brown, etc. I couldn't wait for Mary (or Mrs. ——) to introduce me. I hope to see your wonderful flowers (or quilts or embroidery or lace-work or poetry or whatever takes up the dear soul's time)."

Should Grandma try to monopolize you, just wait until she stops for breath and make an appointment for tomorrow to discuss her pet subject at length. Today you couldn't do it justice for you're afraid you'll be interrupted.

The young people you left will realize that you are not toadying to them if you leave them to talk to someone else. From a dozen different points of view you must pay marked, not necessarily prolonged, attention to the oldsters or the wall-flowers. Something quaint or amusing is usually said by Grandma. This remark you can repeat to those you think it would interest.

Don't be afraid to be alone a few minutes. Get another cup of tea if you like, and sit where you can be seen and can rest for a minute or two. You can spend the time remembering names. Someone will come and sit beside you. You can smile and nod to people who look at you pleasantly, if you feel any sort of bond with them.

*ALL IS NOT GOLD THAT GLITTERS.* Sometimes the most smartly dressed woman present is being pressed by her creditors, and the one you are trying to avoid, because she doesn't look as though she has stepped from the pages of *Harper's Bazaar,* has a yacht and a country estate where she might entertain you if you were a human being instead of a superficial snob. The truly cosmopolitan woman is entertained by all kinds of people. As Kipling puts it, "If you can talk with crowds and keep your virtue or walk with Kings—nor lose the common touch—if neither foe nor loving friend can hurt you—if all men count with you but none too much . . ." This is the perfect attitude.

*DO NOT BE OVER-IMPRESSED BY ANYONE.* Take the attitude that no person, place or thing can in any wise prevent the best expression of your own life. If you are shy or inclined to fear people—say to yourself that there is only one personality in the universe—the divine one and that no human being can occupy that place in your mind.

*DO NOT TRY TO PUSH YOUR WAY SOCIALLY.* Let us suppose you catch the eye of Mrs. Newhigh, who is an important factor in the club or political life of the community. She is dominating, not very well-bred, yet her money and energy are sufficiently useful in good causes to warrant her acceptance by society. She sits beside you for a moment to sound you out and to see if she can use you on her various committees. She is too busy and superficial to change her mind about you later (without special effort on your part). You will probably have to live under her opinion of you hastily formed on five minutes' acquaintance. Actually your social life in the town hinges on what you say and do in the next five minutes. And are you going to make her like you?

Now here is your opportunity to start toward making a place for yourself in the affairs of the community. And you must succeed on your own personality.

Mrs. Newhigh is sitting beside you. She begins, "My son has been telling me what an interesting young woman you are. I came over to see for myself." In this remark she has mentioned her son, you and herself. Your answer must of necessity follow one of those leads.

*PICK YOUR WAY CAREFULLY THROUGH PERSONAL REMARKS.* It is usually a good policy to direct attention to the self of vain persons. They love it. And are quite adept in handling its awkwardness. But Mrs. Newhigh's mention of herself was in connection with her opinion of you. Dangerous ground! You must not appear to be concerned about her opinion of you. If you speak of yourself even remotely you will appear to be justifying yourself somehow in her eyes. So you *must* answer by picking up her mention of her son.

This is almost as good as talking about her. You are fortunate. Sometimes the choice is not such a happy one, nor so easy to find. But, as you do not know just who her son is, you look at her inquiringly and say, "Your son?" Now you have an ideal situation—that of having placed the woman who usually demands explanations under the necessity of explaining to you. It suddenly dawns upon you that the young man with the teacup is Mrs. Newhigh's son.

*GO FROM THE PERSONAL TO THE IMPERSONAL.* Before she has time to realize her weak position and freeze up, you say as quickly as possible, "I should have known that such a resourceful chap would be your son. They tell me there's nothing you can't swing." Here is recognition of her power for which she has striven so many years. But you must not leave her in the uncomfortable position of having to admit or deny it. So you keep right on going, "It was wonderful getting the new wing of the hospital started in spite of the times." Now you are still talking about her accomplishments but the word "hospital" gives her something to take hold of which is impersonal. You have given her a choice at least—herself or the hospital as a subject to discuss. If she is a gentlewoman she will prefer to talk about the hospital. If she prefers to talk about herself she can do it. However, you have been wise and have made it possible for her to be pleased and safe no matter which way she chooses.

*CONVERSATION IS MUCH LIKE A TENNIS GAME* except that in tennis you try to put the ball in the most difficult position for the one who must hit it—while in conversation you must try to put it where it will be easy to hit. *To find an easy answer for yourself in any conversation, listen for an impersonal word in a remark to which you must respond. Take this word as the pivot of your reply.*

For the moment Mrs. Newhigh's pride in the hospital overshadows her vanity, and she begins to tell you the new features of the building. You can show your interest in what she says, but bring the subject back to the human element again, being careful to avoid any mention of pain, tragedy, etc. Also do not dwell on this note if she introduces it. There is the future in which you can discuss suffering, but now you do not want her to harbor a single word in her memory or impression of you that suggests anything to be avoided. In this, as in most situations, *it is the emotional impression that counts—not the mental one.*

So you ask her, "How many beds are there to be?"

Mrs. Newhigh replies, "We don't know yet—but we shall have as many as possible." And you say, "How splendid that so much is being done along that line." An established woman would take you up on that remark and enlist you for the work but Mrs. Newhigh is still estimating you. She has an idea of asking you to come to her committee meeting but is still undetermined about including you on such short notice. She speaks noncommittally. "One must do something."

Well, you have not made much progress, have you? The minutes are slipping by—and here comes an interruption. An unpleasant-looking woman comes directly to Mrs. Newhigh without so much as glancing at you. "Clara," she begins, "the Governor's secretary just wired that it may not be possible for the Governor to dedicate the new hospital wing. We shan't know definitely until tomorrow."

Mrs. Newhigh still thinks it is smart to be indifferent to honors. This phase of pretended indifference is one every inexperienced woman passes through on her way to becoming a real gentlewoman, who is always gracious and appreciative. But Mrs. Newhigh says wryly, "Probably they think the building will collapse if he doesn't get here." Now here is your chance to relieve the situation and once again make her pleased with her own importance. So you say, "Why don't you dedicate it yourself since you are responsible for it?"

*THE INDIRECT COMPLIMENT*. In your remarks you are not saying *personal* things to please Mrs. Newhigh, but rather you are contributing an idea to help solve her dilemma. The cultured woman has learned to give to impersonal topics a twist that *reflects* credit on the other person. If you appear anxious to please, that is, too anxious, you belittle yourself.

The newcomer sees you for the first time and says, with arched eyebrows, "—and if the Governor comes?" You smile innocently and say, "Let him be an honored guest and witness the dedication—perhaps say a few words before or after Mrs. Newhigh." The arched eyebrows come down into a sarcastic smile intended to undermine your remarks to Mrs. Newhigh. Your face is calm and pleasant, though definitely serious, as you wait for Mrs. Newhigh's reply.

She is nettled by the other woman's smiling at the idea of her dedicating the building. Your face is the essence of a dignified acceptance of the idea as a fitting thing. Mrs. Newhigh is won. She sees in print, "Mrs. Newhigh will dedicate the new wing of the —— hospital. The

Governor is expected to arrive in time for the ceremony." She gets to her feet, already bristling with plans. You rise if she is a much older woman than you. She turns to you briefly but determinedly, "Do come to the committee meeting at my house Thursday afternoon at three, Miss Brown. Shall I expect you?"

*TURN THE POINT FROM YOURSELF.* You say quietly, "I shall be so happy to come and do what I can for the cause." Be sure not to stop after you have said, "I shall be happy to come," but indicate the common cause of interest which takes the attention away from the personal by adding—"and do what I can for the cause." Mrs. New-high smiles and leaves. You now have made a good beginning. Don't push!

No doubt there are some people who would call this toadying. But think for a moment—if a queen wishes to accomplish something with human beings she must use her knowledge of human nature to suc-ceed in melting opposition to her wishes. No one lives today who can command ruthlessly in his dealings with others. Even a dictator must keep himself "sold" to his followers. He dazzles them with construc-tive and spectacular psychology. If you give people a vision, you have stirred their energies.

To use this principle only for your own selfish ends will bring but a temporary success. But there is no law, material or spiritual, that condemns you for improving your own situation while you improve that of others! In fact helping other people is the surest way to do either.

When you improve yourself, you have more to give and a more strategic point from which to give it. When you are interested in others, you refine and lift yourself materially and spiritually. This is the way to be a happy human being, successfully dealing with others.

It is fortunate for the world that one of the best ways to improve or hold one's status is to work for charities. Make out a report of your findings in whatever field you select. Get to your feet at the next committee meeting and tell it or read it. If you have not been asked to do so, rise and ask permission to give it. You will be considered then as an active factor. (You will be seen, so be sure not to overdress for the occasion. It is very important to know when to dress and when not to dress. One of the most telling earmarks of the parvenu is that she is apt to be dressed as though she wants to be looked at, when she should at least pretend that she is not thinking of herself, but of the purpose of the meeting.)

It is not expected that all the women and men who may stand on your path to accomplishment—social or otherwise—are "newhigh" or interested in hospitals, but there is always something an active woman is pushing.

*DISARM THE ANTAGONISTIC PERSON.* The unpleasant-looking, rather rude woman, who brought the news about the Governor, realizes that a choice was made between her idea and yours. If you do not dissolve this unfriendliness now there will always be a contest and some enmity between you.

*YOU MUST QUICKLY MAKE HER TALK* so she cannot let her feelings crystallize into a conviction against you. So you say, casually and pleasantly, "Would you be kind enough to tell me where to find Mrs. Newhigh's house? How does one get there?" Even if she is not gracious you must ignore the fact and proceed to melt and win her.

*KEEP HER TALKING.* So few people can think and talk at the same time. "Is the committee active now or is it just being organized? What are the duties of the committee?" Ask for her opinion about something! Ask her to advise you! There is no one in the world so hard or so vicious and selfish that he will not respond to consideration of his opinions.

*THE PARTY IS BETTER IF YOU MOVE AROUND A LITTLE.* Remember though, no audience of one or more will call for an encore if you give them all they want. Hit-and-run driving of an automobile is criminal—but hit-and-run conversation is desirable. By that I mean, make a pleasant impression and don't outstay your welcome. Move from one group to another when you can do so gracefully, giving little sympathetic or amusing pleasantries, or merely listen pleasantly to first one group and then another.

You may often find yourself saying your "charming" speeches when other people are trying to say theirs. Don't be determined to have your say—stop—and let the other person make that lovely speech. Two people determined to be the star of a leave-taking sometimes have all the charm of two people diving for a dropped handkerchief—result in both cases—bumped heads.

To mingle well, one must be able to amuse oneself. If we are self-sufficient we have more of value for others. And yet so long as Charm demands that we remind others of their strength, sometimes the most effective thing we can do is to lean on that strength. So self-sufficiency becomes the art of knowing how to meet the moment.

*ARE YOU ALONE AT A PARTY?* When you have gone alone or find yourself alone at a party you have recourse to either of the methods discussed—going on your own or leaning on someone. It is hard to say which way is the better. In my own experience I recall the result of the latter way at the wedding reception of Bebe Daniels and Ben Lyon. I had gone alone and found myself one of about two thousand people. Lew Cody, famous host as well as actor, a man who probably knew as many people as Wilson Mizner, had entered alone. So after a pleasant and cordial greeting I said, "Lew, I feel feminine and fragile tonight, not at all like breasting that tide alone. I want you to look after me. Farm me out. Bring people to me—but adopt me, please." And the charming Mr. Cody seemed to enjoy making me popular. He kept me supplied with partners that would be any young girl's dream—from Walter Pidgeon to Mr. Hearst—from the Governor to Goebel, the aviator, who had just made the first flight from San Francisco to Hawaii. Only the circumstances can dictate one's way of going. Sometimes one way will work better than the other.

But if you have groomed and polished yourself to the point where you take yourself for granted, the task of adjustment to any situation becomes comparatively easy because your mind can be completely on it. Attention is all that matters. Do not bother with concentration. It is too brittle, too tense. Give your development your persistent, absorbed attention and you will enjoy most remarkable adventures in effectiveness.

*LEAVE AFTER A REMARK OF YOUR OWN.* Unless you are especially invited to remain, it is a good idea to decide to leave while you are talking to a group; then you can say goodbye to those around you (without shaking hands unless you especially wish to). If you decide to go when you are deserted, you look and perhaps feel that you are leaving because you are not having a good time. Just say anything from, "I ordered my car for six o'clock. My husband is waiting for me to pick him up at the club,"—to—"I'll just have time to rush home and get the can-opener out before my husband arrives for dinner. I'm so sorry I must go. It's been such a pleasure to know you." Go to your hostess and tell her you have had a wonderful time, say goodbye, shake hands and go. *Don't linger once you start!*

Don't stand with your hand on the door-knob and start another conversation! And if you can possibly avoid it, never issue an invitation to a couple who have especially pleased you, in the presence of people who are left out of your invitation. If you are a new-comer the first invitation must come from the people of the community.

Now get your coat and go, without hurry. Be sure to let your face and manner radiate friendliness and happiness when you tell your hostess you have had a good time. It is not necessary to say goodbye to anyone but your hostess—but it seems gracious to speak to those you have met if they are near as you leave. It is gracious to look back as though admiring the scene you are leaving.

## INSTRUCTIONS

*Review all the instructions of each chapter.* Remember that in your hand and wrist exercises the wrist always leads. Practice reaching for an object and handing it to someone (wrist leading each way). Your wrists should be loose and supple. You need never even concern yourself about the position of your hands, if you have trained them to be lovely and graceful in whatever they are doing. Remember that age folds the hands together resignedly, while youth seldom has the hands together.

On the stage an actress playing a youthful part will move her wrists a great deal. To look old she will keep them perfectly rigid. Stiffness and rigidity in the body indicate age, or self-consciousness, or the wish to hide something. Suppleness and freedom of movement indicate a free mind and a clear conscience.

Anything that is young, alive and free of inhibitions *moves*. Therefore, the charming woman will do well to keep her body responsively supple and let it express in fluid movement her keenness, enthusiasm and interest in other people. A gesture, even of the hands, should ripple through the entire body. *Every gesture should start from the floor!*

# CHAPTER NINE

## *The Little Things That Count*

### 1. HELP THE OTHER PERSON SEEM CLEVER AND IMPORTANT

At a tea at the White House, I had the opportunity to enjoy Mrs. Roosevelt's always delightful manner and the way she keeps other people happy and entertained. I told her of an actual occurrence in New York during the winter when Mayor La Guardia had such a dreadful time getting the snow and ice off New York streets.

On the slight hill at Park Avenue in the Eighties two cars had slid together, locked, turned partially around, and another car had jammed into them, making quite a tangle. A crowd paused on the side-walk to watch the mêlée. A messenger boy laden with boxes peered over the top of his load and finally yelled out to them—"Ain't nobody but Roosevelt can get you outa that mess!" Mrs. Roosevelt laughed heartily and afterward repeated the story several times, making me feel very important.

How gracious, I thought, to repeat the amusing remarks of other people. I made a point of listening to the most charming people I knew and discovered something that in all my years of study had eluded me—nearly all the successful people I knew repeated the bon mots of other people, giving them full credit. It's a very easy way, too, of having something to say.

The person whose very name makes you glow with pleasure is the one who has supported you and kept you from showing a weakness. Most of the world lets its members ride out on their own in full testing glare, daring them to fail. Then a great chance for all who will listen is to do as the angels do, "Bear them up lest they dash their foot against a stone." There is so little that we can do that everybody else isn't doing. This is a very simple but unusual way to serve and make yourself beloved.

An amusing example, rather an extreme one, occurred years ago during the first World War. One Sunday at the old Triangle Studio at Culver City, built by the late Thomas Ince, now the Metro-Gold-wyn-Mayer, only one company was working. I was the leading lady. Prince Albert Caillaix had come over from France to observe American preparations and to act in other international business. As a respite on this Sunday he was brought to visit the studio. Because I was always studying a French grammar while waiting on the set, someone seized upon the idea that I could talk French to the handsome blue-clad officer. So he was brought over to me with a flourish and the remark, "Miss Wilson will speak French with you." I looked at him in dismay and told him that I was only a student of his language and knew only a few sentences. He said quickly, in French, "Say them and we will pretend to have a conversation. It will be a good joke and they will think you are a good linguist." So, with no further ado, I said, in French, with great animation, a sentence on page three of my grammar, "The pupils have not their books today."

Whereupon he went off into ecstasies, twirled his mustache and laughed as though I had just said the wittiest thing he had ever heard. He paused expectantly, so I said, "My father is in the other room (*Mon père est dans l'autre salle*)." He greeted this with a show of dramatic amazement and another deluge of response. Then I said sadly, "The windows are closed and the doors are open." Once again there were peals of laughter, very honest, no doubt.

After about ten minutes of this kind of ridiculous talk he took his leave, bowed over my hand, kissed it admiringly and told my companions I spoke beautiful French. The studio people were very proud of me and treated me with a new deference after that. It was the beginning of a charming friendship between Caillaix and myself. And yes, you guessed it, I began to study French very seriously and have had a thousand occasions to be grateful that the Prince was such a kind vis-à-vis. The French that I have gained has been of inestimable value.

## 2. BRUTAL FRANKNESS

The modern cult of brutal frankness as affected by some of the so-called café society is doomed to failure as it has been since the beginning of time. It is retrograde and decadent as a practice—and takes the individual back to a two-year-old mentality. Only those who are supported by other people's money can indulge in it. They would soon cut off their own incomes. But because people still keep smiling at them (because there is something to gain by it) they fancy they are virtuous and charming in their brutal expressions. But soon or late they destroy themselves.

History's pages are full of such attempts by individuals. Beau Brummell was one of them. Secure, so he thought, in his success, he began speaking his mind, holding nothing back. For a time the courts of Europe laughed, his words were repeated everywhere as bright bon mots—then first one person and then another began to cut him. The fat Prince of Wales, his greatest supporter and benefactor, who had countenanced his insulting candor, heard one too many remarks about his fatness, and he too cut his gay protégé. So the beautiful and fashionable Beau Brummell died in pitiful poverty with no friend to mourn him. He had cut himself out of the life he loved by the sharp knife of brutal, childish and barbaric candor.

Let me repeat, the people of my acquaintance who indulge in this kind of "truthfulness" are always supported by others. A suave and candid gentleman I know is married to a very rich woman. Another candid creature is the wife of a very successful physician. In other words one must not be dependent upon the favor or friendship of other people if they are to be insulted with impunity. In your town the woman whose tongue is feared most is spending money *she does not earn*. And the man whose tongue is barbed must be in a position to grant favors, and heaven help him when he slips out of that position!

Check on this statement and you will find it true. Men or women, such people must get behind somebody else's protection before they can throw their rocks.

People never get by because of their frankness. They succeed (if they do) *in spite* of it. But we really should pity them. It is because they have been badly hurt sometime in the past that they wish now to speak without regard for anyone's feelings. They would be horrified to know that they are small children hitting back.

After listening closely, one observes that these personal insults are almost always prefaced by the same words, "If you don't mind my saying so—." You and I can take serious warning. Whenever you hear yourself saying or thinking, "If you don't mind my saying so," just *stop* right where you are. *Don't say it.*

Unpleasant things are not "truth" anyway. They are only half-truths or temporary situations in the progress of individuals. The real truth about anybody is that he is passing along the road of experience exactly at the point where you and I have been or will be in our own evolution. What a waste of time—what an impediment to nail upon him some curse of judgment. One may well ask, "Who and what is this person who judges?" We are told to judge—in "righteous judgment"—but we should be sure we have *all* the evidence—and when we have that we have the divine and perfect as well as the human and faulty before us.

Socrates was once asked where he acquired his wisdom—and he replied instantly, "From the blind, who never take a step until they have felt the ground before them." Mentally follow your words and imagine how they will fall on the ear and the heart of the hearer.

## 3. TACT AND CORRECTNESS IN LITTLE THINGS

*MAKE YOURSELF KNOWN FOR SOMETHING YOU LIKE.* If you are known for something you like rather than for something you do not like, you will be a far more interesting person. Have a favorite flower, a color, a food, an author—or let it be known that you like poetry or prize-fights. You are much more of an individual if you impress your *likes* upon people—not your dislikes.

A hostess, an employer, anyone will remember more vividly the person who had an enthusiasm for some special thing—rather than the person who was merely displeased about a number of things.

*YOUR PERSONALITY IS COMPOSED OF YOUR LIKES.* Your dislikes represent what you are not—and if you are *not* more things than you *are,* you are not positive enough to be remembered. So if you want to impress your personality, advertise what you like— what you accept, approve, enjoy.

*WHAT IS A YES MAN?* He is supposed to be a person who, without character and for profit, will say "yes" untruthfully to a powerful person or employer who can favor him. As such he is rightfully an object of contempt.

*WHAT IS A DIPLOMAT?* He is not worthy of the name unless he can say "no" and make the other person like it—or at least not be offended by it. How much better the world would be if everyone were something of a diplomat.

During the World War number one, Marshal Foch was entertaining an American who had tactlessly said, "Why do you French bother so much with all this courtesy? It seems very insincere to me, just a lot of air." The great Marshal smiled and said, "That is what your pneumatic tires are filled with—and it smooths the rough road of life."

People who do not want to use any art in making contacts with other people less harsh should be compelled to live in houses without ornament, to sleep in beds without springs, and eat out of horse troughs. Why should we be artful about all of life except other people's feelings?

Wilson Mizner, a worldling if ever there was one, was once talking to Elizabeth Marbury, that remarkable woman who for three decades was the liaison between business, literature, politics, art and society. They were discussing the small gaucheries that shunt promising people into the discard. Miss Marbury said, "It's usually some small irritating matter." And Mr. Mizner replied, borrowing an ancient Persian proverb, "Yes, it's a tiny pebble in the shoe that raises a blister—makes one lame."

So, in this chapter we discuss a few of these so-big small matters this worldly pair touched upon.

*SALT CAN BE INSULTING.* For instance, at table do not criticize your hostess's food by vigorously adding salt and pepper as though it were a great deal of work to make the food edible. If you must use salt do it quietly. There is always a charming, kind way to do everything.

The ease that is desirable in entertaining gives many liberties, but no license. To abuse the absolutely carte-blanche hospitality of today's hostess is to cut oneself off from further invitations. No matter how formal the occasion may be, never seem stiff, studied and formal.

Practice in front of a long mirror to see that your manner is *casual*. I should say this is the major requirement of a successful week-end visit. It makes everyone comfortable. We spend hours shopping for a becoming color in a hat or a frock. No one considers that deceitful in trying to appear to be what one is not. We get menus and table decorations together that are attractive. We practice the piano hours on end—no one says we are trying to "put something over" on the world. Why then, isn't it our duty as well as our privilege to lift, perhaps color and shape, our own manners so that they may color and gladden our corner of the world? But never practice, pose or listen to yourself in public.

*BE CAREFUL WHAT YOU SAY LAST.* Be sure that your talk is always constructive, always kind. In leaving anyone you wish to have remember you pleasantly (and this means all the time), let the last phrase you utter be something that will linger pleasantly in the mind. *Always let your conversation end on a constructive note.*

In effective conversation as in effective writing put your best points at the beginning and at the end of a paragraph. Try to have the last few words of a sentence convey the meaning to a reader or a listener. If you cannot do this, then see that the last word or phrase is what you want to have most deeply impressed on the person or persons you are addressing. This is necessary in all dramatic writing or speaking, which is only effective when close attention has been given to holding the interest of the audience where it is wanted.

For your best effect you want to have that final impression a pleasant memory of you—but that is not enough. You must never descend into satisfaction with being just "a sweet girl." You want to leave the impression of constructive energy that stimulates and inspires. You must stimulate people's imaginations before they will seek you again. They may like you because you are sweet but they will not make an

effort to know you better unless you *do something to them.* So inspire
them by inspiring words—not necessarily wound into rhetorical, high-
flown oratory, but leave them with a word that suggests the possibility
of building, of healing, of action that is fun and healthful, of pleasure
in harmony of one kind or another.

*WRITE YOUR OWN—NOW.* Now, instead of giving you set
phrases and sentences I am going to ask you to write your own. I have
steadfastly refused to give lists of remarks, for that does not develop
your facility in expressing yourself. But I have tried to train your
mind to find conversational material for yourself. I can't imagine anything more static and uninteresting than a roomful of people who
have read my book saying things to each other that they have learned.
The prospect is laughable. But no matter how many of my readers
should meet, each will have the ease of expression that comes from
personal preparation to talk.

The best thing to do is to discover how many words you know that
have a stimulating and constructive or pleasing effect. So I want you
to make a list of them and study their meanings. I want you to see
how far I have stirred your imagination and how boldly you now take
hold of concrete expression for your lifted and soaring ideas. For
Charm is a magnetism that draws the mind away from the pain, lack
and negative conversation of the uncharming person.

*WRITE DOWN ON PAPER AT LEAST FIFTY WORDS*
(more if you can think of them) that carry constructive suggestion.
Here are six—building, growing, courage, love, cure, beauty—now you
continue the list to fifty or more. Here is an example of their use. You
may say, "John has more courage than anyone I have ever seen." It
will be a much stronger remark if you say, "I have never seen anyone
with so much *courage!*" If this is your last remark you add "goodbye"
and go. You have left an impression of mental vigor and appreciation
of someone else. Yet the quality you have given John becomes a part
of the impression you left of yourself. And it is true that you actually
have the qualities you see in others.

*LEARN A LITTLE TECHNIQUE AND THEN FORGET IT.*
The inexperienced woman is so eager to be correct that she gives every
little formal move an extra flourish as though glad to get that done—

as though she hoped everybody saw that she knew what to do. The best manner is quite unconscious of being "correct"; it casually conforms to what is expected as though by second nature.

*FOUR DESIRABLE ITEMS.* Be proficient in as many sports as possible. Next in importance is adaptability. Leave all your set notions and your pet rules at home. Don't try to bring a pseudo elegance into an informal atmosphere.

*EXPLOSIVE LAUGHTER CAN BLOW YOU OUT.* Learn to laugh heartily but never loudly. Many a woman has let a boisterous laugh keep her from the social position she was otherwise qualified to hold. Her unrestrained howls sound as though she were enjoying the relaxation of being her real and common self. The injunction not to collapse, duck or double up with laughter seems easy to obey. Yet you would be surprised if you knew how many men and women have to learn to laugh in an upright position. Learning to laugh may seem utterly ridiculous, but if one needs to know, his lack is anything but funny to him and his friends. An artificial ripple down the scale is deadly and mirthless. Far better to laugh on one note in the throat. No grown woman should giggle or laugh through her nose. To change a disagreeable laugh one should practice a substitute expulsion of air from the diaphragm in short jerks, in other words, train a different set of muscular contractions. After a while habit makes it natural. A laugh can be hearty, bubbling or rippling without being too loud or coarse.

Inexperienced people go from one extreme to the other in manner— they either are stiffly formal or, as a child put it, fall all to pieces sprawling and yelling. One should be easy in manner in the drawing-room as on a tennis court. Smart people sometimes say and do what is shocking to staid conventionality, but they do it or say it and go on. They do not stop to grovel in the risqué.

Youngsters should not imagine that smartness can be attained by copying the vices of the boldest and least secure of good society. People retain their positions in spite of their laxities, not because of them. If our young people are going to copy these people, tell them to copy also their culture, their generosities and their many refinements.

## 4. PHYSICAL CORRECTNESS

*BODILY POISE AT ALL TIMES*. In sports it is quite possible to give an impression of grace. You can even stoop gracefully to pick up something from the ground or floor if you will bend your knees, let the left one drop almost to the floor and depend upon your right leg for most of the leverage. Never bend over from the waist leaving your hips up in the air. When sitting on the floor keep your knees supporting your weight as you rise. Never get up back end first like a camel. These matters seem small but one ridiculous pose can shatter the most carefully built-up illusion of grace.

Whether or not we ever attain real physical grace, we can at least avoid the awkwardness that sets at naught all our other good points. It is really so simple to handle your body *well*. Then you enjoy yourself more and others enjoy you too.

*COME TOWARD YOUR AUDIENCE*. In making a public appearance an important point is this—always enter a platform or stage far back enough to enable you to come *toward* the audience as you come to the place where you will stand when you speak. If the platform is so small that you can take only one step toward the audience after you have reached the center—then take that one step. You look as though you have something for the audience if you come *toward* them. It helps to rivet attention on you. Then take a deep, long breath before you begin speaking. Some speakers stand just to one side of center, leaving the middle for their subject as it were.

Marian Anderson, the wonderful colored singer, does not come toward her audience until they begin to appreciate her. She stands coldly aloof as a person until she is established as an artist. As the audience unbends, she does also. This is excellent psychology for her— and for anyone in a comparable position. The "going toward" people in no way means that one must ever leap at others like a mastiff puppy, knocking them over and greeting them with a warm, wet muzzle. The attitudes we discuss are merely gracious, inviting, but impersonal.

*LISTEN WITH YOUR BODY.* Suppose you are seated talking to someone and have decided to be a good listener and draw out the other person. Your physical posture will aid you in getting a response. You must listen with your body by leaning a little forward. You must "expect" with your body by leaning a little forward. Listen with your hands by keeping them still (don't *ever* fiddle with a necklace!) and listen with your eyes. A child once said to her mother, "Mother, listen to me!" The mother said, "Why, I am listening, dear. What is it?" The child replied, "But you're not looking at me. Listen to me with your eyes!" And quite as important—you must listen with your *breath*. Watch people in an audience listening to something in which they are intensely interested and you will find them leaning forward, eyes absorbed, hands absolutely still, the mouth soft, sometimes the lips parted a little, and the breath a gentle, long inhalation, just as you breathe when you smell the fragrance of a flower. This way of breathing seems to say, "I want to keep the atmosphere of this delightful moment passing over the sensitive nerves in my head so that I may enjoy it to the full." Exhale more quickly. A trick? Yes. But it is exactly what you do when you are sincere. This way of breathing actually clears the head, thereby making you quicker-witted. When you first try it, it may make you dizzy.

*WHEN IN DOUBT—TAKE A DEEP BREATH.* Whenever you are confused, angry, self-conscious, or simply wish to collect yourself, take one or more deep breaths. It helps to bring you power and poise. Confusion, anger, fear, cause you to breathe short, gaspy breaths. By making yourself breathe long and deep you assist in reversing the feeling. A great many times this, alone, will completely change the emotion. No one gets oxygen enough!

*RENEW MIND AND BODY WITH OXYGEN.* Take a deep, long breath before you enter a room where there are people you would like to impress. Take a long, deep breath as you go forward to meet someone or greet someone. *Breath is life!*

Much power attaches to the breath. It carries all the qualities of your personality. The breath of an angry person can wither a flower. See that yours carries the magnetism of unselfish interest in others. See that it is sweet with the sweetness of health and cleanliness.

*BREATHE FOR INSPIRATION.* When you are alone taking your exercises and deep breathing for health, magnetize your breath as you inhale by thinking of constructive things.

Think definitely of what you want to breathe in from the universe and say inwardly, "I am breathing in love, friendship, health, etc. I am breathing in all the elements necessary for my highest expression of myself. With this breath I am drawing to myself opportunities to develop in mind, character and body. I am drawing opportunities to help others—to brighten their lives by my own radiance. I will radiate to all the brightness I have gained because I am in touch with the inexhaustible source, knowing that the more I give out the more I can take in!"

Soon your body will tingle with the joyous message, which the re-vitalized blood is carrying throughout your system.

*RAISE YOUR CHEST* and give your lungs plenty of room to expand. Nothing vitalizes you like plenty of oxygen from fresh air in your body. *Magnetism depends heavily upon vitality!* So take excellent care of your health. See that you get sufficient rest. A tired body means tired nerves, hence irritability and no magnetism. A sense of well-being contributes generously to charm.

Now here is a most important point. No matter what the condition or appearance of your body you can so magnetize it by constructive thoughts and habits that you can be most attractive. No matter what your apparent limitations seem to be, *you cannot be limited by anything but those things you accept as limitations.*

## 5. THE ADAPTABILITY OF CHARM

If you say, "I can't become or do so and so because of this or that," you have dammed yourself from all expression in that direction. Never feel that others can blossom forth more easily than you can because of some strange quality of theirs which you do not possess.

Human beings are as much alike basically as peas in a pod. They are different only as they have accepted this and rejected that until they have formed many different personal habits. Provided they are in their right minds all have equal opportunities. The ones who apply themselves along a given line get results along that line. Those who fail to pay the price of study and application are only fooling themselves when they claim inability or unresponsiveness. This applies to everything in life.

NEW LIFE CAN BE YOURS. New cells are constantly being formed in your body—your reaction to life is being impressed constantly on your subconscious mind, where it takes root and *produces after its kind*. Your body and personality are now the result of the strongest impressions your subconscious mind has received.

YOUR PERSONALITY IS ALWAYS IN THE PROCESS OF BEING MADE. Make yours what you wish it to be by permitting only the seeds of loveliness to be planted in it. They will grow and astonish you with their blossoms. Remember that no matter how great the failure, the laws of creation, growth and development are still at work—so you can always, *always* build anew. *We tire of life only as we forget this.*

Many of us derive a sort of dramatic satisfaction from self-pity, and though we say we want to be free and glorious we will not give up even this petty pleasure for the larger glory. You can never be free from limitation until you are willing to recognize that you and you alone are responsible for what you are. After you have passed infancy you are not a victim of anything but your own thinking.

So sit down in front of the mirror and make a pact with yourself. Promise yourself that you will never again put a single limiting thought on yourself or anyone else (which is really on yourself for *you* are doing the thinking!).

If others, through jealousy or envy, are apparently opposed to your progress don't stoop to resent their attitude. Don't be weak enough to be hurt by it. Send out a kind thought to nullify a vicious one. One little candle can dispel a great deal of darkness. And if you have learned much from this book you will be clever enough to make others pleased with something about themselves.

Choose some fine point about them (everybody has something fine) and tell them that if you only had that particular thing it would make you happier than anything in the world.

If you love people enough and are interested enough to make them happy, you will not be annoyed by jealousies. Anyway there will be no room in your mind for any negative idea.

Don't bother to resent anything. Resentment is an animalistic tendency we should be civilized enough to discard. When you resent other people you are attending to something that is none of your business, or at least you are attempting to. Your business is to free others and to free yourself from any sort of condemnation.

Don't try to run other people. If you go about your own development sweetly and quietly, soon your life will become so filled with friendship, attention and love that you will be amazed. But don't watch for results in the mood of *daring* the principle to work.

Just plant your seeds, knowing that, in the due course of time, according to natural laws they will bear fruit. Be sure to keep the weeds pulled away—the weeds of doubt, fear, anxiety, inferiority, selfishness, arrogance and anger, for these are the greatest enemies of charm and happiness.

It is very difficult to hide your thoughts, for the tiny, sensitive muscles of the face, particularly about the mouth, betray them. I would not trust the most honest-looking eyes in the world if the mouth beneath them were loose, cruel and sensual.

*ARE YOU HIDING OR EXPRESSING?* When a woman is doing things, large or small, that are at variance with her conscience, her face begins to resemble a battlefield. Her personality becomes negative because all her energies are bent on *concealing something* instead of *expressing something*. Always remember that I am talking from the standpoint of charm. When our lives conform to standards of loveliness and beauty, there are no barriers that stop the flow of charm, which in the last analysis is the delight of uninterrupted divine force operating through us and out to others.

If we have this charm, our faces have the shining, open beauty of countenance that my mother has called "the pearl." Any face can be illumined by this "pearl," which is more beautiful than beauty itself. Its possessor will attain a reputation for comeliness, regardless of the shape of her features.

It is really the light from an inner fire of beauty that draws the world to its warmth and comfort. Not only is it attractive to look upon, but it lends the face a fineness as distinguishing as a family tree.

The technique of Charm is a continual adaptability. This does not mean that you are constantly to reflect others and thus ruin your individuality. Truth sometimes sounds paradoxical—but the Bible presents the truest paradox in the world—"He who would lose his life shall find it." This is true in society. The strongest individual socially is the one who flows most smoothly and harmoniously with those she meets —but, by the strength of that same harmony, calls everyone gently up to her level by asking them mutely to live up to their best.

## 6. GIVE COURAGE TO OTHERS

Tact will prevent you from talking in a rudely stimulating way to friends who are ill. You can, however, direct the talk to things that are mentally diverting rather than to physical activities. You do not talk of the joy of victory to a war widow. Rather do you discuss the dignity of valor. People do not stop to analyze why they like you or want more of you. They simply say, "Isn't she charming!" And indeed it is charming to "touch the wounds of others with healing fingers" to make them forget their shortcomings and remember their good points, to give them back their shaking confidence.

Life pulls at bewildered humanity in so many ways! Blessed is the woman who makes her life a career of stimulating the courage of others.

We do not faint and fail because we have no more strength, but because we have no more courage. Courage and confidence send the blood racing swiftly through the body, carrying off poisons and building new cells. No matter how tired you think you are—if someone stimulates your good opinion of yourself, you arise immediately and go into action. Bad news chokes and kills. Good news lifts the clouds and starts the machinery of our minds and bodies working swiftly and efficiently.

If it is hypocritical to be a bearer of good news to everybody about themselves and all else—then let us have more hypocrites! It is quite possible to give constructive criticism if one is clever enough not to

**disturb** the ego of the person criticized. (Remember the hat conversation in Chapter Eight.)

*YOUR HIGHEST GOOD.* The charming woman approaches
people generally with this in her mind and heart: "To meet another
person is a great opportunity for two splendid achievements.

"First: I shall leave this person in a better state than I found him
even though we talk but two minutes. Second: By so doing I shall
carve a path for affection and friendship to return to me until my life
is rich and full."

To leave people better than we found them is not to preach but by
suggestion to attract and urge them up to a fuller realization of power.
You need not be personal and direct. By radiating joy in your face
and well-being in your attitude you suggest to any beholder that life
can be a very delightful thing.

The inspired mind does not confine beauty to delicate things. It is
also in greatness, in the towering structures of steel and stone with
which men have pierced the sky to defy their own insignificance.
Find beauty in gameness. For if we appreciate that the strong, sturdy
and magnificent things embody the elements of prettiness simply on a
grand, breath-taking scale, then we find this great truth: *Back of the
gentle fineness that charms there must be the steel girders of character.*

We can afford to be gentlewomen because we are strong women.
It is only weakness that is loud and boisterous, cruel and grasping,
for weakness feels that it must snatch while it may. The strength of
charm builds the solid foundation for the symmetrical structure of
personality that daily can reach on up and up and up, and yet remain
as homey and comfortable as a pair of old shoes. By conforming to
laws of harmony one's personality remains poised, and stands before
the world as a symbol of beautiful balance, the wonder of which is
Charm.

## INSTRUCTIONS

Compose ten sentences having the important words at the beginning and at the end. (Note my example using the word "courage,"
a few pages back.)

# CHAPTER TEN

## *And These Above All—*

### 1. THE VALUE OF PERSISTENCE

Few people know of the vastness of the Russian successes in colonizing the Arctic regions. Even though they may have read of it, it just hasn't registered as a reality. In Smolka's book, "Forty Thousand Against the Arctic," he tells the romantic and almost unbelievable story of large settlements of civilized men maintaining themselves in the far north region. They have established towns, industries, lines of communication, air bases—and have even grown crops in the earth.

Intelligence, science and art can work with any materials and bring from them a satisfactory yield. Man is indeed given dominion over all the earth—if he knows how to exercise his gift.

Naturally, with the short Arctic growing season, seeds that are especially treated are used for a garden or a crop. Special methods of production, housing and community cooperation are used.

But the principal point proved is that the most forbidding places and circumstances can be made to blossom. Artfulness, work and patience can transmute frozen wastes into warmth of living production, human accomplishment and gaiety.

Whenever any of us become discouraged with the seeming unresponsiveness of our own situation, let's just throw our heads up defiantly and say inside, "If the Russians can make anything out of the Arctic, I can certainly make something fine out of myself, my home, my situation in life." Of course, it takes courage and ceaseless work—but there is no satisfaction on earth quite so thrilling as to see the fruit of your efforts begin to take shape. That is a joy worth working for.

So make out a program for yourself. Set down on paper what you hope to accomplish in the next year—or is yours a longer plan? Include in that program the further development of some skill, such as a better game of bridge, quicker sight-reading at the piano—quicker and better attention to your friendly correspondence.

And above all, lay out a line of reading for yourself. And learn how to make something, whether that means knitting or cooking or carpentering or dyeing or weaving—anything that you didn't know before.

Also, on your program, be sure to put six new friends in the coming year. Never mind the reasons why you can't. Do it!

And on that program put a few definite choices and decisions.

Decide to be healthy. The moment you take a definite stand, the methods and means seem to gravitate to you. Seek advice and use it—mental and physical.

Decide to be happy. There will always be two ways (at least) to look at every point in life. Happiness is a simple decision and gets to be a habit, like anything else.

No matter what cataclysmic occurrences shake the earth, you will always be able to decide how *you* will react. *No one can decide for you.* You can be persuaded, coaxed, cajoled, taught, urged, pulled and pushed, but the final *decision* as to what you will feel and think is your own—and no one can deprive you of that.

So never feel victimized by world conditions. It's easy to blame too much on general conditions. It's easy to throw up one's hands and consider oneself helpless. It may be extremely interesting to discover how much of beauty and comfort can be achieved with meager materials.

I remember one fall in the country when the garden was parched, ragged, neglected, a large number of guests arrived unexpectedly. I thought, "What an ugly bare table we shall have—no flowers—and what plain food—these people will be very disappointed." But I reckoned without the ingenuity of my cook. When we came to the table there was a charming centerpiece of tan and purple and red weed-heads arranged gracefully in a crystal bowl—one of the most beautiful decorations I have ever seen. On another occasion she used a handful of dried tall grass in a bowl with a little china figure of a wild duck. The salad was served on large grape-leaves. For dessert she had whipped and frozen a tapioca concoction into something that tasted like nectar.

The whole meal and scene had been fashioned of left-overs, seemingly worthless things. An unimaginative average person would have sat down hopelessly and said that there was nothing on the place to do with.

In the future we shall not measure the value of things by their cost, but by their honest worth. It has been said that Americans throw away and destroy more than they use. It may be that we shall, through economies and artfulness, achieve even greater effect with the sparse materials we shall be able to get. For according to what is said of us we shall really enjoy as much as we enjoy now with less than half of the actual goods.

In our house we have an expression that is not so elegant as it is effective. "Just keep on punching," we say to each other under any circumstances that seem to require a bit of keeping on. We owe the expression to Mercer, my driver and man-of-all-work who is well known to many clients who have come to me. It came about originally because of the stubborn rocky terrain of Connecticut. We had decided to make a garden and all hands were enlisted to get it under way.

Progress was slow, so it seemed, in clearing the ground of stones, yet when evening came quite a large area was ready for use. "How in the world did you do so much?" I asked. "Oh," said Mercer proudly, "you can get quite a ways if you just keep on punching."

And more than once when I have been swamped with work and burdened with many things of various kinds to do, and have sat quiet and concerned in the back seat, Mercer has said quietly, "Just keep on punching, Miss Wilson, and you'll get on top of it." Watching the lives of others, by the thousands literally, one must admit as a fact that there isn't much that will not yield to persistence.

I once asked Mr. A. R. Nicol, retired president of the A. G. W. I. Steamship Company, what he considered the most valuable asset one can have—and he replied instantly, "Energy!"

As we pursued the subject I said, "Do you mean that just doing anything, even wrong things will result in success?" "Not exactly," he replied. "But if a person will just keep on going he will profit by his mistakes and one day he will do enough of the right things to bring him success. If he has energy he will persist. That is why I say that energy is the most valuable attribute one can possess."

Certainly almost every woman has in a bathroom closet half-forgotten jars of cold cream and lotions that she bought one day in a fiery but fleeting determination to care for her skin. In the depths of some drawer is a piece of material bought, perhaps cut out and basted, and there it lies unfinished. And that same woman probably has a stack of French lessons gathering dust on the library shelves—or some *gros point* chair covers that got so far and no farther.

Ten to one she thinks life has played her a sly trick in never letting her become a great singer or actress or sculptor—when truth to tell, life hasn't played her false—she just didn't keep on punching.

## 2. HOSPITALITY, ENTERTAINING AND BEING A GUEST

*ENTERTAINING.* A good rule for a hostess is the Golden Rule. Look after the physical comfort of guests *thoroughly*. Make it possible for them to know where there is a bathroom or lavatory, for they will not ask you until they are suffering. Keep cotton balls for powder available for feminine guests, also keep needles, thread, straight pins and tiny safety ones, as well as several corsage pins where the guests can see them. For men, keep a few extra collar-buttons and cuff-buttons, razor blades, etc. A thoughtful hostess prepares for any emergency so that nothing can disturb the serenity of her house or a guest's mind. In every guest-room, put books, *new* magazines, a good light, writing paper, ink and a pen-that-will-write. Then see that the guest has, out of every day, at least two hours, preferably four, in which to be alone, to rest, read or write. Provide games for your guests but do not insist that they play. Men particularly like "something to do." Many successful hostesses let guests follow their own inclinations. This is becoming increasingly popular. In the old days an energetic hostess could wear out strong men by rushing them from one compulsory activity to another. However, whenever one of those negative moments arrives in which no one will take a choice of several proffered games, trips, etc., then the hostess should take the lead and settle the matter without letting it dangle until it is too late to do anything. In some large houses, especially in the country, a bulletin of the day's activities is found posted where all may see it—then each guest can take this and leave that, according to his taste. In a small house, or in a great palace, the actual relation of guest and hostess is the same, though, of course, the service and manner of entertainment may be as widely different as the poles.

*THE MATTER OF RETURNING HOSPITALITY* is exactly that—"returning *hospitality*" and not necessarily returning an entertainment with a like entertainment. So many women feel that they should drop out of social life altogether if they cannot entertain as lavishly as their friends do. I admit it takes a stronger and a more charming woman to keep her head up with a reduced income, but here is another case where your own attitude toward yourself is the pattern that your friends will accept. I know a young couple who go and go to others' houses but give only one or two parties a year themselves. And these are the simplest sort of teas. Fifty people are not too many to invite to a tea in a small apartment and you may serve nothing more elaborate than a hot and a cold drink and some sort of wafers. In New York people will stand talking for two hours with no more than this to bear them up. There is more intimacy, of course, in a tea for a dozen or so, but to wipe out a long list of social obligations there is nothing so easy and so effective, also so inexpensive, as a "tea." In giving a tea for someone always ask for your guest's list or have her help you make yours. Those who come to honor your guest are not later obligated to you socially. However, in this way many women have successfully enlarged their acquaintance among desirable people. The invitations are your visiting cards on which you have written above your name, "To meet Miss ——" and below your name "Tea, five to seven," or "Tea, four-thirty to seven-thirty." If you are also to have bridge or dancing, write in the other lower corner "Dancing" or "Bridge." However, it is not obligatory to mention them. Such cards are mailed in tiny single envelopes. Well-bred people usually reply to every invitation as soon as possible, whether or not a response is requested. If the answer is a regret a visiting card should be included with the note. For a quick entertainment, naturally the invitations are telephoned, "I'm having a tea Thursday afternoon for Mary Jones (if the person to whom you are speaking calls her "Mary," otherwise, Miss or Mrs. So and So). Can you and —— drop in between five and seven?"

For a house with one servant or none, the buffet dinner is becoming increasingly popular. The guests help themselves from an attractively arranged table in the dining-room or one end of the living-room or whatever space is allowed for it. They carry their plates anywhere to eat, but if there is to be bridge following they sit at the bridge tables, the two men acting as waiters for the ladies for coffee, dessert, etc. I know one house where a hundred persons are served buffet dinner on Sundays and no provision is made for the eating. The guests take their plates and roam over the grounds, into the halls, sit on the steps —in fact, there seems to be an enormous amount of fun in trying to find a place to eat! I recall a particularly famous intellectual solemnly eating from the mantelpiece! The servants are kept busy supplying the main table and picking up dishes. In a tiny house the guests do this work for themselves and like it!

In regions where there is snow a clever hostess with modest income might delight the smartest people, as a friend of mine does, by giving a hay-ride in the winter. The guests come by motor to where the huge wagon on runners drawn by work horses awaits them. They ride sitting in the hay for several miles to a spot where a huge bonfire has been made or is built for them, perhaps at the edge of a lake where they may skate; or they tell stories around the fire while hot coffee is served and marshmallows are toasted. Old-fashioned fun and old-fashioned games are being revived. Today's hostess needs but to oil her originality to "keep up with the Joneses."

If you are charming and your presence adds anything whatever of interest or value to a party (rest assured your hostess thinks so or you would not be invited) you should not feel that you are under such terrific obligation that you cannot carry on. If you are a delightful person your hostess might be perfectly willing to pay an enormous sum if she could be like you.

*DON'T PERMIT YOURSELF TO LAG AND DROP OUT OF THINGS*. And never discount sympathetic, affectionate consideration in your invitations. Let love bring you its gifts, which also bless the giver, and give your fair exchange in charm and loving tact. If you do this your hostess, so far from wishing something from you, will feel grateful to you!

If you are the hostess you will quickly reach out for charming guests if you wish your entertainments to be successful. You will not be interested in their bank balances! Whether you are rich or poor, you will find life much happier, simpler and smoother if you will see that your social currency is based on the heart standard rather than the gold standard. You will rise much more quickly and be much more likely to "stay" up if your demands are cultural rather than material.

*BEING A GUEST*. The guest will also solve all her problems if she takes the Golden Rule for her motto. One who is careless with lovely things usually has never had any of her own.

Never correct another guest for *anything*. If a matter arises that you believe demands attention go quickly to your hostess and tell her (or your host). But most such matters are best ignored. You will not be pleasantly remembered as a tattler or a busybody.

Remember you have been invited to enjoy yourself and to make others happy. Your duty is to *look* entertained even if you are bored to death, and if you do not contribute to the happiness of the other guests wherever you can, you may not be invited again. Loyalty to a hostess is demanded by good taste.

Loyalty anywhere is one of the strongest factors of charm. There is romance in loyalty. There is character in loyalty. To offend loyalty at any point is uncharming.

What is more lacking in charm than a girl criticizing a parent, even though that parent be a criminal? What more soul-stirring than the loyalty of a young girl to her parents? The less they deserve it the greater her glory! The clever girl will let her voice take on a deeper tenderness when she says, "My mother" or "My father."

Loyalty between husband and wife is a fine, charming thing. Certainly as guests they should *never* let an instant's friction become apparent. It is unfair to place people where they must "take sides" between them. It is the height of bad taste and disloyalty for a man to criticize his wife. And so long as a woman bears a man's name she *must not* criticize him openly.

A bridge table is a poor place for a family argument. Well-bred people do not wash their "soiled linen" where others can witness the washing. Even intimate friends are made uncomfortable. It stamps the offenders at once as gauche, vulgar, crude and supremely selfish and undisciplined.

When you arrive as a guest anywhere, any time, find your hostess and make your presence known in the pleasantest way possible. Conform not only to good taste and social usage while under her roof, but conform also to the time demands of the household. Do not make your hostess face disgruntled servants thrown off schedule by your thoughtlessness.

A Senator's wife once said that by being ready ahead of time she had had some of the most interesting experiences of her life. However, never arrive ahead of time for anything at a private house. *Kindness* should make you timely.

A charming guest never arrives without bringing something, not necessarily a tangible gift, but a new story, an amusing anecdote, stimulating news (nothing disagreeable) or a new point of view. A new book, a new game, an amusing gadget show that you *thought* of your hostess. This is not etiquette but charm!

If there are children in the family, it is quite as charming to ignore grown-ups and bring something for the "little folks." Anything except candy! The success of such a gift often depends upon its cleverness rather than its expense. I recall a book costing only a few cents that kept two four-year-olds busy for two days. It contained things to cut out—to paint—to make—and two masks that were hilarious fun for the little tots, the grown-ups enjoying their boisterous delight.

Present a gift yourself with no particular emphasis or flourish and whatever you do, don't belittle it. One amusing friend of mine used to say, "I could neither find nor afford anything worthy of your acceptance but I hope you like this."

In receiving, for instance, a box of candy, smile and say something like, "How nice! What a thoughtful soul you are!" To which the donor may say, "To start my visit by acquiring virtues is a good beginning. I hope I shan't give way under the strain." Then go right on without waiting for any further personal remark, "Odd how they keep the same box all these years," or "I believe there is a slight difference in this one, etc." To which someone can say, "Almost everything is changing its face these days—even (mentioning something of general or local interest)." Thus an animated conversation is on its way.

If you have a talent and feel that you are invited only to entertain, don't waste time feeling hurt about it. All of us are veritable "Little Tommy Tuckers" who must sing for our suppers. No guest has been invited (except those with the claim of affection) who does not contribute something to the gathering.

If you are able to play, sing, or read, always do it without much coaxing. Nothing is sillier than the self-conscious parlor entertainer who, after much urging, gives a mediocre performance. If you sit down casually at a piano at the first suggestion, and strum even carelessly through a ditty no one will consider your shortcomings—but if you yield only after coaxing more will be expected of you as you have made a show of the temperament that goes with serious study.

A note of appreciation is always charming when you have enjoyed *anything* from *anybody*—but you *must* write the hostess under whose roof you have stayed.

In large houses, after an overnight stay, the guest tips only the servant or servants who have served her personally. In small houses she leaves something for each. She should not feel embarrassed if her purse will stand only one dollar or less for each servant after a week-end visit. Usually an individual tip does not exceed two dollars—except for some extraordinary service, or a lengthy stay.

## 3. CLOTHES

A delightful guest is one who is appropriately rather than elaborately dressed. Cling to simple, untrimmed clothes of good material and becoming line, long enough to be graceful. Necklaces, earrings and bracelets should be chosen carefully for *accent* rather than for decoration. Many times when you know you do not look smart, you can correct everything by removing *all* your jewelry except *one* piece, and by dressing your hair close to your head.

If you wear earrings then be careful of a necklace. Never have your fingers full of rings. Don't wear a necklace *and* a breastpin unless you put the pin at your belt. It is smart to wear just one unusual piece that belongs with what you have on; hence the vogue for costume jewelry. It is all a matter of taste, not expense.

In a perfectly plain gown an older woman can get by with more jewelry (if it is real and beautiful) at a formal occasion than can a younger woman.

It is smart to travel and visit with few clothes these days. Only people who have never traveled before or who are insensible to smartness will appear in a different get-up every three or four hours. Sport clothes of the sort that are also appropriate for street, and evening clothes are enough. It is not necessary to have a different gown for every night.

You will find a lace gown always dependable and useful, for you can, in a pinch, wear it without pressing the first night of a trip or a week-end. Then you can get your things pressed the next morning when the servants have time to attend to you. It is unkind to send a gown down to the back of a house that is concerned with preparations for a big party.

Convertible dresses and combination outfits are practical for packing. If you plan your clothes in the same color, preferably a neutral one, you can always give them life when and where you want it by the use of jewelry, gay handkerchiefs, scarfs, etc. A trimmed dress, a trimmed hat, a trimmed pocketbook, trimmed shoes and a fur neckpiece constitute an ensemble of the worst possible taste.

If your clothes are plain *you* will shine forth better. Clever women feature themselves, their carriage, their expression, their hair, their skin, their hands, their voices. If you dazzle the eye with finery, trimmings, broken lines, and jewelry, no one can pick *you* out of the scramble. Your clothes should be an integral part of *yourself*.

At a tea in New York early arrivals will perhaps have on street clothes, late arrivals may have on evening clothes if they are going on somewhere for dinner. Wear what you like to a tea. At other times wear what is appropriate to the hour and the occasion.

Prominent people are supposed to have a sense of leadership and responsibility for their fellow men. Hence the fashionable interest in charities. Great extravagance and much display are therefore in worse taste these days than ever before. Smart debutantes in New York are sitting in the balcony at the theatre, riding street-cars and busses and laughing over their "finds" in the ten-cent store. The saving, if any, is given to the Red Cross or used to buy Defense Bonds.

So simple clothes are smarter than ever. This goes for everybody. You can express your own individuality and type with the accessories you choose. Your pocketbook can be gay or dignified. Your hat can be gay or dignified. Your shoes must never be gay unless you want people to look at your feet instead of your face.

When shopping, don't be lured by impractical ruffles, buckles, gadgets and fluff for daytime. There is nowhere to wear them. A sport suit, long enough to be graceful, in a pastel shade such as light beige, can be worn for active sport without the jacket, will be pretty at a garden party, and next year you can have it dyed darker. With it you can wear red, blue, green, brown, plum, orange or white belts, kerchiefs, etc.

## 4. YOUR HOUSE

The same principles that apply to dressing yourself apply to your house. See that there are restful plain spaces to give accent to your objects or groups of objects. Beware of hodgepodges. Have either plain rugs or plain walls or both. Don't have several different kinds of figures in one room unless there is much space to relieve them. One clever woman removes all the lolling chairs from the drawing-room when she gives a party. She also takes out some of the ashtrays. Her theory is that guests have an easier, better time if they have some reason to move about—to cross the room to an ashtray for instance—that they find it easier to rise from a stiff chair than from the depths of a sofa. Freedom of movement does add to the success of a party; this we must admit whether or not we agree with the lady. Plain lamp-shades are smarter than ever. Golden light is always flattering to women—not necessarily yellow, but the reflection of warm tans, fawn color, etc. Candlelight is the most flattering light in the world.

## 5. CARE OF SKIN

Your body has an enormous amount of surface. Therefore the skin at once reflects the condition of your health and your habits of cleanliness. Cleanliness, internal and external, is the major requirement for a good skin. Use a soft brush on your body while it is dry to brush away small particles of cuticle that soap and water do not remove. This stimulates the whole surface of the body, evens circulation, gives you energy and makes your skin satiny.

*Drink not less than eight glasses of liquid, preferably water, a day!* Drink lots of fruit juices, soups—any liquids that will dilute and wash away the accumulation of poisons in the system. Eat leafy vegetables and drink a quart of milk a day if you want lovely skin. Milk will not fatten if you remove the cream, and in no other way can you get the balanced ration of calcium and phosphates that are present in milk. Your nerves and your hair, dieticians say, will benefit by these necessary elements so conveniently put together by nature in milk. If your hair is lank, fingernails chalky, skin and eyes listless, go to your doctor for extra vitamins and calcium. Don't dose yourself.

If you use soap on your face, cleanse it with cream before washing and leave a little cream on so that the soap will not wash away all the natural oil in the skin. If you cannot afford expensive skin-tonic, saturate a pad of cotton with ordinary witch-hazel (which is the base of most of the good skin-tonics) and pat your face with it. An over-dry or over-oily skin is the result of the same cause—lazy pores. Wake up your skin by smart patting not heavy enough to break the tiny veins just under the surface. Ice used on your throat and neck (where you may pat as hard as you care to) will tend to make the contour firm. Pat gently around the eyes, for the skin here is thin and delicate. Use good creams and pure powders made by some firm or person in whom you have confidence. Wipe excess cream from your hands on to your elbows instead of a towel. Do the same with excess hand lotion. Every night put a dab of oil or cream on the cuticle around your nails; then you will never have dry cuticle or hangnails. Large pores can be corrected by extreme cleanliness and the persistent use of astringent creams and lotions. Pimples show an impure bloodstream, an acid condition of the body, or both. Persistent cases should have the care of a physician. No woman can express charm fully if she is conscious of a skin that shows lack of care and cleanliness.

To preserve the chin line sleep with a silk stocking under your chin and tied over your head. Such a support is soft and caressing.

It is not necessary to go through a trying menopause. Every physician is equipped to supply the aids that will keep you normal and even refreshed through this bodily change. Remember that in any time of change we can improve our situation!

### 6. THE CHARM OF REMEMBERING NAMES

You can remember names if you *say* you can. You can't remember names if you insist that you cannot. Try making a direct suggestion to your subconscious mind just before you go to sleep. Talk to your subconscious like this: "You know these names, you've heard these names and I expect you to send them to my conscious mind when I want them." For years I went about proclaiming that my memory was poor. Then I saw a girl, whose mental development was far less than mine, benefiting by the charm of remembering names. I decided that if this girl could do it, I could too—and in one week of concentrated suggestion to myself I changed my reaction to names. Demand and expect things of your memory, of life and of yourself and watch what happens. To remember names is a great social, business, political and personal asset. Remove your negative thought and let your memory function. Stick to it until you win!

### 7. HOW TO TAKE A COMPLIMENT

When some honor is conferred upon you or you are suggested for some honor, don't squirm or simper. Let your face reflect your intelligent interest in the matter in hand and rise very simply and casually to respond—let it be known that you are honored, but let the general impression be that the accomplishment back of the honor is your principal interest.

When you are complimented don't blush and squirm—look delighted and say, "Thank you so much. I'm glad you like it." I heard a young girl who was being complimented on her eyes say, "Isn't it a mercy? It's nice to have a few 'breaks' in life. But my dog has the loveliest eyes I ever saw." And the conversation veered off to dogs. Other compliments called forth such remarks as, "You are very kind (or generous)." "It is so sweet of you to tell me." "You have given me a great deal to live up to." "It makes me so happy to know you think such nice things about me." Or facetiously, "You'll have me believing that if you keep on saying it." "I always like to hear pleasant things. Keep it up." *Never* say derogatory things about yourself in answer to a compliment—or at any other time!

It is not "smart" (meaning fashionable as well as clever) to be cynical. Psychologists tell us that cynicism is an admission that we have failed somewhere along the line and are a little bitter about it. This is not charming. So you see there are logical reasons, deeply scientific ones, for being at all times sweet, full of joy and faith and love. It is not necessarily goody-goody or even semi-religious unless you wish to make it so.

## 8. GIFTS

This, as you know, is not a book on etiquette, but on *Charm*. I cannot take up our time with all its phases, but I have touched a few that concern charm. However, I feel that I must speak of the etiquette and charm of gifts. The most difficult gift to choose is the one a woman gives to a man. The safe gift is a book, on which you may spend fifty cents or five hundred dollars. If your friendship is broken, the books may remain without being a reflection on your taste. Never give a gift or write a word that could embarrass you if you and the man should ever lose your friendship.

Flowers are always a perfect gift—when in doubt send flowers (but not to a man unless he is ill). Although it is not always possible to afford a gift, everyone can give the gift of attention by a charming, newsy, amusing letter when a friend is leaving or on any occasion when a gift would be appropriate. A gift, after all, is simply a token of esteem. You can express your esteem on paper if you are unable to do so with an object. Give an expensive wedding present to a poor girl, a modest one to a rich girl if you would be kind and charming. Send graduation notes or presents. They are also big bargains in charm, for they will be remembered a lifetime.

## 9. CULTURE

*APPRECIATION OF ART, LITERATURE, AND MUSIC.* Every cultured person must know the history of the world, at least in a sketchy way. I know of no book so valuable for this purpose as H. G. Wells's "Outline of History." The first two or three chapters are dry but it will pay you to force yourself to read them. From there on the book is fascinating, as the author has chosen only the most dramatic incidents to illustrate each era.

Look at great pictures and listen to great music as a child would— to see what they have to *tell* you. Great things simply *say* more than the others—usually in the simplest way.

To have a haughty, highbrow attitude because you are familiar with classical art is immature and silly. Learn to be humble before its beauty—learn to find that beauty within yourself—this is the meaning of art. Learn to see wind and sun in paintings, in music. Emotions and thoughts should be read into art of all kinds if you would find their cultural aspect, their thrill, their story and their part in your own life.

"Culture" is an *attitude* fed and nourished by information. Information alone will not give it. However, if time is an object with you and you want to get a sketchy history of art, music, and architecture, you may have these for a small sum in books like "The Modern Self-Educator," truly an amazing book. Another excellent one is "The Book of Culture." From these accurate if sketchy accounts you can branch out into the phases that interest you most. They are splendid for quick reference and should be added to the most extensive library on these subjects. "Culture" today is not a matter of money—the wish and will are about all that is necessary. The Delphian Societies will be glad to form a cultural study group in your community if a certain number of women will enroll. If such study causes you to put your head up in a superior way it is better let alone. Knowledge should make you richer and mellower and more human, therefore more charming.

You have heard the saying, "A man is what he thinks—what he eats and what he drinks." But almost more important, he is "what he reads." The constant pouring of suggestion into the reservoir of the mind where it in turn becomes a part of response and reaction, cannot be overestimated.

The richest personality is likely to be the one who has added the world's finest books to his own store of natural charm. For the more he knows, the more his judgment has to play upon, to compare, to find a parallel for conversation—or for his own quiet entertainment.

If one has missed social advantages and classical schooling, there is no need to accept the inferior position and go through life with pride at half-mast. The generosity of books written to give you much for brief attention will fill the gap amazingly well and surprisingly quickly.

Anyone can easily read fifty books in a year—really read them and know them. And if those fifty books were chosen for their informative value as well as for being well-written and entertaining, the reader will have brushed intimately with the world's finest minds. What could be more stimulating?

The salient points of the world's cultural information can be had today—in extremely compressed form—between the covers of a single book—and from this précis of learning he can follow the subjects and the authors that interest him. A single slight volume on art appreciation might forever remove him from the abyss of ignorance to a place where he could at least listen intelligently and begin to form a taste of his own. And so with music, literature, poetry and history. So, a year or less of intelligent reading could give any earnest person a handle on all so-called cultural and classical knowledge.

The history of our own country is rich and fine in dramatic incident and colorful personalities. Ask a good librarian what novels best depict

it. The Bible, Shakespeare, mythology, these alone would give a foundation surprisingly complete, for so much of the rest springs from
them! And the English language at its best would be made familiar.
Read for pleasure—whatever you dig out drearily will never enhance
your personality. But the better things require a tiny bit of attention
sometime to develop a taste for them—like olives. Just nibble awhile—
and to your own surprise—you will want some more.

Read good authors, rather than good subjects—for a fine writer
cannot help pouring his own background into whatever he does. More
often his side remarks casually dropped are more valuable than his
treatise.

You need never sigh for a generous friend and teacher—everything
you want is right at your hand in a book!

## 10. THE HARMONY OF THE WORLD REFLECTED IN OUR ACTIONS

This is the last chapter of PART ONE. Much ground has been covered. Yet I want to penetrate further into all the finer points of personal effect. So PART Two that follows offers the reader a more ex-
haustive study of the fine elements of personality in relation to successful living.

If you will train your body and your mind with the exercises set
forth in these ten chapters, you will be free from awkward restraints.

You know that the laws of etiquette are but avenues in the city of
Charm. Instead of having policemen at the corners, we turn left or
right only on the dictates of good taste, which include sympathy, tact
and appropriate fun. Be natural, but cultivate yourself physically and
mentally to the point where it is "natural" for you to be graceful and
gracious. Then *stop wondering what others think of you;* concern
yourself with what they think of themselves. There really aren't any
rules! A fine point of view is the only desirable basis.

*THE GREATEST PROTECTION.* Therefore, how much greater
protection we shall give our children if we teach them to desire beauty
and æsthetic balance in all living, than if we try to keep the whip-
handle of parental authority over their blind obedience to our wishes

and to law in general. Since respect for authority and all sorts of standards seems to be as unsteady as other world conditions, let us strive to strengthen our children's characters (as well as our own) by educating their emotions and instincts along lines of symmetry and harmony.

Let them understand that cooperation and teamwork give real reasons for obedience—that each member of the baseball team is a part of the harmony which must exist if the team is to succeed—just as the notes of a chord combine in teamwork for a rich, musical harmony. Show a boy a massive, smoothly working piece of machinery and point out that the whole machine is useless unless every small piece comes into place at the right moment with perfect rhythm and without friction. He can understand this and will respond to life with greater obedience—whereas preaching and moralizing may leave him cold and even more determined to have his own way regardless of others.

*TO INFLUENCE THE YOUNG.* If a young girl can be made to see that proper behavior is not so much a matter of morals as of a "sense of the fitness of things"—and of good taste—she will then more readily guard her life so that her experiences come where they belong for beauty and rhythm in living. Tell her that few things are evil—actually—but that they become so by being ill-timed and therefore discordant, destructive of rhythm and harmony; that she is permitting herself to be robbed if she disobeys the laws of life, experience and society.

Let us teach our young people and ourselves that the whole universe—all nature—is rhythmic, harmonious and dependable. The tides ebb and flow, the days and nights follow like regular pulse-beats, Halley's comet comes every seventy-six years—that within ourselves we are attuned to this great pulsing harmony. But because we have the power of choice we must consciously choose to ally ourselves with rhythm before we can reap its full benefit to us. Once we become sensitive to it, we find this rhythm in everything until all nature becomes for us a great, superb and sublime orchestra, the harmony of which is as little disturbed by the discord of mankind as is the Philharmonic by one broken string on one of its violins. Yet if we will, we may become one with the *great* harmony and thrill to its might as well as to its melodies, both of which will be reflected in our faces, our personalities and our lives.

Large thoughts? Yes, but we need them. All of us must breathe deeper, fire our imaginations and lift our heads with brighter eyes and become more alert, more electrified, more magnetic every time we think on this grand scale.

Then bring this fine principle to bear on our daily living, and we find loveliness coming to us from all sources. The purpose of these lessons is to teach you how to preserve this rhythm in your own life, and how to guard against the things that threaten it daily.

The principles of Charm as outlined in this book are designed to make you more *at home in the world;* for this, indeed, is the pinnacle of personal success. Study it and restudy it from time to time, beginning at the beginning and taking the exercises regularly just as outlined until they are a part of you and you are the personification of them. Put the book away for a while and then get it out again so that there will be a fresh impression. Grasping after charm too strenuously is like trying to catch a sunbeam. You squeeze it out of a hand that closes on it tensely.

May these principles bring you greater joy and happiness than you have ever known. For service is joy and he who would serve best must fulfil himself! No matter where you are, feel that I am taking your hand to wish you well—to tell you that I am glad you are joining me in this common sisterhood for the beautifying of the world, that you are dedicating yourself to be a channel for the beauty that longs for expression.

*Part Two*

REFINEMENTS OF CHARM

# CHAPTER ONE

## *Cosmic Consciousness*

### 1. YOUR KINSHIP WITH THE UNIVERSE

Roland Hayes, the Negro singer, has overcome racial prejudice and has sung, sometimes against threats of race riots, in the greatest concert halls of the world. At no time has he tried to force his way as a person. His mother, who washed clothes to pay for his music lessons, always admonished him to avoid any sense of personal pride, but to make himself a humble vessel for the spirit of music.

He was to sing in Berlin at Beethoven Hall at the time the Germans were so bitterly opposing the policing of the Ruhr by Negro troops from French Africa. There was resentment in the German press that plantation songs were to be sung in the hall named for the great Beethoven. Against official advice Hayes went on with the plan.

The great hall was filled to overflowing but they had come merely to be in at the kill. When he appeared there were hisses and boos that lasted for more than ten minutes. The Negro singer stood as was his wont with hands clasped and eyes closed praying that music and not he as a person would become paramount.

He asked his accompanist to play Schubert's "Thou Art My Peace," a lyric prayer that begins almost in a whisper. The crowd grew still. The program continued. Appreciation grew to enthusiasm. The audience forgot the war, personalities, and accepted with cheers two French numbers, beautifully done.

As the last note of the last number died away, the audience realized how both he and they had been unselfed, and in their wild demonstration of approval he was carried on their shoulders around Bee-

thoven Hall twice before their fervor was spent. They had met on the
common ground of music.

When common ground, a single purpose, is hit upon for all the
world, there will be no more wars. To find the common denominator
of life is the goal of science as well as governments and individuals.
They know there is, of necessity, some single element from which all
the rest emerges. Searching the microcosm as well as the macrocosm,
the farthest reach so far has found the electron, an infinitesimal charge
of electricity existing in all matter. In the mental realm, the farthest
reach has been called Cosmic Consciousness. Stripped of mystery and
cant, it is a simple recognition that we all emerge from and share in
the *mind* in and over all—that we are conscious of it—and benefit by
it—as well as contribute our best to it.

This sense of largeness will help us in the small matters of our lives
as well as the more important ones. The sense of warm kinship with
the whole universe gives a glow to the eye and a disarming sweetness
to the personality. Lincoln had this pervading sense of kinship. Walt
Whitman, Charles Schwab, D. W. Griffith, Martin Luther, Florence
Nightingale, Sarah Bernhardt, Thomas Jefferson, and Dickens are
just a few of those who possessed and were possessed by this feeling
that warms and persuades others by its very presence. How it smooths
our path—enables us to calm the small storms of life, comes to our
rescue continually.

Try it! When a difficult person is in your way, don't brace yourself
against him—that is expensive and time-consuming. Just look at him
and think, "I shall spare a minute to see through this surface nonsense
to the true nobility of *you* and to that I address myself."

In business or wherever this sense of kinship with *allness* enables
you, as modern slang has it, to cut your problem or adversary down
to your size, then you can *think your troubles down*. So long as you
look up to them, they will tower above you. So just be still a moment and rise mentally to a point where you are above or at least
level with the person or difficulty.

It helps to bear in mind too that to this universal mind in which
you live and move and have your being, there is no great or small.
There is only demand and supply. It answers every call. Don't trip

over the details of how it works out. Just cling to the principle and you'll have some pleasant surprises.

Lest universal mind become merely a grab-bag from whose mysterious depths you can always bring up a prize—remember that you are necessary for its expression or you wouldn't be here. And therefore you are a channel, an adequate one, if you make yourself so, for this mind to flow through. Make yourself a conscious instrument for the destiny and purposes of universal mind. Open up to it and it will unself you into a fineness and largeness that will astonish you. Make that contact at all times.

As people who wish to dedicate our energies to a more gracious, beautiful living, we might well take for our motto that of the Olympics: "Citius, Fortius, Altius!" (Swifter, stronger, higher!) Swifter in loving tact, stronger in poise, higher in our aims of self-culture. All this that we may put our own houses in order and become citizens of the world.

If Democracy should fail, it would be because we had been so lacking in self-discipline that our personal problems had taken all our substance and energies, leaving us nothing of value to contribute to the commonwealth.

Let us get a tremendous vision of our part in the affairs of the community, the state, the nation, the world—and the *universe*.

The soul of a country (like your own soul) is created and nourished or starved by the quality of every individual contribution from its many parts. What sustaining vibrations go out from you to uphold the hope and vision of those you contact? Is the great collective soul of humanity lightened or darkened by you?

Just as the radio catches vibrations out of the air anywhere, everywhere, *instantly,* your vibrations can help to bring light to heavy hearts across the world from you, or next door. Your *very desire* to see the world healed of misunderstanding, to give weary minds a vision of the beauty they can create and claim—I repeat, this very desire, emanating from you, produces after its kind in the great subconscious mind of the world.

I am convinced that unhappiness, awkwardness, self-consciousness and any sort of lack of Charm are primarily due to lack of *vision*. "Without vision the people perish." And the largest vision that is practical to us at this point of our development is the vision of what is known as Cosmic Consciousness.

When you have projected your mind helpfully into the sustaining body of world thought, you have linked yourself consciously with the constructive force of the universe—for when you enter into it, it enters into you. You feel its power tingling through your mind and body. Something of its largeness and grandeur becomes your own and you can never again consider yourself or anyone else unimportant . . . nor will anyone else consider you unimportant. There is a flash of something more than temporary life in your eye—and the world will try to get close to you to see if it can discover the source of the magnetic fire that draws them within the great circle of its light and warmth. This is the truly magnetic personality.

This does not indicate that I want you to become ascetics or mystics, or to don dark robes and spend your lives in prayer and meditation. Not at all. But I want you to understand the mental and psychic mechanics of Charm. A great singer must understand the mechanics of music before she can wring your heart with a beautiful aria.

An untutored girl of the wilderness may have a beautiful voice and a sense of melody that enable her to sing enchantingly in a wild "natural" fashion. *But* she must sing alone! If she tries to harmonize with other singers, or even to have an accompanist, she leads them into confusion and the result is discord.

We cannot live alone—therefore we must learn the technique, the rudiments, the mechanics of living before we understand the *art* of living. If we do not, our lives become discord and friction.

To understand the technique of anything is to learn how to adjust the various parts in their relation to each other for the most harmonious, pleasing result. In music we must learn the rules of combinations of notes and their timing for rhythm. In life, correct combinations of people and things and the proper timing of our speech and acts make for rhythm and therefore success. In this respect, if we do not know how to create harmonies we can, at least, avoid discords.

## 2. SUBMERGE THE SELF IN SOCIAL CONTACTS

*NEVER BE EMBARRASSED BY "DIFFERENCES."* In giving a dinner party, your success will depend not so much on the elaborateness of the service as on the congeniality of the guests. Very few hostesses are clever enough to compel the lion to lie down with the lamb. However, I know a woman whose personality is so warm and whose hospitality so enveloping that it fuses persons of conflicting temperaments into a unit of graciousness and they really have a good time. Instead of getting panicky when her son or husband brings home people who do not "fit"—instead of trying to make them fit, she brings out the entertaining interest of contrasts.

*SPEECH-MAKING AND CONVERSATION* are two different things. You may be able to entertain an audience with your wit and brilliance and still lack the ability to be one of the cogs in the machinery of conversation. The charming person creates a rhythmic harmony of talk by knowing *how to give place to the other fellow.*

*DON'T BE THE STAR OF THE PIECE.* It is a little-known fact that some of the best actors in Hollywood have refused stubbornly to be starred. They felt that in supporting roles their names would be as important, their salaries as large, and that their careers would not be as brief as those at the mercy of the public's idea of their glamour. Wallace Beery, Lewis Stone and Jean Hersholt are three fine actors who have made a business of acting rather than of glorifying themselves. They actually fought stardom.

Those who wish to consider life a solo performance should buy an island and live on it alone. The "highest civilization" means the development of this knowing how to "fit in," to mingle, to stimulate by aggression, to rest before it goes beyond the point of good taste—to furnish a background and support for others' ideas, while they in turn form a background for yours.

So, if you wish to be charming, make way for the other fellow. This is possible at every point. Here let me quote from my book "Charm" —"A good talker does not drip over with the desire to express a thought too fully, but tries to paint word-pictures that the hearers

can complete in their own minds, and thus the interest is held. Probably one of the reasons why gushing is so unattractive is that it leaves
nothing for the listener to do."

While one should always express oneself clearly, it is certainly not
charming to take up time telling obvious and uninteresting details
that complicate rather than simplify a story.

To stimulate the imagination of your hearers gives them the impulse to tell something of which they are reminded. You should give
them the opportunity to express themselves before this impulse has
died down. Many a woman, in an effort to prevent silence, keeps on
talking and passes the point where her listener was stirred to contribute something to the conversation. Therefore, no matter how
much she talks, her guest is still silent.

So always try to finish a remark or a story on a general note rather
than on a small personal detail. For instance, I once heard a girl
trying to draw out a quiet young man in this wise: "Do you like it
here?"—He: "Yes, it's a nice place." Silence.—She: "I saw you downtown today with Judge Allen."—He: "Did you?"—She: "He's your
uncle, isn't he?"—He (beginning to feel cross-examined): "Yes."—
She: "Is he your mother's brother or your father's brother?"—He
(plotting escape): "Mother's." She kept up this sort of thing, neither
of them enjoying it because they somehow couldn't get together over
the cold facts of his connections. If she had introduced a reason—a
motive for her questions—she would have loosened the young man's
tongue. Then he would probably have given his whole family history
spontaneously and proudly, as he did half an hour later to another
girl.

She: "Everyone is prepared to like you for your uncle's sake. Do
you deserve it?" (Men admire a mild audacity.)

He: "Probably not, but I'll be duly grateful." (Picking up her
ironical mood.)

She: "Well, just to be nice, let's say you do. There must be something in heredity. They say boys resemble the mother, isn't that
it?"

He: "I wouldn't swear the rule is infallible, but in this case it happens to be true. The Judge is Mother's brother, you see, so I have a perfect right to resemble him."

She: "There is a pair of twins here who don't resemble either the mother or father, but look exactly like the nurse who brought them up."

He: "That's a point in favor of those who believe in environment. Don't look at me so suspiciously. I was brought up in a Christian home and I'm very kind to children and animals."

She: "Well, that means all of us—humanity. We're all just children and animals."

He: "Maybe that's why children like animals so. When I was little we traveled all the time and I was never very closely acquainted with animals,—and how I missed it! You see, Father inherited a major interest in the —— Co., and he gave up a small-town law practice to look after it, and it took us pretty much over the world for years." (And he proceeded to tell his entire history.)

The first girl said she never saw such a cagey, unresponsive man. The second said she never saw such a friendly, communicative man. The second girl had introduced subjects of general speculation and interest, therefore the young man was eager to express his opinion of them and almost unconsciously used himself as an example.

Now, I almost hesitate to say this because it sounds a little tricky. Always try to get others to talk about themselves in this general fashion (without prying questions) *but don't you do it!* Don't be one of those people who will on the slightest provocation bring a vast subject down to their own individual experience. On the other hand, don't be afraid occasionally to tell of your experiences where such a thing seems appropriate, but don't monopolize the floor too long.

Try to keep the pronoun "I" out of your conversation, but when you must use it don't get flustered about it. Try to train your talk away from "I" in general. Often, it is just a stupid addition to a sentence. Imagine that you can say "I" just a limited number of times—save these for personal anecdotes—keep them out of casual conversation. Above all, say "I think" as little as possible. Don't say: "I think this is a lovely room"; say: "This is such a lovely room." This remark includes the world in general by inference. It indicates that others might think so too, and as you are doing the speaking it is taken for granted that you are expressing your own opinion. Don't stamp yourself an egotist, or even an egoist, by too much mention of yourself, even in relating your own experiences.

How many times have you heard someone say something like this: "Just as I came out of the door, I saw a beggar passing, and I thought I had never seen such a pitiful fellow—I felt so bad that I was almost crying when I met Jane, and she said—'Whatever is the matter with you?'—and I said, 'I . . . ,'" etc.? The pronoun "I" has been used nine times so far. Also you are convinced that she is more concerned about herself than the beggar.

She might have told her story this way: "As I left the house this morning a beggar was passing by. Such a desolate, dirty, ragged fellow! His utter helplessness was touching and the tears were in my eyes when I met Jane, who wanted to know what the matter was, and when I explained she scolded me for being so sentimental." Now, whoever she is talking to might make the mistake of saying,—"I think you are very sweet to be so sympathetic,"—instead of simply,—"You were sweet to be so sympathetic." Even in public speaking it sounds much more elegant to say: "To be chosen to bring this important subject to you this evening is an honor, a deeply appreciated one. Thank you." This is better than the "I feel that I have been honored in being chosen to . . . I appreciate it more than I can say." Four "I's" where none is needed.

In answer to his hostess's request that he relate some of his travels, a clever man once said, "To begin with, the French Line had made quite a bid for our party, and as there is no denying the excellent food on French ships, we booked our passage on the *Ile de France* and sailed the fifteenth of May. On our first night out a chap sitting at the Captain's table kept staring in our direction. Finally he came over and then I recognized him—a friend of college days whom I hadn't seen for many years! There was so much to say that the voyage was all too short. It is such happenings as this that add to the pleasure of travel."

A less cultured person would have made this story a veritable orgy of the personal pronoun "I." Even in answer to a direct question, such as, "Mary, what do you think about ——?", we should consider our reply. Here one is certainly privileged to say deliberately, "I believe— I think—I am in favor of ——." But it is not necessary unless you wish to take sides on a question in a very personal way or to come personally to someone's rescue. Even so, you can say, "Since the facts in the case are so-and-so, it seems Mr. ——'s plan is the best solution," —instead of the usual "I think, etc."

Never forget that the more civilized we are the more we are concerned with the other fellow. Therefore, a conversation too filled with "I" is uncivilized; in other words, uncultured. Also, the less you disturb your hearer's interest in his own *reactions,* the more charming he will consider you.

### INSTRUCTIONS

1. Select a dozen sentences in which you customarily use the pronoun "I." Write all these and add just below each sentence a revised version of it, eliminating the "I." Look these over every day and add to them until your conversation contains only the necessary minimum of "I's."

2. See if you can make someone tell his past without asking direct questions. Practice this point whenever possible. It is not intended to make you an expert pryer, but to develop your ability to handle people and to entertain them by touching the mainspring of their emotions—*themselves.* Also, it takes your mind away from the narrow limits of self into the larger, freer and more dynamic forces of universal significance. *The reward is a thousandfold.*

# CHAPTER TWO

## *Enthusiasm*

"People extremely reserved are like old enamelled watches with painted faces that prevent your seeing what time it is," said Walpole.

"But what shall we be enthusiastic about?" queries Voltaire.

"And how enthusiastic shall we be?" asks the modern girl, who tries to find a balance between the coldness of some successful women and the grins and gushing of others equally successful in their own field.

The answer is—"Be enthusiastic about anything to the extent that you are sincere." Nothing ends more ridiculously than a pretended enthusiasm—it can get one into amusing as well as serious muddles.

Years ago, at a friend's house I was served a pink lady cocktail, a concoction of cream, grenadine syrup and several other items very sweetish to my palate; perhaps it is the richness or the sweetness—at any rate they completely destroy my appetite. But fifteen years ago when I saw a tray of them being brought by my smiling host I admired the pretty pink color of them and the froth on top and trying to be pleasant I exclaimed, before I tasted it, "Oh, how pretty!" My host, from that brief ejaculation got the impression that I was very fond of the cocktail. And always since, whenever I am at that house, my host or hostess will ply me with them—always announcing that they have them because I like them so much. See the trap I set for myself!

I couldn't on any of these occasions tell my smiling host before guests that such was not the case. So, I have downed the sweetish things when I didn't want them, lo, these many years.

And see how a lie winds on and on—these devoted friends often bring them to my house—and it is their thoughtfulness and caring that seals my lips again. If they read this they will be first angry and then will laugh for a very long time.

Then too, it is possible to oversell oneself on an idea, as Rousseau did. It was extremely pleasant to live in Paris and speak so eloquently of the simple life close to nature that a cult sprang up—a cult to which Marie Antoinette made the amusing gestures of bucolic charm around the Petit Trianon. But Marie Antoinette adorned even the country scene with ribbons and bows, tying huge bows on the cows' horns and providing silk lace aprons for the milkmaids—of whom she became a most picturesque one.

But one among Rousseau's friends and followers took him too literally and actually gave him a tiny cottage in the country such as he had described with lifted eyes and beatific expression as the ideal. There was nothing for him to do but live in it—there was no logical way out—and the poor soul nearly died of ennui. The country people did not understand him and gave him a wide berth. Gone were the admiring cliques of flattering and fashionable ladies, and their envious gentlemen. They didn't follow him. The donor, Mme. d'Epinay, never knew that her gift was not appreciated.

It bears repetition—never pretend an enthusiasm you do not feel.

Enthusiasm is a moot question. We must find the middle path between those circumspect souls who preach that any show of enthusiasm is evidence of undisciplined, uncivilized minds—and those frantic, restless folk whose empty, jumpy enthusiasm simply bespeaks nervousness.

First, let's examine the case for enthusiasm as one of the most attractive attributes of Charm—later we will discuss how to keep it tempered by good taste and tact, also how to turn it off effectively when it may be misunderstood.

CONSEQUENCES FOR THEMSELVES. But none of its ramifications, its subtle uses and abuses can overshadow the fact that enthusiasm is a fire and, like any fire, always draws a crowd. Any kind of enthusiasm draws attention. Even the sort that keeps an employee working after hours without hope of reward creates comment. A new enthusiasm often changes a personality.

*ENTHUSIASM DOES DOUBLE DUTY.* A meek little man who was uncomfortable in the presence of other people decided to give up human society entirely and devote himself to the insect world. It fascinated him so that his studies made him a great authority on the subject and he was dragged back into society and lionized! No more did he feel ill at ease. In fact he didn't think about himself at all. His mind was filled with (pardon the pun) bugs. He became a huge social success!

Let us analyze this two-fold action of enthusiasm in the life of the meek little man. As he had shrunk away from people originally (we need not take up the reasons why) or had been so crude in his advances to them that they had not responded satisfactorily, he, no doubt, had developed a feeling of inadequacy, and had come to the conclusion that he did not possess and was not capable of generating that nameless quality which makes one able to mingle easily and attractively with society. (Bear in mind that thought always precedes expression on the material plane, just as an architect sees a building mentally before he draws his plan or places a single brick.) The little man felt himself to be out of step, misunderstood, a lone wolf—a man apart. He became convinced of it. He accepted mentally the inability to adjust himself to other people, thus cutting off all mental vibrations that go out to others, taking the unspoken message of his eagerness to be friendly. He destroyed, or at least abandoned, any plan either to give or to take anything from human relations. The result was that since the idea of sociability was not animated by the enlivening spirit of mental acceptance, nothing of its warming magnetism emanated from his physical body to attract others. He became so negative to people mentally and physically that he could be in the same room with others without their even seeing him.

Thus we see how necessary it is to stir the mind to start sufficient movement within itself toward a desired object, else it will never reach outer expression. Any activity of mind or body bespeaks life within it. Such activity interests others because they know intuitively that any activity is really the creative urge (one's share of divine nature) beginning the fascinating process of making something, becoming something, expressing something.

*THE MIND MOVES FAST*. So, if there is something we want to be or to accomplish, it is plain that we must first start that thing moving within our minds, not with vague hope, or timid desire, but with full acceptance of its entire possibility. In other words, if we keep the true spirit of a thing alive in our minds we have set forces into operation that will carry it into full experience. The thoughts of today we meet in the street tomorrow—and sometimes sooner!

But the ego of the negative little man was insulted by the indifference of those who ignored him and, naturally enough, he did not blame himself, but them. *They* did not understand him. *They* were too crude to appreciate his fineness. *They* were, therefore, unworthy of any further recognition from him. He would turn his life away from human beings to the world of insects. Yet, deep within him was the desire to assemble information and scientific facts to give to the world, mind you, the same world of which he disapproved! Inconsistency, thy name is humanity! There really is no way to refute the truth that everyone wants the approval and affection of his fellows and really would like to help them.

The herd instinct is primitive within us. Some people with an entirely materialistic, brutal idea of life say that it is merely for self-protection that man herds together, to fight dangers with greater strength. This is true, but it is not all, for life cannot be explained in merely physical terms. We know also that man is bound together in spiritual reality, that basically we are one substance, like emanations of one spirit, first causation. Some call it God. So when we separate ourselves from others through disapproval, criticism, or condemnation, we become correspondingly unhappy because of maladjustment to the fundamental forces of life. It is this sense of separation that gives us the feeling that we are struggling alone. The socially-minded people (and I don't necessarily mean party-minded) feel that there is always someone at hand to help. Sometimes it is necessary for you to withdraw from external contacts and refresh your mind and soul with a thorough contemplation of your own real self. This does not mean drawing your spotless skirts aside contemptuously—but rather that you prefer to be alone while taking your spiritual bath, just as you prefer to be alone in your bathtub. Both of these keep you personally fit and prepare you to make a much better impression on others.

*WE MUST BE ALONE, AT TIMES.* We must refill ourselves, silently sometimes, when we have emptied our forces out in contacts. True, we gain from these outer contacts, but only when we examine quietly what we have gained can we properly value and use it. Nevertheless, our withdrawal must not be a critical one if we wish to magnetize our personalities. But the little man of our story withdrew critically and cut off almost entirely his mental contact with his fellows. Thus his complete social separation soon followed. This is the mental attitude of the suicide.

But the life forces within us urge us, compel us in a thousand ways into activities that bring us again into harmony with others. These forces, steady, quiet, persistent, pressed upon the consciousness of the little man with their demand that he take an interest in the world about him. Presently the dying spark of enthusiasm within him was fanned into flame by his fascinating discoveries in insect life. It is plain that the *lack of enthusiasm* and the *renewed interest* had lived in his mind, generated by *himself!* He *chose* to react as he did to human beings and to insects. No one else could do that for him. You and I *choose* to react as we do or we couldn't do it.

*WE DELIBERATELY CHOOSE OUR WAY.* Certain psychologists tell us that the mind must agree to death before the body expires —that the nervous woman says to herself, "Now I'll have hysterics," or she couldn't have them—that the high-tempered person *decides* (however quickly and briefly) within himself to lose his temper and to fly into a rage. We must have our own consent before we do anything. This fact is so plain to doctors and scientists that their cure of nervousness and insanity often is based on this knowledge. We must decide what we will manifest in our relation to others in order to live beautifully and harmoniously.

To say, "I could live such a beautiful life if it were not for my family," is simply "passing the blame." If you really did live beautifully and uncritically within yourself, you would be lifted bodily out of the conditions you now condemn, or they would melt miraculously away. That is why I continually urge you to keep your own thoughts so high and fine that you practically do not see the ugly things that exist around you. Like your radio, you will get what you are tuned in to.

In times of national emergency or world demands we are naturally called upon to share the common experience—but even here our individual performance colors the whole matter. Instead of thinking, "What difference does it make now what I do?" we should all think, "What a magnificent opportunity to project my entire strength and expressiveness, creativeness, courage, time, and energy, for the benefit of all!" More than ever we need then to accent every personal skill, technique and excellence.

You cannot control the whole universe, cannot have every influence just what you want it to be—but you can control by selection and by acceptance what you will respond to, register, make your own. Realize that the air you are breathing right now is filled with many sounds that you cannot hear, music slow and swift, intense, kind and murderous, screams and groans, happy laughter, the tinkle of ice and crystal at lovely parties, love poems, speeches of all kinds—but your radio picks up only those of its own wave length!

*YOU WILL FIND WITHIN YOURSELF THE DOOR* that leads out into limitless marvels, powers, beauties and accomplishments when, and only when, you accept *full responsibility* for what you are and for *all* your experiences (not just some of the nice ones).

When we are old enough and smart enough to criticize our environment, we are old enough and smart enough to rise above it or change it. When we can judge it we can be independent of it!

When we moan overmuch about the obstacles in our lives we might as well say, "I never had the energy to do much about it."

There is a spirit within man which enables him to surmount any obstacle of heredity or environment! If he will keep the candle of devotional concentration and attention burning before the altar of his desires there is no power on earth to prevent his realization of them! The integrity of the universe backs him in his efforts just as it backs all who comply with its laws of "Like attracts like," "As ye sow, so shall ye reap," "I came not to destroy the law but to fulfil it," and "As a man thinketh in his heart, so is he."

How many of us really believe with all our hearts in our good? Isn't most of our thinking along this line sort of a sketchy, surface, vague hope, the sort of thinking that is meant in "Who by taking thought can add one cubit to his stature?" But when our thoughts become convictions and take root in our emotional acceptance of them, then, and only then, are we "thinking in our hearts"!

When we add real heartfelt enthusiasm to an idea we give it an impetus that may cause it not only to "come real" but also to ring around the world!—and perhaps other worlds? For in dealing with the great forces at our command we are as babes crawling on the floor.

*HARMONY IS ALWAYS ATTRACTIVE.* Enthusiasm gives life to everything it touches! There can be no enthusiasm where there is not complete acceptance. No friction or difference exists between you and the object of your enthusiasm. Therefore, when you are enthusiastic you are giving a display of harmony. Any type of harmony is admired by others. Instinctively they feel that though their days may be discontented, it is a joy to see someone in complete harmony with life even in a trivial matter. This is why adults are refreshed and renewed by watching the enthusiastic, absorbed play of children. The impressions of these early enthusiasms usually mark the character of the individual all through life.

Wake up! Get yourself a pet enthusiasm—get several of them if you have time. There is so much to be done and so much to do with. The world (and everyone in it) is so full of tremendous possibilities that it is like a six-ring circus. One hardly knows where to look. And yet, would you believe that people come to me and say, "I'm bored. I'm tired. I've lost my interest in life." My reply is always the same. "You haven't lost anything but your vision. You are not really tired— you are only weary of looking not six inches in front of your nose." You are not bored if you have a sense of humor and if you have that you will see that you look like a sheep caught on a bramble bush, and thinks it must stay there. You know, sheep *do* stand and starve in a field of plenty, when a slight wrench would free them from the thorns that they *think* hold them.

Find an enthusiasm! The little man found one in bugs. He forgot for a while to *condemn* people; his time was taken up by *approving* his discoveries.

As any constructive thought can fell millions of destructive ones, just as a tiny candle can light the way through a huge dark space, his personality was gradually lighted and fired. By what? Why, his enthusiasm, of course! It flamed so intensely that he "forgot to remember" past discord and maladjustment. He became completely filled with interesting things he had learned and his interesting new experiences. No matter what is wrong enthusiasm can turn it away.

His work took him to out-of-the-way places to search for other kinds of bugs. Necessarily he often stopped at resort hotels. People saw this eager-faced, bristling, busy little man, fired by enthusiasm, and *they wanted to know him!* On one occasion the manager of a hotel asked him to speak after dinner to the guests about his interesting findings in insect life. He accepted before he fully realized the situation. Then he felt the old panic coming over him, the feeling that he might say the wrong thing or make himself ridiculous and he wished the earth would open up and swallow him. He heard the words of the manager introducing him to the guests. He had to rise, and a saving thought darted through his mind—"I have not been asked to talk about myself—I have been asked to talk about this work that I love better than anything else I have ever known." So he thought about his work—he forced his mind away from himself—he began to talk. He had never made a speech before in his life—but he held his audience spellbound for more than an hour. His enthusiasm for his subject kept him from even apologizing for the fact that he knew nothing of public speaking. Enthusiasm had given life to his words, continuity and interest to his explanations. His fame as a speaker spread. He wrote books and became a great scientific, financial success. But greater than these achievements he became a happy man in his new and harmonious adjustment to other men. These are just some of the rewards of the revitalizing influence of enthusiasm throughout the entire person—mind, soul and body.

Now, anything can be misused. Most of the conqueror-destroyers of history have been enthusiasts—about themselves. Most outlaws, adventurers, gangsters have decided that the world *was free, for and to them*. But there is a law of life that cuts across the laws of even enthusiasm and self. That law says, as an officer once remarked to an inebriated citizen, "Your freedom stops where my nose begins!"

But their lives prove, rather than refute, that within moral limits an enthusiastic, ambitious program is entirely possible of achievement.

*OVER-ENTHUSIASM BECOMES GUSH,* which leads into inelegant intonations as well as into the use of empty-sounding words. The average woman, when she becomes unusually excited or interested, lets her voice slide up and down with too exaggerated an emphasis. No one values the opinion of the woman who constantly says, "My *dear,* it was *per*fectly *won*derful. I *nev*er saw *any*thing *like* it." Overemphasis of some particular phrase or word is shunned by cultured people.

The English language is supposed to have words enough in it to convey every degree of feeling. The fine woman tries to select those words that express her meaning thoroughly. Sometimes she can express more with one word spoken quietly but intensely, than the gushing woman can with much raving. She can, with an expression of fervor in her face, utter the word "wonderful" in such a way that the hearer really feels the meaning of the word.

*SHE DOESN'T TEAR UP HER FACE* by lifting and lowering her brows to add to the intensity of her words. It has been said that profanity is the outlet of those who have a limited vocabulary. One certainly gives the impression of not having words enough when one resorts to overemphasis and too much facial expression to add to the dramatic effect of what is being said.

Now you may be one of those women who hasn't expression enough in her face and whose intonation is too monotonous. If you are, you need to loosen up and become more expressive. But for every one of you there are many who overemphasize to the point of bad taste.

*GRACIOUSNESS IS ALWAYS DESIRABLE.* Often a woman says, "I was quite cool at So-and-So's party because I didn't want her to think that I thought such a lot of her invitation." How much better to be the same, eager, responsive person on all occasions. Personally, I would not let "So-and-So" realize that she or anybody else would cause me to be different from my ideal of myself.

Even when some talkative person monopolizes you it is not necessary to freeze him out. You have two roads of escape. The first is to say deliberately, "Sorry to interrupt you but I want Mary Brown to hear this. She is so interested in this sort of thing. You come right along with me and we'll find her." Mary may not thank you for dumping your bore on her but that is *her* problem.

The best way, however, is to lead the bore to talk about what you are interested in. This is quite possible, even though it does require some ingenuity and full knowledge of how one subject can lead to another.

Elsa Maxwell says to "put all your bores together at a party and they will be clever in self-defense."

Here you will appreciate the conversational exercises in the previous chapters. For instance, if your bore keeps on talking about her housework and won't stop explaining the fine points of scrubbing floors, you may appear very much interested by asking her what kind of floors she cleans. (You might, though, pick up some ideas.)

If she says "concrete," you can ask where local people get their concrete, and thus almost instantly find your conversation directed to some remote place. Or you can ask her what she uses to clean her floors (after you have exhausted concrete or wood—as if you could). She will probably name some well-known product and you can say, "What an enormous amount of advertising that company does! Do you find that you buy advertised products more than others?" Or you can discuss the advertising business in general and then take up a discussion of any advertised product or person.

You can switch any conversation to those subjects you want to discuss or hear discussed and your partner will never know that you led her away from her favorite topic. So, if you are bored at a party, it is your own fault! Remember that the universe is reflected in a dewdrop!

The question of just how enthusiastic one may be over a man is quite a question in the average woman's mind. This is so broad and intricate a subject that I give an entire chapter to it.

## INSTRUCTIONS

1. Brush up your enthusiasm and get a new one.
2. Practice guiding a conversation to subjects that you want to discuss. Try this on three different people every day for a week.

## CHAPTER THREE

# *Men*

This chapter about men opens me to criticism, as the subject is one of great controversy. So I ask you here not to quote me unless you are sure you understand the situation I build up around any given remark. It is unfair to quote anyone unless you can accurately reproduce the spirit in which the remark was made.

A tone of voice—a different facial expression can sometimes mean the difference between a compliment and a criticism. Of such flimsy material is often conjured the unkindness of gossip. So let us approach this subject at leisure and with open minds, remembering that my object is to put fundamentals in your hands, giving you only "sample" applications of the principles to guide you in making your own use of them. It is not my desire to put words into your mouth from my mind, but from your own.

*WHOEVER TRIES TO WRITE OF LOVE* simply babbles like a child. None but a lover knows what the writer is talking about— and he doesn't need it. But whoever tried to trick or trap love is the biggest fool of all. For love, however delicate and ephemeral, comes head on and strips the mind of pretense.

Certainly, for those who have missed love, the chess game of co-quetry, lure, sense, the chase and the catch and all the pretty pretending is as exciting as any other game—and about as satisfying. Like all errors, there is just enough truth in it to give it whatever substance it has. Like costume jewelry, it will fool you if you don't know better. But since there is a great deal of delight in costume jewelry, why should we completely ignore it?

*IS IT LOVE OR VANITY?* One thing I know, the person who thinks life is not worth living has never loved. It is wounded vanity that wants to shuffle off this mortal coil. And when a man or a woman writes me a long letter of details and explanations of someone and then asks, "Am I truly in love with this person?", the answer is "No." One does not have to inquire if one has fallen in love—any more than one needs to ask if one has fallen downstairs. Though one might dazedly ask, "Where am I?" the answer to that foolish one is, "As close to heaven as you will ever get."

*"CAN IT HAPPEN MORE THAN ONCE?* Or have I a soul-mate?" are just two of the questions I try to answer with a wise look while my mental knees bump together in a fearful uncertainty. Whether it can happen or not, it does, once in a while. Naturally so momentous a matter couldn't happen frequently, as in the Hollywood kaleidoscope, but to say that one loves only once and never so completely as the first time is just a lot of words scrambled like the alphabet in soup. It is what people say to seem superior when they have lost a great love and do not find another.

There seem to be as many different kinds of love as there are notes on a piano—one thing they have in common—they are all allergic to selfishness.

*MOST NORMAL PEOPLE CAN LOVE AGAIN.* One must be lacking in imagination or to have lost some element in oneself—lost the impulse to trust or share or believe—to feel oneself incapable of true love. To feel that there is no one extant fine enough to appreciate one's sensitiveness is absurd.

The average person does not have sufficient inflow of joy from some mysterious contact with the fresh source of life to keep himself from being impaired by life's encounters—therefore perhaps he can't love again. But for any person intact mentally, psychically, spiritually and physically, love is possible. From its very nature I should say that real love, even unrequited, is more nourishing and building than consuming—that it gives back infinitely more than it uses up—like a seed planted in the earth. Love is never destructive. It blesses, soothes, unifies, even while it disturbs.

*WOMEN ARE MORE CONCERNED WITH LOVE THAN MEN,* not because their hearts are constructed differently—but because their natural job in life is more concentrated around the family, children, and the home. The lives of men are just as much molded and influenced by love as are women's. A man is no more a complete being alone than is a woman. It is easier for him to put aside the cloying details of domesticity when there is trouble and seek the more suave contacts of the outer world, but of all the empty escapes this one is the most farcical. Usually if he were as suave himself at home as he is outside and his wife were as suave to him as she would be with a new man, they could become re-enchanted. It is said there is nothing deader than a dead love. Like all pat phrases this is erroneous. For love, new or old, is where the heart pours itself out in love. Old melodies stir the heart more than new ones. Familiar roads are invested with a vast sentiment.

*OF COURSE, NOT EVERYONE CAN LOVE,* any more than everyone can sing, paint china or break eighty at golf. And it is these sad souls that need a chart of technique in handling the other sex, who, lacking reality, must make an artful substitute. There are rules only for synthetic love—but since most of it is synthetic, the rules apply quite generally.

*JUST WHAT ARE MEN LIKE?* It might be well to begin with a cursory analytical survey of them. Men are no more the natural enemies of women than is the law of gravitation. From a woman's standpoint men are a factor in life that must be dealt with. The happiness or hurt she experiences through these dealings is largely a matter of whether she has considered the laws by which they live, move and have their being—or whether she has tried to force them into the way she wishes they would go.

Men are simple and direct as a child is simple and direct. Most men (almost all) are surprisingly immature emotionally. I mean they react immediately and inevitably on what the psychologists call the "pleasure and pain" principle—especially in their contacts with women.

*MEN ARE NOT ANALYTICAL ABOUT WOMEN.* The most brilliant man apparently shuts off his mind when in the presence of women and reacts as a child would who is sampling things in an old-fashioned grocery store. He finds some of them candy, some of them pickles, others dry but good crunchy crackers and so on down the line.

The most tremendous injustices women suffer at the hands of men are not injustices at all from the man's standpoint. How can there be an injustice without violation of reason and balanced thinking? The man's mind has never been involved in the matter. So, therefore, he has not been unjust!

To be sure, mental companionship is entirely possible between a man and a woman. But when it exists, it is the whipped cream on top of the dessert and not the body of the thing at all. It should never be depended upon to carry the burden of a union for very long. It is, indeed, a thing to be striven for but not to be relied upon for permanent happiness.

*LIKE A CHILD, A MAN DEMANDS PHYSICAL AND MENTAL COMFORT* or he will be cranky and unreasonable. Women will torture themselves in body and mind to gain a certain end or effect. But not a man! This is why the preservation of a marriage or the life of a love affair is up to the woman.

Whenever you attend a golden or a silver wedding you may write it down on your cuff that here is one more woman who has found ways and means (not words) to make her man believe that her way was *his happiness*.

I do not mean that men are not capable of great sacrifices. They will go to war and die in patriotic glory. They will burn at the stake for religious convictions. But they will be uncomfortable around a woman—*unless* their pride is somehow fed.

*HE JUST WANTS TO BE HAPPY*. So long as a man is pleased he isn't very particular just how it is accomplished. This knowledge gives a woman about her only great advantage. I mean if she can soothe his ego, amuse him and keep his mind entertained with an image of himself that makes him fairly purr with satisfaction, she may deny him other things he thought he wanted.

*DON'T OVERDO PUBLIC COMPLIMENTS*. Extravagant praise that would insult a woman's intelligence is welcomed by men if it is given in private. Many women make the mistake of loudly praising a man. This only embarrasses him, as the man does not wish it known

that he is as gullible as he really is. Therefore, when he is faced pub-
licly with extravagant praise he is more apt to be offended than
pleased. Try this out on growing boys and you will get the exact reaction that men feel, because the boy has not learned to hide what he
feels.

Men are more comfortable in the presence of others when they are
allowed to merge into the general atmosphere. They do not wish to be
singled out conspicuously by a woman! A man feels like a fool when
a woman calls him wonderful while others are listening—ah, but
when they are alone and the atmosphere is right, he expects it of her.
Then her most fantastic admiration finds a lodging place in his heart.
But she must not give her admiration too freely.

*HYPOCRISY AND INSINCERITY HAVE NO PLACE IN
CHARM* and no place in building happiness. But the best way of expressing thoughts for the best effect on the matter in hand is merely
using one's intelligence for the good of all concerned.

*MEN ARE INTERESTING AND WONDERFUL CREA-
TURES.* When one considers that so little is demanded of them
morally and spiritually, they seem truly wonderful. Whatever virtues
they have are expressed because they wish to express them. Therefore,
their goodness is even a higher type of goodness than that of a woman
who is good simply because she realizes the advantages of being good.

A fine man may be a rare discovery but, once located, it is worth
any real woman's time and thought to capture him. Any man is aware
that managing mothers and yearning maidens are after him, that is,
if he is eligible—and what a galaxy of men are squeezed into that
elastic term "eligible"! So he has learned to be wary, not only of
insincere anglers, but of marriage in general. His freedom is very
precious to him. He will walk safely around any trap—unless the trap
becomes to him a means of obtaining something that he believes is
more precious to him than his freedom. It is senseless to pretend that
the trap isn't there. Your only sensible attitude, and also one that
intrigues him, is your frank indecision as to whether he is worth your
bait!

*SHALL A WOMAN TAKE THE LEAD IN ROMANCE?* Now
we come to one of the most delicate points in the whole matter. Will

a man value a woman who throws herself at his head, who takes the lead, as it were, in courtship? The answer is "No," in almost every case. (There are occasional exceptions.)

But do not make the mistake of jumping to the opposite and false conclusion that indifference will get you anywhere. The "I'll show him that I don't care" attitude may temporarily pique the interest of a stubborn man, but it will bring neither of you happiness. And what is the sense of going out of your way to capture unhappiness?

*DON'T CRY, LITTLE GIRL—MUCH.* On the other hand, if a sniveling, over-sentimental woman sobs out her love through a hanky, the man is disgusted. Not that tears haven't an important place in love. A man will worship a woman who is tender enough to cry over someone else's troubles. He will treasure the tears she sheds over the aching, exquisite beauty of some unearthly ecstasy in music or a sunset. But it takes an exceptionally beautiful or an extraordinarily winning girl to "get away with" tears shed over him. The average woman weeping over romantic love is not romantic. She is messy. The man may be moved to compassion the first time, but after that he merely plots escape. Why? Because he has been made uncomfortable. He is called upon to face a situation that he does not wish to face. He is angry that the woman has upset the harmony between them—he is disappointed that she has wrecked his mental picture of her as a creature of poise and allure.

*MANAGE TO BE A MINOR PROBLEM.* A man, however, does enjoy coping with a problem in connection with a woman. This is an important phase of keeping a man interested after you get him. But even this problem must not make him uncomfortable or he will balk.

*LET HIM SEE YOUR INTEREST IN HIM—BUT—* The clever woman makes every man she meets feel that in him she has made an interesting and important discovery. She makes him realize that she is looking for love—and perhaps he is the one. Perhaps! But he is not the only interesting thing in her mind. In fact, after she has made him talk about himself and she has been fascinated by it for a time, her mind just goes on to other interesting things, how the Joneses' house is built—houses are such fascinating things—politics, if she has a flair for them and isn't offended when she is disagreed with—anything to show she is interested in what goes on about her.

In other words, she gives him a little competition right in her own mind. Then watch him strive to keep her mind on him!

He will try various and sundry ways to keep that close, eager attention that shone in her eyes during that rapturous half-hour before she got Cézanne or the one-over-one bid on her mind. She doesn't slight him. She just makes it hard for him to keep her attention. She is all approval, sympathy and understanding when she does turn to him. When she does think of him she is completely absorbed in him—for a time. That is what is so fascinating about her. He comes unconsciously to the conclusion that a fellow has to be up and doing to hold the happiness of her interest. Here is something worth a man's effort!

*A MAN MUST HAVE A FEELING OF CONQUEST OR HE ISN'T HAPPY!* A wise old gentleman once said to me, "Margery, women will save themselves many heartaches if they will remember these words, 'A man loves pursuit—a woman loves possession.'"

On the other hand, if the woman makes no move to get the man she wants, she often finds herself married to someone else. The clever woman will find ways to bring herself to a man's attention and build up a competition for him as well! To try to excite a man's jealousy before you have his interest is ill-timed. To excite his jealousy after you have his interest is evidence that you are not very sure of your own value. Though don't forget that men want what they see other men admire. The competition of other men is stimulating to a man just up to a certain point. Then he becomes disgusted and indifferent.

The point is—never bank too much on a man's interest in *you*—lay your plans around *his interest in himself!*

The average man is more romantic and idealistic than he wants to admit—often more than he knows. True, some of them are so thoroughly on earth that you can get their thoughts no higher than their appetites. Even then, such a man has an unspoken vague notion of his ideal woman and if he finds her he sometimes develops æsthetically. This is the reason some homely woman who keeps a man's imagination working along lines of a lifted vision, spiritually, and his own possibilities, has him so engrossed that her more beautiful sister may flirt with him in vain.

The pretty girl who has come to regard herself as a prize package is in danger of having her heart broken in marriage. Her adoring bridegroom, once he possesses her, still hunts for a soul satisfaction—an inspiration which he fails to get from her. She thinks only of herself, her looks, her clothes, which are but one-fourth of being a woman.

A woman may be very spiritual, that is, religious. She may love good books and have high thoughts, yet fail utterly to inspire a man with them or through them.

To influence men you must reach them on the plane where they now function. The average male may have noble yearnings he doesn't understand, but his definite interest is in worldly activity of some sort. If he has gone in for athletics, or walking, or games, you will be wise if you try to get him to be active. Take an interest in watching him at sports. Physical activity is stimulating. Men love exercise. And if they associate you with their memory of pleasure in outdoor games and hikes, they will like you better.

Take your man on long walks—play golf with him—but always let him excel. On a long hike, be sure you get tired first. But don't carry this to an extreme.

A man likes a woman who is just a little below him in physical strength, but he has no use for a whiny kill-joy. If you excel in sports, then have some other weakness. If a woman exhibits just a little physical weakness she appeals to the man's protective instinct, which he enjoys. It makes him feel important. Some big, strong women appeal to a man's protective instinct by being squeamish about unpleasant sights and sounds—tenderly emotional, etc.

The largest, handsomest woman I know has a husband whom she has convinced that she must be protected from every unpleasant thing in life. He babies her and she knows it looks silly but feels that the game is worth the candle if it keeps her husband interested. To be sure he grumbles sometimes about it, but in his manly heart he enjoys being the big, strong, wonderful protector. The truth is women *are* uneven in their bodies, minds and abilities. And men *should* know it and help them.

All of this may not sound very modern, but neither is human nature. Human reactions remain about the same whether our houses are built in straight lines or curves and whether skirts are knee-length or ankle-length. The fact remains that in order to make a man feel necessary and important a woman must lean on him at some point.

*A CAREER AND DOMESTIC HAPPINESS.* A successful business woman I know has an adoring husband. People have wondered how such an aggressive, efficient woman can keep her fine he-man interested. And here is the secret. She's afraid of mice! She mustn't be left alone in their apartment for a minute without his protection. She flies to him hysterically at the sight of a three-inch mouse. Of course, it's absurd! But aren't we all? You can't make your own rules in life. Only a few adult men admire adult women.

The strongest, finest men are usually interested in the weakest women, whereas a strong woman usually attracts weak men who are looking for a "soft spot." This woman I mentioned is having a magnificent career in the advertising business and by being clever she is also having a happy home life.

*CAREER MARRIAGES COME TO AN ABRUPT END WHEN THE WOMAN NO LONGER STAGES HERSELF AS BEING WEAK AND FEMININE SOMEWHERE.*

In this modern day when women are shoulder to shoulder with men, a picturesque relationship takes a little more thought than it used to. How can a brisk, bright, efficient woman appeal to the chivalry of men and keep their business respect at the same time? By getting the men around her to do things for her! She should not impose upon them and make a nuisance of herself. But at least once a month, she should ask the boss to do something for her, if nothing more than to move her desk a quarter of an inch.

Never, never, never let a man see you exert yourself physically, such as moving a heavy piece of furniture (unless he knows that you have a weak back, so will scold you gently). You may work your head off all day, but when your husband comes home—stop. You can better afford to leave the furniture in the middle of the floor than to take out of his mind the impression that you are exquisitely feminine. Tell him you have been waiting for him all day to fix the piano right—the moving men are so stupid—they're strong enough, of course, but this job requires an artistic sense as well. He may fuss and grumble but in his heart he likes it.

Don't impose on him. Just one little thing is sufficient to make him feel his manly superiority. When you call on a man's superior strength don't stress it enough to make him suspicious of your flattery. Just go on talking about something else. Enough that he associates you with his pleasure and happiness! And last, but by no means least, make it possible for him to have complete peace at times.

*FEMININE FOIBLES AMUSE MEN.* The unmarried woman must use these same tactics in getting a man's interest. But while they are laughing or smiling over your little weaknesses they straighten up their manly shoulders and are willing to strive to the death to maintain the situation that makes them feel so manly. Oddly enough, a man so appealed to will find his greatest urge to accomplish things. He will benefit more by a woman's dependence upon him than he will by her being shoulder to shoulder with him—unless she learns to call upon him in other ways.

Manliness degenerates very quickly around women who provide no romantic flattery for masculine strength. Now here is an important point. It does not please a man to have a girl throw herself at him. Wherein lies the flattery? He's more apt to feel like "any old port in a storm." It pleases a woman to be told she is one in a million. It annoys a man and frightens him off. Never give a new man the idea that he is the one you have been looking for. But let him know that you think he is your sort—and leave it to him to prove it!

*CHALLENGE AND CHIVALRY.* I know of one romance that started by the girl's saying lightly, "If you're what I think you are, I need you desperately." The first part of her remark was a challenge and the last part a call on chivalry. Both of them stirred him so that he never forgot the occasion. Never end this remark with any suggestion of loneliness but, rather, a complimentary call on the man's surface chivalry. Keep heaviness out!

*MEN ARE CONVENTIONAL AT HEART.* Though he wouldn't for the world admit it, the average man is more conventional at heart than is the average woman. A woman's innocent mind lets her accept and pass over conditions that a man will condemn, and she will thus open herself to criticism. The man's worldliness leads him to suspect the worst wherever there is any questionable situation. I do not mean that all women are innocent and all men suspicious. But the very fact that so many women have thrown aside the old-fashioned virtues makes it increasingly hard for those who cling to them. Therefore, even though you may do unconventional things, see to it that you keep yourself out of situations that could possibly bring you unhappiness through the loss of the confidence of your suitor or husband. Always remember that men are conventional animals at heart. They will break their own laws but appearances must be maintained!

We see some oddly assorted couples in the world and many of them are true romances that last. Many that, to all appearances, seem ideally mated, go speedily to the divorce courts.

The things that attract a man to a woman are inner things, most important of which is his conviction, conscious or unconscious, that she is his complement—that without her he is incomplete. It is up to her to cause him to realize this. He will seldom discover it by himself. He mustn't be told such a thing. Men like to feel that they make their own decisions.

Few men seriously set out to find a wife. If they did, they would make more appropriate choices. Therefore, they cannot be impressed, at first, by a woman's fitness for the job. It is usually some superficial thing that attracts a man at the beginning. Therefore, the worthiest girl who carries herself in a stiff, self-conscious prudery with the serious responsibility of the world in her face will hardly be noticed by men.

MEN ARE ATTRACTED BY HAPPINESS as flies are attracted by sugar. This is why the look of expectancy, of happy, alert interest in something or everything is useful. A graceful walk and alert poise bespeak a happy frame of mind. To get harmony and rhythm into your mind and body, and consequently into your face, shows forth a happy adjustment to life.

Men are not analytical about women. They move toward women or away from them largely by instinct in their search for happiness.

Remember our very nation is founded on the right to life, liberty and the pursuit of happiness.

*IF YOU CAN BE GAY AND AMUSING* with jokes and fun, by all means do so. But the girl who makes a joke of everything pushes romance away from her.

Any girl can cultivate the radiance of an inner happiness that will be quite as effective. Men grope toward such a girl almost unconsciously because she stimulates their imaginations. It is no pleasure to a man to be seen with a girl who looks bored with him. He likes his friends to see him with a girl he can be proud of and who is, at least, politely interested in his society. Too much interest embarrasses him. And how he shuns possessiveness!

*NEVER EXPECT A MAN TO FIT IN WITH YOUR MOODS.* The male has no understanding of such things. You must fit into his. Sorry, but that is the way it is! Learn to find out what sort of man you are talking to and approach him on that level.

Important men usually admire a spirited woman—by that I do not mean a loud wit. Being spirited means that you are not overawed by their importance—and they do respect any woman whom they must work to impress. A small big man wants to be admired and yessed. A truly big man is entertained by a certain disregard for his importance—temporarily.

A certain important ambassador married a comparatively insignificant girl who after listening to someone list his diplomatic achievements had the courage to say, "And what does he do for exercise?"

*ALL MEN ARE REPELLED BY SELF-CONSCIOUSNESS.* It makes them uncomfortable. They feel somehow responsible for the girl's obvious discomfort and subtly resent the blame. This is one of the many reasons why it is absolutely necessary to train your mind away from yourself and have such control of it that you can *keep* it off yourself around men.

All of these things are, of course, generalizations, and so I assume there are exceptions to all of them. But I have never seen one. Even a shallow woman's posing and flirting will not be effective unless she is more interested in the man's reactions than in her own performance.

As we said in the last chapter—any kind of enthusiasm will draw attention, but the attention soon drifts away when it is discovered that a girl's enthusiasm is centered on herself and her interests. This unconscious display of selfishness is one of the reasons we lose our friends.

*DON'T BE A DOOR-MAT.* Now we come to an interesting point in our relations with men. Since we know they are not analytical about women, there is absolutely no sense in expecting them consciously to realize what we do for them. Our little self-sacrifices and abnegations that make our men feel so grand will be taken for granted like the air they breathe unless we find ways to bring our unselfishness to their attention. You may quickly become a door-mat unless the man is made to understand that a definite plan of living for the best of all concerned is being worked out by you. This is as much for his sake as for yours. For if you fade into a nonentity in his eyes he has no one by his side of whom he is proud.

While a woman should play a passive role to a man's positive one, it must be a positive passivity, and not wishy-washy. Every few weeks remind your man (in a kind, casual way as though you were gossiping about someone else) of your value in his life. But don't overdo it; just let him see your point and leave the subject. Never complain about your position as helper and do not let your mention of it leave him in a weak or accused position.

One wife I know brings the matter up amusingly by pretending to read a newspaper item. "Wife again saves husband's dignity! Destruction of happiness was averted by the quick wit and heroism of Mrs. So-and-So. By giving a pint of her own blood she saved her husband's importance. No medal was awarded. Hence this honorable mention."

*MEN HAVE MANY FACETS.* Remember that a man is a many-sided animal. He is moodier than a woman. His complex ancestry has given him a variety of leanings. Sometimes he wants to take root and build his life and house brick on brick to endure forever. Again he is perfectly willing to abandon the work of years to follow a nomadic urge. Sometimes he wants to fashion things with his hands. At other times he wants to sit back and plan with almost military tactics a scheme that will take generations to materialize. Man is both a doer and a dreamer. *The clever woman will encourage him in all his moods and provide opportunities for the expression of his natural leanings.*

His nomadic urge can sometimes be satisfied by a trip through the *National Geographic Magazine.* I have yet to meet a man, young or old, who isn't fascinated by it. His urge to do things with his hands can find expression in art, picture puzzles, cellar carpentry, or tinkering with machinery. His desire for physical activity should be encouraged. It is unnatural for a man to want to sit still all the time. Sports, dancing, hikes, work in the garden (if he likes it) all have their place in romance. A pot of paint is sometimes a challenging thing in the spring.

*MEN EXPECT WOMEN TO HAVE SOCIAL SKILL.* Comparatively few men have the social instinct, but they want their wives to have it. They expect it of a woman, and if a girl doesn't run about all the time and get a reputation for being a "party-hound," it is an asset in their eyes.

No woman can occupy a man's thoughts all the time. She is but a part of the vast expression he must have to be a happy man. The sooner we American women get this into our heads, the sooner the divorce rate will be lowered.

She can successfully keep his mind off other women if she will make it her career to see that his complex nature is expressed as fully as possible. When a man is thoroughly expressed and happy, he is singularly loyal.

Men love to get into a rut if it is a pleasant one. A man will go to the same lake or stream to fish year after year if it is a good one. He will eat in the same restaurant interminably. He will play the same golf course a lifetime if it pleases him.

It takes brilliant bait to shake the average male out of his routine. To begin with, his vanity is such that he doesn't like to admit that his choice in anything can be improved upon.

The clever woman will keep the basic urges of his nature expressed so that he is content with her. What are these basic urges? They seem fairly simple in a list. But to work them out cleverly is a complicated career for any woman.

First in importance put *hunger*. Most men love to eat and nearly all of them have a sweet tooth. They don't want to be urged to eat as if they were animals being placated. They want to be well-provided, well-served and let alone. So whether you live in a palace or a hovel, "feed the brute" often and well. This can have many ramifications. Most men adore an open fire (another primitive tendency). The tang of bacon fried in the open remains a pleasant memory of the senses. Many a young man has turned to call at a house because he knows delicious sandwiches or some sweetmeat, the thought of which makes his mouth water, are sure to be found on a table in the living-room. He does not even admit to himself that this is the reason. So far as he thinks the matter out, it's just a nice place to be. And it is true that a woman thoughtful enough to provide these little things usually has other qualifications to draw his interest. If hospitality at home is im-possible, then take your man out into the woods and feed him from a lunchbox.

His next most important urge is vanity and this includes all else. To a small man, speak of skill and brains—never let the conversation dwell on physical strength. To a clumsy man, don't speak of dancing. The average man does not understand himself and is quite fascinated by a woman who convinces him that she does.

You remember my telling you that unfinished conversations bring men back. Long ago I gained the devoted friendship of a certain man by saying to him during the first evening I knew him—"You don't know much about yourself, do you? Why, even I, who never saw you before, know more about you than you do." This was years ago. He still comes to see me whenever possible to talk about himself.

*KEEP HIS MIND ON HIMSELF—IT'S FAIRLY SAFE THERE.* A man expects so many things of a woman that he is easily disappointed. This disappointment causes him instinctively to search again for the mythical ideal he has built up in his mind. For this rea-son the woman who can keep a man's mind on himself, rather than on her, will hold him tighter and longer. The woman who can go with a man, even as an audience, in his strenuous athletics, who can amuse him with small feminine inconsistencies (a man doesn't want a woman to be consistent—they never admire consistent women, other than theoretically) who leans on him a little (not too much), who

feeds him, body, soul and mind, who makes herself lovely and graceful, who is so in tune with life that she affects him like the rhythm
of a waltz—this woman can wrap her man around her little finger!
Need such a woman be beautiful actually? Read the papers! Daily
they record such women stepping into important marriages while
their sisters, content with their beauty, get what is left.

Charm that is a happy synchronizing of heart and brain, trained
to work in unison, will carry any woman to personal triumph.

The next chapter will continue on the subject of men and the *unconscious demand*.

# CHAPTER FOUR

## *The Unconscious Demand*

*"WHY SHOULD WOMEN HAVE TO PLEASE AND PLA-CATE MEN?"* I am constantly asked.

Because both women and men get more out of that arrangement than from any other. Experiments over thousands of years have produced no improvement over the woman attracting the man up to the best of himself for the best good of society.

It has been argued that chivalry and feminine modesty put women in a very insecure position in human society, put them where their lives are at the mercy of some man's fancy, where they must be chosen, where they must attract, lure, cheat if necessary, capture—and then hold only by grace of the man's caring and whim. Put that way, it isn't very attractive or dignified for the mothers of the race.

Such an arrangement makes man-catching and man-pleasing the bulwark of a woman's life. Bad enough in itself. But wait, what of those women who fail in even this unfair miserable game? Not everyone can win a race or a prize. What are the losers in the man-race to do? Live meekly with relatives on a kind of tacit charity—with every utterance of the handle "Miss" a fresh accusation of her failure in life's game for women?

What then is the solution? As a bald economic matter, the woman who is not supported by a husband, and doesn't wish to live with relatives, may support herself, so we have the woman in business. Some women have both careers and husbands. With the greater acceptance of the business woman in the national pattern, the woman is lifted out of her exaggerated femaleness. War lifts her out of it still further.

But still she hopes for romance—and is in a stronger position to wait for the right one—to choose more fully—if choice there be. And if not she can pretend, and maybe she means it, that she prefers her independence to the quasi-slavery and indignity that she sees her married girl-friends subjected to in some cases.

THEN SHE HEARS OF NEW SOCIAL SET-UPS, where women are the charges of the Government, no longer at the mercy of a chance male (that sounds pretty good), where mating and child-bearing are government, not family, matters, and where except for such minor inconveniences she is labeled worker, her child a labeled, catalogued, numbered government asset.

Neither the male nor the female has any responsibility in the matter other than biological functions. They have no personal interest in each other (here the whole scheme begins to look a little tarnished and shabby). She begins to question about the where and the why of the mating in which they both go scot-free eventually.

Assembly-line children, she thinks to herself—not even the dignity of the jungle where animals choose, mate, fight for each other, live together—where the male finds food and protects his offspring. Though at least, it is an escape from the humiliation of personal failure and the struggle of success.

But what is the price of this escape? Nonentity! Well, she admits, she can't eat her cake and have it too. To feel no pain one must be unaware, unconscious, nonexistent—ascend or descend into a kind of Nirvana or nothingness. That may be "heaven" for some people—but as it is a type of failure why is it any less humiliating than any other kind, she asks herself?

Her pride begins to assert itself. Better to try to win in the old selective way—and if one loses to bear one's losses bravely. She doesn't wish to be blotted out in a merciful, legal nothingness.

The male too, in his normal state, is willing to abide a measure of pain, embarrassment and boredom. If he is even near mental maturity, he knows that ideals do not come in neat cellophane packages, but are carved from chaos. What is the world coming to if women have to be saved from men by acts of parliament? A sad commentary on our men!

The male would eventually get the worst of such "freedom." Very few males would be needed in a purely physical society. All materialistic schemes kill off or enslave whomever they do not need. Now he comes to the illuminating, clarifying truth that men need women as fully as women need men—not merely for biological necessities—but far more deeply. The masculine mind gropes upward and outward with even more intensity than does hers.

His need of confirmation and encouragement is almost greater than hers. He needs her to admire him, to point to the distant height that he alone can scale, discover, harness—to steady him when he falters—to light his path when it grows dim—to talk to him in those clammy stretches of doubt—and to ornament him in his triumphs—she and her child justify him. He needs the warmth and nearness of her mind as well as her body.

So then, she sees attraction in a higher light—she doesn't want a husband now, so much to keep "Miss" off her tombstone—as to fulfil herself *and him*. She begins to feel that she fulfils herself more truly by helping him to fulfil himself. Strange how personal success is so dry to a woman, after a while.

It isn't so humiliating to attract a mate in order to be his complement as it was just for her own support, vanity or gratification. Why, she could be positively *scheming* about making him see what she could do for *him!*

Why, after all, should we ask to be *given* security (indeed it doesn't even exist) when the elements and prizes of life lie all about us waiting for us to discover the ways they best work and fit together? A woman wants courage, not a panacea. She sees an open road, a high road of great beauty as well as stones and briars.

Yes, she says, let's have security for the young, the old and the ill, but let the rest of us explore life's possibilities. And down in her heart, when she stops fear and panic there, she knows that every woman can get a man—some kind of satisfactory male, without half trying. The real job is to do her duty by him afterward. There are modern partnerships that work—if the woman is clever.

She can pack away her bait and air her idealism. She can be herself. With his need of her, her child's need of her, the world's need of her personal contribution of color, poetry, kindness, soft judgment, shelter in weakness, her position as a woman begins to look very glamorous.

My heavens, she tells herself—you can get morbid about anything if you're determined to! Or you can see that all of life is available at any point within itself. At any rate, she is too high-minded, too red-blooded, to become a national, legal nonentity. That would be the real embarrassment.

Then too, she really doesn't have to please men any more than anyone else—say, a customer, her guests, a puppy or her little sister. Besides, it's fun pleasing men. They are usually very responsive and appreciative—quite interesting and wonderful beings.

In another way of regarding it, she tells herself that, to an almost startling degree of accuracy, she receives from anyone, men and life itself, what she unconsciously demands. In the ordinary pattern of life, aside from pestilences, hurricanes and wars, she receives very nearly her unconscious demand. The steadiness, the potency and merit of one's deep and honest expectancy is about what one meets in experience.

To lift, to enlarge, to ennoble that expectancy is the whole effort of this book. Not hope, which is but a light in the dark, nor anxiety, nor frenzied concentration and nervous work accomplish much. The crux of the matter is deeper in our accepted and admitted valuations—which, thank heaven, we can change, through persistence.

*DEMAND DOES NOT MEAN COMMAND.* Let us be clear about this word "demand." I mean it only in the sense that we speak of hunger as a demand for food. The spoken demand usually is denied. Do not confuse "demand" with "command." The imperious, commanding woman is as outdated as hoopskirts. The successful woman's demand on life is made up of her qualifications to expect a favorable answer to her unconscious demand.

By this time, I feel sure that you have straightened your life, your habits and your disposition into a semblance of your own ideal of them. But I am hoping that now, having gained your own approval of yourself, you will not become smug and *self-satisfied.*

When one becomes satisfied with oneself, the magnetic emanations that go out to others are short and weak. Just as short and weak as are those of the self-conscious person, and for the same reason—the mind is on the self! Consequently, mental and physical vibrations circle about the self instead of surging out freely and easily in long wave-lengths to other things, other people, larger issues, big conceptions or the more immediate, intimate interest in your friend's point of view.

*WOULD YOU LIKE A RECORD OF YOUR THOUGHTS?* If our thoughts could be taken down by a stenographer just as they race through our minds, we could read them at leisure and we should understand just why we affect or fail to affect people as we do. Eugene O'Neill's "Strange Interlude" was a concrete example of how the mind can instantly reverse something the tongue has just spoken.

In like manner, we often speak or think a hope or some constructive thing—then immediately think of the impossibility of it, or some ugly criticism, doubt or fear creeps in. This *frictional thinking* burns up a lot of personal magnetism, misuses our natural power and diverts and minimizes the effect of our physical presence by shortening our "wave-length" into negativity.

*NEGATIVE THOUGHTS QUICKLY MAR THE FACE.* For instance, you are talking with a man you hope will like you. You are discussing a play you saw the night before. You say, "All evening I kept wondering how you were liking it. It seemed that you, of all people, would enjoy the high drama it climbed to occasionally." The man is pleased with this and searches your face to determine your sincerity.

While he is looking at you, a thought I call a "tramp" thought flits across your mind. You think—"Why does he shower attention on that odd-looking Smith girl when I am really so much nicer than she?" Your face instantly loses the warmth it held while you were thinking of the interesting values of the play. Your open, enthusiastic expression narrows with criticism and envy.

It is as though a light had been snuffed out, or as though a lovely girl had been looking out a window and suddenly a hag replaced her.

The young man, not being analytical of women, is disappointed, he knows not why. Your thoughts, being on yourself, do not reach out to include anyone else. Not even he can feel any warmth from your mind. There is none. The girl he saw in your face, who attracted him, has "moved out."

Not only does the young man feel mistaken in his original estimate of you, but he instinctively mistrusts anyone who can change under his very eyes into another sort of person.

Now you may have supposed that your sly little thought was harmless enough—and certainly very human. But these little negative, bitter, critical, envious, selfish thoughts are like rodents that attack the roots of rose-bushes, causing the foliage and blooms to droop and die while everything on the surface is apparently in fine condition. The flowers' beauty has been sapped from within.

We should really spend a little time in going over our mental habits to determine how often we shorten the wave-length of our personal magnetism by unlovely thoughts, and especially selfish thoughts.

We all know selfish women who seem to get everything they want besides having many friends. I sometimes wonder if these women are really as selfish as they seem to be. Perhaps their unconscious demand on life is greater than yours.

*BUILD UP YOUR UNCONSCIOUS DEMAND.* Remember that the unconscious demand is stronger than the conscious one. The woman who wishes to be effective must build up her unconscious demand for the best things from life, being willing, of course, to give the best of herself. If, in her heart, she demands that men be chivalrous, her manner toward them will be one of expectancy and they will respond if no other thought crosses and cuts the current of her demand.

*WHAT TYPES OF WOMEN STIR CHIVALRY?* I have taken a class of girls onto a street-car to see which of them had the quality of stirring chivalry in men sufficiently to have seats offered them. Now, of course, we all have something more important to do with our womanhood than merely getting seats on public conveyances, yet it is when little courtesies are dropped that an element of charm and joy and self-respect is lost between men and women.

It is far easier sometimes to perform some task than to wait for a man to do it, but remember that:

*A MAN LETS GO TO THE EXACT EXTENT THAT A WOMAN TAKES HOLD.* Common sense dictates that when a tired husband comes home he should be given every comfort and consideration, but he should never be allowed to lose, for very long at a time, his sense of responsibility as a male protector in *every* way.

In times of war, women step into men's civilian jobs, and in air-raid work they are often shoulder to shoulder with men—a work for which they are not fitted either by nature or temperament. All such effort should be regarded as one of the unpleasantnesses of war. It is this accepted lack of poetry and proper balance between men and women that is largely responsible for the inevitable post-war coarseness. Women should learn to preserve all they can of femininity at every point. There is no point in being mannish or coarse or bold because we are being helpful in an emergency. Why be leathery about it? It is worth a deep plan and constant effort to keep as normal as possible at all times.

Ideal femininity helps to preserve civilization and lifts it. Oddly enough the highest peaks of civilization and accomplishment have occurred when women were most highly valued and cherished. The opposite point of view, however logical, seems to lead to excessive brutality or indifference that ends in collapse.

The points I mention here are perhaps adapted to general experience. They are chiefly interesting as psychology tests.

If a man can get a girl to drop her eyes in slight embarrassment before his ardent gaze, he has the satisfaction of having been noticed as a man. If she simply regards him as she might a sign-board or a strange animal in the human zoo and keeps all criticism and guile out of her expression, her face is merely mildly curious and her gaze as disarming as that of an observing child.

If the man looks encouraged at all, he is easily squelched by a stifled yawn and the slow removal of the eyes to someone or something else. In other words, you haven't in the least recognized his presence as a man. If he rises to give you his seat, thank him briefly and do not look at him again.

*HAVE YOU NOTICED THAT WHEN YOU DROP SOME-THING IN FRONT OF A MAN,* the act of picking it up and handing it to you may inspire him to complete his courtesy by giving you his seat? The man with any training and education whatever does not enjoy sitting down while women stand. He argues with himself in justification during the trip or buries himself in a paper. We were much amused when one girl reported that she had brought a man to his feet by appearing to calculate the breadth of his shoulders. "If they are narrow," she said, "he wants at least to act like a great fellow who can afford to be chivalrous. If they are broad, he becomes conscious of his great bulk at rest while women lurch about."

I used afterward to think that it was rather mean to make a tired worker relinquish his seat simply as a tribute to femininity. But invariably I could remember that any man who had been chivalrous for any reason, looked pleased with himself, held himself straighter, regarded himself more highly and walked away with a lighter step.

*IT ADDS NOTHING OF VALUE TO THE WORLD FOR WOMEN TO MEET MEN ON THEIR LEVEL.* Even if there must be equality in business and in other walks of life, the demand for chivalry should be maintained for the greater happiness of society in general.

Men are chivalrous (when they are) because it pleases them to be so—*not because it pleases the woman*. This is another proof of the fact that you must depend upon a man's interest in himself rather than his interest in you.

*MEN SOON LOSE INTEREST* in the woman who makes things so easy for them that they have no chance to enjoy being manly. For this reason, I heartily disapprove the bad habit that tried, fortunately without success, to fasten itself on the younger set several years ago. I refer to the girls' meeting the boys at some central location, and going from there to an entertainment. Occasionally circumstances do alter cases, but only the greatest emergency should bring about this practice.

I remember an instance in which the young man asked the girl to meet him in the lobby of a down-town hotel "to save time." She asked my advice. I replied that I did not think time as valuable to a woman as the preservation of the idea that she must be treated as something very precious. I suggested she tell the chap that some day when he had more time and could come and get her she would love to go with him. As it happened, he came after her and in a short time asked her to marry him!

*DECIDE ON AN ATTITUDE AND BE WILLING TO PAY FOR IT*. To return to our unconscious demand—we must remember that we can't have everything. One thing is bought at the expense of something else. We must make up our minds what it is we want from men and then do nothing, say nothing, look nothing and think nothing that would interfere in any way with the accomplishment of that purpose.

You must decide whether you want to be "one of the fellows" or a "lovely lady," an "amusing gamin" or a "restful woman." The average woman is not clever enough to combine all these in her personality. When she tries it, she seems to a man merely an undependable contradiction of herself.

To avoid monotony, one may have unusual ideas about literature, politics, the theatre, art, etc. You may have amusing moods—and dress to suit those moods. *But you can't be crudely frank with a man* on one occasion and expect him to take your next romantic mood very seriously.

If you must have outbursts about the sordid side of life that has occupied recent novelists, it is safer to keep a diary than to mar some man's picture of you as an idealist. You might also vent your disillusions into a dictaphone and then smash the records after you have heard your own tale of bitterness played back to you.

Men have looked to women to be the healing factor in society, to soothe and smooth and encourage them. In other words, men want women to *be women* and hold up the ideal of life to them so that they may stumble toward it in their own expression.

Men can be interested in religion unless it takes up too much time with the life to come. Men are here-and-now people. They will follow gladly the woman who wishes to make this life as beautiful as possible and will gradually accept that woman's opinion of spiritual values in daily living, if she is clever about it.

It is a large order, but a great deal of permanent satisfaction awaits the woman who will trouble herself to be a woman and demand that men be men.

Marie Antoinette's failure was largely due to her being so conscious of herself as Queen and her demands that others be likewise conscious of her royalty,—while Victoria's security lay partially in the fact that she was so sure of herself that it was seldom necessary for her to make a royal gesture. She ruled without strutting and waving her crown to draw attention to it.

Just so, women in private life will retain their Court longer if the Court is not too much aware of paying homage. The clever Queen lets others point to her crown. She doesn't do it.

*A VICTORY MEANS A VANQUISHED.* It never pays to dwell on a victory of any kind. For wherever there is a victory there is also a vanquished. In a community or family matter the vanquished is also a member of the family. To have his failure held before his eyes, especially for the purpose of aggrandizing someone else, angers and eventually estranges a man, a woman or a child.

As all living is for the purpose of growing and developing, every human being feels a right to make a certain number of mistakes. To have these mistakes magnified and perpetuated by nagging kills the value of the experience, which otherwise might have added to his wisdom.

*DO NOT DWELL ON YOUR OWN VICTORIES AND DO NOT DWELL ON ANOTHER'S FAILURES.* Some women, in their efforts to show their own high standards and refined tastes, fall into the bad habit of biting, acid comment concerning whatever falls below their admiration. They forget that a real woman is a citizen of the world, a tolerant, cultivated, constructive person. They forget that no really educated, enlightened individual ever stoops to unkindness even in words.

No "lady" finds it necessary to build herself up by the faulty method of contrasts and competition. She *is* a "lady." Everything about her proves it. She does not have to proclaim it. Certainly sarcasm and ridicule of others prove nothing except her deplorable state of development. It is clear that this woman is making a conscious demand for recognition that she should be able to win without so much conscious effort.

As a rule, men respond rather quickly to a woman's unconscious demand. They balk stubbornly in the face of conscious demands. This explains the difference between women to whom the good things of life seem to flow and those women who struggle and struggle to reach the same point, but whose very struggle defeats their end.

Merely to want something is not enough, though it is a necessary starting point. Neither will you receive it by merely going through the external motions of obtaining it, though this is absolutely necessary. You will not win it, at least not permanently, until you unconsciously expect it and take it for granted.

To take something for granted does not mean that you cease to appreciate it or that it becomes less exciting and colorful. We take the sun and air for granted, yet there is no sensitive person who does not feel a thrill at the beginning of each day.

To expect unconsciously the good things of life whets your appetite for them rather than dulls it. It is as though you said inside yourself— "I like this so much I must have some more of it."

Even in a restaurant, the one who enters as though fully expecting the best of service will get it. In trying to cultivate this manner, many people ignore the maître d'hôtel and the waiter as much as possible, apparently believing that haughtiness will cause them to realize the importance of the guest. I have seen such persons sit and sit waiting for service.

Going to the other extreme, there is the person who assumes an unwarranted intimacy with the head-waiter in the hope of wheedling consideration and service out of him. This over-familiarity is resented as much as haughtiness.

To the man and woman of the world, dining is a pleasant function. They regard the maître d'hôtel with confidence, often asking his advice, but always with a calm, intelligent, expectant manner. The preferences of such people are given instant consideration even though their tips may be smaller than those of their less confident neighbors, who wonder "how it is done."

To begin with, the waiters in a fine restaurant look forward to serving you well. They are well-trained and regard their profession as highly as you do yours. Naturally, they will enjoy serving people who allow them to do their utmost and seem pleased with the result. A cantankerous diner must have a fat pocketbook.

For the sake of your digestion, and also your future comfort in attaining service, be pleasant at meal-time. An expression of a fine appreciation of a sauce or flavor will go farther to show that you are an epicure than will all your high-tempered complaints.

*DON'T WEAR A PERMANENT SMILE.* It is time now for another warning. Having decided to meet life positively instead of negatively at every point, beware of getting a set, empty, professional smile on your face. A look of eager attention is much more pleasant to behold than a trained grimace that holds neither the glinting light of happiness nor the sparkle of real fun. It is much better to be sincerely, earnestly serious than to be forcing a smile. Men are particularly sensitive to sincerity. They instinctively feel artificiality as a child does.

No amount of telling a child what a dear little thing he is will gain his friendship. But, if you, under his appraising scrutiny, go naturally about the business of being a friend, he will respond naturally and happily. To learn about men, study a little boy. Men never grow up emotionally. It is one of their most charming and most exasperating attributes. The exceptions are too rare to consider here.

Speaking of smiles, they can be made to say many things. But to bring a hurrah kind of smiling, back-slapping attitude into anyone's sorrow is certainly overworking a smile. You can help your friends out of dark moods by first respecting their feelings and then by letting them understand that you *expect* their strength and nobility to assert themselves in courage and sufficient consideration for others to throw off the darkness. One of our best reasons for being constitutionally happy is that these adjustments to life are always possible.

*HABITUAL SADNESS, HABITUAL UNHAPPINESS, HABITUAL SELF-CONSCIOUSNESS* are nothing in the world but habitual selfishness! How, then, shall we be unselfish and at the same time get things from life that we want? How can we keep our thought away from self and at the same time gain or protect our personal interests? In the first place, there is no way for you to lose what is definitely yours. A negative acceptance of something, even over a period of years, does not make that thing yours in reality.

Again, there is no law known to life that can prevent you from attaining what, in your inmost soul, you know to be yours! What then is gained by standing on guard mentally to see that no one trespasses on your preserves? It may be necessary at times to rout a stray marauder from the sacred precincts of your private happiness. But it is certainly a waste of time and energy to spend much effort in suspiciously ferreting out people's motives if they are unworthy.

Our protection from discord of any kind is to be so filled with harmony that nothing else can affect us—to wear such a bright and shining consciousness that, as darkness of any kind approaches us, it is lighted by our own light—then it is no longer darkness. We will waste no time in envy, or jealousy, if we honestly believe that there is wealth enough of all kinds to go around, enough happiness for everyone.

Then too, we must learn to be positive in our unselfishness, instead of negative. I don't know why the popular conception of unselfishness demands that one abandon all hope or desire of personal gain or happiness—that one is to cease to exist as an individual and merge one's life into others in a complete suspension of personal reactions—a sort of Hindu Nirvana.

I do not consider it a very superior unselfishness that says, "Well, having failed to get anything out of life for myself, I shall now help others try to find something." The noblest sort of unselfishness is the kind that knows that there is little interest or pleasure in hovering over the pronoun "I"—that the drama of life moves out and out in ever enlarging circles from the personal consciousness—that the largest and most glorious personal happiness is in projecting the receptive, sensitive self as far as possible into the highways and byways of human expression and experience.

Every modern invention is evidence of this urge of mankind to project itself far beyond the limitations that we now think bind us. Mechanically we have the means to defy space, to conquer distance, to penetrate stone walls with a song—so why should we longer confine ourselves as individuals to the outworn limitations of the self that remains in the cellar of self-unfoldment and hugs itself in the dark?

We are only in the first stages of beginning to realize that the pronoun "I" is but a springboard from which we get an impetus to personal expression in enlarged experience.

And if we will remember that *all of life is everywhere present,* we will stop thinking that we lack opportunities where we are, that our environment is against us, or that somewhere else we could be better and different people.

The point is, be better and different and your environment will change accordingly. Don't get the cart in front of the horse. In other words, you can stay right where you are and change your life and yourself almost beyond recognition if you will put the necessary effort and conviction to work for you.

I have seen women who were apparently trapped in the most closely interwoven nets of obligations and conflicting affections—caught in situations where it seemed that there would be no release until someone had passed on—actually walled in by circumstances. But after a few months of determinedly constructive thinking and joyful living, I have seen them absolutely freed—without hurt to anyone—without loss to anyone—and, therefore, without the feeling of having bought their freedom at someone else's expense.

I tell you that opposition melts before constructive thought! I tell you that personal happiness is preserved when the "I" becomes brave enough to trust its strength in broader interests that leave pettiness behind.

*THERE IS NO TURNING BACK* when once you set your face to the light of beautiful living. You may falter and fail temporarily but you will rise and walk on, head up and heart singing. I ask no greater happiness than the privilege of striking this flash of light across your mind, or, if you have had it and temporarily lost it, that this book may give it to you again. Then it is that you stand free—as a potent, powerful person, able to project yourself over or through the things that seem to hold you back. In my own life I have seen the most impossible situations melted; they have fallen from me, as a worn-out garment, and I have stepped from them.

It isn't easy to keep our minds on grace, beauty, loveliness and honor when we are touched daily by the opposite of these. But it only puts lines of battle into our faces to fight these things on their own ground in our revulsion to them. The only way is to fill ourselves to the brim with what we do admire—steadfastly to build beauty within ourselves until we no longer look at ugliness critically but see it merely as an opportunity for beauty to be there also!

Try to think of your thoughts as boomerangs—that is actually what they are—except that our thoughts multiply and each returns to us with a brood like itself.

To be sparing in criticism and to be joyful in spite of unpleasant things is not to be stupidly content—it is really working most scientifically toward a complete reconstruction of things in so far as they affect us. The woman who has found her power in her own inner kingdom, has a peace, a poise and a light in her face that make others want to learn her secret. It is to be hoped that she remains very feminine in her gentle, quiet strength, for if she permits herself to advertise her strength she will find that she has attracted many weak people who want to lean on her. If she becomes merely a shining example of what personal development can mean to the individual, then people seek to be like her and find their own strength.

Is it not true then that the noblest assistance a woman can give to others is to show what the use of constructive principles can mean in every way? I recall a client whom I had freed from the most malicious mental tangles, who finally stood before me sound, sane and so firm on her own two feet that she stated she no longer needed me. I nearly wept for joy!

The woman who succeeds most in influencing others does so by virtue of what she is and not by what she says. Words and rules are important but they are dead and fruitless without works. Words are only sign-posts that point the way. If we sit under sign-posts and do no traveling, we will never arrive but will forever be at the crossroads.

However, we should remember that words are one of our sign-posts by which others judge our direction and then determine whether they want to go our way, to be our friends. So we must learn to say those things that attract and please others.

But when a woman depends too much on external effects, she is apt to neglect the more important elements of personality.

What she *is* represents her unconscious demand, which is to be measured by the weight of the majority of her thinking. If most of her thinking is about herself, she will have a short-wave magnetism that reaches no one. If most of her thinking goes out from herself she will have a long-wave magnetism that embraces almost everyone in its sweep. The breadth of her interest is her unconscious demand.

But see for a moment how easily she can betray herself. The mind is subtle and our old faults have many ways of perpetuating themselves. Suppose she says to herself, "Indeed, I shall keep my interests away from myself because I lack so much as a person that I fear my ability to be interesting." What has she done? Has she not condemned herself and gone to other things to escape what she does not like?

This type of thinking will have small effect on improving her personality, because her poor opinion of herself becomes a dam which stops the flow of long-wave magnetism from her. Any thought that might be construed as a snag which stops the outrush of flowing acceptance of experience—which necessarily includes experience with self—is a detriment to charming magnetism.

But the woman who will trouble to do the things and think the things that make her glad to be a vessel for life and then turn her mind to the interesting world of people and things outside herself, will give off an uninterrupted, easy, harmonious, long-wave magnetism of Charm. Others will respond because then they feel the full force of her unconscious demand.

I want you to understand why you do what you do and what definite results you can expect. Watch your thoughts carefully. It is a good idea to make a little chart of them as doctors do a temperature, and mark the line upward for constructive thinking and downward for destructive thinking. It may surprise you.

# CHAPTER FIVE
## *The Art of Compromise*

Good and quick judgment is necessary for tact and many other expressions of Charm. We can gradually form the habit of thinking quickly and kindly. *Habit is really the accumulation of responses along any given line until action becomes automatic—until conscious mental or physical effort is no longer required to start an act or idea*. We can use this law of habit-responses to help us build our charming personalities. In fact, we can't build Charm without it.

If we must continue to decide to be selflessly interested "in other people and other things"—if we must always *conclude* to be pleasant when we feel like snapping someone's head off—if our smile continues to be a matter of immediate policy—we are on our way, but, we have not yet *arrived* at Charm. The charming woman's smile is bright with sunniness inside!

Years ago it was claimed that three weeks was sufficient time in which to form a habit. Certainly, with reading and re-reading this book, any number of constructive habits can be formed. Even though you are not entirely faithful in doing the exercises every day and using the principles outlined, you will gradually absorb their benefit.

*For once you have turned your face toward beauty, there is no turning back!* No matter how often you fail, how weak you may seem to be occasionally, you cannot abandon the ideal. It will never let you alone. And you will never let it alone. It is clear, then, that the only sensible thing to do is to enter into a regime of self-discipline that will more quickly bring you success and satisfaction.

*WE KNOW THAT THE MIND LEADS*, creates the pattern and starts the force of accomplishment into action. But we must also recognize that a great deal of help can be had from a body that is functioning properly and easily.

Just as I have been concerned with removing the ideas that impede your mental progress in Charm, I am now concerned with helping you to eliminate the bodily deterrents to your progress. If any function is to be quick, smooth and efficient, its way must be cleared.

*THE VICIOUS CIRCLE.* You will find your judgment better and self-control easier if the bloodstream that nourishes your brain is free from poisons. It is an accepted fact that destructive thinking and emotions are detrimental to health. We are also told that poisons enter the blood from a clogged digestive and elimination tract. These may befog the brain and slow its processes, causing moody discouragement, which brings more poisons into the blood, which brings more discouragement—and there we have a *vicious circle*.

*THE FRIENDLY CIRCLE.* On the other hand, by keeping our thoughts determinedly bright and high with plans and expectancy and by keeping our bodies clean inside and out, we can establish a *friendly circle* which assists our lofty aspirations, causing the body to rebuild and refresh itself. Then our minds climb happily to new heights.

To this end, purify your bloodstream. It makes your mental work easier. So see your doctor and take every means of keeping your strength as high as possible.

Elsewhere in this book I have begged you to drink lots of water. I never see clear, fresh water without thinking how much of life, health, charm and success it controls. If we get to be sun, water and air worshippers, as Hippocrates, the father of medicine advised, we have a better chance to develop that freshness of mind and body that is a faithful dynamo of magnetism.

I believe that every dark or confused thought is either caused or encouraged by poisons reaching the brain cells. Often our minds are slowed down imperceptibly, just enough to impair our vision and judgment. Then it is we miss many opportunities for advantage.

*FATIGUE IS THE BODY'S WARNING* of accumulated waste in the system. The quickest way to help recovery is to sip a glass of water and lie down for two minutes if you can spare no longer time.

It bears repetition that there is no artificial stimulant that will give you the added energy generated by a glass of water with a bit of lemon in it (no sugar), a hot bath with soap and brush, followed by a cool or cold shower and a brisk rub-down with a rough towel.

*BEAUTY IS FAR LESS IMPORTANT TO CHARM THAN IS WELL-BEING.* A clean body, refreshed and smoothly functioning, not only gives off the vibrations that make one's physical presence felt and admired, but gives speed and accuracy to thought.

Fatigue is also injurious to posture and, as we already know, posture is very important to Charm, because by its position the body "talks." It doesn't help very much to rest a brief time on a soft bed that yields and accepts the position of the tired body.

For a quick come-back rest on a hard surface, where the back *must* straighten out and the vertebræ of the spine find relief. When the days are crowded and exacting I often lie on the floor for what might seem 'a mere instant, but even in that brief time a certain relaxation and regeneration begin that enable me to go on for hours. A rested, clean body is the best foundation for the good nature, the selflessness, the tact, the good judgment, the good taste, and the quick sympathy of Charm, to say nothing of the brighter eye and the surer grace of true beauty.

In other words, the woman who would be charming must "have her wits about her." The clever woman grooms herself for her job of being a charming woman, for physical and mental efficiency. Then, and only then, is she ready to learn the art of *Compromise.* For only a clear mind has clear judgment.

Someone has said that all of life from the cradle to the grave could be summed up in the one word "compromise." This is the backbone of all harmony in contact with others.

No one can ruthlessly go his own way regardless of others, for very long. Therefore, when we consider someone else and are influenced in our thoughts and acts by that consideration, we are "compromising." But not the sort indicated by the bride who said—"So we compromised and did it my way."

The graciousness of giving way in part to another's point of view is a major point in savoir-faire. Some people cannot concede without loss of dignity, sometimes loss of temper. The cultured woman is able to make concessions to the immediate situation, no matter what, without losing her individuality. "How very interesting," she may say, "I had always supposed the opposite to be true."

To understand the art of compromise will help one a great deal in conversation. It is far from being a namby-pamby yessing which thoughtless people consider it to be. It is really stimulating to good talk.

Compromise yields only a point at a time. If several people are discussing a certain subject and they all agree entirely about all of it, an awkward silence is likely to fall and someone will have to find something else to talk about.

However, if each flatly states a different opinion, that too may end the discussion or bring a discordant feeling or a quarrelsome argument.

Sometimes crafty people compromise elaborately on minor points and carry the major ones as they wish afterward, as though they were quite unimportant. Wives have been known to do this successfully with husbands, and likewise husbands with wives and parents with children.

There is hardly a point in life where compromise is not valuable. To capitulate graciously and without criticism is one of the abilities of the charming woman. She cannot expect the world in general to have her high ideals.

If she lets herself be critical of others, she will spend most of her waking hours chafing against the crudity, thoughtlessness, awkwardness and tactlessness of the average mortal. And Charm will slowly expire under this mental attitude.

She will protect her personality only by a great tolerance and sympathy for those less advanced on the path of development than she. She will draw no direct comparison between herself and them. She will realize that they may have fineness in other directions and perhaps a noble unselfishness in other ways than those indicated by her standards. She views the world as every cultured person does—as a passing show of great interest. She is willing for each person to have his opinions and individual characteristics—as she is willing for a leopard to have his spots and an elephant to have his trunk. This very willingness is part of the elegance of compromise.

*REMEMBER THAT LIFE IS GROWTH AND CHANGE.* We cannot force our standards upon others. Sometimes the people who rest on their self-styled superiority watch with amazement a family for whom they have no respect whatever, prosper and become prominent in the community. Sometimes the girl who was ridiculed for her slowness in school has a much more successful life than teacher's bright pet who thought her smartness a sufficient weapon with which to meet life. The only way to live successfully is constantly to advance with an open mind. Whenever we "peg" our own superiority we are apt to wake up some morning and find ourselves outdated with a static opinion, while life, love and living have passed by—perhaps failing humanly but trying again, scrambling along, progressing at a surprising rate. It is this "livingness" that is the warmth of a charming personality. To gain this attitude, we must know the art of compromise.

*BE TOLERANT BUT DON'T PULL YOUR IDEALS DOWN.* We must never compromise with ideals for ourselves but for others. In other words, we must expect infinitely more of ourselves than we do of others. If we are really superior, we won't mind doing this. It will not be a question of fairness or justice in our minds. It will be a question of capacity. Certainly the strong should carry the greatest burdens—and what nobility is there in strength if it is not willing to be strong, graciously and with a sense of responsibility?

*AN OPEN MIND IS A CIVILIZED MIND.* We are realizing as never before that life is a moving, fluid thing. There is little that is not subject to change. So don't get brittle, unchangeable opinions about things. Keep stiffness out of your mind as well as out of your body. The only thing that should be unchangeable is our "direction" in living, which should be determinedly constructive.

A story comes into my mind from my childhood. There was one old lady who was always making excuses for people, always saying something nice about everybody. She got a bit tiresome to one critical old man, who snapped at her one day—"Oh, your opinions don't matter. You'd have something nice to say about the devil himself."

To which the pleasant old lady replied—"Well, I can't think of any-body who attends so strictly to his own business."

The cultured woman never snubs anybody. She doesn't let "un-profitable" people take much of her time—but for the few minutes she is with them, she is thoroughly understanding and gracious. She lets each person feel that she understands his point of view. The college man feels that she understands his intermittent despair about prepar-ing for life. She knows that climbers don't want their small victories pointed out. She knows that people of position like to discuss enthusi-astically their new flowers, the new chair, or the success of their stables. She knows that old gentlemen like to tell of their successes. She knows the farmer likes to talk about the weather. She puts herself, however briefly, in the place of those with whom she is in contact.

When Lola Montez practically forced her way into the presence of King Louis I of Bavaria and they started talking "as though they were merely resuming a conversation" these two people had found in each other that rarest of all human discoveries—someone who is instantly and completely responsive. Most of us must make an effort to find and touch the other person's interests.

I once asked a friend of mine how she was able to adjust herself so quickly to anyone she might meet. She laughingly told me the story of the lost horse that all the smart people in the village couldn't find. Finally the village half-wit produced the horse. When he was asked how on earth he found it, he said—"Well, I just said to myself, 'Where would I go if I was a horse?' en I went there, en there he was."

I'm not telling you these old stories to amuse you. I am repeating them because they so graphically illustrate my points. We can all say to ourselves on meeting a stranger, "What would I want to discuss if I were in your place?"

TO FIND A SUBJECT, SEND UP SEVERAL TRIAL BAL-LOONS. Bear in mind that lots of people go out socially to get away from their professions, to hear what the rest of the world has to say. Bachelors often like to talk about how children should be reared and the doctor might like to discuss old tapestries or the plague of termites. But a safe start for conversation is usually something relevant to your usual interest. Unless it is responded to with some degree of interest, you can easily switch off to another topic by our "association of ideas" formula.

*WITHOUT COMPROMISE ONE IS MENTALLY RUDE.* To the stubborn person, "giving in" means almost a breaking of pride, which is really a one-character, internal drama that no one sees but the solo owner-performer. Such pride is but a dam over which the flood waters of a larger point of view must flow, and thence out to mingle with the world where it finds its level by performance, not policy.

To the cultured woman, compromise affords the opportunity to show her command of every situation by her wisdom in meeting contacts with the good taste that smooths the way for herself and others.

*GRACIOUS PEOPLE DO NOT BLOCK OTHERS, MENTALLY OR PHYSICALLY.* The knowledge of how to give way without loss of dignity is largely a matter of gracious intent. For instance, the courteous, well-bred woman simply *couldn't* stop in the doorway of a shop to chat with a friend while people try to squeeze past her. She *couldn't* inconvenience and block other people on the street, either walking or motoring. Some prominent women, and other thoughtless ones, imagine that because their husbands pay their bills they own special rights in whatever place they happen to be. If special rights and extra service are a compliment, rather than an answer to a vulgar demand for attention, they will offend no one and be more apt to assume permanency.

Haven't you noticed how a well-bred woman goes her way quietly, sweetly, almost unobtrusively? Yet her very presence, her tone of voice, her attitude of simple assurance get more courtesy and helpfulness that is genuine because everyone wants to pay his respects to—what?—her *Charm,* of course!

*IN CHARM IT IS THE INNER ATTITUDE THAT COUNTS.* This is the reason we often find charming women among ignorant people—and sometimes uncharming ones among those who have had many opportunities.

No one wants to cultivate diffidence. But we do want to cultivate a deep recognition of the rights of others. This does not mean that we should stand aside always and let others take the lead. As a matter of fact, it is only the woman or man who knows how to make others happy and comfortable who is fitted to lead!

We have seen that people in general like to be told what to think, that in their opinion of us they largely follow the opinions we give them. Not because they are weak-minded, but because they are un-interested, really. Remember, we learned early in these pages that *people usually put the same construction on your life and acts that you put on them.* The world is busy with its own affairs. Therefore, it is simpler and more usual to accept suggestions given off by others than to conjure up our own opinions. Now, suggestion can be used in many other ways to greater good if we do not overdo it and become obvious.

*CHARM IS A LIGHT AND A LIFT.* When a woman's person-ality suggests loveliness to the beholder, the benefit is mutual. The charming woman not only smooths her own path by drawing the best to herself but she has unconsciously done a favor to those who express their best to her. Thus she starts a train of constructive reactions that may be endless, going from person to person, even from generation to generation. Knowing how definitely our facial and physical expres-sions, as well as what we say, affect those with whom we come in contact and even those who merely glance at us on the street, it be-comes our *responsibility* to give always a constructive impression—if we are to help ourselves and to help others.

*THE FASHIONABLE ATTITUDE OF THE FUTURE WILL BE AN EVEN MORE CONSCIOUS RECOGNITION OF OUR RESPONSIBILITY TO OTHERS.* But until education along this line becomes more general it remains for those of us who do know to be even more watchful of our thoughts and deeds. It is so easy to slip into discouragement. It is so easy to slip into destructive expres-sions of all kinds. It takes a great deal of moral strength, a great big WANT TO and a truly aristocratic acceptance of responsibility to keep ourselves and our attitude towards others always ideal. Yet we must serve the ideal if we wish the ideal to serve us. It is human to be buoyed up by constructive effort for a few days and then to sink back into destructive attitudes through mental and physical laziness and through our inherited animalistic tendencies to resentments.

Knowing the great reward of staying close to ideal thinking and

acting, still we do not discipline ourselves sufficiently to attain perfection. We fall asleep, as did those who set themselves to watch while
Christ was in Gethsemane. His gentle reproach when He found them
was simply, "Could ye not watch with me one hour!"

Yet the constructive forces of the universe are so eternal that we
may fall away from them a thousand times and still return to ally
ourselves with them. I do not mean this in a religious sense at all. I
mean it from the psychological point of view.

Do not be alarmed by the idea of a large body of destructive thinking in your immediate or long past which you think must bear fruit
until it has spent itself in your life. This is what most people actually
mean when they speak of "judgment" and "punishment." Millions of
people in India are enslaved by this idea of Karma. As though the
universe could not right itself!

Even though disaster were on its way to you and rightly so, ful-
filling the law of cause and effect, it is possible to avert its blows, to
transmute its force into something higher, by turning the light of
constructive thinking into its dark path. You may thus change the
experience entirely. Christian "forgiveness" is a mystical statement of
this fact.

Remember that you always have the power to rise above discord of
any kind by the unbelievably simple expedient of replacement of ideas
and acts. Every minute constructive forces are at work for you. If you
cut your finger the healing process begins at once. It is only in the
mind of man that disaster is followed by disaster. Nature is always
forgiving, rebuilding, beginning anew.

To be bitter and discouraged over the failure of anything is certainly very short-sighted. The thing you grieve for is not the first of
its kind. The world is very old. After your first disappointment, to
feel that the next thing you build toward is just a second-hand make-
shift is also very short-sighted.

Your new idea, your fresh start, is just as new and fresh as the first
one—unless you deliberately pollute it by bringing the dregs of the
former failure into it. That is up to you. If you will get this fact firmly
embedded in your mind, it will save you much heart-ache and help
miraculously to preserve your poise. When you are nursing your

wounds overlong and indulging in self-pity overmuch, you simply perpetuate the idea of sorrow. You owe it to the world, as well as to yourself, to get back to constructive ideas at the earliest possible moment.

This does not mean that you are to cultivate an indifferent, callous, "don't care" attitude—but rather it emphasizes the necessity for a deeply rooted understanding of the healing and building forces that are here for our help and progress. All of this is intended to give you a firmer foundation of character so that through your inner development you can keep your life flowing more smoothly in pleasant ways. If we have these more serious matters thoroughly understood, the smaller aspects of Charm seem to flower more easily. This inner strength also promotes the feeling that we can well afford to learn the art of compromise. Having your feet on the firm rock of a deep understanding helps you to compromise more gracefully than if you just do it "to be sweet."

*DON'T EVER DO ANYTHING JUST TO BE SWEET.* This attitude softens the personality instead of strengthening it. Don't ever do anything from the weak, mushy, namby-pamby, negative wish to be "sweet." Do fine things from the wish to be fine. Then you will keep the high light of a great consciousness in your face and bearing, the nobility of the truly enlightened person.

The very word "enlightened" fascinates me. It is so very appropriate. Culture—mental, physical and spiritual—is a great light that illumines the faces, bodies and lives, as well as the minds, of those who absorb and express it continually. They become not only enlightened but gradually one with the light itself!

Then it is we do not need so much conscious training of our thoughts. Our habit-responses will have made us "naturally" attuned to high ideals. Then we can depend upon our emotions to help us rather than to trick us as they sometimes do now.

Do not imagine that I place thought on a higher plane than emotion. Thought and emotion are interdependent. One is born of the other. They play upon each other, each lending reality and substance to our personalities. Thought alone may make us brittle, cold and mechanistic.

It is quite possible to carry the order and rhythm of mechanical perfection into the spontaneous warmth of emotion. It is emotion that sweeps the world into one psychological unit. Therefore, it is precious and extremely valuable to anyone who wishes to influence others. Emotion carries a strong vibration.

Even a salesman at your door cannot get your attention unless you see that he is really "worked up" about the thing he wants to sell you. His carefully thought out, craftily worded speech will leave you cold if it does not carry emotional conviction.

A pupil once wrote me, "I am too emotional—I spend myself so unnecessarily. Can you help me to curb or kill my emotions?" I have no doubt that she was very much surprised when I wrote to her:

"No one has emotion enough. I most certainly will not help you curb or kill your emotions. I shall help you direct them. In your new development of poise, it should be much easier for you to think clearly and to see that you perhaps waste your precious emotions on unprofitable things and perhaps 'over-emote' along some one or two lines. Try to focus your interest and enthusiasm and emotion on matters, things and people that have a constructive place in your experience.

"By this, I do not mean to enthuse over just those things and people that bring you profit. It is quite as important to your development to bring profit to others, bearing in mind the warning in CHAPTER TWO of PART ONE.

"Spend your emotions in getting sufficiently worked up over posture and health, to take your exercises and to attain regular habits. Spend your emotions on beauty and in creating all sorts of loveliness around you. Spend your emotions on charitable work. Learn a foreign language."

Emotions are really energy born of interest. You can direct them into constructive ways that will make your life rich and full. Cultivate grand emotions—so few people really feel anything unless they themselves step on a tack.

It is the feeling nature that carries the stimulating message of living reality from your consciousness to another's. It seems almost wicked to think of curbing or destroying emotion when the whole world has such a great need of its warmth and fusing power.

Nourish, encourage and cultivate your emotions, but guide them! It is on pure emotion that the great beauty of music, of poetry, of color, of the whole panorama of the earth and sky, swings through space to touch our hearts with a stirring message.

We want to be more alive, more sensitive, more keen—but only to constructive things. It is plain that, unless one is able to keep poised constructively, great sensitiveness is a curse. Perhaps thick-skinned coarseness and stupidity are nature's protection while we learn the lesson of educating our wayward emotions.

Yet, as we develop and grow in understanding and spiritual strength, we want to be sensitive so that we can feel and hear the highest and finest things. We want to prepare ourselves so that we shall be entrusted with powers that might be dangerous for ignorant people to touch. As we solve each problem of self-control to win an ideal life, new doors appear before us to which we may earn the keys as we step forward in faith—faith in the integrity of the universe and its laws of building and progress. We win our power day by day as we win control of our lives.

Thus we see that we do not draw on some remote source of power, we go deeper within ourselves, making a larger channel for that which we *are* to come forth into expression to heal and to bless *every life*.

This is your destiny, your right and your reward! No one can stop the progress of humanity. But we can speed it up.

You will walk firmly and beautifully straight toward the light of idealism from henceforth—all the shadows falling behind where they belong—and you will face the happiest and most useful period of your life.

*Part Three*

EFFECTIVE CONVERSATION

EFFECTIVE CONVERSATION

# CHAPTER ONE

## *How to Make Your Talk Serve Your Ends*

There is more pleasure and profit in the study of conversation than in any other single subject. Surveys have shown that successful and effective people have one thing in common—facility with words.

Here the study has been made as effortless for you as possible, but you are asked to apply yourself to the few simple exercises given. They have been chosen for their direct and surprisingly swift results over many years of research and experience. Try it! But try all of it.

If we are really interested in communicating more satisfyingly with other people we will find keen delight in the small as well as the larger points. All of them are important.

For *good* talk we need ideas, words and the impulse to express ourselves. If back of these there is the desire to be companionable, sympathetic and refreshing, behold the *perfect* conversationalist!

Many people have good ideas for talk but lack the words and the ease in using words that would give *expression* to their thoughts.

Facility in talk is gained usually only through knowledge and experience. Yet through conscious study of the principles of conversation one may gain as much knowledge and experience in a few weeks as could be gleaned in a lifetime of striving without guidance. We will begin at the beginning. We must first sharpen our tools before starting to build any worthwhile creation. Upon this *preparation* lies the final result. Instead of scanning these lessons for the "high spots," you will be happier, in the end, if you will go carefully from beginning to end as I have planned it for you. Even though some of the material may be familiar to you—it will pay you to polish your ability to use it.

Control and rhythmic distribution of power are necessary for a smooth performance of any type of energy. For the moment we will profit by thinking of conversation as an expression of energy—energy born of interest. Upon the amount of this energy depend our vivacity, our wit and our responsiveness in general.

## 1. BREATH

In talk the power back of the energy is *breath*—so this must be our *first consideration*. As every message must have a carrier, every train a track, every journey a route, so our words must have the proper breath on which to ride out to the ears of others.

Your breath, coupled with the *emotional force* back of it, is, then, *your power*. Control of it is necessary for smoothness, for poise and continuity that hold the interest of others. An uncontrolled breath spills the meaning of words and their emotional force, just as carrying a glass of water in a wobbly fashion spills the contents.

The first way to insure *controlled breath* is to see that there is plenty of room in one's body for the necessary amount; so *look to your posture*. At first glance there may seem to be little connection between interesting conversation and posture. But remember that a lake is dependent upon the streams that feed it, and there must be a dependable source of water or the lake will deteriorate to a boggy swamp. For good conversation there must be a dependable source of breath, namely *well-expanded lungs*. Good posture insures room for lung expansion. I am going to take one minute here to tell you of the many other rewards of good posture.

A raised chest endows its owner with the appearance of well-being, success, triumph. Other people are much more interested in you if you look as though you have *something for them*. A low-chested person doesn't look as though he has anything for anybody. There is no place to have it!

I have often thought how appropriate is the word "chest." I would like to go a step farther and call it "treasure chest." For we human beings involuntarily and unconsciously value each other (perhaps for primitive and prehistoric reasons) by the height of our chests. You can experiment with this strange and interesting fact to your amusement and your profit. Try entering a room making your chest sunken, breathing in a shallow way, and no one will notice you. At best you will get slight consideration. Go back out of the room and come in again with chest raised, head up. Pause in the door and while you draw a long deep breath look slowly and cheerfully about the room. A number of people will get to their feet to greet you. *They will value what you have to say!*

*AN EASY WAY TO BETTER POSTURE.* One of the finest ways to improve posture is to lie on the back without a pillow with a large book placed directly under the "wings" of the shoulder blades. It is almost impossible to accomplish by muscular effort what this simple act will do. Five to fifteen minutes two or three times a day will bring swift results.

Do not try to sit and stand with your shoulders held rigidly back. You will look stiff and awkward if you do. Let your shoulders be free and relaxed and *down*. Never raise them in a nervous hunch. But raise your chest as though you were suspended from the ceiling by your breast bone. UP and UP and UP! This posture will improve your figure at the waist and flatten your abdomen. Do not even let overlarge busts keep you from gaining the benefits of this posture! Large bosoms are in style again and let us hope they will remain. You are a woman! Why should you be ashamed of it? Raise your chest as high as possible! Do you feel and look a little stiff when you first try it? A little trick to remedy that appearance is to *put your head slightly on one side*. All the stiffness is removed and you *look* as though you were graciously interested in whatever claims your attention. A man without good posture and controlled breath seems somewhat less than a man.

The flattering complement of *complete attention,* as indicated by this posture, is a valuable point in *listening* which is an important part of good conversation. Have you ever noticed that you really do put your head on one side when you are watching or listening to something in which you are intensely interested? You have, of course, observed that all animals, and children as well as grown-ups, put their heads first on one side and then on the other when they are regarding somebody or something that piques their *absorbed interest.* You may recall the little dog before a phonograph, listening to "His Master's Voice." His ears were "cocked" and his head was on one side indicating his alert interest and complete attention. In all matters, if we will stay close to the *natural* reaction, we will have real conviction in what we say and do.

Aside from the health value and the better appearance of good posture, it also has psychological value beyond the telling. So get a good posture, and expand your "treasure chest"! The additional oxygen you will take in will help to *clear your head,* thus enabling you to *think more quickly,* to be more *alert,* thus more *tactful* and more *poised.* Never forget that the suggestion given by your posture is just as effective on yourself, your own mood and feeling, as it is on others. And if you wish your conversation to fall with force on others' ears, it must be fraught with force from within yourself. By force I do not mean loudness or overemphasis. I mean that it must carry conviction and life if it is to awaken conviction and life.

Breathing for speech is much like breathing for singing. It is impossible to take in quickly through the nostrils alone breath enough for a long phrase or sentence. So, while speaking or singing, breathe with the mouth open a trifle—the merest bit will do. This opening can be scarcely perceptible. Avoid a gasping look. See that your shoulders do *not* go up and down as you breathe. Posture should *raise* the chest and breath *expand* the ribs. Neither should move the shoulders.

One is not aware of the breathing of a good singer or speaker, but to see some people struggle with air is to witness physical gymnastics that no lady would indulge in before an audience of one or one thousand. There is a smooth effortlessness in any good performance, no matter what or where.

There is an undeniable charm in the broken-up-by-breathing-and-giggling talk of a child or schoolgirl under eighteen, but beyond that age it is merely untutored, uncouth and silly. No one with any claim to poise will permit herself to breathe in gasps. Since *breath is life,* one's control of breathing is very apt to indicate one's control of life. When a pupil sits before me the first time, she is often amazed that I can tell her so much about herself after watching her for a moment or two. One woman thought I was a fortune-teller. But I was merely reading from her posture and her breathing the facts they betrayed.

To a discerning person nothing is hidden. And even to those less discerning consciously, our outward expressions carry emotional impressions more potent than mere logic. *An impression of poise is given only when the breath is even and without jerks, gasps or flutters.* A sentence that carries the assurance of the well-bred person rides out of the mouth on an unbroken stream of air. The words, though each is clearly enunciated, as perfectly made and finished as a pearl, follow each other with a smooth connection.

*A SENTENCE IS LIKE A STRING OF PEARLS.* The string is the necessary unbroken stream of breath, the pearls being the words that are strung upon it, lying closely and *comfortably* touching one another. But first we must have the even stream of air, the string.

*SPEAK ON AN EVEN STREAM OF AIR.* An exercise that will quickly help you to school your breath in just the proper way is to blow slowly and evenly through your pursed lips. Or better yet, get some ordinary soda-fountain straws and tear them into four-inch lengths. Put a length into your mouth as you would a cigarette, except that it must be in the center of your lips. Now place a forefinger in front of the straw, but not quite touching it, and blow your breath *slowly* out through the straw. With your finger you can judge whether you are expelling the air evenly. When you need more air, part the lips slightly and breathe in through mouth and nose. Then repeat the exercise. Do this ten times twice a day, more often if you have the time. This exercise accomplishes a number of fine results. From it you gain *breath control.* You begin to be conscious of the lips as the focus of speech, which will help to prevent you from trying to articulate back in your mouth and throat as the average person does. Once you become *really lip-conscious* most of your voice troubles and your pronunciation difficulties will be at least half over. But we are getting a little ahead of the point here.

*MAKE YOUR DIAPHRAGM DO THE WORK.* In expelling the air from the lungs *use your diaphragm* as your bellows. The diaphragm is located between the lower ribs. To be sure you are breathing from the diaphragm put your hand over it and say "Ha" in a very breathy and explosive manner. *Repeat* it several times. If your hand feels the muscles draw *in* as they push the breath *out,* you are breathing correctly.

If you are breathing and speaking independently of these muscles, you are not getting the value of your voice. So put them into use *consciously* and soon you will be doing so *unconsciously. Rich tones can be produced only with a body breath.* The cold, flat, tinny tones of the disagreeable, or at best uninteresting, voice are the result of shallow breathing, tight throat and cold head-breathing. The body-breath seems to have been *warmed* by your own heart and it vibrates with emotional overtones that are magnetic, warm, human, sympathetic. This breath is an absolute carrier of your finer impulses.

*SHALLOW BREATHING SHOWS UNEASINESS.* What you say with a body breath behind it seems literally to come *straight from the heart.* Your words seem to have borrowed warmth from the heart as the breath rides past it. When we are greatly stirred by beauty, laughter or sorrow we nearly always breathe from deep in our bodies. Fear, dread, hurt, feelings of inferiority and inadequacy are invariably expressed in shallow breathing. Therefore, if we wish always to give the impression of living fully, of being keenly sensitive to life, of being greatly alive, we should cultivate deep and rhythmic breath. A little attention to the exercises to accomplish this breath will suffice. The correct way, after all, is so much *less trouble* and so much less exhausting than the incorrect way. We are required to give persistent attention for a brief time only at the start to establish the correct way.

*YOU WANT A FLEXIBLE VOICE.* You will quickly gain a steady and controlled breath—then you will find that you have a flexible instrument that you can bend, mold and modulate to express every shade of feeling. A tight head-voice is unwieldy—but a relaxed body-breath voice can have a great variety of tones.

*KEEP YOUR THROAT FROM INTERFERING.* Now let us dispose of the throat with one fell swoop. The only office of the throat in good voice production is to *stay out of the way.* It is merely a place through which the breath passes on its way in and out. The throat and the head are only sounding boxes. The best way to help your vocal throat is to relax it and to enlarge it with yawning. The throat of a good singer or speaker is a large cavity.

*THINK OVER THE MECHANICS.* Now think of the stream of your breath as coming from the diaphragm—coming out along the floor of your throat and mouth. The only muscles that should be used in articulation are those of the tip of the tongue and the lips. The voice that "doesn't carry very far" is usually articulated in the throat. *Do not use your throat at all in speech!* Practice using your lips in an exaggerated way to be sure you are using them instead of your throat for articulation.

## 2. YOUR SPEECH DESIRES

Perhaps the next point of importance is to be sure that what we have to express is *worthy of expression.* You want to be a good conversationalist, I hope, because you want to be thoroughly at home and in genuine accord with other people of fine expression. You feel that you should live life on as high a plane as possible, mentally and spiritually as well as socially. And you want, I hope, more than the "loaves and fishes" of material and worldly gains through better contact with others in conversation, the æsthetic joys of *doing something well—* to enjoy the pure art involved.

This latter motive will enrich the mind and heart, the best assurance of good conversation. While on the other hand, if one regards the art as merely a scheme to gain one's own way and material advantages, the selfishness of such an attitude impoverishes the very talent we are striving to nourish. At least in part we should strive for *beauty for beauty's sake,* rather than for admiration—in speech as well as elsewhere.

## 3. THE SIMPLE INTRODUCTION

It seems logical to begin our actual conversational instruction with the subject of introductions. The correct forms of introduction and all points of etiquette should be reviewed in my book, "The New Etiquette." However, we will touch a few of them here that bear directly on getting the right start conversationally.

I am sure you *never* introduce a woman to a man, but always present the man to the woman regardless of age, unless the man is a

Cardinal or ruler. And who does not know the one formal expression, "Mrs. Smith, may I present Mr. Jones?"

But the usual and continually acceptable form on every occasion is merely to call the names of the persons you are introducing, looking at each as you speak the name, mentioning the woman's name first, "Mrs. Smith, Mr. Jones." Or, if Mrs. Smith has two daughters with her, "Mrs. Smith, may I present Mr. Jones to you and your daughters." After Mrs. Smith has acknowledged the introduction, she glances from the man to her daughters and says, if one of them is married, "My daughter Mrs. Angel," and glancing to the unmarried one she adds simply—"My other daughter—Alice, this is Mr. Jones." *This does not give Mr. Jones the right to call her by her first name.*

Do not call your own daughter or your husband Mr. or Miss except to servants. Say, "Mrs. Jones, my husband—or my daughter." Neither does a man refer to his wife as "Mrs." except to a servant. He says, simply, "My wife." Even when the man is the guest of honor, and a distinguished one at that, he is still *presented to the ladies.*

*ONLY OCCASIONAL ROUND-ROBIN INTRODUCTIONS.* Most of you nice people do not parade a guest around a large room introducing him or her to everyone. One introduces several people near at hand so he will have someone to talk to and lets the other introductions occur when he finds himself with others he has not met. A guest who has just met the stranger is at liberty to introduce him to others, when it seems desirable. Under a mutual friend's roof people may talk without introductions. If they wish they may introduce themselves.

In a small room where one need not shout to speak to everyone present, where there are only a few people present *and* there is only one conversation going on, the new-comer may meet everyone in the room from one position, shaking hands with those near—merely bowing to those a little farther removed.

It is the woman's privilege to extend her hand to a man or not, as she wishes. There is no offense in her not doing so. Usually she does not extend her hand. (Do as you like. There is no rule.) The man must not extend his hand first to a woman—but he always shakes hands with a man.

A hostess extends her hand to each arriving guest. The guest, as a rule, extends her hand on leaving. Never say, except for some very special reason, "I want you to meet Mrs. Jones." Never say, "Let me introduce you—" or "Meet Mr. Jones."

## 4. OPENING CONVERSATION

Most of us are familiar with the idea of giving *some little clue to the interests of the people we introduce* so that they may start talking more easily. But it is such an important point that it bears repetition. *Bring out the strongest point of probable mutual interest.* "Mrs. Smith, Mrs. Jones." They both say, "How do you do?" (This is the only known acceptance of an introduction. There is no use trying to vary it.) You continue the instant both of them have spoken. "Mrs. Jones would be so interested in your collection of old etchings, Mrs. Smith, for she has written a book about etchings." Or, "Mrs. Jones used to live in the old Parker place when she was a girl." Or, "Mrs. Jones is a dear friend of Amy Wadsworth." Or, "Mrs. Smith is a cousin of your devoted friend, Amy."

I was very much amused one day when a pupil said, "And then what do you say after that? I met a man from Cuba the other night. My hostess explained that he was connected with the sugar plantations down there, then turned away and left us. All I could think of was, 'How do you do? I take two lumps.' So of course, I didn't say anything." As a matter of fact her remark might not have been bad. Sometimes little, unexpected, amusing things are far more stimulating to talk than the merely "correct" thing.

*THE AWFUL PROBLEM OF "I."* Graciousness dictates, however, that one *leave reference to oneself out of conversation as much as possible.* Few people ever learn to handle the personal allusion with skill. There is something so attractive about the pronoun "I" that once the inexperienced talker gets on the subject he doesn't know how to get off. If one can adroitly mention "I" and veer the talk to another topic or point before an answer is necessary, its use often adds *conviction* and *verve* to a discussion. Perhaps the best way is to learn to talk *without* "I" and then gradually mix it back into your conversation in small and homeopathic doses. After all, it isn't so much *what* we do and say as *how* we do and say it.

Let's return to the tongue-tied girl and the man from Cuba. As she said nothing, in all probability he said, "You have been to Cuba?" She could have answered, "Yes. It's heavenly down there—when it's peaceful." He—"It is heavenly anywhere there is peace." She—"That remark indicates that you are either a bad soldier or a pacifist."

Note that in her first remark she avoided answering his personal question with "I"—also, her second remark put him, even though amusingly, *on the defensive,* where a woman should always have a man, at least in their first few conversations. For a man on the defensive wishes to prove himself. Naturally he wants his "accuser" for an audience.

*MEN USUALLY ARE AMUSED WHEN ON THE DEFENSIVE.* A girl can keep herself supplied with beaux by this simple method, though different men will react in different ways, and for varying lengths of time, to this type of stimulation. As a rule a very important man enjoys the woman who *can* put him on the defensive. The young inexperienced man reacts similarly but for a different reason. He thinks he *must* prove himself.

*SYMPATHY VERSUS CHALLENGE.* The man who responds to sympathy rather than challenge is usually someone who needs the sympathy, either because of tragedy in his life, failure in school, illness or some business struggle. Sooner or later, in every friendship with a man, the girl must take the sympathy "tack," but he is more apt to feel stimulated at once by her if, in their early acquaintance, she challenges him. *All spirited conversation is challenging to something or somebody*. Challenge is a good opening anywhere. We will elaborate on this idea later.

Note also that her last remark gave him his choice of three topics to discuss: 1. He can talk about himself—which he probably will do— 2. Soldiering, or 3. Idealism. A good rule for yourself is: *Listen for an impersonal subject in your conversational partner's first or second remark and snatch it before it floats away in a stream of personal nothings*. For example:

Mr. Brown, an average, tactless, well-meaning young man who presents many conversational dilemmas in his efforts to be agreeable, has just been introduced to Miss White. Mr. Brown—"I've heard so much about you."

One can answer with the usual bromide, "I hope it was all good," which will be quite all right. But it is certainly a little more imaginative to say something like, "A reputation is usually based on trifles." Or, "I hope you were duly credulous." Or, "My faith in my friends is perfect and my enemies may do their worst."

If the young man (or anyone, for that matter) goes on with the complimentary hearsay one may say, "Your informers (or call them by name) were very kind." Or, "Mary is so lovely herself, that she looks at everyone and sees her own reflection." Or, "What a heartening thing to hear about oneself. Thank you for telling me."

Never seem deliberately to dodge mentioning yourself or to object to an allusion to yourself, but get off the subject as quickly as you can do so without too much obvious effort. Mr. Brown continues, "Now that I've met you I know it is all true. I wasn't told half enough." One can only flash the young man a brief, but not coy or flirtatious, smile of reward and answer, "All of which reminds me how much there is to know about ——." This blank can be filled in with a subject of current or personal interest.

You have taken the first possible opportunity to switch the talk. You might have switched earlier if you wished by going from the mention of the name of his "informer" to some activity or attribute of this person. If in the early conversation Mr. Brown had said something like, "There really should be some pomp and ceremony to welcome you, but the only drums we could find are our palpitating hearts. Can you hear them?"

Then one might take the first IMPERSONAL word as a cue, saying, "Of course I can hear them! Speaking of pomp and ceremony, you should have seen the elaborate manners of my Pullman porter on this trip." Everyone will immediately remember some story of his own experiences with porters and the talk may last all evening. There are so many such stories! I do not mean to advocate porters as a preferred subject of discussion, but it is one of common experience. All such topics are rich sources of sustained talk.

Always try to introduce something of *common experience*—or go to the opposite extreme and speak of something extraordinary and unusual. The common experience brings about a feeling of kinship at once and knits together in spirit everyone within earshot. The extraordinary and unusual topic stimulates wonder and calls for strongly expressed opinions which help very much in relieving self-consciousness.

Let us consider other ways of opening conversation. Suppose the person or persons you are meeting are strangers, that your introduction has been a mere calling of names and you have no clue to their interests—nothing on which to base a start. You have said, "How do you do?" There is a moment of silence. Evidently you are the one who must begin. You envy the Kentucky mountaineer's custom of looking suspiciously at a stranger and demanding that he state his business at once. However, this is not your privilege in good society. You have a choice of three ways, as a rule, to start to talk. It is well to have all of them ready so that you can use them alternately if you are meeting a large group of people:

FIRST, and always dependable, is a brief remark about the weather. Regardless of how many jokes you have heard on this subject, it remains a topic of continual discussion everywhere. "Unusually warm today, isn't it?" or "It seems quite chilly today, doesn't it?" or "Well, everyone is grateful for the rain." Or, "What a surprising change we've had in temperature! One scarcely knows how to dress for such weather," and similar remarks are heard daily. Since humanity is more or less at the mercy of the weather, there is no way to avoid it as a conversational subject—and no one wants to do so.

SECOND, and equally popular, is a brief allusion to someone who is either present or expected to be present. "Have you seen Mr. Jones about?" Or, if you have just bowed to Mr. Jones, "Remarkable man!" Or, if you have just bowed to Mrs. Jones, "Mrs. Jones is such a darling —or so wonderful—or so heroic! Do you know about the splendid things she has done for the —— cause?" The only risk here is that you may be talking to the sister or brother of her divorced husband—and they would scarcely enjoy hearing her praises sung. However, such a chance is remote, and in any event an enthusiasm for another person is very becoming.

THIRD, and useful at all times as well as for a beginning, is to show eagerness for more news of some current excitement occupying the public attention or that of your group at the moment. "I wonder if *you* have heard any further developments on the —— matter." Or, "Are you as interested in the outcome of —— as the rest of us are?" This last one always fits in.

*HAVE A LONG LIST OF SHORT EJACULATIONS.* Then of course, the short ejaculation is always a comfortable reliance. "Lovely party!" "Wonderful voice!" "Interesting place!" "Pretty child!" "Divine music!" "What a night!" "Perfect garden!" "Grand game!" "Good riding!" "Smooth playing!" I often ask my pupils to write down a list of twenty-five such ejaculations for opening wedges and for silences. It is a splendid idea to do so, and to repeat it at intervals.

An amusing woman looked anxiously at a celebrated man she had just met and said, "I don't think you are having a good time. Come over here and sit down with me and we'll play guessing games. That will be fun." Of course it takes courage for a woman to say such a thing to a great man, *but I have yet to meet a "great" or any other kind of man who doesn't enjoy being treated as if he were a little boy.* The only exception is the young man who is really a little boy and wants to be treated like a great man. To him, say "MR." very loudly and listen gravely to his opinions, nodding your head occasionally in agreement with his sage remarks.

English women understand so perfectly how to treat young people with the dignity they love—even though they may have had a pillow fight fifteen minutes before. We Americans are so apt to rate the young by their lowest level of expression rather than by their highest. Europeans make allowances for human lapses and permit people to climb back on their dignity. Over here, it took Will Rogers years and years to convince us that comedy can be profound, whereas we have always slyly hoped that the profound might be comic.

In some instances the opening of a conversation is a sort of sparring match to see which of the two contestants can find out the most personal facts. It isn't exactly good taste anywhere and is positively dangerous in places where some of the guests are celebrities whose faces are not familiar to you. Questions like, "Is this your first visit here?" and "Do you intend to remain here long?" are asked only by impatient members of the rocking-chair brigade at summer resorts. Naturally a hostess trying to arrange an entertaining program for a guest might ask if the guest were familiar with the countryside and the diversions it afforded.

If you have a motive in asking for personal information, state that motive so that your questions do not sound prying. But never bother to explain beyond a simple statement of your purpose. Never say, "I hope you don't think I'm prying."

It is poor taste to assume that your hearer is critical of you. The assured person is careful not to go beyond certain lines in making personal remarks and never apologizes for what he says or does unless it is definitely rude. *The assured person never belittles himself, compelling his hearer to dash to his rescue.* This last point is very important.

*WHEN YOU CAN'T THINK OF A SUBJECT.* One clever girl, when she finds an opening remark failing her, turns frankly to her partner of the moment and says engagingly, "What would *you* like to talk about?" or "What shall we talk about?" The only unfortunate aspect of this question is that a man always feels compelled to answer, "You." Then the girl spends as much thought getting off that subject gracefully as she would have had to expend in getting on an impersonal subject in the first place.

If he happens to answer with the mention of some very intellectual or scientific subject, she can say, "Then you'll have to do all the talking and I shall probably learn a great deal. I can't even remember whether a molecule is larger than an atom, or the reverse." Or if she is familiar with his subject she might say, "How fortunate, I've just majored in that—or just finished reading a book about it." or "Blank's book on the subject is very stimulating. Do you agree with the theory that . . . ?"

Naturally, if you are a guest for the first time in a house, and have been invited there because you are a friend of one of the family, you will be asked politely inquisitive questions, which are nothing more than a *show of interest* in what manner of life you lead at home. Usually people are eager to know if you deserve the affection of their own loved one. This desire is very natural. Instead of resenting it, you should, as quickly as possible, tell as much of the relevant facts of yourself, your people and your background as you think would satisfy or interest them—never at any time stooping to brag or, on the other hand, to assume a false modesty. So, of course, you must talk about yourself. If you are not proud of your background, never explain about it as though admitting you had an infectious disease. Just casually and frankly tell the facts about yourself.

Many of the wanted facts about your life can be given in anecdotes that spare you the feeling of being cross-examined or of being compelled to give a police record of yourself. For instance, you can almost at once say, "What a lovely cat! So much like the one Mother had at the beach place this summer. We had gone from Chicago where we live to —— and we inherited this cat with the rented place. Mother, my sister Mary, Ted, the baby of the family and I were there for some time before Father and my older brother, Ken, joined us. By the time they arrived we had taken the cat as one of us and named it "Also." We stayed down there an extra month partly because we disliked to leave the cat and partly because rents were a little cheaper than last year."

Naturally, you would *never* mention money directly, except to people who have the right to know whether you have much or little. Do not speak of the cost of things unless to gloat occasionally over a bargain, but even this must not be overdone. It is a safe rule to leave money out of conversation. In anecdotes you may tell as much or as little of yourself as you wish.

Emily Post suggests an actual personal sketch of oneself as a solution to the question of opening conversation with someone about whom one knows nothing. Her example is refreshing and amusing, as well as helpful. "I live in the country all the year round. I have three small children. I am interested in gardening and I love music. My recreation is hunting, and reading all the new novels. My husband neither neglects me nor misunderstands me. Now tell me about you!" Such an opening would certainly simplify what is now a mysterious art to most people. A further simplification would be to add, "I am an ardent Christian Scientist—or Catholic or ——." Or, "We subscribe to no particular religion. We are devoted Republicans. And we are on the Hay diet." Then plenty of talk should be available, likes and dislikes understood.

Yet, the real art of conversation lies in lighting a tiny blaze of interest in the minds of others that will burn without consuming any of the hair or skin or clothing of those who warm themselves at its flame. It is not quite mature to *depend* entirely upon personal facts to keep interest alive.

Children use the personal with un-self-conscious directness which is simple and charming. Grown-ups are often better off when they remain equally simple and direct. A child will eye a new child and his next impulse is exhibitionism. Often his first remark will be, "Look how far I can jump." Or, "Watch me climb that wall." Or, "I'll bet you can't do this."

Conversation, today, is by no means the formal circumscribed matter of other years. Spontaneity seems to be the god worshipped by the younger set. Therefore a wave of candor, of extreme frankness, seems to have possessed them utterly. When it is tempered by their really electric intelligence and the innate kindness of gentle people it seems very sensible as well as stimulating. I have heard a young girl say to a man whom she had just met, "You've a job before you. We don't match as we are. Either you must convert me to your pleasant mood or I shall probably drag you into my glowering one." To state a difference, which is not a rude one, always stimulates talk.

*SOMETIMES SURPRISING CANDOR IS DELIGHTFUL.* At a formal dinner a distinguished man answered his partner of the moment with, "But, you are not the type of person to hold such views. You have surprised me and I don't quite like it." He was amused and delighted when the woman replied with equal candor, "At the moment my views are influenced by two very tight shoes." He laughed, "Enough to bias anyone's opinions. Perhaps it's going to rain. My left foot is giving me fits too." And he continued to talk in the most absorbed comfortable fashion.

Later, in the drawing-room his hostess said to him, "I've never seen you so interested in a young woman. What in the world were you talking about?" He looked at her solemnly and said, "We were discussing the influence of one extremity upon another." To which she replied, "Well, Man's extremity is God's opportunity." And he answered, "At least I have had the opportunity to talk with one completely honest and natural woman. I consider that God-given." She said, "Don't you think it would be nice if each of us knew what the other meant?" He answered, "Not especially. I never consider it necessary to inquire deeply into the motives or meaning of those I trust." She said, "Then you trust me?" He bowed, "Certainly." She smiled, "That's too bad. Too much responsibility." He said, "You don't like responsibility?" She answered, "That's beside the point. I don't like to be pigeon-holed." He said, "The trouble with you nice women nowadays is that you want to eat your cake and have it too." At this point they were interrupted and she asked her next vis-à-vis, "Do *you* think that modern 'nice' women like to eat their cake and have it too?"

This conversation is quoted at length to show you the *ease and humor* with which sophisticates say what they please, toss the personal back and forth like a tennis ball, with a general topic so closely in the background that one can hardly tell whether they are really discussing themselves or just using themselves as a screen against which to throw their pictures. *Small talk usually smacks of this smartly impersonal persiflage.*

## WORDS TO WATCH

The question of accent and particularly the sounding of the letter *a* which "places" one as English, Western, Southern, Bostonian or whatever, is always a moot question, but we may as well deal with it and get it settled in our minds. To take the middle path is to be inconspicuous and to fit in with anyone from anywhere. I happen to admire the broad *a* of the English and the Virginians, who really brought it over from England. Though I was taught it by my parents and my Virginia grandparents as a child, I learned, as I grew up, that in the rest of America, it was considered an affectation.

*THE MIDDLE "A" IS BEST.* I have found a nice compromise by pronouncing the *a* in words like *half, calf, afternoon, can't* and *bath* as I pronounce the *a* in *at* which is a little more soft and round than it is usually spoken, but is not broad enough to attract notice.

Nothing places one so quickly as the pronunciation of *water,* which all really cosmopolitan people sound as though the first syllable were *awe* with a *w* in front of it—*wawt-uh,* accenting the first syllable.

The word *educate* may be more commonly pronounced *ejucate,* as given in the dictionary, but, more often than not, cultivated people pronounce it as it is spelled, *ed-u-cate,* with no suggestion of a *j* sound.

Also the word *detail* is pronounced *deTAIL.*

The most common expression of quick apology in England and in cosmopolitan centers where English is spoken is the single word "Sorry." The length of time and emphasis one gives to it indicates the gravity of the offense. It suffices instead of the moot "PARdon me or Pardon ME!"

Also, the well-bred cosmopolite never accepts the slightest courtesy, even that of someone's moving aside to let her by, without a word of gratitude, "Thank you." However, most of the time it is so cool and so brief that it becomes the mere syllable "—cue," the word "thank" merely being given time in space, as it were, but no articulation. It is one of those rare instances where the rule of perfect pronunciation is broken. Though, remember that there are still old-fashioned ladies who abbreviate nothing!

# CHAPTER TWO

## *Get Ready to Talk*

The desire to be capable of the best self-expression in speech is a splendid motive that drives one to sharpen one's tools for the making of good conversation—but cold perfection will never warm the hearts of your hearers. You must strike the spark of *animating warmth* born of a pulsing human *urge to share* what you feel.

This spark comes from the fires of a burning desire to draw closer to the mind and heart of your neighbor, to give him solace when it is needed, encouragement and sympathy always, also *gay laughter* to brighten his spirits and to lighten his load. And when I say "neighbor" I do not mean merely that person whom you would like to cultivate for social or material reasons. I refer to *every life that touches yours*.

*ALWAYS END ON A NOTE OF ENCOURAGEMENT.* If your words and your manner do not shed light as you walk through life, you are misusing or failing to use the power of language. If faces brighten, backs straighten, chins go up as you approach you will know that your words have been found lightening, heartening, constructive. As you create this atmosphere for others, you automatically bask in it yourself, and life has a richness, a sweetness and fullness that satisfies your heart.

The loveliest pool must have an outlet if it is to stay fresh and lovely. Learn to *give* the treasures of your thoughts and reactions and to *accept* eagerly those of your friends.

*CULTIVATE AN ENJOYMENT OF CONVERSATION* if you wish to talk well. Let your character, your impulses and your desires *flow out to others* in a charming freedom of words, unhampered by the chilling, binding, deadening grip of self-consciousness and that awful "back and forth" wondering how your words sound to others. Don't talk unless you have something to say; and *if you know your words to be kind,* sensible, appreciative, and neither boastful nor critical, speak freely. Often the strange little thought that "scurries across the mind like a frightened mouse only to disappear into a hole" is a charming little whimsy that should be captured.

"Think before you speak" is not half as valuable to a talker as "Feel before you speak." To be sure, thoughtless, cruel people *should* think before they speak, but I am addressing this lesson to those quite capable, thoroughly kind persons who crowd words back from their lips when they should be spoken—also to those who through timidity or lack of practice never get their words even that far. Silence is golden only when one should be listening, meditating or protecting the confidence of someone else. *It is through speech that we come to know and be known.*

*WHEN SHE LEARNS HOW TO TALK* a chatterbox will talk less. Likewise, one ceases to fidget and to have awkward mannerisms when one learns to dance and to control and use the body with *understanding and grace.* We do not wish to be so consciously perfect that our hearers "spot" us at once as people striving for perfection. We must never lose sight of the fact that speech is utilitarian and is meant to serve the purpose of *conveying ideas.* If a bit of slang (the tiniest bit) expresses what you mean, then use it.

*DON'T BE STUDIEDLY PERFECT.* Do not let study and *awareness of words* make you stilted or overcareful when you speak. To do so will rob you of spontaneity which is the charm of conversation.

*DO NOT LISTEN TO YOURSELF TALK* except when you are exercising in private, but do plenty of that. Also as you find greater fluency, beware of "showing off." The temptation is very great to overexercise a new accomplishment. And others quickly feel that you think you are quite excellent and are *comparing* them with yourself to their disadvantage. Charm flies instantly!

> "A little murder now and then,
> A little bit of burglarizing,
> Won't earn the hate of fellow-men
> As much as being patronizing."

*DON'T ADVERTISE YOUR VIRTUES.* To quote H. L. Mencken: "The moment a man lets it be known that he has more in his head than the general, they (the common people) begin to scrutinize him with sharp and bilious eyes and if the chance ever offers—and it usually does, for he always does something foolish soon or late—they fall upon him with loud hallelujahs, and, in the vulgar phrase, 'tie a can to him.'"

*DON'T BELITTLE YOURSELF. But* to belittle oneself, or one's situation or belongings, reminds us of the Chinese story of the man whose guest, standing in his garden with him, admired the moon. Whereupon the host said, "Oh, no! You embarrass me with your generosity. This is only the common moon of my poor hovel." He should have said, "Yes, isn't it beautiful?" "We are so fortunate to have it. I'm glad you like it. It gives us a great deal of pleasure." Any such remarks are equally appropriate when any aspect or privilege of one's situation is under complimentary discussion.

*BE TRUE TO YOURSELF* and do not lower your standard of talk to fit others. As G. K. Chesterton says, "There is more simplicity in the man who eats caviar on impulse than in the man who eats breakfast food on principle." Avoid, at all times, a studied and artificial attitude and speech. Naturally, in learning any new thing there is that first period of *extreme awareness* which passes off shortly as we grow accustomed to it. We shall always be learning if we are open-minded men and women. Therefore, we shall always be faced with the necessity of needing a *proper manner* with which to try our new ideas and discoveries.

The best manner is one of frank curiosity and interest in what is new to you.

Above all, do not pretend to be something you are not or to know something you do not know.

A certain woman was trying to pretend by inference that she knew England very well, though she had never been there. A friend spoke of the Church of England and the pretending woman said, "Oh, isn't it beautiful, so majestic, standing there in London like a sentinel of souls!" Naturally everyone within earshot laughed. It was as though someone had complimented the Methodist church in America. The woman was so embarrassed when she realized that her pretense was exposed that she left the town.

I once knew a man who said that Socrates was his favorite philosopher and often quoted him or so he thought. But the cat was out of the bag one day when he made the mistake of referring to the *writings* of Socrates. Socrates left not one written word, that has come down to us. We know him through the writings of Plato.

*PRETENSE KILLS THE EMANATION OF WARM SINCERITY* that draws others to us, and often makes us objects of ridicule. On the other hand, a better type of speech is almost always a more correct presentation of the good qualities of the average person.

So many perfectly worthy men and women leave speech to chance and therefore underrate themselves every time they open their mouths. Sometimes I think that good, clear, correct speech is like a pipe-line that carries fresh water from the spring of life—and that we may have just as much and give just as much of this life-giving refreshment as we provide the pipe for. *Our speech is the channel through which we both attract and give the best things of life.*

*LEARN NOT TO BE EMBARRASSED* over a mistake or a faux pas you may make. Remember that all human beings make mistakes and you have just as much right to make yours as the next person. And write it down on your cuff that no matter how perfect and formidable any person may seem to be, his path has been strewn with mistakes. Learn to laugh at your mistakes, to acknowledge them and *go on.* If you do this people will laugh *with* you, not *at* you.

*PEOPLE RATE YOU AS YOU RATE YOURSELF.* Remember the princess who fell during an impressive ceremony but because she was un-self-conscious and treated the matter so casually *she saved the whole party embarrassment?* This illustrates the point that people invariably put the same construction on your acts (and on your life) that you put on them. If *you behave* as though you had made an unforgivable error, you *convince others* that you have. If you remain relaxed and regard it as just a natural, human thing to have done, others will regard your mistake or whatever, in that same light. The average person is so self-centered that, ordinarily, he gives little or no energy to analyzing another's situation. Consequently, he follows lines of least resistance and takes his cue from the other person. Practically always!

*DON'T HAVE A BARE CONVERSATIONAL CUPBOARD.* Resolve here and now that you will *never again* say, "I just don't know what to reply when someone says so and so to me." You would not say this unless you had experienced *a number of times* the awkwardness of having no answer. No woman would permit her bread box to remain empty if she went to it time and again and found nothing in it. Yet many men and women permit their conversational cupboards to stay bare. They seem to live with the vague hope that some day words and sentences will pop out of it even though they have put none in. Unfortunately, this hope is not founded on fact. Before another day passes over your head—sit down with a pencil and paper and *write several replies to all the awkward questions and conversational dilemmas that repeat themselves in your experiences.* You can start with the list of questions given at the end of this chapter.

*IT PAYS TO FORCE YOUR THOUGHTS INTO WORDS ON PAPER.* Even though you may never use exactly what you write, you will have gained the boon of greater facility in expression. Most of us think of such clever things to say after the opportunity to say them has passed. If one can think of a good answer at *any* time it is possible to think of it at the *right* time. Practice is the only way in the world to gain quickness in transposing a situation into thought and thought into words.

Before you appear in public you have groomed yourself—you have put on clothes that you planned thoughtfully—obtained them by laborious shopping or standing for long fittings. You have prepared yourself to be pleasant-looking. Since so much of your attraction for others is based on the smoothness with which you handle the small but important problems of conversation, isn't it rather stupid not to have some *equally careful preparation* for them?

*WRITE OUT* replies not only to the questions that "stump" you continually—but *make up imaginary ones.*

If a man should tell you how beautiful you are—what would you say? Write your answer and rehearse it. If it sounds silly to you—change it until you are satisfied that you would acquit yourself with un-self-consciousness, fitting appreciation and a *deft turn of the talk away from yourself*. You might say, for example—"Thank you. What a pleasant person you are! Everything seems to be pleasant today, in spite of the weather." To which the young man could reply, "I don't mind being classed with the weather if you will admit that I, too, am unusual."

It will be well to bear in mind that we are studying the *principles* of conversation and that the actual remarks I give you are but *illustrations* of the points involved. You will note that my examples take a light, amusing, pleasant turn if possible.

To be sure, there are times when one must be sympathetic and serious and these occasions will be discussed later as special subjects. The occasions where extreme seriousness is necessary are *rare*. The charming and popular person is the one who can be *depended upon for apt pleasantries*—at least in good society.

The very young people of today are, for the moment at least, taking themselves very seriously. Naturally, one must not joke with the pet subjects of these young Atlases who feel that they are carrying the world on their shoulders. To talk to these fledgling intellectuals one must brush up one's history, philosophy, modern art and social economics.

*THE MATURE POINT OF VIEW.* More mature people realize that the world has always been in a state of upheaval, change and growth—and while they are deeply concerned with the seriousness of the present changes, they refuse to allow any condition to change their own mellow tolerance for the chaos we call life, which they have found deeply poetic, romantic and more than a little funny. They feel that people who see life from one little crack in their minds are *immature* and somewhat *fanatic*. So unless you have a flair amounting to genius for some special cause *keep your attitude toward the world in a pleasantly fluid state*. Then you run less risk of being outdated by the rush of events. You run less risk of becoming brittle and unwieldy in personality and conversation.

*UNDERSTATEMENT IS MORE EFFECTIVE.* One of the many minor rewards of keeping our general attitudes in a "pleasantly fluid state" is that the resulting poise will *protect us from temptation to overemphasize.* Wouldn't it be nice if most of our acquaintances would clear their speech of opinionated overemphasis, which is very bad taste and leads subtly to exaggeration?

Haven't you at least one friend whose remarks you always discount because of her (or his) habit of laying too much stress on words to make them seem more important? Should that day ever arrive when she did not exaggerate you would have no way of knowing that you were hearing the truth. Knowing the lack of confidence you, yourself, have in this woman, I feel sure that you will not indulge in overemphasis and exaggeration.

If our usual conversation is based on truth, we inspire confidence, faith, love and respect. Not only that, but our listeners give each of our spoken words their true value, so that when we say something is "good" it will have more weight with them than if someone else shouted, "Marvelous!"

*A WORD SHOULD ALWAYS HAVE ITS FULL VALUE.* We can, by proper dramatic feeling about what we say, add to the effect of ordinary words. Later I shall have an entire lesson devoted to this phase of conversation. Now I am more concerned by its broader lines, its sweep of psychological effects.

*"DO YOU TALK TO HEAR YOURSELF TALK?"* If you should ask some voluble friend this question, you would, no doubt, offend him. Yet, many people talk for their own ears, rather than the feelings of others. But we, who are giving speech our attention, want our words to stir agreeable emotions in our listeners, so that they will seek us and be enchanted in our company. Sugary compliments are not always pleasing and one can easily become surfeited with sweets. Then what is our best dependence? The answer is—*stimulation through challenge.* But it should be used with *discretion.*

Everybody has noticed the naturalness of the child in greeting a newcomer with, "I'll bet you can't do this." The same thing in "grown-up" terms accomplishes the same result that it does for the child. Challenge of any kind helps to eliminate self-consciousness, because it brings *action* to the fore (if only in words). We are not nearly so apt to be self-conscious if there is *something to do.* Otherwise, we are afraid we are being misjudged and underestimated if other people are basing their opinions of us merely on our appearance.

The desire for action and accomplishment is really *man's defiance of his limitations!* Through action he flings his influence out as far as his ingenuity will permit. The "show-off" is a potentially powerful person, though somewhat misguided. These ideas will help to explain the popularity of games and puzzles. Each of them challenges us in some way.

"I'd tell you a secret, if I thought you deserved knowing it," is a challenge that can have amusing and interesting results. It can be said immediately after an introduction. The secret can be some trifle of the moment.

"I wonder if you are as nice as you seem to be," brought chuckles from a bishop, and, to my knowledge, he has spent years in trying to show how nice he is.

"To feel that one is understood always loosens the tongue. I could be very entertaining if I thought you could appreciate me," was the impudent opening of a conversation that ended in a wedding.

"A man of great courage and broad sympathies is needed now. Is such a man to be found?" This is a remark that can be used both seriously and frivolously.

"I have a dilemma for you—and our hostess has a cocktail. Which will you have first?" He will probably suggest that the cocktail will help him solve your dilemma.

Mark Twain, who knew the human heart in its sublimity as well as in its absurdity, has Tom Sawyer stand on his head to win his childhood sweetheart. Challenge, in one of its many phases, might prompt all the Tom Sawyers in the world to stand on their heads for their ladies. Believe me, they will be much more fascinated by your ability to cause them to *show their ability* than by all your beauty and wiles.

The principles outlined here are applicable not only to the genus male, but to every living person. All of us are children in that our emotions are untutored and immature. Therefore, we respond to these basic urges of our egos which are in conflict with our limitations.

The person whom we *stimulate to his best effort* and to whom we then *give admiration for that effort* will always come back—especially if we have been tactful, sympathetic and truly constructive in our motives.

It is quite possible to trap a man into matrimony by knowledge of his weaknesses. But such a procedure usually ends unhappily. Instead of starting out deliberately to trap a particular person, why not build your own character and self-expression to the point where you will *attract* a fine man—who will be a natural complement of yourself? What is gained through trickery is lost by the same means. Such a marriage is not worth having.

It is quite ethical to use any honorable means to add to your social life and your business advantage—but, in marriage, you want only what is *really yours*. Only in this way can you have peace and security. True, a strong woman often marries a man almost against his will and makes a man of him. But, she is the exception that proves the rule. Besides, the woman's motive may be largely unselfish. This case is quite different from those in which the woman is merely self-seeking.

*USE CHALLENGE*—as an opening remark with most men and with all children—except where through inability to meet your challenge your suggestion would be cruel. Do not use challenge in the process of a long, monotonous pull. Use it to spur a man on to his goal when he is exhausted but near the finish. Your challenge, then, is evidence of your faith in him. And usually, just a little more faith, just a little more effort and just a little more patience would take him to success. Some great man has said that most of us fail because we stop two feet from our goal. There is a great need for challenge in the right place in our lives.

*USE SYMPATHY* where there is a hunger for understanding—when it is time to comfort and soothe a friend and to "touch others' wounds with healing fingers." Use sympathy when someone's life-work is being discussed—to indicate your understanding of his problems—and in all conditions of ill-health. Sympathy is not necessarily pity. Its truest meaning is "to be in accord with" and "to share the feelings of" another. Thus we can show great sympathy for the winners in life as well as the losers.

The woman who can make others know that she feels as they feel, is a popular woman. Sympathy, in the sense of pity, is softening and destructive to men when carried too far. Pity should be saved for the very young and the very old. It eats at the self-respect of able-bodied men and women, even while they enjoy its brief comforts. It is well for us to understand the needs and wants of the human heart before we can essay to satisfy them with words.

Many a woman has wasted her life giving out sympathy where it was ill-considered—and she has been baffled by the lack of permanent good she has accomplished. Usually, such a woman attracts around herself a collection of weaklings, male and female, *and keeps them weak and soft by her misuse of sympathy*. One's own intuition must dictate the exact moment to turn on challenge—but in a general sense, use it when the performance of your children or friends is below par through lack of interest and mental energy.

We have seen that challenge is a stimulus to friendship in its earlier stages. It is also a stimulus to conversation that needs new life at any point. To challenge an idea in someone's remarks is not necessarily to disagree with him, but may mean also that you wish him to clarify a point, to cite his authority, or to prove his hypothesis. If one just agrees all the time there remains nothing to discuss and the talk comes to a sweetish and soggy stop. But if you say to Mr. Agreeable, "I don't understand your use of the phrase, 'the best there is.' Do you say that arbitrarily as your own opinion or do you mean that certain people of your acquaintance thought —— was the best there is?" you will not only stir up new comments from Mr. Agreeable, but you have also introduced the subject of opinions and how they are reached. With a group of fairly intelligent people this subject will last an entire evening.

In your own conversation be careful not to make broad statements that invite challenge, unless you like being on the defensive. It is always more courteous to say, "In my opinion" or "We always thought" or "Everyone seemed to agree that it was the best."

However, there are many times when an out-and-out statement of approval is more pleasing. If you are discussing something of great personal importance to one of your hearers, then you should not be slow to proclaim its goodness. "It seems to me" or any other hesitant statement of its virtues becomes a dubious compliment, a little worse than saying nothing. To be "damned by faint praise" is the most abysmal condemnation.

*DON'T SPLIT HAIRS TOO MUCH.* However, never confuse challenge with an annoying habit of splitting hairs which always takes the conversation out of its sweep and narrows it to lifeless minutiæ.

*IN BUSINESS,* using the principle of challenge and likewise inviting challenge sometimes gains a business advantage because most human beings react almost instantly to its touch. But old established firms of great dignity are more impressed by one's background of manner, character and "tone." They will usually prefer an approach like this: "Your Company has always been one of the verities in my life. My ambition has been to be a member of your staff. To this end I have made a study of your methods in the such-and-such department and feel that I am ready to serve you. Naturally you have been unaware of my deep accord with all that you stand for, but I know that after I have been with you for a time you will recognize the harmony between my abilities and your own aims."

*TALK ABOUT THEIR PLANS AND NEEDS FIRST.* Some psychologists teach that one should never introduce the pronoun "I" until the end of a business interview or letter. This idea is also splendid: "Since your —— department is the finest of its kind in the world, you naturally wish to keep it always the leader. You will be interested to know that certain tests have revealed an opportunity to step still farther ahead of your competitors. I shall be happy to give your firm the benefit of this information (or service) for it seems to belong to you. Moreover, it has always been my ambition to be allied with you."

Some clever salesmen and other men who are trying to put over a deal will save challenge for their final fling. It is really the most obvious attack but because it is so effective it is in constant use. Therefore, many people prefer to make a more dignified contact first, then later, if necessary, bring in the challenge.

*LISTEN TO YOUR SUCCESSFUL FRIENDS.* Bear in mind that the principles back of a good letter or introductory conversation will continue to hold good in your later conversations. It will behoove you to study closely the manner and conversation of your successful friends and to analyze them for the principles involved, though your friends may be unconscious of what they do. Then, using those same principles in your own way, you can meet your own problems with greater success.

*BUSINESS CONVERSATION AND LETTERS* are less stilted than formerly. In both of them avoid such expressions as "the above," "your letter to hand and contents noted," "yours of the fourteenth inst.," and any others that seem to indicate a desire for a lazy brevity. You can be concise without these indications of your wish to dismiss the matter as soon as possible.

Will Rogers said that whenever he got a letter with "dictated, but not read" at the bottom of it, he always sent it back to the writer in an envelope marked "opened, but ignored."

In spite of the popularity of the informal visiting card for brief messages, a folded note paper with but two lines written in the center of it is more gracious than scrawlings that crowd a correspondence card and leak over its edges. Such a card seems to shout, "Well, I had more to say to you than I thought I had." However, when traveling, some people do send their friends picture cards of the places they are visiting. These seem to be "in" again.

*DON'T BE A SUPERIOR TRAVELER.* Please, after you have studied with me, never return from a trip with that look of having become a triumphant thing apart from those at home. The most charming attitude of a returned traveler seems to say, "The nicest thing about traveling is coming home. Mary, one of the madonnas in the Sistine chapel looks just like you and she made me very homesick. Of course we had a marvelous time, but, oh, it's good to be home!"

*TAKE CAREFUL NOTE OF WHAT YOU SEE.* Learn, by practice, to describe what you see in your mind's eye. A good exercise to help you accomplish good descriptions and to acquire a ready use of adjectives is to force yourself to think of two descriptive words every time you look at any object or person. As you ride downtown, as you enter a building, as you stroll the countryside, wherever you are alone, mentally describe what you see. In your room at night before you turn out the lights let your eyes wander about the place, describing what you see. Look at your walls. Think, "high, plain." Look at a book. Think, "thick, red." Look at the curtains. Think, "heavy, soft." Look at your mirror. Think, "clear, truthful." Common words? Of course! But they paint pictures and this is what conversation is.

*A GOOD WRITER OR TALKER* merely forces himself to describe what the average person has never thought worthy of description. Most of the people we know recognize these ordinary adjectives when they see them, but they have no common use of them. Therefore they have no words when they would like to say something about ordinary, familiar things. Later there will be more about the use and abuse of adjectives.

A stimulating talker is able to make you see the object he is describing, to make you think his thoughts and to cause you to feel as he feels. He has trained his imagination to see quickly for him and thus he is able to describe quickly and with ease what his mind contains.

Thus he has the power of giving an accurate description which will protect him from the effusiveness which is the bad habit of the inexperienced or aimless talker.

*IMAGINATION IS VALUABLE* not because it creates what does not exist, but *because it develops the power of visualization,* without which one can describe nothing. Imagination gives color and ease to descriptions.

## WORDS TO WATCH

An important telltale error lies in not using a possessive pronoun before a present participle. How many, many times do you hear otherwise good English marred by this: "Imagine me doing that!" The correct way is: "Imagine my doing that!" Do not say—"Imagine him coming at this time!" The correct way is: "Imagine his coming ——." (The word "her" is both a possessive and an objective pronoun.) It will be clearer to you (in case you do not use the correct form) if you will understand that the coming, the doing, etc., are the acts of persons and as such belong to them; hence, the possessive, "my, his, her, its, their."

*Exquisite* is pronounced *EX-quisite,* accent on the first syllable.

*Perfume* is called *PER-fume,* accent on the first syllable. Never say *per-FUME.*

Never say *PRO-grum* when you mean *PRO-gram.*

Never say *tasty* when you mean *delicious. Tasty* is taboo!

Never *reside* anywhere—just *live* there.

The word *enough* should always come *after* the word it modifies. Never say, "We have *enough* bread." Say, "We have *bread enough.*" However, it is quite correct to say, "I have *enough,* thank you."

Unless you have been brought up in France, it is dangerous to use any French word when an English one will do. For instance, the word *lingerie* is almost impossible for an American to pronounce as the French do. Say *underclothes,* instead.

The correct pronunciation of *lingerie* is *lan-zhery*—with the accent on the first syllable. The *a* is sounded as in *at.* All too often one hears it as *long-zhe-ray.* The *n* should be almost omitted.

*Hors d'œuvres* is pronounced *or-DERVE.* The *s* is not sounded. This is one of the French words it is difficult to dodge.

By the way, *Roosevelt* is pronounced *ROSE-a-velt,* with the accent on the first syllable. The first four letters must not sound like the beginning of *rooster.* This name is very commonly mispronounced, and all members of this famous family are too polite to correct the person who pronounces their name as if it were *RUCE-velt.* But since you may meet some of them, it is well to remember that *ROSE-a-velt* is correct.

Do not correct other people if you hear them making this common error. They will probably not believe you. But if they hear you pronounce this word, or any other word, correctly just once, the chances are that they will remember it, will make some inquiries, and will follow your example.

And by the way how do you pronounce words like *new, institute, reduce, avenue, duty,* etc.? For all such pronunciations take the word *few* as your pattern. You would never dream of calling it *foo,* would you? Yet many people call the word *new* by the strange sound of *noo.* Even many New Yorkers call their town *Noo York.* These same tongues say *Dook* for *Duke* and never realize that they are putting themselves on a level with Jiggs of the funny paper. By eliminating a few vulgarisms the average person's pronunciation takes on a new interest. Usage may make *oo* acceptable.

As I suggested in this chapter, make a practice of *writing* your replies to questions that have found you speechless—also to imaginary ones. You may take the following list for a start. You should write this and similar exercises *as often as possible* with but one point in view —facility.

## WHAT WOULD BE YOUR REPLY TO THESE REMARKS?

1. "Don't you think your neighbors are dreadful people?"
2. "How much do you like me?" (A married flirt speaking.)
3. "Have you ever traveled in Switzerland?"
4. "Mr. President, this is my cousin, Miss —— ——."
5. "I've made an engagement with Mary, but I'd rather be with you."
6. "How does it feel to be the winner today?"
7. "My, but you're beautiful!"
8. "What makes you behave so strangely tonight?"
9. "You look tired. Aren't you well?"
10. "I'm sorry we couldn't have seen more of you while you were here."
11. "I think you're prettier than your sisters!"
12. "I love you!"

Put your answers away and save them until you have finished the book. Then turn back to this chapter and answer these questions again. It will be interesting and encouraging to you to note the difference in your replies.

# CHAPTER THREE

## *Helpful Speech Habits*

If you are really applying yourself, you are already experiencing greater ease in establishing *warm contact with other people through talk*. Please do the exercises religiously even if you think you do not need them. Inspect your foundations, repair them or enlarge them by doing all the things I ask you to do. My aim is not to give you a few tricks and suggestions, but to build within you the complete structure of charming conversational ability.

Often a pupil says, "I find myself out of place in talking to women of my own age. They are unable to discuss anything but clothes, the domestic machinery, the baby's antics, movie stars and cosmetics. They think I am trying to be 'highbrow' when I talk of anything else. What is one to do? Is the feminine mind really so earthbound and narrow that it cannot speak of something outside its daily experience?"

*ALL TRULY FINE MINDS CAN RELATE THE GREAT TO THE SMALL.* As a matter of fact, the subjects she mentioned are not bad starting points, for they are *common experiences* that invariably make talk easy. The learned one can, if she wishes, lead the conversation gently around to more abstract themes. Perhaps, if her mind is so "narrow" that it excludes babies and cosmetics, she may lack the human touch that alone can give warmth and meaning to theories.

*TAKE THE COMMONPLACE AND ENLARGE IT INTO WORLDWIDE ISSUES.* In doing so you give your hearers a fine feeling of importance, which, in turn, makes them more receptive to other large ideas. Without once offending the woman of "little" interests you can help her to a broader vision of life and therefore conversation. She will feel that you see her as the romantic, dramatic figure she really is—a torchbearer—a tender of the fires of human continuity, human faith—the maker of a home, that sacred cradle of human destiny. Such an attitude will not only stimulate her but will give you her undying friendship and loyalty. After all, *what are friends but those who see us through magnifying glasses slightly tinged with rose?*

Suppose a woman insists upon telling you what an expense her children are. You can say sympathetically, "Yes, indeed! They require so many things. Just keeping them clean is no small matter. The average little girl must soil at least seven dresses a week." No matter what you say afterward this woman has been convinced that you understand her problems, therefore she will more *readily follow your conversational lead*. She will probably continue by telling you that she has her laundry done at home. Then you should ask her what she considers the best washing-machine.

Once machinery is brought into the conversation you are freed from the commonplace if you wish to be. The talk can then go easily and naturally to new heating systems, the improvement in the appearance of automobiles and all utilitarian objects. Isn't it only human to tell your neighbors about something you have found helpful? Then you are off around the world as one topic suggests another!

*START WHERE YOUR HEARER'S MIND IS!* Do not try to *jump* into a new topic, especially if it is an alien one. Actually, there are no alien topics to a clever conversationalist. He can blend the most widely differing ones with but two or three steps of transition.

Perhaps the best mark of the "educated heart" is *not to seem to hurry past others' interests*. We should establish a bond on common ground before we can expect others to go with us anywhere, even in conversation. This is the first lesson of tact. It takes only an instant of undivided attention and absorbed interest in the concerns of our friends to satisfy their need of understanding. Surely all of us can give that instant. Such attention warms the chilliest atmosphere. It begets admiration and cements friendships and gives you the reputation of being gracious.

*LOOK THE PERSON YOU ARE TALKING TO SQUARELY IN THE EYE,* especially at the moment of greeting. Even if fifty people are waiting to speak to you, do not shake hands with anyone while your eye roves the crowd. The cultivated woman never seems to be in a hurry.

BEWARE OF HURRY. Hurried speech gives the impression that you are disposing quickly of non-essentials. You have experienced the rudeness of this behavior if you have ever held the hand of a person whose eyes were elsewhere and who disposed of you with a quick, indifferent smile when she finally did look at you for an instant. Such a woman will seldom have the second chance to insult her acquaintances. She is catalogued instantly as a boor.

BE TACTFUL. The next point in tact is to avoid the assumption of your friend's inferiority even in health. TACT says, "How well you look!" THOUGHTLESSNESS says, "How much better you look!" Though both of these remarks might have come from a kind heart, "I've never seen you looking so well!" implies that ordinarily your friend is considerably below par. A stranger might well suppose that the person you are talking to does not usually look smart and attractive or well and lose interest accordingly. (If one has been dangerously ill and now is well his friends will please him by remarking it.)

"You looked so stately sitting in that chair," implies that out of the chair you do not look stately. "You looked so stately," is sufficient. A tactless young man once said to a young lady, "Wear that brown dress. You look wonderful in it." A gallant young man said, "Wear that brown dress. It looks wonderful on you. What you can do to a brown dress!" A tactful girl once said to her father, "Sit here in this blue chair, Father, your hair is so becoming to it!" Amusing and pleasing.

## VOICE AND ENUNCIATION

Of course, you have been taking your breathing and vocal exercises. If you will apply yourself to them you will find your assurance and your poise very much strengthened. *A clear mind is necessary for tactful conversation.* Anything that tends to help your own sense of well-being will be an additional asset. Therefore, anything that tends to purify your bloodstream, anything that cleanses your system of waste-matter, carrying poisons away so that they cannot befog your brain, will help you toward quick thinking and tact.

Drink a great deal of water. Get sufficient rest. Take invigorating physical exercises. As your voice improves you will find that it sounds more musical, deeper, kinder and more understanding. A nasal, flat voice sounds hard and cold.

*TO RID YOURSELF OF NASAL, HARSH TONES* and to improve the voice open the throat widely and imitate (as though joking) the open tones of an opera singer. If you are a bathtub singer, you can use this exercise for amusement and diversion.

*YAWN* first, hold your throat in that position and sing your little joking imitation. Then, with your hand on your diaphragm say "Ha." Then "what, what, what—this, this, this, this—that, that, that" (pronouncing the final *t* and *s* in an explosive way in order to be sure that you are using your tongue instead of your throat). Now say, "mood, mood, mood" (pronouncing the final *d* explosively). Then try to say "mood" three times in a natural way *with the words smoothly strung together,* being sure to pronounce the *d* distinctly.

*PREVENT THE DROPPING OF LAST SYLLABLES.* Here is an exercise that will prevent you forevermore from swallowing the last syllables of words, which is the most common fault of slovenly speech. If you feel stilted and artificial when you pronounce the last letter of a word distinctly and find it difficult to go on to the next word smoothly, do this—imagine that the last letter of the word is the first letter of the second word. Say, "moo-dmoo-dmood." A trick? Of course. But it will make clear enunciation simpler for you. It will pay you to take this exercise at least a few times just to be sure that your tongue has not grown lazy.

*ONE MUST HAVE ALERTNESS* and spirit or be considered dull and ininteresting. A lilting voice, enthusiastic conversation, and a good posture that makes you feel and look "alive," add force and interest to your presence and weight to your words.

*WHAT PRICE VIVACITY?* The cultivated woman knows that vivacity is not so well expressed by a jumpy body as it is by an intensely interested, alert mind, and a clear, animated speech.

*CLEAR PRONUNCIATION ADDS LIFE* to one's speech. Practice for finely cut words with sentences like, "Seven silver saplings sank in the sand." "The monks made a marvelous monument to those of the men who merited commemorating." "Wonderful women gave gallantly to poverty-stricken public charges."

However, listen carefully to your speech to determine whether your delivery has a *bell-like clarity of tone and enunciation,* or if it is merely choppy with an unpleasant, incisive, instead of a concise, effect. If words are pushed out with an explosive, choppy sound they indicate irritability, impatience, coldness and seem thoroughly opinionated.

*SO PRACTICE TO EMPHASIZE THE VOWELS OF WORDS* instead of the consonants. Say, "People pondered the policies of the powerful politicians." Speak it thus—"pEople pOndered the pOlicIes Of thE pOwerfUl pOlitIcians," and *go from vowel to vowel with the least possible interruption by the intervening consonants.* This exercise will give your speech a caressing smoothness and fine continuity. And in broadcasting it will prevent "blasting."

How to judge your voice? If you are unable to criticize your own speech, you will be able to *form an opinion of it quickly by noticing how other people react to you.* If you do not hold your friends, it is probably because your manner of speaking indicates that you are so absorbed in your own affairs, ideas and opinions that there is scant room for theirs. Your *enthusiasm* may hold them for a while—but they will drift away when they discover or come to feel that this enthusiasm can be kindled only when matters of personal interest to you are being discussed.

*IF YOU FIND PEOPLE REACTING TO YOU UNPLEAS-ANTLY*—examine your voice for an accusing whine, for flatness, coldness or dictatorial irritability. A diplomat's manner of speech conveys his sympathy with and acceptance of your ideas even though he may actually be denying your request. Whereas, a person whose speech irritates you may grant all you ask at great sacrifice to himself without making you feel pleasant about it. See that your manner of speech is a *balm to the nerves of others* and not a needless bit of sandpaper. People seek again and again the warmth and cheer and hospitality of an open fire—just so, *they seek the warmth and enveloping pleasure of a caressing voice and speech that is leisurely enough to seem to have time for others.*

## THE LOVE OF WORDS

The cultivated person also takes the time to gather words for the enrichment of his vocabulary. Love of language and words is one of the marks of fineness.

And so it is with our vocabularies. *If we learn to love words, they will come to us easily and readily.* But if we simply gather them in our minds coldly we will increase our vocabularies only with great effort. Probably the one who loves words spends more energy on them than the person who merely wishes his vocabulary to be respected—but all the effort expended is a labor of love and as such will bring a much richer reward.

*A WORD IS A MAGICAL THING*, a wonderful thing. Almost every word in our language has a long ancestry following the road of human experience back through adventure, dramatic national changes, and years of slow growth in civilization. A language is a living thing born of necessity next in importance to shelter and food. For, in these days, at least, one must have words for every situation. It will hasten your ability to talk well if you will *fall in love with words*. If you haven't a good dictionary, buy one at once. I keep one in almost every room in the house so that when a word of which I may not be sure enters my mind, I can reach at once for my dictionary and in a few seconds learn not only the word's meaning, but often its source and *all* of its uses. A dictionary that is too brief is of little use!

In reading, choose an article or story that interests you and mark with a pencil all the words in it that you think are beautiful. Even though you may think you know what they mean, *look them up in the dictionary.* You have many surprises ahead of you if you will follow this practice. The reason I suggest that you choose words that to you are beautiful is that through them you will be much *more easily fascinated by words.* Then your mind will more readily follow your desire to know the *entire* meaning of other words.

Most of the short, one-syllable words in our language are of Anglo-Saxon origin. Those crisp, short, forceful words that *express with one sound a complete situation* come from those direct, blond giants who preferred to fight rather than to talk and had little use for argument. Their needs were simple and direct and so was their speech. Modern students of words are developing a growing respect for the art with which these ancestors of a part of our language could *express so much with so little effort.* Modern journalism and modern speaking recommend that we *use the dramatic force of short words.* There is strength in words like *kill, eat, come, go, die, run, fight, look, see, get, hit, sleep, food, deep, high, low, quick.* Rigamaroles of long words are coming to be regarded as archaic. To be sure, there are times when only a long word will say what we mean. Then, by all means, use the long word without self-consciousness.

Sometimes there is a lilt and rhythm in a long word that is wanted for euphony. But where you can *substitute a short word for a long one* without losing any of the meaning of what you are trying to say, choose the short word. It adds force and vigor to your speech. Sprinkle your speech with such *nuggets of directness* as GOT instead of *procured*, DEATH instead of *demise*, BOUGHT instead of *purchased* (however, the things you have bought may be referred to as *purchases*), GAVE instead of *donated*, WENT instead of *departed*, SIT instead of *be seated*, DRINK instead of *imbibe*. A friend of mine has been arranging a dictionary of one-syllable words and when it is ready for publication I shall most certainly ask the privilege of recommending it to my students!

*GREAT SIMPLICITY APPEALS TO EVERYONE.* The greatest sin among cultivated people is affectation of any sort, especially in words. If you want to hear speech that is the height of elegant simplicity, listen to President Roosevelt. Even though you may not agree with him you will hear English that is fine, direct—the language of the educated mind which contains the simple vigor of one who is living life finely and well. The speech of the uncultured person falls offensively on learned ears. But the speech of the cultured person is *so completely without pretense and furbelows that the untutored per-*

*son hears nothing unusual in it.* Most things that are great and fine carry a message for all men—not just a select few.

A truly great painting attracts an ignorant man (who has any awareness of beauty in his soul) almost more than it does the man who understands the mechanics and technique of its creation. In the Metropolitan Museum, I once followed a laborer dressed in worn corduroys and heavy boots just to see what kind of pictures and sculpture would appeal to him. Invariably he stood longest before the finest works—twisting his dilapidated hat in his hands. They touched him deeply.

I became more than ever convinced that if a message cannot *convey its meaning* to the simplest of us it has no great value for any certain "class" of humanity. The educated heart and mind express a *knowing simplicity.*

Affected speech is the one thing that well-bred people make open fun about. They will accept the mistakes of ignorance sooner than the airy effusions and mincing handshake of the one who thinks she is acting and sounding like a member of good society. You should take hold of simple words as firmly as you would grasp the hand of someone you are welcoming—naturally, sincerely, honestly!

## ACCENT AND CONTINUITY

I have no doubt that you are impatient to get on with more actual conversation. But you will be much more successful and more pleased with your final effect if you will do more than a little toward preparing yourself to talk. Look first to your *breathing,* then to your *voice,* then to your *articulation* and *enunciation.* Then you are ready to enter the fascinating realm of conversation.

But first, here is *one of the most important points* to be learned about conversation. You can put it into practice at once. *Do not drop your voice at the end of a sentence!* To do so gives an air of finality with which shy or uninterested people do not care to cope. Dropping the voice on a period (as all of us were taught to do in school) is death to continuity in conversation. Even in public speaking it is hard to hold your audience's interest if you keep finishing your talk by dropping your voice. Dropping your voice sounds opinionated, final, as though your remarks closed the matter. In conversation, *keep your voice up* as though the matter were not closed, and thereby indicate your interest in what someone else has to say.

President Roosevelt is (consciously or unconsciously) a master of this simple device. He does not drop his voice. Therefore, his listener *feels included in his thinking,* and invited to contribute something to the subject. This point is an almost magical and never-failing way to keep conversation going—assuming, of course, that there is something to talk about.

*A SENSE OF CONTINUITY—OF MORE TO COME.* We have spoken of the value of prolonging vowel sounds and minimizing consonants. Not only does this type of speaking sound softer and lovelier, but it also gives a *feeling of continuity* to what you are saying, thereby holding the attention of your hearers. Continuity has a great charm. Everyone in the world loves to hear a story or read a story in which the continuity draws the interest along irresistibly. With sufficiently well-drawn continuity an ordinary story takes on a great deal of dramatic pull.

The first step toward establishing this feeling of continuity that intrigues and fascinates is to have your voice flow from word to word with smooth, unbroken force. I asked you to practice exhaling your breath *evenly* through a straw, so as to develop emotional continuity in your speaking.

*IT IS NOT NECESSARY TO BE BRILLIANT.* If you will listen to the talk of fascinating speakers you will note that what they say is not necessarily brilliant, but that their manner of speech makes their words important. Often the most trivial chitchat takes on great interest when its continuity is implied by the breathing and the delivery of the speaker.

*GIVE ACCENT TO MEANINGFUL WORDS.* Suppose you were saying, "A very delightful thing happened today." Usually these words would cause your listeners to wait more or less eagerly for what you were going to tell. But if you should drop your voice at the end of this remark, their eagerness would be dulled at least fifty percent, perhaps more. If you spoke these words in a flat, nasal or cold voice, it would sound as though there was no real conviction and that *"delightful"* was just a word that you were using carelessly, without meaning. Your hearers might conclude from your unconvincing use of the word that you didn't know what was delightful. Again they just wouldn't be stirred to think anything—except perhaps to note your negativity.

Anyone who is careless with the real meaning of words might easily be careless with the truth, also. Of course, your hearers do not bother to think these things out in so many words, but the emotional impression is there just the same!

But, how different, if with chest and head up, you should lean forward slightly with an expression of animation on your face and say, with the words riding out on a warm body-breath, *"A very delightful* thing happened today." Or, "A very delightful thing *happened today!"* In either of these treatments there is drama; more of it, however, in the last one, *because the verb is accented.*

DWELL ON VERBS IF YOU WANT TO BE STIMULAT-ING. Just think this through for a moment. A verb denotes action. Even in motion pictures the eye follows movement. And in talk the mind follows movement because it denotes life and animation.

Repose is fascinating (if and when it may be considered so) because it represents a *pause* in *activity.* The activity is implied just the same. How can there be rest if there has been no action?

A painting of an old woman (like Whistler's portrait of his mother) sitting quietly with folded hands makes you glad she is resting at last. But, bear in mind that the drama of the picture still centers about her former activity. Unless a phrase, a picture, a sculpture or any work of art makes you conscious of action either past, present or future, neither you nor anyone else will be interested in it. For this and other good reasons *always accent your verb* for it is the *action* of your remark.

Suppose you say, "One morning he came, looking like a saint." You would accent either *one* or *morning,* according to the facts of the story, but for emotional effect you would accent *came* and *looking.* Try it both ways and see the difference. Also, you would let your voice caress the word *saint* by dwelling on the vowel a little longer than ordinarily and letting your voice be very warm on that word. You can dramatize any word by the amount of breath you put behind it, the softness or quickness with which it is uttered and the amount of propulsion given it. You can also intensify it by making it *higher or lower in tone* than the words that immediately precede and those that follow it.

To simplify this thought for you—let us imagine that all descriptive words and all verbs are *light* or *dark* in color. For instance words like HEAVY, DEEP, SLOW, DARK, SAD, BROAD, are dark words and should be spoken with low chest tones and some of their heaviness expressed by taking a little extra time in uttering them.

On the other hand, words like BRIGHT, GAY, LAUGH, WHITE, SPRING, HIGH, QUICK, THIN, etc., are *light* words and should be spoken in a higher tone of voice with a clear, bell-like quality.

Far from being artificial—this is the emphasis and the manner you use (or anyone uses) when you are interested enough to describe something effectively. It is what you "naturally" do when you are at your best.

*WHEN ONE LIKES TO LISTEN.* Whenever it is said of someone, "I love to hear her talk. She just makes you see and feel what she is talking about!"—you may know that the woman mentioned gives every word she utters its full value in her speech. Therefore, what she says is *real, alive* and *interesting*. The person to whom people do not like to listen is the one who gives no emotional value to her drone of flat, colorless, nasal words, the woman who says she was so excited in the same tone of voice she uses when she says she is going to take a nap!

Bear in mind that I am not trying to train you to become an actress or an orator, but when all the smoke is cleared away from any sensible discussion of speech you will discover that there is only one kind of good speech and that is *effective speech*. It matters not whether you have an audience of one or one thousand. Public speaking should not be very different from private speaking.

*PUBLIC SPEAKING IS JUST GOOD SPEAKING.* If you learn how to speak effectively to your husband or your beau, your children and neighbors, you will be a very effective public speaker if you wish. The same principles obtain in any situation where you want to convey what is in your mind to the mind of someone else. It does not matter where or to how many people you are talking.

If your child is a bit dull in some subject at school, do not conclude that the child is stupid. Usually the subject has not been sufficiently dramatized for the child, to intrigue and to hold his interest. *Pause to let an idea soak in.* Go over the details of it with him, using an interested manner of speech and with a *sufficient* number of pauses (not dropping your voice on them) so that he has time to picture what you are saying. Then he will follow you and renew his interest in the subject.

*ALWAYS PAUSE AFTER DESCRIPTIVE WORDS* so that your hearers can form a mental picture of what they hear. Otherwise, their more or less indifferent minds become cluttered with words which all sound alike and they lose interest as a consequence.

If you expect your hearers to keep on listening eagerly, you must see to it that they follow you with their imaginations and emotions. They can do this only if you give them time to keep up with you. By this, I do not mean that you must talk slowly and drag your story out—on the contrary, you can talk quite fast if you wish, if you will pause often enough to let your hearer *visualize.* You will not be interrupted if you do not drop your voice.

In these pauses, do not be guided by written punctuations. These are for the eye. In speech, you should divide your phrases, considering only emotion and imagination, regardless of where the commas and semicolons come.

Of course you are not going to perfect the use of these principles in five minutes or five days—but a little *persistent,* private attention to a few sentences will implant the ideas in your subconscious mind from where they will gradually grow into your ordinary conversation.

Let me repeat that *this is not an artificial, theatrical manner of speech I am teaching you!* What I have described to you is nothing more nor less than the way you actually *do talk* when you are interested and interesting. The point is that by training yourself to *talk well at all times* instead of just on those occasions when advantageous circumstances surprise you into your best, you can, by these methods, always be at your best.

*IN ORDER TO SPEAK WELL AT WILL.* It gives you power to know how to reconstruct a fine effect on those occasions when your mood may be a little under par and yet you must rise to the moment creditably, whether in a personal, social or business interview or in a public speech. If you do not know *how* you are effective, you are at the mercy of circumstances. If you do know *how* to create the effect you desire, you are in command of the situation.

Exercise: No laborious study or great length of time is required to apply these teachings. Select for exercise one sentence from the paper, magazine or book you are reading and practice reading it for the difference in its light and dark words, letting your voice go *up on the light words* and *down on the dark words*—making pauses after two or three descriptive words. Pause just *before a verb,* if you wish to give it a great deal of importance; just *after a verb,* if you wish to make it dramatic from a physical standpoint.

For instance, "We *struggled* (pause) up the hill," brings a mental picture of the actual physical struggle involved. Whereas, a pause before a word indicates deep feeling, shows that you are affected by what you are about to say and are approaching the subject with some awe and regard, perhaps even reverence. A perfect example is, "I (pause) *love* you!" It is the way a truly loving person would probably speak.

*WE SHOULD DO OUR STUDYING WHEN WE ARE ALONE,* letting our subconscious minds work our new knowledge into our habitual expression. If we exercise enough in private we shall not have to listen to ourselves talk in public.

*PRACTICE AND THEN BRUSH IT OUT OF YOUR MIND.* Of all the ineffectual things in the world, the speech of someone who is obviously striving for an effect is the worst! A musician does not practice his scales before his audience. Likewise, we should not practice our speech before our hearers. Learn how to talk and then *forget* it!

## WORDS TO WATCH

*Acclimated* is pronounced *ak*-KLIME-*ated* and not AK-*kli*-MATE-*ed*.

*Chaise-longue* (long chair) is pronounced *shez-long* and not *shaze-lounge.*

One refers to the hangings at a window as "hangings," "draperies" or "curtains." Do not call them "drapes."

*Inquiry* is pronounced *in*-QUIRE-*y* and not IN-*queery.*

*Stimulant* is pronounced as it is spelled, accent on the first syllable, and refers only to material things. "Alcohol is a STIMULANT."

*Stimulus* is pronounced as it is spelled, accent on the first syllable, and refers to a mental and spiritual stirring. "These ideas are a STIMULUS to ambition."

Watch carefully how you use the word "got," which is the past tense of the verb "to get." Never say, "I've *got* a new dress." Say, "I *have* a new dress." However, you may say, "I got a new dress," indicating that you did the getting. "To get" means to obtain or to acquire. It does not indicate possession as "have" does. Never say, "I've got to ——." Say, "I must ——."

# CHAPTER FOUR

# *What to Say–to Whom*

There is very little difference between conversation at a formal dinner and conversation across a back fence, if the people doing the talking are experienced enough to be *easy and natural,* to keep their troubles to themselves, to lend a sympathetic ear, and to have a *well-mannered interest* in the world about them.

Looking back over my own life, I conclude that the most profound conversations I have ever been privileged to share were around a camp-fire on the Western desert. And some of the emptiest, most superficial ones I have been compelled to endure have been in the best society. This is not to say that all roughly clad Westerners are profound, or that society is superficial. Neither is true. I merely cite the point to assure you that *there are no special topics that must be discussed at any given time.* Within the broad limits of selfless good-taste, the whole world is yours in talk!

## 1. TALKING TO A MAN

Good conversation is an opportunity for the freeing of the mind to let imagination and fancy soar entertainingly. Imaginative talk is much more attractive to everyone than discussions of dry facts, but it is especially agreeable to men. The cultured European woman can talk of governmental matters, scientific findings, or social economics, but she does not ride a hobby horse to its and everyone else's exhaustion. She can switch the talk charmingly and instantly to poetry, music or more graceful and feminine topics. She has learned the hitherto more masculine subjects in order to be *companionable* to men, but she knows that her fascination for them lies in being able to spin attractive "nothings" into *amusing and relaxing conversation.*

The American woman is shoulder to shoulder with the men of her acquaintance a great deal of the time. Politics, athletics and business are now her province too. She considers herself the mental equal of men. Often she shares the economic burden and sometimes carries it alone! Therefore, it is hard for her to perceive the necessity of leaving serious opinions to men (in conversation). It is hard for her to suppress her quick logic in order to make the man of the moment seem important. It is difficult for her to marvel at the deductions of some mediocre male in order to seem feminine in his eyes.

The American woman is distinctly *at the crossroads* and in a quandary as to which way to go. She wants a fling at complete and unhampered self-expression—yet, in quiet moments, she doubts whether she will find happiness down that road. However, she frequently experiments in brusque frankness and in treating men as though she and they were exactly on the same level in every way. Gradually, she begins to miss the little privileges and favors she enjoyed as a "feminine" type. Men begin to reduce their courtesies to a minimum. Her worthwhile beaux *pay compliments* to her brains and good sportsmanship, but *marry* the Misses Nitwit, while our fine, modern girl cries quietly into her pillow and throws herself with added zeal into her career. She gets a little hard and nervous and crisp.

Or, perhaps she marries her man. But two egos fighting for supremacy under one roof are just one too many, so the judge tells them a year or two or three later. But, she says to herself, "Everything is changing. I don't know why men can't accept women in a new light too." The stubborn fact remains that human nature changes very slowly. Perhaps millions of years are required for even slight differences in reactions. In my opinion, the modern woman is very foolish to sacrifice her personal happiness as a woman on the altar of a mere theory of the changed relationships between men and women. One robin does not make a summer. And neither wars nor depressions remake men and women (fundamentally) into new types.

In this year and for yet a few years to come, *happiness will be found by a man and a woman when one is the complement of the other* and not when they are two contestants for the same prizes. Even when a woman is doing a man's work *she can be feminine about it!* And in no other way does her femininity assert itself so revealingly as in her conversation.

My conversations with men as given in this book are based on the premise that the *greatest success,* the *fullest happiness* and, in the end, the *greatest opportunity for self-expression* are to be had *when the woman keeps the man pleased with himself,* when she inspires him and guides his energy with her gentle, pervading feminine strength.

Yet, at all times, she must avoid a cloying sweetness. She should have a gurgling (not giggling), wholesome humor that plays around the obstacles of life as a brook plays around the stones it encounters and flows laughingly on. Happiness is attractive to everyone, but it draws men as flowers draw bees. Keep your petty annoyances to yourself as a rule, yet lean heavily, *but briefly,* on the men among your friends when you are in real trouble. Men like to be heroic comforters for a couple of days, but they have no talent for a long-drawn-out sacrifice of happiness such as women make without a complaint.

*BE A SMALL PROBLEM TO HIM.* I have spoken of challenging a man on *first* acquaintance, then *later* being sympathetic to him. The third and most advanced stage of *holding the interest of a man* is to be a problem to him in some small way. In a sense, this is a return to the challenge, for his ingenuity is taxed in handling the problem you present. If this problem does not take too much of his time or rob him of too much happiness, he will enjoy coping with it (even though he grumbles) for it makes him feel very manly to be able to meet the condition.

The woman who continues to make life too easy for a man is in danger of being ignored and taken for granted. Worse yet, she provides no stimulus to the man's pride of accomplishment by calling on his physical, mental and spiritual strength. The two problems that a man will *not* cope with are nagging and too much domineering. I refuse point blank to name the ways in which a woman may be a problem, for the circumstances vary so much with each different individual that one must sense rather than know just how far and in what direction to go with the idea.

A man often complains, in confidence, of his problem with his wife, but he seldom, if ever, divorces her on account of it. Often, her claims upon his patience (or whatever quality she taxes) bind him to her with the strongest cord in the world—*dependence*. He will endure a great deal if the foundation of the whole matter is flattering to him. The male energy must have a problem. If the wife does not supply it there is a danger that some other woman will.

Another interesting point is that if a woman *satisfies a man's ego on small points* she can, usually, have her way in large ones. It really takes so pathetically little to please a man. An admiring glance at the right time, deference to his opinion of the proper degree of heat for coffee, having his papers where he likes to have them, are often sufficient to make a man feel important in his home life. Once he is pleased, you may move him from one spot on the earth to another and influence him in the major aspects of his life. Too much admiration given at the wrong time fails in the end.

*NEVER DWELL ON A COMPLIMENT YOU GIVE TO A MAN.* Go immediately to some other topic. If a man is very handsome and is being complimented or admired and sought for his appearance, *you* must not be impressed by his looks. Compliment his tennis, or his mind, or his vocabulary, or some *accomplishment* of his. He will then understand that looks alone will not impress you and will feel that friendship with you would be real.

Look at men with a clear, open countenance. Never let your eyes waver, flutter or flirt—nor do anything that appears self-conscious. Never drop your eyes. Move them coolly to the side when you look away from the gaze of a man. A queen does not drop her eyes. Every woman should have a queenly bearing and manner. One of the most impressive lines in "Anthony Adverse" is, "She occupied space as though she had inherited the right to do so."

A man is charmed by the woman who regards men simply as a natural phenomenon and not as the chief end of her existence. They like to be treated as though they are entertaining, slightly alien creatures about which she has a *mild curiosity*. She should look at them with about the same degree of *casual fascination* with which she regards the animals in a zoo—something to hold one's interest, before one passes on. But be sure *you* pass on! Never cling socially to a man, or to anyone else, for that matter. Neither should you lean backward self-consciously and fail to make friendly and kindly overtures when they would be appropriate. It is always appropriate to be hospitable and to do and say those things that will make others happy, whether they are men or women.

Suppose you are expecting a young man to call. If you have a servant, he or she will answer the door, take the young man's hat and coat and place them in the guest closet if there is one—if not, on a hall chair or bench. If you are going out together immediately, the young man will say, "I'll keep my things, thank you. We are leaving at once. Will you tell Miss Smith that Mr. Newfriend is here?" And he waits in the hall with his coat on. Or, if he takes his coat off, the servant shows him into the living-room and announces him to you, unless you are in the living- or drawing-room where you greet him at once. Either is correct. If you have answered your own door you might say, "Hello, John," or "Good evening, Mr. Newfriend. Won't you come in? Has it started to rain yet? It surely will before long— the sky has been threatening for hours. Lay your things on this chair." "What did you think of the —— game today? Did your team win?" Or, "Wasn't it bumpy driving up this block? I hope they get it fixed some day." Or, "Did you find the place easily? A description of how to get here sounds like a design for a pretzel. You must have some of the instincts of a Northwest mounted policeman. I hope you can as easily find the solution of the puzzle I'm working on. Have you ever grappled with a so-called simple puzzle?"

The man, unless he has had a thorough training in resisting a witty remark that would be tactless, might make the mistake of saying, "The only simple thing about them is the person who tries to work them." And then add lamely, "Pardon me, I couldn't resist that. You led me right into it." Well-bred men and women do resist the temptation to say cutting things for the sake of a laugh. Sarcasm, bitterness and personal puns are *absolutely taboo*.

*EASY BEGINNINGS PRESENT OTHER SUBJECTS.* Other questions to start the talk after arrival might be, "Did it take you long to come? Traffic is so heavy at this hour." Or, "As you came along did you notice a small garage under a willow tree on the left of the road?" The man may say, "Yes, about two miles back I saw a picturesque little village-smithy effect, and ever since I've been trying to recall all the verses of 'Under a spreading chestnut tree, the village smithy stands.' Can you help me out?" You may laugh and say, "Isn't it strange how it bothers one to try to remember something that won't come back. I won't trust my memory. I'll look it up for you." He answers, "Good! In the meantime, tell me what you started to say about the little garage under the willow tree." "That," you laugh, "is one of our points of interest we always show to visitors. Charles Chaplin once bought gasoline there—and really, you'd think it was another of George Washington's headquarters if you could see the way the local people, and tourists too, marvel at it. Such is fame!"

NOW YOU CAN TALK ABOUT FOUR THINGS—poetry, trees, memory and fame, which, with their associated subjects, might take up two or three hours. Your visitor has just about gotten into the living-room by this time. (The well-bred man does not seat himself until his hostess has indicated, with a gesture, the chair he is to sit in; then he stands until she is at least half-way seated.)

Already you are launched on poetry. You can go over the verses you both learned and loved as children for half an hour and be thoroughly entertained. Likewise, all men love trees and will usually talk until they have told all they know about them. Memory is a good subject because everyone can tell amusing stories of occasions when they forgot something important, both as children and adults. Fame suggests actors, politicians or major figures in history.

Such a well-started evening of talk should prove to be very entertaining, and lacking in those awkward personal allusions and self-conscious moments. Then the man can express himself readily and easily and have such a good time that he will want to come again as soon as possible.

One excellent rule to gain and to hold the interest of a man is to keep his mind off you while you keep him busy and happy in your company. In this way you gradually make yourself necessary to his happiness.

*LOCAL HISTORY ALWAYS YIELDS GOOD SUBJECTS.*
You will never have difficulty in starting a conversation with newcomers if you *learn your local history thoroughly.* No matter where
you live on the face of the earth, your local history contains amusing,
poignant, quaint and dramatic incidents that are well worth repeating.
A man I used to know had learned so much of his local history that
he entertained visitors by taking them to the cemetery and telling them
stories of the people buried in the ancient graves! He made it so fascinating that one always forgot the sad or morbid part of the excursion.
Once when I was with him he noticed that a very old tombstone had
fallen over. He pointed to it with his cane and said, "I must send my
gardener over to fix that stone. That man was the tailor who made
the trousers I wore when I went out into the world." A friend who
was with us said, "Really, Colonel ——, you have the most extensive
graveyard acquaintance of anyone I ever knew." Now I am not advocating that you entertain your friends in the cemetery, but I am
striving to emphasize that *stories of people, real people, are always
interesting,* so interesting that it doesn't matter *where* they are told.
In every community, large or small, local legends abound. Gather
them as you would fire-wood to warm your hearthstone in the
future.

I suggest that, whenever you have an engagement, you sit down
and make a list of subjects you can lead the talk through. One would
not dream of building a house without a plan, yet we spend hours of
precious time in the most aimless and haphazard danger of dullness in
conversation *at just the time we should prove ourselves interesting.*
If the talk takes its own spontaneous turns, so much the better; but
if it does not, you are prepared to save your evening from being a
dull failure.

It is your place to ask a man to call. When you say goodbye to
a young man you have met and enjoyed, and if he paid you interested
and marked attention you should say, "Goodbye, Mr. Likable, do
come to call on us when you are in the city again." Or, "If you will
let us know when you will be back, we would like to have you come
to dinner." Or, "I'm having a party on the nineteenth and would
like to have you come. Where shall I send your invitation?"

Naturally, you would not invite anyone in the hearing of someone else who is left out. If necessary, send someone to the man with the message that you would like to speak to him and thus remove him from the hearing of others.

Suppose a young man you have known but casually and at a distance all your life suddenly comes to call. It would be vulgar to reproach him for not having called before. You should *go right on talking naturally* of the things you are both familiar with, avoiding mention of the fact that you have not always enjoyed them together. Perhaps the young man will leap all those years with one sentence, "You're the loveliest thing I've ever known. Think what I've been missing all this time!" You should simply smile openly (not coyly!) and say, "Thank you," which is sufficient reply to any compliment. This "thank you" should be said with genuine pleasure in your face and voice, but also airily and gaily if the compliment is a fluffy, pretty one. If it has to do with a more serious quality you should answer, "Thank you," in a deeper, slower voice. Then go on with whatever you were discussing.

*AFTER A COMPLIMENT AND YOUR "THANK YOU," YOU SHOULD GO RIGHT ON WITH CASUAL TALK.* "By the way, that was grand tennis you were playing today." Or, "I have something really lovely to show you. You used to draw quite well, if I remember correctly, so I know you'd like this illustration of Dan Content's. It's one of those strong things that I think you could have done if you'd stuck at it. Have you given up drawing altogether?"

*ALWAYS TAKE AN INTEREST IN THE ABILITIES AND CAPACITIES OF YOUR FRIENDS.* Then your friendship has something under it to support it during those periods of personal negativeness. Romantic affection has its periods of blankness and even repulsion that must be tided over if love or friendship is to live.

Or you might say, "Do you read much now? You used always to carry a book around. I was a little afraid of the great amount of learning I was sure you had." He may say, "So you're not afraid of me any more?" You reply, "Not exactly, but there's something just a little breathless to me about the way men go at things—and their endurance is simply unbelievable."

The following conversation took place between a great man and the girl he afterward married (though for years, he said he would never marry). They met at a tea. She said, immediately after they were introduced and left together, "How in the world do you find the time to do so many things in twenty-four hours?" He answered, "System." She: "It's like living several lives in one. Do you think it's good for you to drive yourself so hard?" He: "I never think of myself in that way. I simply do what there is to be done." She: "Well, you certainly seem to stand up under it beautifully. You don't look any worse for the wear. So I think I'll stop worrying about you. Tell me about your system. Can it be learned or is it a mysterious gift?"

He (looking at her suspiciously): "Are you, by any chance, making fun of me?" She (greatly surprised): "I! Making fun of you! I wouldn't dare!" He (dryly): "No, I suppose not. Back in your eyes I can see you laughing." She: "On the contrary, I'm ready to cry over your unkindness. But I suppose a man with a system couldn't be expected to be very tender or understanding. Heavens! I've known you exactly one minute and we're rude to each other! Please tell me about your system. Perhaps that will be a safer topic."

He: "So you think that having a system for business accomplishment robs me of sentiment." She: "I have no way of knowing that you had any to be stolen. However, few people are successful at more than one thing. You have your system. It must be a great comfort to you."

He: "See here, young woman, before you've known me much longer you will have learned what sentiment is. You're going to dine with me tomorrow, next Sunday and the next Wednesday, and then I'll tell you what else you're going to do." She: "A masterful man! How lovely! Now will you please tell me your system, M'lord." He: "No, I intend to demonstrate my system to you." Three months later they were married.

This conversation illustrates perfectly the typical feminine interest in a man's welfare, humor and challenge. I doubt if the man lives who is not fascinated by this combination in the talk of a charming woman. Or, perhaps because of her talk she becomes charming in his eyes.

## 2. EXAMPLES OF CONVERSATION

Now for a few concrete examples of some of the principles we have touched so far in the lessons. Don't you find it fascinating to apply them? I'm sure you have better taste than to misuse the pronoun "I"— nevertheless, I thought it would be helpful to give you these illustrations:

### EXAMPLES OF THE USE OF THE PRONOUN "I"

WRONG: "I looked out the window and I thought it was such a beautiful day that I thought I'd go downtown as I felt I would get better bargains if I went to the sales, myself." (Seven references here to yourself!)

RIGHT: "The soft air coming in the window indicated that the day was beautiful, so balmy that it fairly invited one out, perfect weather in which to go downtown and take advantage of the bargains advertised on sale. I found some splendid values. One dress was a real find." (One reference here to yourself!)

EXERCISE: *Write down ten sentences* in which you customarily use the pronoun "I" too often; then revise them, eliminating all but one or two references to yourself. A little practice will correct this bad habit that cheapens your conversation. Even when you are telling a story that concerns your own reactions to a sequence of events, it is possible to convey what you mean without an orgy of "I's" and too many references to yourself.

However, *do not efface yourself entirely* for that would be just as self-conscious as too much mention of "I." Feel perfectly free to mention yourself, but let it be known that your mind is more concerned with "other people and other things."

### EXAMPLES OF VARIOUS GREETINGS

TO MRS. GRAND (who has just opened her country place): "How do you do, Mrs. Grand? It's so nice to see lights in Stoneleigh again. The whole countryside seems more cheerful now that you're back. I'm coming over to see the new colt tomorrow, if I may." (Do not leave the conversation on too personal a note. Here you slid very nicely to the subject of the colt. When you stay on personalities the conversation quickly degenerates to fatuous compliments.)

EXERCISE: Write down a number of greetings which entail a small personal discussion, then *veer smoothly* to another topic. In other words, accustom yourself to invent subjects. You will be surprised how thinking this out about ten times will clarify the point for you forevermore.

TO YOUR EMPLOYER: "Good-morning, Mr. Preoccupied. Is the change of tariff on leather(?) going to be favorable for us, or will it invite greater competition?" Or, "I suppose you saw in the morning paper that the —— company is planning an improved program. Is it going to affect us?" Use the words "we" and "us" even with the most formidable employer. Also, gradually convey the idea that the welfare of the company and all that concerns and influences it is *a matter of importance to you.*

TO A YOUNG MAN: "Hello, Bob. You look much too cheerful after our dreadful game yesterday. Shouldn't we be in sackcloth and ashes? Why didn't you jump out on the field and magnificently save the day?" Or, "Hello, Bob. Wasn't it thrilling! I shouted for us till I have no voice left. Fancy my being crippled like that! Come over at five for a dish of tea and congratulations. Bring your shadow along. What's his name? Oh, yes. Fred Smith. Is he as nice as he looks?"

TO A MIDDLE-AGED MAN: "How do you do, Mr. Mellow? Fine day! Makes one want to—well, what does it make you want to do? Climb a mountain or loll under a tree? I'm betting on the mountain."

TO AN OLD MAN: "How do you do, Mr. Experience. Did you hear the commotion last night?" (Old people always hear noises in the night: the wind, the fire-engines, or the neighbor's baby.) "There's been nothing so violent for years." Here you will be stopped, for the aged one's memory will furnish his tongue with similar and worse commotions until you will need to find a clever excuse to go on about your business. Listen as long as you can, though. There's always an *interesting kernel* in the oldster's stories that *you can repeat later.*

TO A YOUNG GIRL YOU'VE JUST MET: "How do you do?" (There is some difference between saying, "How do you do?" to a young and to an older person. To the younger person you do not say it so deliberately and slowly as to an older person. It can be said so casually as to sound almost as familiar as "Hello.") "A friend of Mary's? Then you must be a grand person. Mary is such a peach, isn't she?" Again, you do not leave the talk on the person to whom you are speaking, but go at once to the subject of Mary. However, if other people insist upon making personal remarks to you and do not change the subject for you, simply say, "I'm glad you think so. I'll do my utmost to preserve your illusion. Speaking of illusions, I'm glad magicians have come in style again. But perhaps actual facts have become even more wonderful than pulling rabbits out of hats."

TO SOMEONE WHO SPEAKS TO YOU WHILE TRAVEL-ING: "Nice journey so far. All sorts of people traveling. Interesting types, don't you think?" Do not let yourself be drawn into a conversation that seems to assume that everyone else present is beneath your notice.

People who are not sure of themselves express their superiority (?) verbally and with lifted eyebrows. To the cultured traveler, the world is a parade which he has bought a seat to see. He is no more critical of it than he is of an elephant's trunk. It is simply there as a *natural phenomenon.*

It hurts no one to be casually polite to every human being. If you do not care to talk to others, then bury yourself in a book.

Your manner, voice and attitude will attract to you your own sort of person. Remember that water seeks its level. It won't run uphill unless it's pumped. To be agreeable on a ship, a plane or a train entails no further social obligation on either side.

It is always well to inquire about the health of a child, a parent or someone dear to the person you are greeting. *Do not comment on the appearance of an older woman who is more or less a stranger to you.* But, with younger women whom you know quite well, a personal compliment or a comment on a costume is only natural.

Unless a man is in a uniform new to him as well as to you, do not comment on his appearance, especially in front of others. To do so implies that he does not usually look well-groomed.

This point is easily understood by the daughter and the son who have added special touches to their usual toilet in honor of some visitor, only to have their thoughtless mother or small brother say, "My, how slick you look." Their discomfort is evidenced by reddened ears and the murderous glances sent to the offender when the visitor isn't supposed to be looking. However, if you can avoid the implication that today is a special sartorial day, a compliment on appearance can be welcome, just as a compliment on food can be acceptable. "Mary, you look so lovely. You're always such a refreshing sight." "You were a beautiful bridesmaid! Phyllis was wise to choose so decorative a wedding party." "Such a delicious dinner, Mrs. Hostess!"

In a restaurant it is quite all right to say, "These shrimp are unusually good," but in a private house do not say that any excellence is unusual, for it might be misunderstood. All of *these subjects require a little tact,* without which they are best left out of the talk. "Such perfect grapes!" "Marvelous wine," "Such handsome celery," "Wonderful sauce," are expressions heard at the best dinner tables, but they are said only occasionally, not all at once, and *only when they can be used truthfully.*

Often pupils write asking me to explain why I suggest that they say "house" instead of "home." My answer is, "Suppose you had an apartment in New York, a country place in Virginia, a cottage on the Riviera and a house at Santa Barbara, California, what would you mean by 'home'?" To the cultured person whose consciousness has widened to take in the world and the universe, "home" is wherever he hangs his hat. "Home" has a spiritual significance. "House" is a place. Always refer to a "country place" and not to a "country estate," except in a literary or legal sense.

Many people are now referring to their thoroughly formal country palaces surrounded by acres of landscaped gardens as "the farm."

*All expressions that sound in the least impressive, formal, stilted or in the slightest degree affected are falling rapidly into disuse.*

The hostess is passé who introduces a guest with, "Mr. Jones resides in the nation's capital and maintains a home also in the West and is engaged in prolonging the usefulness of food."

A modern hostess, who felt that she wished to explain her guest would say, "Mr. Jones lives in Washington, has a ranch out West and runs a canning factory where the most scientific and latest discoveries are used. Your chief interest in it is the research department, isn't it?" Now the people introduced *can talk without having to brush aside the personal* as though it were an annoying mosquito. Never introduce anyone as "the brilliant writer," or "the smartest girl in school" or "the handsomest man in town."

The fatuous hostess celebrating her guests sometimes reminds her mildly surprised celebrities of the story of a minister's eulogy at a funeral. The young widow and her mother, unable to recognize the deceased husband from the clergyman's description, sat through another funeral before they discovered their error.

Never refer to any man as your "boy friend," or as one with whom you are "keeping company" or "going steady." Unless you are engaged, in which case you refer to him as your "fiancé," he is merely "Bob" or "John" or "a chap I know" or "a friend of mine." You "saw a lot" of Bob this summer. You didn't "go steady" with Bob. He may have referred to you as his latest "rave" or his "new heart" but you were not his "girl friend." Don't say, "I like Jim better than any of 'my men friends.'" Say, "I like Jim better than any man (or than any of the men) I know." "Lady friend" and "gentleman friend" are too funny to be considered at all.

Never thank a man for taking you out. *Thank him for a lovely evening,* but *emphasize your enjoyment of some phase of the evening* rather than your gratitude. He should be the grateful one. "It's been a grand evening. I've had such a good time. It was good fun, wasn't it? The best show ever! Your friends were so interesting." "I've enjoyed all of it, but thank you especially for the flowers. They're my favorites." Use these and similar remarks where they are appropriate.

Never invite friends *for* dinner because they might object to being eaten. Invite guests *to* dinner. And by the way, you don't "take dinner," as if it were a pill! You *dine*. Or *have* dinner.

No matter how much we study conversation, our talk will always be a reflection of our character and intent. So vitalize your thinking with cheerfulness, hold your head high with the joy of living and maintain a fine expectancy toward life.

## WORDS TO WATCH

*Canape* is pronounced *can-a-pay,* no accent. The *s* of the plural is not sounded.

*Menu* is pronounced *men-you* and not *MAY-new*. A *menu* is a complete, arranged meal—in a restaurant *table d'hote,* pronounced *tah-ble-dote*. One orders at random (à la carte) from the "carte du jour" (the card of today). In most restaurants you are given both a *menu* and a *carte du jour* (pronounced *cart doo zhoor*).

*Demi-tasse* (half cup) is pronounced *der-me-tahs,* no accent and not *demmy-tas*.

*Petit-fours* (tiny fancy cakes) is pronounced *petty-foor*. Do not sound the *s*.

*Au gratin* is pronounced *oh-gra-tan* barely sounding the *n*. No accent.

*Farther* is pronounced as it is spelled and refers only to distance. "Farther from here."

*Further* is pronounced as it spelled and refers to something additional or to ideas. "Her interest furthered his career." "Pursuing the subject further—."

*Chauffeur* is pronounced *SHOW-FUR* and not *SHOW-fer*.

Never be guilty of saying, *"One of THOSE kind."* You should say, *"One of THAT (or THIS) kind."*

*Masseur* is pronounced *mass-SIR* and not *mas-SOOR*. A *masseur* is a man.

*Masseuse* is pronounced *mass-SIRS* and not *mas-SOOSE*. A *masseuse* is a woman.

*Amateur* is pronounced *ama-TER,* the *ter* as *her.* Do not say *"ama-TYURE"* or *"ama-TOOR."*

*Chic* is pronounced *sheek* and not *chick.* More acceptable words to describe someone or something having style are, *smart* and *good-looking.*

Don't say *"stationery"* when you mean *writing, letter* or *note paper.* Stationery really refers to all the things a stationer carries.

*Lay* and *lie* are often confused. You *lay* your hat in the chair. You *lie* down to sleep. You were *lying* down. The book has been *lying* where you *laid* it. You should *lie* as you *lay* yesterday.

Use the word *lay* when you *put* or *place* something. Use the word *lie* when you mean it *rests upon* or *stayed* there.

*Route* which is a line of travel, is pronounced *root. Rout* sounded like *out* with an *r* before it, means to chase something or somebody away.

*Either, neither* and *each* should not be used with the word "one" following, except for special emphasis. These words are complete designations. Do not say "either one," or "neither one," or "each one." When you have a choice of two things say, "Either will do nicely" or "I will take either you suggest." Never say, "Neither one of them came." Say, "Neither of them came." Never say, "The visitor gave each one of the children some candy." Say, "The visitor gave each of the children some candy."

*Or* and *nor.* Say, *"EITHER this OR that," "NEITHER this NOR that."*

*EYE-ther* and *EE-ther, NIGH-ther* and *NEE-ther* are all correct.

*Precedent* is pronounced *PRESS-i-dent,* but *pre-CEED-ence* and *pre-CEED-ing* are correct.

*Strata* is pronounced *STRAY-ta.* All too many people speak of "this strata of society" oblivious of the fact that "strata" is the plural of "stratum" pronounced *STRAY-tum.* They should say, "These strata" and "This stratum."

*Data* is pronounced *DAY-ta.*

# CHAPTER FIVE

## *Talk at a Dinner or Party*

Certainly there should be no dearth of conversational material today when there are so many interesting developments in everything that concerns living. Yet, since many pupils ask me *how to decide upon a topic and to launch it in talk,* it may be well to cover this point before going on to other aspects of our subject. There are ways to discuss unfamiliar as well as familiar subjects.

## 1. DEVICES FOR CONVERSATION

Let us say, for example, that you know a great deal of the theatre, architecture and designing. Suppose a group of people are discussing music, and perhaps your knowledge of it is somewhat limited. Yet, you fear to say what you *do* know, thinking that it may reveal the depth of your ignorance (this applies to any subject), so you say nothing. Presently you realize that you are quite "out of it." You are not even regarded as a listener since people discussing a subject in its technical phases ignore one who does not, at least, seem sympathetic by nodding, or making short remarks that *show recognition of the facts or opinions expressed.* Of course, no one admires the pest who keeps yeaing and naying every few seconds while someone else is talking. Yet, *we must find a way to remain a part of the talk* or we gradually fade out of the situation and are left sitting on the edge of the circle feeling, as the younger set expresses it, "most unnecessary."

If you keep yourself a part of the group you not only can learn a great deal, but you also have the opportunity to switch the talk to some topic you can discuss with more freedom. An experienced conversationalist never has to use more than two transitional topics to lead to his own pet subject or the one he wishes to discuss at the moment. But he must be a part of the conversational group before he can bend the talk at will.

So while someone else is talking, you can show your receptiveness by an *occasional short remark* such as, "That's true!" "How sensible!" "Indeed it is!" "I hadn't thought of that!" "That's most unusual!" "Very clever!" "How nice!" "How dreadful!" "Extraordinary!" "Wonderful!" These remarks, however, must be used with discretion and with genuine feeling. *The things we say solely for effect usually fail of that effect.*

My object throughout these lessons is to teach you *how and when to say what you really feel.*

You may also show your responsiveness to what is being said *without speaking a word!* When something is said of which you heartily approve or in which you are intensely interested, you can *indicate your interest by leaning forward,* looking intently at the speaker and nodding a little. The movement of alertness in your body will be as expressive as a spoken word!

*DO NOT SIT WITH QUIETLY FOLDED HANDS WHILE YOU LISTEN.* If you do you are in danger of looking much older than you are and dully resigned to your fate. A gesture of animation that appears to have been stirred by the remarks you are hearing is a flattering compliment to the speaker. You should not move so much that you seem restless. Carried to this point, animation might indicate that you were uncomfortable physically or mentally bored. But you should move enough to *seem responsive* to what is going on about you. Listen with your hands as well as your breath and your body!

Now, here is an important point. Once you have become a vital listener, *withhold your approval* except when it is really earned. The speaker will begin to work for your interest unconsciously. By this simple device alone you can build a temporary respect for your opinions, strengthen your influence with a group or an individual. This is the method used to train seals and many other intelligent animals and it works very interestingly with human beings.

At the first opportunity, give a taste of pleasing and flattering approval, which would correspond with the first fish the trainer gives a seal, then afterward give reward only on merit. Incidentally, this procedure is excellent psychology to use in the training of children. And whatever works with children will usually work with grown-ups.

One may not, of course, be exasperating enough to withdraw one's approval *suddenly,* to draw the shades down quickly over one's interest and to go abruptly from an animated position to a slouch of indifference. But, if you wish to keep others coming toward you, just make reward for their effort a little harder to win.

Please understand that all of these deliberate devices are to be used only as a matter of attraction and defense in the *early stages* of a conversation or a friendship. They are meant only to keep you in touch with those you desire to know better until you *do* know them better and are thus able to decide whether you want them for real friends. *True friendship and true love need no such machinations to perpetuate them.* But, it is perfectly legitimate to use any means that are not ignoble to keep in touch with others until deeper understanding ripens or until you have decided you do not wish it to ripen.

## 2. HOW TO PARTICIPATE IN CONVERSATION

Certainly *you must participate in a conversation* in order to influence it. Let us assume that even though lacking familiarity with all the musical terms in the talk, you still have kept yourself in the circle by noticeable and audible appreciation and responsiveness. You need not *confine* yourself to short appreciations.

*WITHOUT TECHNICAL KNOWLEDGE ONE MAY STILL STAY IN THE TALK.* We are now face to face with a profound truth that applies to every aspect of conversation. Though you may not be able to join in the discussion of technical terms and highly specialized knowledge, you still may add your comment if it applies to the *emotional effect* of the type of music being discussed.

You can become and remain a part of any highly specialized discussion, regardless of your ignorance of its fine points, if your comments give voice to how you or others *feel* about it.

You may listen to engineers explain the latest scientific findings in relation to speed and weight shown in a new design for trains. You may know nothing of the details and yet be perfectly sensible in remarking how one might *feel* when riding in the new contraption. You can say, "What a thrill to shoot through space like that!"

You might listen to a group of medical men discuss the newest serums for children and be quite in the talk by commenting on the probable *emotional reactions* of mothers in their acceptance or refusal of its use. You can say, "What a merciful thing for all the mothers in the world!"

If, in the musical conversation, someone says, "Gershwin made a fetish of chromatics," you, perhaps, may have no idea what that remark means. Still you know how you and others *react* to his "Rhapsody in Blue" and you can say, "Well, whatever his methods, his things are perfect tone-pictures of our times. His precise rhythms are like the insistent progress that beats through our lives and compels us on, even though it tires us. The recurring discords certainly picture our confusion. They seem to be seeking a solution to life and never finding it. His ending always on a higher or even tone, instead of a lower one, affects me as a question mark does. (Laughingly) I think I should answer him." All of this can be said without knowing one single note of music or any of its professional phrases or phases.

Any of these ideas can be expressed in your own words and, of course, they need not all be said at one time. More than half the time *when someone brings in the subject of "emotional effects" the conversation turns to them as a topic.*

Someone may answer your remarks with, "One gains much the same impression from Ravel's 'Bolero.' Always, in periods of transition, primitive strains replace somewhat more refined melodies. I can shut my eyes while listening to the Bolero and sense how close barbarism lies to the surface of our so-called civilization." (By now, you are tired of music and would like to talk about houses.)

A cynic present may say, "I think it is savagery behind a thin silk curtain, isn't it? They say that 'Music hath charms to soothe the savage breast,' but I think that should be changed to, '*Some* music hath charms to soothe the savage breast.' Other sorts perhaps have power to stir the beast awake."

You may say, "Which only proves that music is but a form of expression that can be used to express whatever the composer wishes to say with it. Music, after all, is just a general subject under which are grouped variations of sounds. The term is as general as painting or food or houses. All buildings can be called houses, but each may be a different man's dream."

A young woman wishing to be less serious, says, "A dream house, then, need not necessarily be the home of a bride and groom. Another illusion shattered. I think I'll go home. This conversation borders on the positively wicked and I don't think you are a good influence for me."

Someone says, "Don't go! We'll build you a dream house and play paper dolls with you if you'll only stay. We need you to keep us wholesome."

The young woman replies, "Then I'll stay if there's really anything noble in it. At my age, you see, one must have a cause." A worldly young man says cynically, "Perhaps you'd like to have us talk about that masterpiece of composition, 'The Maiden's Prayer.' By the way, who wrote it?"

Whereupon, you (who are eager to talk about houses) can continue with the musical discussion if you think the others would enjoy it more—or you can turn the talk at once to houses and architecture.

You can say, "No, the agreement was that we would build her a dream house. Now, everyone here has a dream house. 'Breathes there the man with soul so dead, who never to himself has said, "This is the house I would like to own."' So gather round the table, right this way, ladies and gentlemen, and each of you contribute a room—your ideal room—to this dream house for *Ruth*." It is great fun actually to do this. It will keep all classes of people interested for hours! And you are now on your favorite subject, architecture.

This conversation is a very clear illustration of getting on a topic you wish to discuss. Naturally, conversation does not always take this same turn. But in any conversation, it is possible to blend into the talk *the name of your favorite subject*—and once it is mentioned it is easy enough to take it up as soon as possible and to continue with it.

However, if music remained the subject of the conversation, other composers would be brought into it. You might say, "All the moderns seem to lean to impressionism. What could be more descriptive than Ferde Grofé's 'Grand Canyon Suite'? Even children can understand those passages where the donkey walks along."

Someone may answer, "But Honegger reached the peak of this craze for impressionism with that interesting impression of a train. What's the name of it? Oh, yes, 'Pacific 231.' "

Someone else adds, "But Gershwin's 'An American in Paris' is the best of that school."

Then you may say, "And Gershwin's 'Concerto in F' proved him capable of deeper things. But, after all, wasn't the forerunner of this modern trend dear old Debussy? It seems to me that a lot of the things one hears today were inspired by his 'Claire de Lune' and the 'Golliwog's Cake-walk.' "

Someone says, "Of course, we are always pouring new wine into old bottles in spite of all instructions to the contrary. All new things are tinged with the old, even new loves."

Another says, "And even new lives. They say the next life is to be measured to us according to the flavor and color of this one. And the reincarnationists say that this one is flavored and colored by the last one."

The young girl says, "What dreadful people we must have been in the life before this one."

Someone asks her, "Then you don't think much of us in this life?"

The young girl says, "I can think of lots of improvements to make, but on the whole, we're not a bad sort, are we?"

A gallant young man answers her with, "It's kind of you to group your virtues with our wickedness in your inclusive 'we.' I'm sure we could pass any judgment bar if allowed to walk closely beside you."

The young girl says, "How beautifully old-fashioned—and much appreciated," sweeping him a little curtsy.

Someone begins to laugh heartily. The young girl says, "Is it nice of you to laugh at my pretty compliment?"

The laughing gentleman replies when he can, "But I am not laughing at your compliment. I assure you it didn't say enough. I was laughing at a sudden mental picture of your leading us all into paradise as though we were a sightseeing excursion. Do you suppose we'd need tickets?"

The first young man says, "My good fellow, you are now simply advertising your thoroughly materialistic mind. We were soaring, wandering in Elysian fields, and you have brought us down to earth with a thud."

The laughing young man jumps to his feet, "Tickets! That reminds me. (Turning to the young girl) I'm to pick up our tickets on the way down. I hope *you* don't object to tickets. They're really necessary, you know."

The young girl says, "As a matter of fact, a ticket is a badge of qualification. Good ones are nothing short of a triumph. After we get them, let's pin them on our chests and show the world what superior people we are. (Offering her hand to her hostess) Goodbye, Mrs. ——, I've had such a good time. It was sweet of you to ask me to come."

Mrs. —— says, "We were so happy to have you, Jane (or Miss ——)."

The young man says, "Goodnight, Mrs. ——. Thank you for the most marvelous evening ever. Sorry to take Jane away, but I'm sure you can handle the spiritual welfare of the others single-handed."

Mrs. —— says, "Well, of course, I couldn't be expected to fill Jane's shoes, but we'll get on somehow." The others call "Traitors! Deserters!" after the departing couple and are rewarded only by superior smiles.

This is a very good average of conversation in a normally intellectual and pleasure-loving group of mixed ages, showing their humor and information. It shows that when people have found their tongues that the question of "What to talk about" no longer exists. (The only problem then is to see that each guest has an opportunity to say the things that bubble out so naturally.) It shows how *conversation can be switched from topic to topic by choosing a single word from each speaker's sentence to form the basis for the change.*

It would be excellent practice to go back to the paragraph beginning, "However, if music remained the subject of the conversation, other composers would be brought into it." Then write out your own remarks on music. Lead the talk into a discussion of opera or concerts, singing and singers. As a matter of fact, it is really harder to hold the talk to one subject than to switch it, for the average person's mind unconsciously *takes hold of the casually dropped word* to help him start discussing some personal experience or impression which leads *far afield from the starting point.*

There is, of course, such a thing as overdoing it. Talk that trips too sketchily from topic to topic is apt to be flimsy with no real current of interest. When you are hostess, try to prolong the discussions that seem deeply to engross your guests, even though the evening assumes an entirely different tenor from your plan.

## 3. CONVERSATIONAL DUTIES OF HOSTESS AND GUEST

However, when the talk stays wearyingly on one theme, as it may at times, the hostess may say (as a friend of mine once did) good-naturedly, but deliberately, "Now, you can't talk about that any more. Mary wants to hear about the yacht races." Or, "We want to hear about Fred's motor trip into Mexico." Or, "We want John to tell us about that new three-wheeled automobile." Or, "I simply can't wait to hear what happened to Mary last night."

It is the task of the hostess to see that conversation *runs smoothly,* both as to subjects discussed, and also to be tireless in *seeing that congenial partners get together.* Naturally, she should not interrupt a rapt couple who are deep in some discussion of their own, unless their interest has caused them to be conspicuous and oblivious of their social duties.

The hostess whose guests are not "mixing" in a way to keep her party animated and successful has a perfect right to say to a man, "I need you for a bit of rescue work, John, come with me." She takes him over to the couple or group who have been oblivious of the others for too long a time and she addresses the most charming man in the group, "Charles (or Major Andrews), John has been such a good boy that he deserves your chair there by Phyllis, and you're going to talk to me. Won't that be nice?" He gets up with some gallant remark and starts off with his hostess, who continues, "—that is, you're going to talk to me after you've made Miss No-beau happy for a few minutes." If he knows her well enough he may make a little grimace; if not, he will look politely confident that his hostess can do no wrong and make the best of it.

*WITHIN REASON, GUESTS ARE LEFT TO THEIR OWN DEVICES;* but when they are either selfish or thoughtless enough to pursue their own pleasure at the expense of their hostess and the comfort of the other guests, she should and does manage them with cheerful and casual firmness. It is certainly a compliment to one's hostess to assume that *all of her guests are worth knowing,* although in many houses, especially during and after the last war, it was thought smart to leave guests utterly alone—sometimes they caught one or two glimpses of their hosts—for an entire week-end! Often, the guests divided into icy little groups or pairs and many times never learned one another's names.

Fortunately, this mockery of hospitality died out in the high places where it started before it spread into general acceptance. Good-taste and kindness always triumph among gentle people, and though the younger set often goes daringly near the edge of rudeness and vulgarity, it is always whipped back into line by the older guardians of society's standards of its own obligations.

Children, boys as well as girls, should be *thoroughly trained into an acute consciousness of what they owe to other people* in the way of courtesy, with special emphasis on what they owe a hostess. By the time they have grown up entertaining will be far less complicated than it is now when a successful hostess must be part Cleopatra, part wild-animal trainer, and part diviner of man's destiny, in order to blend a lot of carelessly brought-up people (often with good names) into a unified festive atmosphere that should pervade even the most modest of entertainments.

Yet, *the simplest solution for hostess or guest is to hold uppermost in mind the happiness of the others,* each striving to give the "greatest joy to the greatest number." (Otherwise, why give a party or go to one!) This considerate attitude of mind would make a success of any contact between human beings, whether in an office, a store, a factory or a farm.

## 4. HOW TO INTRODUCE A NEW SUBJECT

You have seen in the foregoing pages that in hopping lightly but connectedly from topic to topic, *small matters can furnish as much conversational fuel as greatly important ones*—often more. It is not particularly stimulating to talk for you to say, "It is said that rain falls incessantly somewhere on the globe." Or, "Did you know that Haviland who makes the beautiful 'French' china was really an American, who, lacking recognition in his own country, went to France where his ideas were appreciated?" Or, "It is an interesting and not generally known fact that Samuel Morse, the inventor of the telegraph, was a superb artist, excelling in miniatures. He formed the first society of art in this country and then deserted his artistic career for his scientific one." Facts introduced in such a way may be filed gratefully in the hearer's mind for future reference, but so far as conversation is concerned one might be tempted to say, "And so what?"

But suppose you wanted to talk about Samuel Morse and the existing talk was about physical exercise, for instance. You might say, "Is it true that the body is developed at the expense of the brain—or does a strong body make the mind stronger?" You will receive a number of answers, according to the opinions of every man present. You can continue, "But doing one thing well does tend to bring the ability to do something else well, don't you think?" After that is answered, "Well, a talent, which after all is a type of strength, can usually be expressed in more ways than one. Caruso was also a sculptor. Michelangelo did a number of things. And like him, Samuel Morse combined science with art. Now couldn't other people do much the same thing in a smaller way?" Thus you have a reason for bringing in the *name* of Morse, then the current of talk, in exchange of ideas, is carried right along with the transition of subject.

Really, if you are ever bored it is your own fault. It is quite possible for you to switch any conversation in any way you like if you will take the bit of bother to find one or two transitional subjects so that your change is scarcely noticeable. All that is necessary is a *desire to do so*. No particular ability is required. Like tact, switching the con-

versation is largely a matter of having interest and attention enough
to bring *your own subject* in adroitly. In like manner you can make
talk easy for others by leading the conversation up to *their topics* so
naturally and casually that they will hardly realize you have done it
purposely. A little thought along this line will enable you to throw the
talk to each guest.

If there are no pet subjects it is obvious that a *good general question
is the simplest way to start a conversation.* Some phase of the general
topic will be outstanding to each hearer and in the light of the knowledge of each guest he will make his response.

Some teachers pretend to believe that question-asking is a sign of
weakness in conversational ability. Yet, these same teachers, in actual
practice, use questions profusely, because it is *psychologically correct*
to do so. For the same reason that keeping the voice up at the end of
a sentence seems to include your listeners in your line of reasoning,
*well-timed questions indicate interest in the opinions of others.*

Such interest is polite, pleasing and charmingly considerate. To ask
a man, "Is it true that certain government bonds are to be replaced
by new ones?" is to show pleasing respect for his information on such
matters. Why not add this personal pleasure to conversation instead
of making the flat statement, "The papers stated that certain government bonds were to be replaced by new ones."

However, you must not give the impression of having *no* opinions
of your own. Occasionally throughout an evening of talk, but once
or twice is really enough, you should state an opinion that is entirely
an expression of yourself. "It's the best book I've read in years." Or,
"Hers is the most beautiful house of its kind in town." Or, "The artist
is at his best in this picture." *To commend a thing after careful consideration is quite as much a critical opinion as to disparage it.* If you
are careful not to give your unqualified approval except where it is
merited, you can establish just as much of a reputation for good judgment as though you went about pointing out faults in objects and
people. If you refrain almost completely from derogatory criticism you
will be *more beloved* by others who may respect, but fear, a sharp-
tongued woman. Do not pour out undeserved flattery which is sense-

less to everyone who hears it, but *make a practice of finding the admirable quality;* then base your comments upon it.

## EXAMPLES OF INTRODUCING TOPICS

These illustrations will show you how easy it is, by transition, to switch the conversation from one topic to another—not only to a subject you prefer, but to subjects generally at any time, to keep the talk stimulated.

1. Suppose the talk is about books. You have done no reading lately; therefore, you prefer to talk about gardening instead. *A* says, "Willa Cather's book, 'Lucy Gayheart,' is perfectly delightful!"

After inquiring into your friend's pleasure in the book and hearing her answers, you might say, "Lucy Gayheart sounds like the name of a new rose (or peony, or pansy or gladiolus), doesn't it?"

*A* replies, "It is a pretty name. Sounds so much more appropriate for a flower than Miss Annie Clay or Miss Gussie Coldstone."

You answer, "Why do so many lovely and defenseless flowers bear such long, unimaginative names? It must be because they are named for the person who develops them and all too often the name is absolutely unbeautiful and unromantic. Then, too, they are sometimes named by the developer in honor of someone he or she admires and the result is equally as inappropriate."

*A* says, "Well, you know a rose by any other name would smell as sweet."

You reply, "So says Mr. Shakespeare! Oh, by the way, did you know that, tucked away in Central Park in New York City, there is a tiny, fenced-in knoll called 'The Shakespeare Garden'? In it is grown every flower, herb and shrub named in Shakespeare's plays. How is that for surprising romance in a city of skyscrapers? Why do you suppose gardens have always been considered romantic?"

*A* answers, "That feeling is probably based on the splendid and long reputation of the Garden of Eden."

You can answer, "I wonder if Adam and Eve had to spray their plants as I do to keep the bugs from getting them!" Now here you are at gardens!

By glancing over this conversation you will see that you went from a book to names, to Shakespeare, to gardens. Incidentally, you will find that men as well as women are interested in gardening. It is a very popular hobby. Conversation about gardens grows and bubbles as though it had yeast in it.

*A TRANSITION NEED NOT BE BRIEF.* If *A* was stimulated by the subject of names and took up that topic for a while, you need be a little patient to carry out your transitions to get to your subject. In fact, if each different subject can be brought into talk in an easy, casual way, there will, undoubtedly, be spirited conversation about it— and this is just what you want!

2. Suppose you are talking to an ardent golfer. You may not wish to make the usual trite references to his excellence along this line. Perhaps the man is shy about his accomplishments. He has deliberately changed the subject once or twice when someone tried to make him talk about his golf. At the moment he is talking about young animals, colts, puppies, etc.

You can say, "The young of anything is adorable, isn't it? Even little lion cubs and baby snakes seem cunning and innocent. If they'd only stay that way!"

The golfer may say, "Typically feminine! If you kept your own children in such a mental atmosphere they'd be tied to your apron-strings and grow up to be mollycoddles."

You say, "I don't think a little extra care and cuddling hurts them a bit." Even though a man may argue, intellectually, against such an idea he, nevertheless, is *emotionally impressed* by your *motherliness and femininity*. This impression will remain long after he has for-gotten the cut of your smart gown or the shade of your face powder. Never lose an opportunity to drop a casual remark that shows your feminine, motherly interest in everything and everybody. Such an attitude will often precipitate a desirable proposal. "Well, now just cast the spot-light of your cold logic, Sir, on young Bill Smith. He's trying desperately to follow in your footsteps, but so far, his fourteen years of inexperience make him a caricature of you. If you should feel moved to help him a bit he might make a champion too. What does he lack?"

Mr. Golfer would be unable to resist the temptation to analyze the boy's golfing idiosyncrasies and you will have him well-launched on the subject of golf. In other words, there is always a way, by *indirect approach,* to introduce any subject!

It is always much more polite to draw out any specialist in this way, instead of throwing raw, personal compliments at him and demanding of him a dissertation about his work. A reluctant talker will usually take up any subject quite readily if he is given an *impersonal hold* on it. Later there will be more of this idea in our examples of conversation with a sweetheart.

## WORDS TO WATCH

The "split infinitive" is still avoided wherever possible. "To go," "to come," "to sing," "to work," etc., being the infinitive form, are kept together. Don't say, "I wanted to perhaps buy ——." Say, "I wanted, perhaps, TO BUY ——." Don't say, "If you want to really learn." Say, "If you really want TO LEARN."

*Address* is pronounced *ad-DRESS.* Never say *AD-dress.* Whether you *ad-DRESS* an envelope, an audience, or tell where you live, there is only one correct pronunciation—*ad-DRESS!*

*Piano* is called *PYON-o* (the "on" as in "yonder") among musicians and cultivated music lovers. The *o* which is the last syllable is a round full *o.* The word correctly spoken seems to have but two syllables. Never say "Pi" (as in "pit") "anna."

*Pianist* is pronounced *PYON-ist* (the "on" as in "yonder").

*Concerto* (a type of composition) is pronounced *kon-CHIRT-o* (the *chir* as in chirp), or, *kon-CHAIR-to.*

*Rachmaninoff.* He calls himself *Rock-MON-ya-nuv.* The *ck* of the *rock* is the closest I can come with English letters to the soft throaty Russian *ch.* The *mon* is pronounced as the Scotch say *man.*

*Ravel.* The accent is on the last syllable—*Ra-VEL*—not *Ravel* like a string.

*Ferde Grofé* is pronounced *Fur-dy Grow-FAY.*

*Chopin* is pronounced *Show-PAN,* hardly sounding the *n.*

*Mozart* is pronounced *MOTE-zart,* barely sounding the first *t.*

*Verdi* is said *VAIR-dy,* the *air* as in chair.
*Puccini* is said *Poo-CHEE-ny,* the *chee* as in cheek.
*Wagner* is pronounced *VOG-ner,* the *o* as in odd.
*Debussy* is pronounced *D'BYU-cy.*
*Paderewski* is pronounced *Pada-REV-sky.*

# CHAPTER SIX

# *Hospitality Develops Conversational Power*

## 1. THE COMPLIMENT OF GOOD TALK

One of the greatest *developers of conversational power* is hospitality! Invite people to your house often and provide no entertainment for them after dinner but talk. It is not good taste to keep guests whirling so dizzily from one activity to another that there is no time for sustained talk. *Home entertaining and conversational evenings* are being rediscovered and enjoyed. It is certainly a much greater compliment to a visitor or caller to wish to know him better through talk, than to keep him so busy that he has no time to talk.

*LEARN TO ENTERTAIN EFFORTLESSLY.* Whether you live in a palace or in one room where you sleep on a studio couch—invite friends to tea. Invite friends in to supper, if a dinner is too much for you to attempt. To many a woman, a caller or a guest is "company" for whom she must exert her talent as housekeeper and cook. She exhausts herself by making elaborate concoctions, arranging flowers and straining to put the family's best foot foremost.

It has always been my practice to recommend the *simplest preparations for guests so that the hostess may be fresh, attractive and sympathetic* by retaining sufficient energy to be tactful. Good talk that warms the heart is not born of fatigue.

Any number of clever women have discovered some menu that requires the minimum of preparation and give the same dinner to guests all the time! On the theory that guests come to see her and not to eat, a woman who runs her own house should arrange the "easiest" possible dinner that will spare her for her friends. The can-opener should do full duty.

Even if you have a number of servants, your mind and spirit will be free to *give unreservedly to your guests,* if you know your dinner is simple, "fool-proof" and has no difficulties or "snags" in it.

No one is so poor that she cannot afford a little tea and a cracker or a tiny tea-cake for a caller. You need have no more than this when you have fifty people in to tea. An evening of conversation followed by a few simple sandwiches, little cakes and coffee is often more memorable than a costly party.

Most men like to eat, and think a woman very feminine who recognizes their enjoyment of food. A sense of physical well-being does tend to *set the spirit free* to soar in realms of theory and imagination where the finest conversations are nourished.

A feeling of warm hospitality also *sets the tongue free.* I have never known a woman who knew how to greet people warmly and make them feel welcome in her presence who was not a good conversationalist. Or perhaps, because she always said the right, kind thing that made others comfortable, we thought she was a good talker. Set a fire under your kettle of hospitality and soon good talk will come steaming out the spout! No "buts" or "and" or "I will soon or some day!" The practice of hospitality has much to do with the ability to talk.

## 2. SOME HINTS ON CALLS

In calling on a new neighbor, it is expected that you will first tell who you are and give an account of yourself. "I am Mrs. U. R. New. I live in the third house on the other side of the street. I am President of our Woman's Club and Chairman of the Literary Society. The two freckle-faced boys down there are mine and I have a daughter, Mary, in high school. We have lived here for many years. Naturally, we are interested in new neighbors. I don't wonder that you chose this fascinating place. Did the outdoor fireplace sway you in its favor?"

Thus you do not stop after giving an account of yourself. Else you would seem to be demanding a similar record of the other person. But when you turn to the subject of the new place, the woman can more gracefully answer you and weave into her replies an account of her family if she wishes to do so. Sincerity, honesty and downrightness always make a favorable impression.

The call on a new neighbor should be made while the newcomers are moving in, as a neighborly offer of help of any kind, such as a stepladder or tea for the exhausted family—otherwise, *give them time to get straightened out.*

Prying questions are in bad taste. But if there are children in sight, it is quite natural to say, "Are these children yours?" "I understand that your husband is a lawyer," is permissible, but never, "What is your husband's business?" "We are all so delighted to have neighbors here and we do hope you'll like the community," is really what you came to say, so *say it in words and imply it in your manner.*

If you are one who is called upon as a new neighbor, or at any other time, it is always gracious to say, "How nice of you to think of us. It was good of you to come." Or, "It has been such a pleasure to see you," or, "You have been very kind and helpful."

If one's manner is one of quiet dignity such gracious remarks are *the appreciation of equals.* If one is ill at ease and says grateful things accompanied by too much facial expression and too much bobbing about, it will seem a servile gratitude.

*IN MAKING CALLS,* you can usually find a key to conversation by merely asking yourself inwardly, *"What am I here for?"* Then convey your message and leave. By "your message" I do not mean a mere statement. I refer to the atmosphere of what you wish your call to convey.

*A CALL OF CONDOLENCE* should be just what its name implies. "Con" means "with," and "dole" from *dolere* means "grieve"—to grieve with. It is poor taste to try to change the subject or to "cheer up" the bereaved ones. Such a call should be made immediately upon news of the death, and is merely an expression of shock, of sympathy, and to offer any possible assistance.

Remain only a short while, unless there is some real service you can do. The call that is made a few days after the funeral can be one that tends to brighten the atmosphere, if possible or desirable.

Fatuous compliments are out of place at such a time. Say what you feel. Say what you mean. Where you cannot honestly convey your sorrow at someone's passing, you can always say or write, "My thoughts are with you constantly in your great trial. If there is anything in the world any of us can do, please let us know."

Do not say, "We should be so happy to serve you." Keep the word "happy" out of written or spoken words of sympathy.

*THE HABIT OF PAYING PARTY CALLS,* which often is the mere leaving of cards, is slowly being discontinued, but there are still many fine people who pay such calls and expect them. They are certainly *gracious gestures* of appreciation. With many hostesses, a note or a telephone call suffices. The note is preferable. It can be very brief.

"Your party was wonderful! We enjoyed it so much. John wants me to include his thanks with mine for the happiest time ever. Sincerely, Alice Joy," is a sample of what is expected. You can say as much in person or over the telephone. Notice that the note *begins with "you" instead of "I."* See that your telephone and other conversations begin with the word "you" if possible. In any event, avoid starting with "I" whenever you can.

Never try to impress a stranger with your importance. On the other hand don't assume a mouselike humbleness. Just *take yourself for granted* on all occasions and with head up look at the world with a clear, simple, honest gaze! Be so busy *living life* with all its myriad interests or comfortable routine that *you have no time for self-consciousness.*

*WHEN YOU LEAVE.* In leaving after a call there are just one or two "talking points" to be observed. Unless you must catch a train, do not bolt after someone else has finished a story. Try, if possible, to *start to leave after a remark of your own.* Some people allow their expression of gracious interest to fall off their faces as though it had been a mask, the instant they decide to leave.

Just as one should always give a reason for not accepting an invitation, it seems equally gracious to give a reason for leaving, especially after a brief call. Don't give your reason apologetically, as though it pained you to deprive your hostess of your valuable presence, but just say simply, "I had no idea it was so late. I must do an errand before I go home." (Rise.) Or, "I am expecting something (or somebody) and so I must be at home when (he, she or) it arrives." Or, "I promised to pick up my daughter at the Junior League Building. They have been rehearsing a pageant there this afternoon." Then say goodbye to your hostess (always) and go without lingering and keeping others standing while you try to leave.

H. H. Munro (Saki) has his character Reginald say, "A woman who is careless of disappearances is capable of dying at the wrong moment of an unfashionable disease." Do not "cling" at the last moment. Keep your happy expression on your face until well out of sight, unless it is so natural for you that you wear it all the time. Don't rush either in or out.

It used to be said that in Paris the only women who hurried on the streets were Americans, the dressmakers' midinettes, and those of sinister profession. Often a hurried manner results in ungracious speech. Hurry is merely a habit and a bad one. It saves very little time, is awkward, jerky and unlovely. How often have you seen a woman hold up traffic while she rushed and scrambled grotesquely across the street, only to stop on the other side with a vacant look on her face as though she had no real objective—or else she paused to look in the shop windows! Grace and fineness are characterized by a certain impression of leisure—which does not mean time-killing and lolling.

## 3. CHARITABLENESS AND TACT IN CONVERSATION

Let me point out again the stimulating use of the question wherever possible. Conversation is kept alive if sprinkled generously with questions. I do not refer to personal questions—but rather an upper inflection or actual query at the end of a statement, that either asks directly or implies, "Don't you think so, too?" Even saying, "Doesn't Mrs. Jones look beautiful tonight?" brings an easier response than the mere unadorned statement that, "Mrs. Jones looks beautiful tonight."

Let me repeat that too many flat statements tend to close the talk. This is why a brilliant man with his head crammed full of facts often cannot translate them into the terms of animated, rolling conversation.

*LECTURING ISN'T CONVERSATION.* The learned man has, through study, come into the possession of certain conclusions and definite information. He may parade this knowledge in lectures, but before he can make it a part of live conversation he must learn how to make his listeners take an active part in the examination of his facts. This is best done through well-placed questions and he should be patient enough to endure even the silliest of questions if they *keep his subject a part of the stream of conversation* to which each person present contributes his bit.

The most learned person *must* defer to the intelligence (or lack of it), the mood and the facility of expression of his hearers, else he will find himself gathering dust with his books and they will dry out together. When just a little *effort and consideration* would make his knowledge usable and welcome to others, it is too bad for him to deny the world the benefit and himself the human pleasure of real conversation.

In all general discussions there are times when one must choose between one's pet theories and holding one's tongue to preserve a smooth harmony for the occasion. It is not a happy choice but rather a taking the lesser of evils. One is apt to have a sense of having betrayed one's standards by not defending them. Yet sometimes it is nobler to *preserve peace and harmony* so that your later influence of persuasion may turn a wrong opinion to your way of thinking.

In any event, since the public street is the only place neutral enough to permit a discordant discussion, and since no lady would make such a spectacle of herself on the street—it follows that there is no place or time for her to give anyone "a piece of her mind."

Society is presumably a pleasant association of highly civilized people. It is to be expected that we must make some *personal sacrifices* to keep it so. If we are not willing to make such sacrifices we do not "belong."

*DON'T TAKE SIDES IN OTHER PEOPLE'S QUARRELS.* From a purely selfish point of view it is well to realize that people are growing and changing in their attitudes and opinions, their likes and dislikes. If you permit yourself to be forced to take sides on any moot question, whether it concerns people or issues, you may find later that the matter was settled harmoniously, leaving you out in the cold —that the quarreling friends or relatives have "made up" and you are left "holding the bag."

*TAKE THE CHARITABLE POINT OF VIEW* always, though it need not be so strongly expressed as to be a rebuke to your hearers.

Sometimes, if one does not enter into a conversation of criticism of someone under the disfavor of those speaking, one's attitude is construed as siding with the criticized one. I remember distinctly that through my failing to join in a certain critical discussion of the divorced husband of a friend, she thought I was "on his side," but she has come to understand that I love her no less because I did not wish to add to a belittling condemnation of anyone. One can lighten the matter by some such remark as that attributed to Mr. Goldwyn, "Gentlemen, include me out!"

The more wrong one may be, the more he or she needs helpful thoughts—mind you, not approval, but just to be allowed to go down the open road of experience, learning through mistakes, without the burden of *my* damning thoughts. Another instance of making a choice between one's standards and expediency!

Somewhere I have read a definition of expediency as "the dry rot of the human soul." It is true that every time we compromise with our standards for an immediate advantage our characters crumble a little. Really, nothing is worth it!

*THE BEST EXPLANATION OF YOUR STANDARDS IS YOUR OWN LIFE.* The way you live and conduct yourself bespeaks your opinions more loudly than anything you can say. If you are fine you can afford to be charitable toward those who are not. One can always say, "Perhaps we do not know all the facts." Or, "There may be extenuating circumstances." Or, "Perhaps she (or he) acted under great strain and there is some help we could give."

A good blanket remark that covers all inharmonious gossip or discord without offense to either side is, "It is certainly most unfortunate." And you will have spoken the truth. It is not only unfortunate that human beings should err, but even more unfortunate that other human beings cannot be more kind.

However, since all groups of people have among them individuals who are discordant, one must be splendidly poised in one's own inner harmony and charity, and particularly adept at changing the subject to a more pleasant topic in order to preserve one's own personal integrity, at the same time keeping the friendship of everyone.

This habit of speaking is entirely possible. If you achieve it you will be doing the community a great service—you will have proved yourself a true citizen of the civilized world—and you will have preserved your own forces.

A woman astonished me the other day by saying that she did a great deal of good in the world by telling people exactly what she thought of them. Her mouth was a thin, indignant line. Her movements were jerky little stabs of outraged righteousness. I have no doubt that she does some good, but her method is so faulty and unscientific as to make the effect on others temporary to the point of hypocrisy. And just see what she is doing to herself!

My profession is helping people. Experience with thousands of clients has proved that the lasting influence of a *constructive approach* to the problems and faults of others makes it the only logical one.

You will find your criticism or advice falling on better ground in your family if you will soften the blow by referring first to a good quality and suggest that the picture would be quite complete if this little, insignificant detail (perhaps it is a grave fault, but you must not say so) were adjusted. *People will accept the most important criticism if you are casual about it.*

SPEAK FIRST OF A GOOD QUALITY. Just so, in all conversation, if you will first speak of the good qualities of the room or picture or issue under discussion, your objections to it will not seem harsh, but rather smack of intelligent analysis. If you blurt out the fault first, you seem ruthless, thoughtless and careless of the feelings of those who may admire the object being discussed.

NEVER ATTACH IMPORTANCE TO ANYTHING YOU WANT TO ELIMINATE. You should indicate the ease with which a fault may be corrected if you want to see it disappear right before your eyes. This is the soundest logic and most perfect psychology, and is a workable principle at all points in life. I would like to burn those words into everyone's consciousness. *Never attach importance to anything you want to eliminate.*

*YOU NEED NOT COMMEND SOMETHING BAD.* Even if you have wasted an evening at a thoroughly bad play and it is senseless to pretend to your unhappy hostess that you enjoyed it, you can always say, "On occasions like tonight, the audience is always fascinating. Their faces were a study. Any scientist would have loved the opportunity to note their reactions. And was there ever a finer performance than that of the husband's friend? Too bad he didn't have more to do. There was really a splendid idea in the piece."

A cosmopolitan woman I know takes the attitude that she loves the theatre so much she doesn't care what the play may be. Her childish enthusiasm on this point often causes others to smile and some people do not believe her entirely, but she disarms and delights them at the time she is speaking. She is certainly a comfort to a hostess.

If we wish our words to be remembered they must be pithy. But our *manner of speaking is remembered long after the words are forgotten.* This is why we should train ourselves to be so *habitually gracious* that even in anger our words slant across the sensibilities of the hearer instead of penetrating them like a barb.

The *emotional impression* remains even though the meaning of the conversation may have passed from the memory beyond recall! This is the reason why it is such a poor idea to separate from anyone in anger.

Just the other day I heard a woman say, "I recall only faintly the circumstances you mention. I remember only that I was extremely hurt and angry, but what it was about I couldn't tell you." We are offended or charmed by someone's manner of speaking as a rule. If the issue at hand were as important as we think it is at the time, it would remain in the memory.

The expression, "When you say that—*smile!*" represents the whole drama of human reaction to speech. With a smile one can say things that please and amuse—while those very words said without a smile might bring about a most difficult situation.

You may say with an expression of amused tolerance, "You are the silliest old dear," and it will be considered a caress. Whereas, *if* you said it without the smile and the "dear" you might have a fight on your hands. The principle that applies here might be called the art of disarming antagonism. It is an art worth learning. Its sister principle is non-resistance.

*WHEN YOU ARE TEASED OR CRITICIZED* you can close the matter at once by saying with an open-faced, honest smile, "I believe you're right. I do the funniest things!" Nine times out of ten your accuser or teaser will answer in your defense with, "I wouldn't go so far as to say that. You are one of the most sensible people I've ever known."

I once had a housekeeper who was sometimes a little erratic and difficult. She was tolerated only because of her loyalty and efficiency. One day during one of her "difficult" times, I walked up to her and threw my arms around her impulsively saying, "Oh, Minnie, you're just an old darling. What is the matter?"

To my surprise this adamant creature melted instantly and burst into tears sobbing, "No, I'm not. I'm just a crazy old fool!"

If I had tried to show her how wrong she was, she would have defended herself to the death. Such is human nature! Some glimmer of light is shed by this situation on the Biblical saying, "Agree with thine adversary quickly, lest thou perish in the way with him." It is certainly true in personal relationships.

*THERE IS AN INSISTENT URGE WITHIN EACH OF US TO MAKE OURSELVES IMPORTANT AND DRAMATIC.* When someone else does that for us, we become honestly critical of ourselves. If no one else makes us feel important and dramatic we spend our lives trying to prove the value of our ideas and to justify our hope that we are right, infallible and superior. A clever wife supplies this justification and approval for her husband so that he has his whole mind to put on the task of providing and need spend but a minimum of energy on shouting his praises or angling for the spotlight.

This one great human service is the basis of most marriages that last. Since friendships are but another type of marriage, is it not clear that the same psychology would fit in our most casual relationships with others? A man or woman who keeps others striving for approval over *too long* a time is never capable of bringing out the best in them.

The strain toward the satisfaction of vanity is always present. Any mind *released from this necessity is free to soar,* to be witty, to be helpful, to invite thoughts that never lodge with strain. How it simplifies life to understand and apply this principle!

## 4. THE POLICY OF NON-RESISTANCE

*DON'T BE BAITED.* When one is being patronized the best thing to do is to assume the humble role. Without opposition, the one who is trying to "lord it over you" will be quickly embarrassed. In other words, if you learn to take the fun out of teasing, patronizing and accusation, you will not be annoyed much with it. Just go even further than your accuser goes. Say, "You don't know half of it. You should have seen me when . . ."

I once knew a woman whose unkind mother-in-law twitted her for having twins, trying to embarrass the young mother with the stupid idea that it was animalistic to have more than one child. Imagine her surprise when the young woman said, ignoring the direct insult, "I'm so disappointed. I'd been praying for triplets. But I guess God knows best just how many children one is capable of caring for. Anyway, just having one child seems so inefficient!"

*IT IS MUCH BETTER TO LEARN HOW TO HANDLE DIFFICULT SITUATIONS THAN ALWAYS TO RUN FROM THEM OR TO CONDEMN THE PEOPLE WHO CAUSE THEM.* Evidently the situations of our lives are necessary to our experience, for it is a startling fact that if we should be dropped out of a balloon in a totally strange country we would shortly have created or attracted about ourselves just the same conditions that we left.

*MAKE YOUR PEACE WITH YOUR CIRCUMSTANCES* where you are—harmonize yourself within—and life will then promote you; or you will come to be absolutely independent of environment. If you want to change your life—*change yourself*—and your circumstances will change miraculously.

*DESIRE HARMONY* rather than place and possessions and soon you will find yourself keyed to a different, more elevated vibration that will attract its own setting and happiness.

*RESULTS IN LIFE ARE OBTAINED THROUGH WORKING FROM WITHIN,* not from without. To understand this has much to do with poise in conversation. I have known the development of poise through a real, workable philosophy of life, not only to bring *release* and good speech to normal people, but also to cure speech defects, such as stammering.

Stammering, awkward speech, high-pitched voices, nervous mannerisms and tactlessness are all children of fear. This subtle, insidious fear down within the inner workings of the mind interferes with harmonious coordination of ideas, impulses and muscles. To be sure, this fear has many names and motives, but we can wipe it out of existence and *free our natural forces and talents* if we will learn *non-resistance.* A mind that is resisting this and that and the other cannot be spontaneously, intelligently expressive.

Then, too, mental resistance expresses itself in your body, often encouraging tenseness and awkwardness. The relaxation of non-resistance keeps you supple, young and graceful. And on the spiritual side, you will attract *your own* much more surely and swiftly.

*RESISTANCE AND TENSIONS ARE BARRIERS* that keep the best things of life from reaching you—just as tenseness in a muscle keeps the life-giving blood from flowing through it freely, bringing nourishment and refreshment. Tenseness and resistance keep us thinking and reacting in the same old negative ways and make us creatures of habit to such an extent that we become narrowed down to our own interests completely, finally becoming so limited that one day is just like another, only more so.

## 5. LEARN HOW TO HAVE FUN

Often friendships wear thin through sheer monotony. In this way boredom creeps into marriage. If you wish to enliven any relationship, bring fresh fuel to the fire. If you wish renewed interest, then display a *new interest.*

*PLAN NEW ACTIVITIES.* When affection grows stale, when zest leaves your usual companionship, the best thing to do is to *take the person's mind off you altogether* onto a new and fascinating subject, perhaps a hobby. If you and everyone else are tired of your interest in raising guppies, then change to turtles or goldfish. Discharge your cook and personally fix those dishes that make your husband's mouth water. Make a hobby of finding a new salad every day for a month. Invite all the young men you know to help you paint and redecorate the attic. Invite your friends in to follow fliers on a long trip, reading aloud from the encyclopædia about the climatic conditions of the countries over which they pass, tracing their route on a map or a globe with a pencil. Men adore this sort of thing and every woman with a spark of adventure enjoys it.

Lay out a new design for next year's garden and get everyone you know to offer an idea. Organize a hiking club even though you have to start with two members—yourself and your dog. Start a collection of clever advertisements which will one day be valuable as a picture of this era. Men fall in line with this hobby readily.

If you have been too grown-up, too stiff and dull, give a party where the guests come dressed as children and play children's games —from bean-bag to post-office.

If you want your conversation to be lighter and airier and yet you feel as though you were pumping a well when you try to key yourself up to it—*try standing on your head, actually!*

The world is never the same after you have seen it upside down. You can't stand on your head without laughing, no matter who you are; thus it helps you to get the feel of spontaneous laughter and takes some of the kinks out of your mind as well as out of your body. I am advocating this seriously for anyone who wishes to cultivate a new or different point of view. It helps to keep you supple, tolerant, and brings a new look of loveliness into your face. Lady Mendl and women up and down the social scale have discovered its benefits.

An amusing dinner takes the guests to a different house for each course. Buy some toys and children's games ostensibly for your little nephew, but leave them carelessly in the house where the men will see them. You will find them down on all fours running the electric train—shooting the beanshooter and building a skyscraper out of those smooth, clever blocks that are made to cause grown-ups to buy them just as Farmer Jones bought his wife a Morris chair. Put bowls of fruit and cocktail tidbits in the living-room.

*MAKE LIFE MORE FUN AT YOUR HOUSE*—fun that leaves the personal phases time to refill—perhaps to heal and bloom again.

*CREATE THE ATMOSPHERE OF YOUR TALK OR MERRIMENT FROM WITHIN YOURSELF.* You will find it contagious to others. Humor that depends too much upon others usually falls flat. We must learn not to depend upon environment, but to *create each day for ourselves* as though the thoughts and hours were material which we fashion into a becoming garment, not only *beautiful* but *suitable*. Appropriateness is the watchword of the charming woman.

## 6. POISE AND DIGNITY

*BE APPRECIATIVE BUT NOT OVER-AWED.* Since words are expressions of ideas and since all human beings have the same ideas and emotions somewhere along the path of life, there is no occasion for anyone ever to be over-awed in the presence of another human being, regardless of his title or accomplishments. If we will learn to have a *deep respect for life itself* we will naturally be as gracious in our speech to the humblest person as we are to someone in an exalted position.

This is not "manner," but the very foundation of poise, that enables you to be master of your ideas at all times. Do not have one set of words and facial expressions for one kind of person and another sort of expression for the other people. Have one kind of speech and one manner for all humanity.

Tact and courtesy will bring their reward from the paper boy, the furnace man and the scrub woman as well as from your superiors in age or business. If we have only *one* speech and manner, life becomes very simple for us and our minds are continually free and relaxed in any society. Thus we have a *clear and simple dignity at all times.*

Dignity has many strange interpretations. To some people it is a heavy seriousness coupled with a certain forbidding quality that is unapproachable. Dignity is really the composite quality one gains from *good-taste, respect for the rights and sensibilities of others, mental and physical poise, relaxation* and *the strength of being rooted in a beneficent universe!* One cannot have true dignity unless one is fairly sure of one's source and feels in contact with its *ever-flowing power!*

Many of us find much of this assurance in religion and many of us find it in the laws of life which are not named. Poise emanates like a perfume from the person with mental and spiritual roots.

As Queen Christina of Sweden said, "Dignity is like perfume—scarcely noticeable to the one wearing it." So if we are consciously "high and mighty" we may know that we are not dignified!

One more interesting thought. Dignity is not necessarily solemn. One may be gay and amusing without losing it. In fact the perfect assurance of the one who is *joyous at all times* and in whom one *senses strength* like that behind nimble fingers that fly so lightly over a piano, always gives us the feeling of "background" as important and real as that of birth or education.

*THE JOYOUS ATTITUDE* is always appropriate except in the presence of another's sorrow. Only people incapable of the good sportsmanship of a joyous attitude consider it superficial. Depth and intelligence are not revealed in moaning about life and in a gloomy outlook.

Never, in speech or otherwise, strive for dignity. One may not approach it directly. Dignity is the reward and final effect of other attitudes, convictions and emotions. Dignity and charm are like sunlight. They cannot be grasped in the hand. We can only provide an open channel for them to shine upon us.

If we have physical and mental poise, if we keep our hands off other people, and keep our tongues off the personal, and are joyous and sympathetic we shall have a great measure of both charm and dignity. Expressiveness may be a pleasure to the one capable of it, but it is certainly born of an urge to share as well as to show. On the whole, it is much more unselfish than inexpressiveness.

But, it is better to be sincerely gloomy than to be artificially, emptily and jumpily trying to be cheerful. A joyous attitude cannot be put on like a new hat. It must be *built into one's habitual reactions.*

While I seem to have spent some time and space here discussing attitudes, it is necessary to stroke the fires of our impulses and emotions if our spontaneous expression is to be what we desire. For words must have their source in strength if they are to be effective.

I want you to seek deliberately and hold a conversation with someone who may have awed you a bit in the past. Also, I want you to seek deliberately someone whom you have not considered worth bothering with and hold a gracious conversation with that one. It will be interesting if you will have practically the same talk with both people, so as to prove to yourself your own *universality*.

## WORDS TO WATCH

*Vehement* is pronounced *VEE-a-ment*.

*Gist* is pronounced *jist*.

*Repartee* is pronounced *REP-ar-tee* and not *re-PART-ee*.

*Herculean* is pronounced *her-CULE-ean* and not *her-cule-LEE-an*.

*Grimace* is pronounced *grim-MACE* and not *GRIM-mace*.

*Condolence* is pronounced *con-DOLE-ence* and not *CON-do-lence*.

*Pergola* is pronounced *PER-gola* and not *per-GOAL-a*.

*Gondola* is pronounced *GON-dola* and not *gon-DOLE-a*.

*The Kentucky Derby* is pronounced *The Kentucky Durby*. But the *English Derby* is always *DARBY*.

*Decade* is pronounced *DECK-ade* and not *de-KADE*.

*Pretext* is pronounced *PRE-text* rather than *pre-TEXT*.

*Defect* is pronounced *de-FECT* and not *DEE-fect*.

*Nephew* is pronounced *NEV-view* rather than *NEF-few*.

*Culinary* is pronounced *KEW-li-nary* rather than *KULL-i-nary*.

*Cuisine* is pronounced *kwee-ZEEN*.

*Envelope* is pronounced *EN-ve-lop*. *AHN-ve-lop* is French.

*Decorative* is pronounced *DECK-era-tive* and not *decker-A-tive*.

*Dictionary* is pronounced *DICK-shunary* and not *DICK-shun AIR-y*.

*Secretary* is pronounced *SECK-retery* and not *SECK-re-TAIR-y*.

*Subtle* is pronounced *suttle*.

*Chassis* is pronounced *shassy* and not *chassy*.

*Ingenious* is pronounced *in-GEE-nious* (clever, inventive, resourceful), not to be confused with the next word.

*Ingenuous* is pronounced *in-GEN-you-us* (artless, innocently frank).

*Affect* is pronounced *af-FECT*, not to be confused with the next word.

*Effect* is pronounced *ef-FECT*. (Look up these two words.)

*Expert* when used as a noun is pronounced *EX-pert*, but as an adjective is *ex-PERT*. "The *EX-pert* is *ex-PERT* in his work."

*Hypothesis* is pronounced *high-POTH-e-sis* (facts, real or fancied, that support a theory).

*Orgy* is pronounced *OR-jy*.

*Research* is pronounced *re-SEARCH* and not *REE-search*.

In all pronunciations I have given you the "preferred." One will find some exceptions in high places. I have given the most accepted though there is no point in screaming or fainting when one hears an exception.

# CHAPTER SEVEN

## *Holding Your Own*

### 1. DICTION

Nothing loosens one's tongue like having a good supply of synonyms, enabling one to express an idea in more than one way. For this reason, if no other, *one should read a great deal of poetry*. It is filled with synonyms. Poetry not only adds words to your vocabulary, but it also tunes your ear to words and phrases that flow together musically, thus improving your diction.

The word "diction" is often misused for enunciation and pronunciation. Diction is "the use, choice and arrangement of words and modes of expression." If you have at your command several words from which to choose for any given meaning, *you will naturally choose the most fitting one* if you have that *sense of word-rhythm* that is gained from the reading of poetry.

*READING ALOUD GIVES A THREE-WAY BENEFIT.* It is extremely profitable to read aloud, for you think, see and hear at the same time, besides having the practice of actually speaking the words that you would like to make your own. Reading aloud hastens your complete possession of new words and new ways of speaking.

Find your own favorites among the modern and the older writers, but particularly *read poetry*. Not that we expect to go about spouting poetry, not that we wish to eliminate slang entirely, not that we want to learn to speak as Shakespeare's heroines spoke, but that we may understand the richness and the beauty of our language and have some knowledge of its elasticity and breadth in order to correct the poverty of our tongues!

*EASE IN TALKING AND FACILITY WITH WORDS* are gained as we see and hear beautiful speech. When we say something that is incorrect, or use slang jokingly, we should really *know* that it is wrong or it will not be amusing. Which reminds me of the apt definition of a gentleman—"A gentleman is a man who is never rude unconsciously." In other words, when he is rude *he knows it.*

One should never become discouraged by not being able to acquire lovely speech overnight. A good vocabulary is like a bouquet. The words, like flowers, are gathered one at a time. I strongly recommend "Roget's Thesaurus of English Words and Phrases." It is unbelievably simple and helpful and is found in the possession of nearly everyone interested in words, either professionally or culturally. The best commentators and newspaper writers use beautiful, telling English.

Every new word is worth $100 to you. Add one or two words to your stock every day and you will be surprised how quickly your speech will be enriched. It may interest you to keep an account of your words in a little book and see how wealthy you will become in a short time. And this is a wealth that pays big dividends and has the added virtue of being yours forever. No one can take from you what you know.

## 2. LEARN FROM OTHERS

Learn to learn from other people and you will speed up your self-enrichment. One of the best aids in learning beautiful speech and good conversation is to cultivate the friendship of people who talk well, who have a large fund of information and a background of much experience. As a rule such people are much older than the average student. Some old man or old lady whom you now ignore, may be, for you, a rich source of knowledge. And how they love to talk!

The modest little professor who never goes out socially, will pour a liberal education into your ears if you seek him for a chat once a week. Everyone can tell you *something*. All information can be used for conversational material.

Encourage tradespeople to tell you their problems—they will unconsciously drop information about their businesses that you might have to read two large books to learn. Talk to the elevator man, the laundry man, the electrician, and learn how things are done in the world about you.

When you want special information call up the information desk of any large newspaper office. Talk to the buyers, if possible, in the stores where you shop. They can tell you strange tales of fabrics, raw materials, labor conditions, international laws that affect shipping their purchases from one country to another, and the evolution of types of manufacturing. They have the latest news of commerce at the tips of their tongues.

Several years ago I was puzzled to see the name "Lalique" on the back of some china which also bore the name "Haviland." I had long known of Lalique glass, but had never heard of Lalique designs for china. Also, I knew that Lalique was dead. The saleswoman apparently knew nothing of either so she sent for the buyer.

This charming woman told me that Suzanne Lalique, daughter of the famous maker of Lalique glass, was responsible for the china decorations, that she was married to one of the younger Havilands. She also advised me to cling to any Lalique glass I had, as it expresses, in art and spirit, the work of the "one artist universally acknowledged since Cellini." All of this consumed about five minutes and I have felt much richer for knowing it.

By stopping for a moment to talk with the man who came to take my rugs to the cleaner, I recently learned a great deal about dyes. Friends who came to call later were glad to talk about dyes, chemicals, paints, etc., almost all evening!

Buying petit-fours in a French pastry shop the other evening, I spent an extra five minutes talking to the old gentleman who owned the place and learned a number of interesting things about the making of pastry. *If you haven't time to read and study for an education let other people give it to you.*

Bear in mind, one need not have knowledge of a thing in order to have an interest in it. A question like, "How on earth do they ever make that delicate china lace one sees on Dresden figurines?" may net you considerable information as well as animated talk for your guests. Or an out-and-out confession of ignorance along some line adds honesty to these other profits.

Suppose you say, "I'm ashamed to admit it, but I have never in my life heard the opera 'Il Trovatore.' I don't even know what it's about. What is the story of it?" About six people will start at once to tell the story and you will probably have to select the one you wish to tell it to you—or, you can ask them to portray six of the characters and have a hilarious time as they try to act out the story from memory. Or, "Just what is the theme of Noel Coward's last play? We haven't seen it yet." Or, "What are the new books? I've been too busy to read anything for ages."

## 3. STUDY ONE SUBJECT THOROUGHLY

Again, a wonderful way to gain a great deal of information about a great many things is to study one subject thoroughly. For instance, if you should decide to make a hobby of collecting samples of different kinds of lace and learning about them, you will uncover the most fascinating stories of people and places, of wars and princesses, of peasants, of smuggling, of cathedrals, monks and nuns, of coronations and christenings. In fact, lace has played a dramatic role in world history!

For years I made a hobby of discovering all I could about the lost continent Atlantis. As my friends learned of my interest in it, they, too, would watch for any allusion to it and would send their findings to me. People whom I did not know began to write to me from all over the world.

Others are always delighted to tell you what they know about their special work, interests and findings. Choose a hobby and *follow it through* if you want to intensify your interest to others and to yourself.

Of course, you can never be quite certain about the information gained through hearsay, yet the very uncertainty of its accuracy makes good conversation. You can always present your subject with an honest query. "Is it true that ——?" And someone present will be overjoyed to have the opportunity to verify or dispute what you said, according to his knowledge or opinion.

*KNOWLEDGE OF THINGS OUTSIDE YOUR IMMEDIATE EXPERIENCE IS A GREAT PROTECTION FROM SELF-CONSCIOUSNESS.* It is true that the self-conscious person worries so much about himself that he has no time to be vitally interested in anything else.

Someone has said, "The secret of repartee is repertoire." In other words, one must have something prepared if one expects to be interesting and witty. Having something to say gives you confidence which relaxes your mind for those things that may come to you on the spur of the moment.

Another excellent help in gathering information is to *form the encyclopædia habit*. When some subject is mentioned of which you are ignorant or would like to know more, turn to your encyclopædia and read the entire history of the matter.

Everything in the world has a fascinating story behind it. Read up on perfume, for instance. Forever afterward perfumes will be intensely interesting to you and you will be able to turn the conversation to the interesting things you have learned about them.

Often conversation about matters of the moment turns into an awkward controversy because strong and conflicting opinions are held by different members of your group.

## 4. INTRODUCING CONVERSATIONAL TOPICS

We should *know* what is going on in the world at the moment, and discuss it without rancor, but if it is impossible to keep all your guests in a good humor while talking about the things of this day, isn't it much better to be able to *switch to things of another day,* perhaps paralleling the modern question? Then you can drift off into another phase of some ancient personality.

For instance, if there is a strained discussion of present leaders, you can say, "Some people have likened all leaders to Napoleon, who merely wanted personal power and personal empire. But even he had his softer moments. He was helpless in his love and jealousy of Josephine and he adored cologne—or is that just a legend?"

The personal foibles of royalty have always been a rich subject for

discussion. Here is where a reading of biographies is valuable to conversation. Strachey's biographies of Victoria, Elizabeth and Essex,
Stefan Zweig's Marie Antoinette, Emil Ludwig's Napoleon provide
much excellent conversational material.

Suppose you read one of them and start talking about it. You will
draw your hearers out on the biographies they have read and learn
a great deal without effort, as we have already shown.

Many people enjoy sitting about an open fire talking about government in its most serious aspects for hours and hours at a time. Late
refreshments seem only to give them energy for another couple of
hours. Since one cannot give an opinion without knowledge of the
subject, often one's only hope of entering such a discussion is with
questions—and, as I have pointed out to you before, they are always
welcome.

These deep, serious talks are enjoyable to those who like them, but
a great bore to those who do not. Most people do not like them and
want their social conversation to provide relaxation. The truly charming and smart woman *knows how to make small talk about big
matters*. And for her ability to take the sting, the hurt and the weight
out of the things that have tired him all day, a man considers her
charming and *feminine*.

One may really consider this last sentence a very good definition of
tact—*to take the sting and the weight out of things for other people*.

When in a conversation on government, literature, science, or at
any time when you might appear to be giving information which
would imply that your hearers are ignorant of what you are telling,
you can relieve that rudeness by adding three little words to any information necessary to your story. You might say, "This story was
told of Napoleon just before the battle of Waterloo. *As you know,*
he had . . ."

It was once said of a very charming man that he could give people
more information while flattering them than anyone else in the world.
If any of us feel we must *show off* our information, we should hire
a hall and give lectures and not offend our friends by assuming their
ignorance of what we are telling.

One can say, "I've just made a discovery that I suppose the rest of you have known for ages. I just learned that oriental rugs are named for the places where they are made. Isn't that interesting? Those long names are not just to make them sound expensive after all."

Someone present will be sure to have a story of rugs, or of conditions in countries where they are made and sold.

You can continue, "Well, it really seems logical when you stop to think of it, for a man's invention is usually named after him. There are Pullman cars because Pullman invented them. We have pasteurized milk because of Pasteur's researches in bacteria. My mother used to speak of fletcherizing her food because Fletcher had advocated thorough mastication of food. We see amperes registered on our battery gauges on the dashboards of our automobiles because a Frenchman called Ampère contributed so much to the knowledge of electricity."

The others, then, will think of other products or methods that are named for their discoverers and the talk will go on with animation.

Sometimes when a certain subject doesn't seem to "click" and your guests appear to be struggling with it politely instead of enthusiastically, you should *put them at ease by introducing a very commonplace topic*. Such as—"Well, I wish I knew who invented potatoes au gratin. I ate some last night and was up until three o'clock arguing with them." Such a remark is not supposed to be good-taste but it is certainly good conversation, for it will evoke such a number of enthusiastic responses.

Sit down and, for your own information, write a list of ten subjects of common experience; and opposite each subject *write your sentence introducing it into talk*. Then you are ready in any emergency.

Introduce a *common experience* whenever talk seems stilted or hard to start. It is easy to try again in a few moments to take the talk back to an *abstract topic* that offers less danger to good-taste.

The average man much prefers to talk about science of any kind rather than music or opera. Yet, often, we find ourselves surrounded by men who are so devoted to music that they have followed it until they have acquired an almost professional point of view. Know your man.

Every cultured person knows something of fine music and loves it even though he may not be fanatic. In New York there are young men and old who are as devoted to their favorite singers and conductors as any young girl could possibly be to a motion-picture star.

There is a scene in the old play, "Romance," played so long by Doris Keane, in which she, as a world-famous opera singer, leans from her window and has a hearty chat with an organ-grinder. A friend, present at the time, criticizes her speaking so intimately to a mere organ-grinder—to which she replied, "But, why not? We both make the music!"

There is a kinship and warmth that spring up through a mutual love of music that cannot be replaced in the human heart and therefore in human conversation.

## 5. HINTS ON "DISAPPEARANCES"

Here are a few more thoughts on "disappearances." In answer to someone's conventional, "I'm so glad to have met you," which is always acceptable if true, you can vary your answer with, "Nice to know you!" Any such remark said with a gracious smile and a warm pressure of the hand is agreeable. This same, "Nice to know you!" can be said so casually that it can chill any unwelcome advances. Seldom, but occasionally in public, one encounters undesirable people who cling like burrs, insensible to all the ordinary, tactful ways of eliminating them. Then it is a case of "all rules fail in wet weather."

There comes to my mind the undignified picture of a celebrated matron actually running wildly down a hotel corridor to escape meeting some distasteful individual. Rather than be unkindly rude to this unwelcome creature, she took to her heels. Many modern matrons will be rude where they consider rudeness necessary, but they are usually the newcomers with shallow roots.

Most of the time unwanted "clingers" in business, on the street or at a party can be disposed of by giving them a moment of undivided attention, then turning from them completely. Naturally, one does not wish to squelch any honest overture of a respectable person. This discussion is concerned only with the best ways of dealing with boors, pushers and opportunists. Some women simply hand them over to someone else—either by mischievous introduction or by involving them in a conversation with others and then leaving! Anything rather than open rudeness!

This may seem a strange subject to include in a course on conversation, but so many pupils write me of their perplexity along this line that I thought it might be helpful to many others. After all, there is no such thing as heaven on earth—not now, at any rate. We shall always find a "fly in the ointment." Meeting unwelcome people is simply part of social activity and we must take the bitter with the sweet and be good sports about it. One's greatest protection against annoyance is to feel a real love for all people and to act accordingly. You will find that the encounter is never quite so bad as you dreaded it might be. It never hurts one to be kind and generous. When we become so delicate that we cannot stand humanity as it comes, we should withdraw from it completely and become hermits.

## 6. HINTS ON APOLOGIES

Remember that if you are the offender, you owe it *to yourself* to make a proper apology. So often the inexperienced woman stubbornly refrains from apologizing, feeling that she is belittling herself in the other person's eyes. You will always be in a dignified position if you will act from the *desire to acquit yourself creditably*—to feel that *you have done what you should do* in any given situation.

If you will teach a child to apologize for little things, it will be easier for him to cope with important matters. Just a quick little, "Sorry, Mother," will help to form a gracious habit. However, there is a delicate line to be struck here. There is no more annoying person than the one who abases herself at your feet with disconcerting frequence and dramatic abandon. Apologize *for your own sake* if you wish to be considered civilized!

## 7. HINTS ON ACCEPTING COMPLIMENTS

We have already discussed compliments somewhat and have said that "Thank you" is the perfect answer at all times. Other appropriate replies are—"How kind of you!", "How good that makes me feel!", "I'm so glad you think so!", "You've spoken just in time, I needed a lift today!", "Yes, isn't it lovely!", "You've made us very happy.", "Well, you've certainly set before me an ideal of myself to strive toward."

You should be casual (not cold) in answering a young man's compliment. All references to the Blarney stone or an inherited talent for giving compliments are trite and outmoded. When you wish to be gay and mocking you might say, "Thank you, kind sir," or "What a pretty speech! Oh, please say that again!" You should look very pleased when an older person gives you his or her approval, as though you were glad to have won the approbation of such wisdom and experience.

To a young woman one might say, "How generous of you, Mary, when everyone knows that you have the market cornered on that score." To an old friend, "I don't know what I'd do without your approval and appreciation." To a stranger, the faithful "Thank you" is at all times appropriate. An amusing woman said, "If people don't mean their compliments to me, that's just their hard luck!"

The greatest difference in accepting the compliments of people of various ages lies in the warmth of your manner, the tone of your voice and the quickness and gaiety of your speech. It is to be taken for granted that a woman is accustomed to compliments and takes them as one of the pleasantries of life. It is very second-rate to squirm self-consciously, to dig your chin in your chest coyly and to be thinking whether you deserved the compliment.

You will always be self-possessed and charming in your acceptance if you will at least appear to have your mind on the speaker's kindness and generosity or the value of his or her opinion rather than on your own qualifications. This is just another instance of the cultured person's *always* having his mind elsewhere—anywhere except on himself!

## 8. HINTS ON SMOKING AND DRINKING

This attitude is the background of even the impersonal elegance of doing as one pleases about smoking or drinking. So many pupils write me that they are uncomfortable when refusing a cocktail or a cigarette because they feel that the other guests think that they are trying to be "different."

A self-conscious refusal might draw some odd conjecture in the minds of your companions, but a clear-eyed, casual manner and a cool, "Thank you, I'm not smoking," will be accepted as casually as you say it. If you should say tightly, "I don't smoke," your hearers might even suspect your disapproval of them. "I'm not drinking," instead of "I don't drink," will also pass unnoticed in any cosmopolitan group.

If, by some stated difference, such as not smoking or drinking or for any other reason, you seem to have made yourself conspicuous, you can best handle the situation by taking the spotlight, as it were, and turning it to good conversational account. To shrink from notice is unthinkable! So seize the opportunity to tell a good story, to use your ability to take the conversation to yourself *briefly*, and then switch the talk as I am sure you can do deftly by now.

## WORDS TO WATCH

| *I hope you DON'T say:* | *I hope you DO say:* |
| --- | --- |
| "different than" | "different from" |
| "getting married" | "being married" |
| "got married" | "were married" |
| "get finished" | "have finished" |
| "get through" | "are (or am) through" |
| "party" (meaning person) | "person" or "someone" |
| "dove" | "dived" |
| "lit" | "lighted" |
| "sewn" | "sewed" |
| "proven" | "proved" |
| "smother" | "some other" |
| "c'mawn" | "come on" |
| "jewish?" | "do you wish?" |

# CHAPTER EIGHT

## *Pointers in Persiflage*

### 1. YOUR ATTITUDE TOWARD YOURSELF

The cultured person's attitude toward himself is perhaps the simplest of all his attributes. Yet, it is often most difficult of imitation for the unschooled. It is easy to say, "Oh, just take yourself for granted." A fortunate few may be able to do just that without any further suggestion but some of my pupils have required more specific instruction.

We should always bear in mind that when we deliberately acquire a manner that is foreign to our natures, we may make ourselves ridiculous. At best we shall be unconvincing. *We should always stay close to fundamental naturalness.*

It is not *natural* for anyone to be uninterested in himself. Therefore an assumed false modesty is always unreal. But the cultured man and woman have been privileged to discover what an interesting place the world is and they know that *other people and other things* are more fascinating than themselves.

However, you should never say, "But you're so much more interesting than I am," or "I'm just a little nobody," or anything belittling about yourself. Such remarks cannot fail to hurt you.

Then, too, your hearers are under the unpleasant necessity of defending you from yourself. No one likes to be in such a weirdly false position. You are at once placed as being either ignorant or a hypocrite. Usually, the girl who belittles herself is really trying to make her companions important, but she does it at a price which embarrasses them.

*It is entirely possible to exalt your friends without lowering yourself.* As a matter of fact, it is much more of a compliment to them for you to be thinking of them and their interests than of yourself, even comparatively.

One charming woman I know seems to draw up a chair mentally to drink in the ideas of her friends—just as a child might enthusiastically settle herself with little gestures to listen to a fairy-tale. Her face is filled with a glow of expectancy that makes her guest feel that his words are always delightful.

The cultured person *expects* people and the world to entertain and amuse him. This very attitude of expectancy is the demand of the experienced person, that servants and everyone else seek to satisfy. He has found a few shortcuts to draw entertainment from everyone and every situation.

Suppose in a group of talented people a man says to a quiet little woman, "And what do you do that is exciting? Are you, also, a major influence in the world?" She should not reply as she usually does, "Oh, I can't do anything. I'm just a little, stupid wife—just a home body."

She should say (showing that she doesn't mind talking about herself), "Oh, everything I do is exciting! There's real art in my biscuits—and I'm sure Pavlowa could never have gotten around the corner of a bed as gracefully as I do when I make it. And, if you consider hot cornbread exciting, you will admit that mine is a major achievement!"

The woman who can say some such thing without too much mockery in her voice will gradually draw the interest and friendship of everyone. If her voice sounds sarcastic, she will seem to be making fun of the others. *The unguarded tone* of one's voice is the deciding factor in the final effect of one's speech. For this reason, I advocate the cultivation of warm, generous impulses and finer, more delicate thoughts along lines of beauty in all its phases so that the overtones of your voice that reflect the *real self* will be attractive.

However, sarcasm is merely a small personal fault, *while self-abasement lowers you as a type.* "Don't I look awful?" "I'm such a mess!" "There I go again, always putting my foot in it," are remarks to be avoided, for they are like little vines of poison-ivy that eventually choke the tree of personality.

Even the girl who makes witty remarks about her own shortcomings, causing others to laugh, pays too high a price for the laughs! Among my own acquaintances two girls who say funny things about themselves are still unmarried in the early thirties. I do not mean that everyone should be married before having reached a thirtieth birthday, but both of these girls *want* to be married.

A well-brought-up man doesn't want to marry a girl who can be amusing only at her own expense—and his. Some women succeed in spite of such clowning and not because of it!

But, by no means be serious. One should be as frothy and amusing as the circumstances permit. The experienced touch in conversation is a light one, as I have shown you in the earlier lessons. This point will be taken up from another angle in our lesson on story-telling.

Let me repeat—*it is not natural to be uninterested in yourself.* Therefore, when you are the subject of attention, you should be graciously at ease while you listen and while you reply to some remark about yourself. But, since whatever attribute or quality you have that is worth complimenting carries with it either *the help of other people,* or *the use of tools or instruments,* it is only just to bring them into your answers—thus half the pang of self-consciousness will be already eliminated.

For instance, if you are a pianist and someone is extravagant in his praise of your performance, you can say, "Thank you. It has been a joy to play on so perfect an instrument." If the instrument is out of tune (and is in a public place) you might say, "I should love to play for you sometime on a piano that is, at least, in tune."

If someone says your tennis is good, you can say, "This is a wonderfully resilient court—and thank goodness it runs true north and south, so no one has the sun in his eyes."

When someone compliments your riding you can say, "Thank you. Perhaps some day I shall be a credit to the most wonderful teacher in the world, Mr. —— of Meadowhill."

If someone says, "How in the world did you ever achieve such perfection in your garden? It is too beautiful," you can say, "Well, a good garden is a combination of luck and cooperation. And just loving a garden seems to produce miraculous results. Let me show you the best mulching tool ever made."

If someone insists that the credit for something is all yours, you can turn the talk to some amusing story like the one of the little boy who had made a wheelbarrow and when his family admired it said proudly, "Yes, sir, I made that out of my own head and I have wood enough left for two more."

No one works alone in this world (not even writers, for they can only write of what they experience and feel about things outside themselves). Since we are the product of *all the influences that have impinged upon our consciousness,* a compliment is, in truth, not intended to rest solely upon the august pronoun "I." You can accept it much more gracefully if you will realize this intended distribution of credit.

If someone says you have the deepest blue eyes in the world, why should you squirm self-consciously? You had nothing to do with acquiring them! And isn't it artificial and silly to pretend that you don't think they are pretty, when you and everyone else knows that they are? Why not say, "I'm sure I don't know what I've done to deserve them. Perhaps I was lucky enough to have a Norse seaman in my family line way back somewhere. Have you ever noticed the excellent blue in the new technicolor pictures?" You see where this procedure takes you? Right into a stream of active and impersonal conversation!

## 2. TABLE-TALK

Unless the table conversation were general, you would, of necessity, talk to the person on your right and then to the one on your left following your hostess's lead. It is not unusual for a table of six people to break into three separate conversations and then blend back into one a number of times during a meal.

The informal table is increasingly popular. Can there be a more enjoyable time of the day than that hour when one sits refreshed in mind and body, eating good food and sharing a current of lively talk! There are few rules that govern table-talk.

The few taboos are: anything disagreeable, offensive from the standpoint of opinions, anything repulsive or repugnant and, under ordinary circumstances, death—and too much sentiment.

Love and mashed potatoes just simply don't go together. Either the potatoes or the love will dominate—so why put love "out of key," as it were, or why waste perfectly delicious potatoes? An ardent lover will make his own rules sometimes, but, certainly no woman should try to encourage sentiment at table. Yet, many women make this mistake, trying, poor dears, to take advantage of every moment they are with their beaux. I suppose it is only natural since dining with a man represents a great amount of his attention—in a city.

*LIGHT TALK AT TABLE.* Table-talk should not be profound. As a rule the average person is not interested in differential calculus, or the racial consciousness of the Ethiopians when he is either thinking of ordering or eating mountain trout accompanied by Chablis. Gastronomics and the fourth dimension are poor partners.

Barring business luncheons, table-talk should be absolutely light and more or less inconsequential small talk. *Short observations are the secret of success during the early part of dinner* and on other occasions where at least a part of the attention is claimed for doing something.

*CONVENIENT TECHNIQUES.* A clever woman usually develops four different conversational techniques. One that furnishes her with short observations to use while riding in a car or taxicab, while witnessing sport events or at any time where she cannot expect sustained attention and has no right to demand it by unwinding a long story.

Second, she develops a fund of slightly longer remarks for those occasions when more time is to be devoted to talk.

Third, she learns how to draw people out on their pet subjects for really sustained conversation. And *lastly,* she learns how to tell a long story herself. Strange as it may seem, this last point is the least important one in being considered a good conversationalist.

*TIMING IMPORTANT.* Often a good story fails to draw a proper response, even when it is well-told, if it is ill-timed. Certainly, at a table where one *must* turn at a signal (the hostess's turning) to another talking partner, long stories are out of place.

It requires a woman of great presence and humor to break off a story of, let us say, a fire—leaving the house burning with babies sleeping upstairs—while she turns smilingly to the gentleman on her left saying coolly, "I just heard Mrs. —— say that you have just returned from Costa Rica. I hope you were in a nice, cool place—or do you mind the tropics?"

Then, fancy her later turning back to the man she was telling about the fire (who, in the meantime, has been discussing Oriental religions and the beauties of meditation) and saying, "Now where were we? Oh, yes, the fire was terrible! The servants were in hysterics! The—"

At this point she would probably be interrupted by the man's grinding his teeth and saying, "But, my nerves, Madam, are in shreds. Were those children burned to death or were they saved?"

Whereupon, she would, no doubt, say blandly, "Oh, they were spared, of course." And leave the man wondering why the "of course," and hoping with great fervor that he will be "spared" another encounter with this monster of the dinner table!

A more agreeable woman who was more sensitive to appropriateness might have said when she first sat down, "Such lovely flowers! Aren't they an unusual color?"

The man would answer, "Some new development, perhaps."

She continues, "Probably. Very modern, almost modernistic."

He says, "You startle me. Do you mean to tell me that the modernists have reached out into the animate world and the vegetable kingdom to create new types?"

She replies, "That was your idea, not mine."

He: "Oh, I meant new only in the sense that Burbank presented new things. But when you tell me flowers have gone modern, I can't help shuddering."

She: "Don't be alarmed. I don't suppose they'll ever get the petals to grow in angles or to develop chromium bars. Do you really love old-fashioned flowers so much that you rise in this manner to defend them?"

He: "Perhaps it's just nostalgia for my lost youth."

She: "Perhaps it's just the typical masculine grudge against the unfamiliar."

He: "You're judging me rather harshly. If there is such a thing as a typical masculine grudge against the unfamiliar, which I don't concede, you understand—but, if there is, I do not share it and I can prove it."

She: "How?"

He: "Well, I don't know you, but I hope to remedy that state of affairs. Nevertheless, you are what might be called for the sake of this little discussion, unfamiliar to me—and I swear to you that so far from having a grudge against you, I feel extremely pleasant about you."

She: "You *are* kind. But do you suppose these modernists are to be trusted after all? They are discarding every article, every line and every idea that isn't utilitarian. They call their designs 'functional'; isn't that the word?"

He: "And you're afraid they'll decide that flowers serve no practical purpose and abolish them completely, isn't that it?"

She: "Perish the thought! This doesn't seem to be a very pleasant discussion. What is the matter with us?"

He: "We're talking about very pleasant subjects, flowers—and you."

She: "Well, then we're not doing very well by our subjects. Apparently everything can be discussed from a number of angles—and now I'm going to see what angle is most prominent in Mr. Left's mind."

He: "Perhaps I'll improve before you get back."

She (smiling and turning): "A curious question has arisen, Mr. Left, that Mr. —— and I have been 'viewing with alarm.'"

Mr. Left: "I thought that only politicians 'viewed with alarm.' What is your curious question?"

She: "We were wondering just how far the so-called modernists are going to be permitted to denude us of ornamentation—and just what havoc might result if they aren't stopped."

He: "Worrying unnecessarily! A change may be uncomfortable, but it is never fatal. . . ."

This conversation is a perfect example of the ordinary small talk expected of guests who wish merely to fill the air with agreeable, slightly stimulating talk during a meal. Naturally, there is no rule that compels one to stay to these lines.

One of the charms of any conversation is the unexpected turn it often takes. Many people are very witty at table and because of their ability to pour out short, amusing observations they are often sought as guests. But, the average person with small wit and much appetite can prove to be an agreeable companion if he will learn to spin light talk during a meal.

Some people are able to be very serious at table without once giving the impression of heaviness. But, their seriousness will take the form of enthusiastic opinions, passionately stated observations, or deep convictions, all of which are acceptable from them because they keep the talk in short sentences that do not interfere with the progress of the dinner.

During the kind of talk I have given you here, the speakers could eat an entire meal without missing the full flavor of the food, without interrupting the service and without any particular mental effort.

*AFTER DINNER,* in those few moments of first silence in the living-room, a firm or startling statement tends to put new life and unity into the wandering interests of a group. A clever hostess will have one or two such remarks ready, in case all her guests fail to provide the necessary stimulation. The guest who comes prepared for this emergency will always be welcome.

It is not always the best talkers who know how to keep a conversation going. A clever hostess has found remedies for these recurring problems of talk. They are easily met when one is willing to recognize them and supply a simple colloid to the talk.

## 3. THE GRACEFUL GOODBYE

This subject always brings to my mind a sentimental friend who cannot bear to say goodbye at any time, on any occasion. His wife, being more practical, appreciates his feeling in the matter but thinks he carries his sentiment a bit too far.

Several years ago, she tried to cure him by going to extremes and saying "Hello," as she kissed him goodbye when she sailed for Europe. All the sadness was taken out of the parting for him and her friends as she stood on the deck waving and calling "Hello!" as the ship sailed away. She left a merry, hilarious group standing on the pier.

We have discussed leave-taking somewhat casually, here and there, in earlier chapters, but there are some more definite ideas along this line that I should like to give you. I hope you have decided *not to linger after you have started to go.*

Of course, it is quite all right to change your mind about going and decide to stay another fifteen minutes or another hour, but *sit down* and let it be known that you *are* staying. Don't keep your hostess and a number of gentlemen standing, while you wait for Mary to gather flowers, or for Johnny to find his cap.

Certainly, there should never be an abrupt, businesslike leave-taking, for that kind of behavior seems to indicate that you have something more important to do, but, there is a *nice, middle path of consideration for other people* that should guide your departures as well as all your other behavior.

But, I beg of you, do not become so eager to please other people, or to cause them no trouble, that you tiptoe and whisper about through life as though trying to occupy as little space and time as possible.

Since a knowledge of human nature makes most people distrust such an attitude, we are reminded again of Uriah Heep and his false humility. If your self-abnegation really is sincere, you will, unfortunately, be considered too diffident to amount to much!

Never try to make yourself small and unimportant! Wherever selfishness plays no part, it adds to your *natural acceptance* of the best in everything to *choose it unconsciously.* But, if you scurry with cold calculation in your eye to the best chair ahead of someone else you will have misunderstood my meaning.

Take the best for granted, for and from yourself. Occupy space as though you "had inherited the right to do so" when you arrive and when you leave. These are moments when you are the center of the stage. There is no way to change that fact, and there is no sense in trying to shrink or fade on either occasion.

Settle such matters in your mind *now, once and for all time!* Your tongue will be freer and more tactful if you have no uncertainty about whether your own attitude toward yourself is what it should be. If it is correct, you will not waste perfectly good breath apologizing inanely for matters that are inevitable in social contacts.

*IF YOU HAVE A PROPER ATTITUDE TOWARD YOUR-SELF, THE SELF BECOMES FINISHED BUSINESS AND*

## YOUR MIND IS FREE FOR OTHER MATTERS OF THE MOMENT.

When you take leave of your hostess, you should expect *all* of her attention momentarily and she will gladly give it to you. She will express her appreciation of your presence. "I'm so glad you could come," or, "It was good of you to come," or, "It has been so nice to have you —or to see you again," are appropriate.

If she should say, "We must know each other better," or, "I hope I shall see you soon again," you may answer with "I hope so," which will be quite enough if you *look very pleased* when you say it and hold her eye with an honest look of appreciation while you speak.

When a young man expresses his hope that he will see you again, you might not wish to say, "I hope so" in the same manner you said it to your hostess. To him you can also say with a slightly pleased, more casual interest in your voice and face, "That will be nice. Then we could see what might be done about your—" mentioning some interest or appetite or hobby of his that you had talked about. Or you can say, "Sounds interesting. Come over any time, if you don't mind being left unceremoniously while I attend to my weighty duties."

The formality or informality of your answer naturally depends upon the mode of your life, whether in town or country and how well you know or wish to know the speaker. Formal people consider an invitation with no date attached as "no invitation."

The best assurance in the world of continued contact is to have a possible *continuity in your last remarks*. Indicate something that will be continued in your next conversation. One woman I know has an arrangement with her sisters whereby they interrupt each other in tête-a-tête so that their companions of the moment will have an easy approach to them later by going on with the subject they were discussing.

For instance, if one of them happened to be talking with a young man about childhood escapades, and the boy was relating a story about climbing a cherry tree, the sister would interrupt and take her away. A little later the young man might see her across the room at a moment when he is free and cross the floor to her, saying laughingly, "Well, I'm still up in the tree—aren't you going to get me down?"

Whereas if their former talk had been finished he would feel more constraint about approaching her and their friendship might ripen more slowly, perhaps not at all!

With knowledge of these small points in talk, a girl can *provide easy contacts* in conversation that will multiply her popularity in a few weeks. Unfinished conversations bring people back again—bring them together more easily. In other words, there is a track for their friendly impulses to ride out on.

Remember, it is just as hard for the other person to establish a running conversation as it is for you—probably more so. When you establish a channel of contact the other person will usually flow into it gracefully.

Soon after arrival at a party or tea you might establish three or six broken conversations, thus insuring an active evening through re-contacting these partners later. You will find that you have given your evening a gayer tempo—that people will think your manner very easy and comfortable, that you are approachable and you will also appear to be more popular.

Naturally, your best dependence for continued interest is an impersonal topic. *Men fear the personal* as a basis for continuity of friendship (unless they are talking about themselves). A tried and true impersonal bond is the *borrowing of books back and forth.*

A clever woman can establish a dozen or more impersonal reasons for others to have occasion to see her again. Charity work, games, puzzles, contests or amusing wagers are a few bases for further contact. The girl who expects the selfish, busy, shy and preoccupied people of this modern world to seek her because her hair is curly, or because she dresses well, or is good to her mother, is going to have many disappointments.

The popular girl, consciously or unconsciously, provides easy channels of contact with her. It is possible to do so *entirely with conversation.*

When you must leave a conversation you can say, "Oh, dear, I wanted to hear the rest of that," or, "Oh, dear, I wanted to tell you about the time the elephant walked into our living-room. All right, I'm coming." (Leave.) After some such remark, don't you *know* that the next time you see any of the people in the group who heard you, the first remark will be, "Now, what about that elephant?" You will have made it easy for your friends or new acquaintances to be expressive.

In saying goodbye over the telephone, *do not drop your voice.* Never, in a hurt or slightly complaining voice, remind a young man over the telephone (or on any other occasion) that he has not called on you for a long time. You can always invite your recalcitrant acquaintances to a party or a dinner given for someone else. Another advantage of an *impersonal approach!*

It seems to me that young women make more psychological mistakes with the men of their acquaintance over the telephone than in any other of their contacts. I hope you do not let your voice fairly coo the moment you discover you are talking to the handsome chap you met last night at Mary's house.

Have you ever heard a conversation like this? "Hello. Oh, *Johnnnnnn!* I was just hoping you'd call me. Un-huh. Sure do. Watcher doin'? Whyncher co'mover?" This type of talk is dreadful face to face, but without the alleviating presence of your lovely young face it is *fatal!* Women who use perfect English often make the same mistake.

More conducive to a fine friendship is, "Hello. Yes, this is she. Oh, Mr. New. Well, that's kind of you. I enjoyed it too. How jolly! Of course, it would be nice to see you. Yes, Thursday is all right. Just let me think a moment. Yes, Thursday would be perfect. At eight? Yes. Oh, whatever you like. I'm an amiable soul. Right. Goodbye."

Other endings to telephone conversations with both men and women are: "It will be nice to see you again. Goodbye."—"Thank you for thinking of us. We'll be happy to come. Goodbye."—"That will be lovely. Thank you so much. Goodbye."—"It all sounds too wonderful. I simply can't wait. Goodbye."

Naturally, the warmth of your voice, the laughter in it, the intimacy with the person you are talking to would vary the whole effect of these words.

It should be the desire of every woman to leave a pleasant train of thoughts behind her. Resolve here and now, that as you pass through the world you will leave it brighter, comforted and inspired. This resolve will bring tactful, cheering and *stimulating* words to your tongue.

## WORDS TO WATCH

The use of the word ONLY should be given due consideration by everyone with the desire to speak with any respect for the English language. "I only laughed because he was so funny," should be, "I laughed only because he was so funny." The first way means that you were the only one who laughed. The latter way means that you would not have laughed under any other conditions. "I meant only to tell her a part of it," should be said, "I meant to tell her only a part of it." Take this sentence and place ONLY in four different positions in it and see the great difference in the meanings of each change. Well-bred people are not careless with ONLY.

*Archæology* (study of ancient things) is pronounced *ARK-e-OL-o-jy* and not *ARCH-eology.*

*Derisive* is pronounced *de-RYE-sive* and not *de-RIZ-ive.*

*Abdomen* is pronounced *ab-DO-men* and not *AB-do-men.*

*Connoisseur* is pronounced *CON-nuh-SIR* and not *con-nuh-SEWER.*

*Adult* is pronounced *a-DULT* and not *ADD-dult.*

*Adept* is pronounced *a-DEPT* and not *ADD-dept.*

*Pretense* is pronounced *pre-TENSE* and not *PRE-tense.*

*Preferable* is pronounced *PREF-er-able* and not *pre-FUR-able.*

*Comparable* is pronounced *COM-per-able* and not *com-PAIR-able.*

*Romance* is pronounced *ro-MANCE* and not *ROW-mance.*

It is correct to say, *"The coat HUNG in the closet,"* but *"The criminal was HANGED."*

It is preferable to say, *"We are EAGER to see you,"* rather than, *"We are ANXIOUS to see you,"* unless you really mean ANXIOUS. Anxious indicates anxiety and concern. However, many fine writers use this word carelessly.

# CHAPTER NINE

## *Story-Telling and Drama*

### 1. HOW TO USE AND MISUSE WORDS

One of the most *telling differences* between the cultured woman and the woman who is not sensitive to good speech lies in their *use and misuse of adjectives and adverbs* in ordinary conversation.

Just the other day I heard a lovely, but thoughtless, girl say of her dancing partner, "He's terribly clever." Since "terribly" is derived from "terror," one might have supposed that the young man was engaged in inventing machines of torture instead of dance steps. It would have been much more forceful to say, "He's wonderfully (or very) clever." Remember the force of clear, simple understatement.

While modern usage permits a more lax use of words than has ever been countenanced before in good society, an abrupt line is drawn at too much exaggeration. None is preferable. The sub-deb may be "cute" when she rushes in talking about being "practically dead," and "awfully, terribly excited" about her new hat, and the "too, too beautiful buttons" on Mary's dress, during which recital her voice slides in and out, up and down like a trombone.

In a woman more than twenty, such expressions are indications of illiteracy and an undisciplined, uninformed mind. Lack of vocabulary naturally causes one to overwork certain words. It is a good plan to listen to yourself for a day or two and see what words you say over and over again. *Write down these words;* look them up in a dictionary of synonyms or an ordinary dictionary where you will learn other words that mean the same thing. Then you can *vary* those expressions that have become monotonous to your friends and limiting to you.

*ADJECTIVES ARE USED SPARINGLY* in the best speaking, as in the best writing. Too many adjectives used early in a sentence confuse and *delay* the meaning and it loses force accordingly.

For instance, to say, "The bride wore a lovely cream, stiff, shiny satin" is piling up adjectives that require a *mental effort* on the hearer's part to reassemble into the vision of the bride. It is better description and better drama to say, "The bride was lovely in a cream gown of stiff satin that shone handsomely."

When you say, "The most exquisite, delicate pink carnations, large, blue delphinium and airy, dainty, white baby's breath were placed in a heavenly blue, boat-shaped glass vase in the middle of the table" your hearer must *patiently collect* all the words of your sentence and then form them into a picture in his own mind. An evening of this is very boring. It is an awkward way to paint a picture *unless the flowers themselves were of paramount importance at the moment.*

If you are trying to describe the decorations of a room you would "set your stage," so to speak, *before* you decorate it and then add, "In the center of a table in a blue glass, boat-shaped vase there were pink carnations, tall, blue delphinium and white baby's breath looking very fresh and airy."

In other words, if we tire people by asking them to reconstruct our carelessly blurted out descriptions, they are not apt to be interested. But if you *first present an understandable picture* and then place your people and decorations, your hearer does not have to wait until you have finished speaking before he can *begin to visualize what you are saying.*

This point seems so simple and obvious, yet it is a fault of ninety-nine poor speakers out of a hundred. In other words, *we must make it easy for our hearers to follow our train of thought* or they will not do so for very long.

Make a written exercise of describing an experience you have had. After several attempts, proper psychological construction will be very clear to you. Then it will become an agreeable habit.

## 2. HOW TO TELL A STORY

How many times have you heard someone say, "This is a very funny story I heard today, but I'll probably ruin it in the telling. I simply can't tell a story. You know, some people haven't the gift, but then very few people can tell a story well."

Then she struggles through the story, spilling the point in advance and getting the cart before the horse. She usually closes with, "That's a very funny story when it's properly told," though it would be hard to convince the kind people who have produced various sounds approximating polite laughter that it ever could be funny.

Telling a funny story is not different from telling any other kind of story well. If there are no long delays in moving the story to its conclusion—if the speaker doesn't kill your *first interest* by unnecessary details and dates that do not matter in the least—if his words are chosen so as to *give you a clear picture of each step in the story*—it will be effective whether it is serious or funny.

A serious story can be told carelessly with less harm to the final effect of it because its tempo tends to cover over discrepancies; but *comedy must move forward by direct and telling strokes* to the climax. The man who can tell funny stories can always speak effectively *if he wishes* to talk on serious topics. The same tactics make each of them effective.

People of the stage and screen often have a more lasting success in drama after they have been schooled first in the *direct technique* of comedy. For this reason I advise everyone who is interested in being a good conversationalist to learn the technique of story-telling.

*TO HOLD AND GUIDE THE INTEREST OF LISTENERS* is naturally the very backbone of the art of being an interesting talker. An excellent training for any kind of talking is practice in telling funny stories. I want you to try and keep on trying no matter how "unfunny" you are for the first hundred times. Select a good story from some current periodical, or one that you have heard, and practice telling it. Write it out in your own words and then compare your version with the printed version. In this way, you can discover where you are weak, where you digress, where your words are less forceful, less colorful, less neatly turned than the printed ones.

If people don't laugh you haven't told your story well. Therefore, you would probably not tell a serious story well—for either is simply a case of making the point effective.

Another excellent exercise for attaining the ability *to hold the color and drama of any story* is to use the current news. If possible, find a newspaper story of stirring heroism, read it, put the paper down and write your own version of just what happened and how it affected the people involved. Invent a probable solution to the entire matter and tell it concisely and well.

Alexander Woollcott both tells and writes stories with a heavenly style and vocabulary! Pin one of his stories in your memory and try to tell it afterward—writing it first, if you prefer.

*SEEING YOUR OWN WORDS ON PAPER* gives you a much better chance to judge them and also shows you exactly where you need more words than you have, thus giving you the opportunity to acquire those necessary extra words *for a specific use* rather than just collecting them in your mind like columns in the dictionary.

The words that you learn *for some special purpose* will stay in your mind forever. Work? Of course it is work to achieve any worthwhile goal. But if you make a game, a hobby, of becoming a good conversationalist, your "exercises" will be your entertainment instead of your duty.

Besides, if you haven't sufficient desire to accomplish your end, you will not have generated enough mental heat to give you the energy to pursue your course. *Facility in anything comes only with practice.*

Theories and principles we must have. Without them we have no line of action, no pattern to follow; but after all, they only point the way—we ourselves must do the traveling along the path pointed out to us. The experience must be *our own* and no one can hand it to us.

A good story-teller is a popular person. Yet there is always the danger that the one who establishes a reputation for entertaining talk may gradually monopolize conversation and become a dreaded bore. He can't understand the change in the attitude of other people who shun him—the very ones who used to seek him! But, he must understand that it *is* possible to have too much of a good thing, especially in conversation.

One is sometimes reminded of the story of Samuel Johnson's boredom at a violin concert. His nervous hostess tried to revive his flagging interest in the violinist on the stage. She said, "That is an extremely difficult thing to do." Samuel Johnson retorted, "Madam, I wish it were impossible."

None of us cares about the excellence of a story-teller if he is taking up time and space where the more trivial chitchat of personal banter would create a better atmosphere of warm human contacts at table or in the drawing-room. Along with the ability to talk well one should develop the ability to *sense what is appropriate* at any given time. This sense is, apparently, an extra reward for caring about your speech!

Nevertheless, the good story-teller *who knows when to talk* is the greatest comfort to a hostess and a joy to all his (or her) friends. Story-tellers are *made,* not born. Gradually the unstudied success has come to know, from a sheer sense of drama, *whetted by experience,* just how to tell his story. But one can also *study the subject deliberately.*

While I do not believe in trying to copy someone, it is a good idea to read good writers and good stories in order to *tune your head, your heart and your ear* to just what constitutes effective talk. We shall never be able to label the various parts of interesting talk and mix them with mechanical reliability. The result would be soulless and lacking in that spontaneity which alone can fascinate a listener.

I would not try to convince you that there are but one or two ways to tell a story, for individuality has greater scope in this field than in any other. Most successful writers and speakers *take their hearers at once into their confidence.* This is the most usual procedure and the most dependable—the one I advise the beginner to perfect before trying the other more complicated methods where effect is less sure.

Some writers have established a wide audience through piquing the reader's curiosity by a "mystery" beginning. This attack is all right if it works. But if you fail to catch your reader's curiosity, you have lost him.

Suppose your opening sentence, "A shot rang through the night," brings only a yawn from the reader. The average reader (or listener) these days is tired and prefers to be led along with little effort through an interesting story.

The tired, or only slightly interested, mind is more apt to be intrigued by knowing at once what is going on. You are more apt to hold his interest by, "Patricia Atwater, female, white, twenty years of age, blue eyes, brown hair, five feet one inch tall, watched angrily while the officer read those facts on her driver's license." This sentence is an extreme example of taking the reader or listener into the teller's confidence immediately. You have at once a picture and a situation *without seeming to strive for either.*

However, you may talk about the shot fired if you first give a clue of interest to the matter. (Understand my point of view is the conversational one.) You might tell a story like this: "Well, let me tell you about *our* burglary. We were all sleeping peacefully last Tuesday night (if you aren't sure of the date or time, don't stop to wonder about it or to check with some member of the family—simply say, "one night recently" or "last summer"), when we all were brought bolt upright by a succession of shots fired right outside the house, or so it seemed at the time. We were so frightened none of us could speak.

"I managed to get my shaking legs over to the chest and fished out a revolver buried in pink ribbons and lace handkerchiefs. No one seemed to remember whether it was loaded, but anyway it looked dangerous and protective. Just then a man's voice said angrily, 'There you are, you black son of sin! You'll never wreck *my* life!'

"Naturally, we were afraid to venture out of the room. Somebody had presence of mind enough to call the police and when they got to our place they found the livery-stable man drunkenly gloating over having shot a black cat that had crossed his path!"

It is a good idea to *state the subject of your story* always or nearly always right at the *beginning.* Here are several examples of presenting the picture at once, which is the best way to hold the interest of listeners, and to *go into your story with smoothness.* "Speaking of raising hogs—," or "What you said of coffee plantations a while ago was very interesting. Some years ago, an uncle of mine had a very exciting time with tropical laborers on his place. The whole difficulty came about through his not understanding their religious observances. They believe . . ."

Or, "Since you fly you'd be interested in the new type of plane an eccentric neighbor of ours has designed. I suppose all geniuses are entitled to their eccentricities, but this chap does some very strange things. He . . ."

Consider the last example for a moment. So many thoughtless talkers would garble it in some such manner as this: (Remember, the talk is about flying) "You know we have the funniest neighbor. He's a man and invents things—all sorts of things. Some of them are sort of crazy and of no use to anyone, though he did invent a new door-knocker that everybody thought would sell. But it didn't seem to.

"Most of his things are just little gadgets that don't amount to much. Mary, do you remember that funny sort of a hairpin he gave you when you were in high school? Well, anyway, he flies too. I forgot to tell that and that's the whole point of the story. Yes, he flies, or at least he used to in the last war. He was quite a hero they say, though I've never been able to get the straight of the story." ("Or any other story," the listeners think, while wondering just what in the world she is driving at.)

However, if one has a real flair for making seemingly meaningless remarks funny—in other words, making a "line" of being amusingly stupid and roundabout, even this grave fault can be turned to account. But no one wants to be unintentionally funny, though we often are.

Again, nothing stimulates one's facility with words so much as *reading aloud*. Take a book of current interest or one of the old classics or favorites and have a family circle of reading, each taking turns. If this is impossible, organize a reading club and appoint three or four "readers" for each evening. Meet once or even twice a week. This is an excellent way to combine the social life you crave with the other desire to "get some reading done."

In your own story-telling, beware of exaggeration, for one over-statement can cause your hearer to underrate everything else you say and thus he never enjoys the *full effect* of your narrative. Exaggeration gradually undermines other people's confidence in you and when that happens you might as well not speak at all.

*CONVICTION IS THE ONLY THING THAT SUSTAINS
YOUR HEARER'S INTEREST.* He must believe you. You must
use every device to stimulate his confidence so that every single word
you speak has full effect *with the added force of your own conviction.*
Just recently I heard a man say, "Whenever Mary tells a story, mentally I always divide it by two, fold the remainder in half, put it in
a slot where only one end sticks up and then believe what I see written on the margin." (If all of us did this with all gossip, the world
would be a better place.) When we "put it on too thick" we lose the
effect of dramatic contrast.

As G. K. Chesterton put it, "One sun is splendid; six suns would
be only vulgar. One Tower of Giotto is sublime; a row of Towers of
Giotto would be only like a row of white posts. The poetry of art is
in beholding the single tower; the poetry of nature in seeing the single
tree; the poetry of love, in following the single woman; the poetry
of religion, in worshipping the single star."

However, *never say, "I know you won't believe me but this is really
so,"* or in any way defend the truthfulness of your statements.

We should never make complimentary or uncomplimentary remarks
about ourselves. Either is provincial. "Never" is a strong word and
perhaps should *never* be used, for just after writing the last sentence
I recalled an amusing woman who replied to a compliment from her
husband, "I should say I am a lovely person. I'm the nicest wife *you*
ever saw."

You probably know that the best critics have always considered the
Bible not only the best teacher of fine English (it is said that Abraham
Lincoln got his extraordinary command of words from the Bible) but
also as containing some of the best stories in the world.

At the end of this lesson you will find a list of *twenty great short
stories in the Bible* that everyone interested in either speaking or writing should read. Regarding them purely as stories, removed from religion, you will find them sublime in construction, plot and feeling.

In telling a story, *interest and suspense can be bolstered* considerably
by the *proper breathing and phrasing.* Here our first rule of not permitting the voice to drop is needed. Sometimes it adds suspense if the
speaker takes a slightly audible breath between the phrases of an excit-

ing story—because people *do* breathe audibly when they are excited.

Suppose, in relating an exciting experience, you were saying, "We went through the house." It has little effect of excitement if you don't break it up, but unless it is broken up properly it had better be said all on one breath line.

For instance, "We—went through—the house," is all but meaningless. But "We went—(gasp) through the house," is full of drama. To pause after "went" gives your hearer time to realize the probable danger of your going. "Through the house" seems like an herculean task when said in this way. As we have noted before, all forceful speakers learn to pause after a *verb of action*.

The next time you pick up a book or magazine *read only the first paragraph of each story*. In this way you will become sensitive to the best ways of opening a story—to set your stage, as it were, to arrest instantly the attention of your hearers.

Then read the last page of each story to understand more thoroughly the art of closing a narrative, which is almost as important as the opening. *Always close a sentence, or a paragraph, with the words you wish to remain in your hearer's mind.*

Oddly enough, the greatest protection against any kind of unpleasantness is *humor*. The women who can successfully evade every unpleasant issue are those with the ability to make others laugh—to tell *or to read* an appropriate story that breaks the pressure of the moment and often clears the air.

Amusing people apply themselves just as diligently to *the art of laughter* as they do to the art of dress, make-up or speech. It is a mistaken notion that one is born funny or another is born serious. Sometimes I think *too-serious people just haven't cared enough about others* to bother to learn the most useful of all social arts, *humor*.

Someone says, "But my stories always fall flat." Then repeat other people's stories, cut stories out of papers and magazines and carry them around in your bag to pull out and read when you need one! If absolutely necessary you may break into a tense discussion and say, "So sorry to interrupt, but I must go in a few minutes and I want to show you a little thing I cut out for you this morning."

One of the grandest ways to develop a charming sense of humor is to begin by realizing what a great variety of people, ideas and all manner of things there are in the world—by realizing that *nothing is absolute except the urge toward growth and life.* If one's humor is sardonic, sarcastic or sadistic, it may be worldly, but it is not charming. The charming person has a *sense of fun* also, which some people say is distinct from humor.

Rowdy, clamorous, boisterous laughter is to be avoided as much as practical jokes which are always based on someone's discomfort. Let yourself laugh heartily, relaxedly and naturally.

The humorous touch of the modern woman who is also charming, is light, carrying a "touch and go" style. She does not labor for a point. It trips off her tongue, not naturally, but *through practice.*

You can accomplish two things at one time if you will go to call on some elderly person to practice your humor, or try it on children. Besides *benefiting your conversation* you will have done a kind thing and added to your reputation for charm.

No matter how awkward you are in being amusing, keep on trying *until you gain some ease and facility* in light expression. In the first place, the light touch will keep you from being long-winded. It will train you to go directly to the pith of the subject under discussion, which is a most desirable goal if you wish your talk to be *alive.*

To talk interestingly one must be effective, and to be effective one must learn and then *forget* the technique of the effect. In telling any kind of story *eliminate non-essentials.* Say nothing except what carries your story definitely forward to its climax. Amusing side-speeches are to be attempted only by experts.

Most stories are strung out too long in the telling. Yet, a spellbinder always has a *leisurely way of speaking,* though he really wastes no time in coming to the point. Never appear to be hurrying through to the conclusion because of fear of losing interest. If you do a little observing and studying of the openings and endings of good stories you need never fear lack of interest.

But, never permit yourself to enjoy the sound of your own voice so much that you just drone on and on because you can and people are kind enough to listen. People who do talk interminably cause one to think of a man who had his portrait painted and was disappointed in the finished canvas, saying that he liked it better when the artist said it was only half-finished, and adding, "It really takes two people to paint a portrait—one to do the painting and the other one to knock the painter on the head when the picture is finished, before he spoils it." Sometimes a story-teller could use an assistant of this sort.

If one has studied the construction of stories and phrases that are effective he will be in less danger of wandering aimlessly and boringly. We are not born with even the ability to walk—yet many people think they should talk "just naturally" and usually such talkers "just naturally" bore people. Even a little attention to story-telling will pay great dividends in additional facility to you and additional interest to your hearers.

If you are casual in your speech, the most involved phrases and words seem natural and acceptable. Often a young pupil writes to me, "I admire good English, but when I leave slang out of my talk and substitute proper words and phrases for it, my friends think I am putting on 'side' and make fun of me. For instance, if instead of saying something is 'gosh-darned grand,' I say, 'It is exceedingly good,' they rag me about it. I want to talk as you want me to, but what shall I do?"

My reply is, "Speak casually, and the correct words you use will not seem stilted. If you speak naturally without undue emphasis, your words will be heard *for the meaning they contain.*"

Have you ever noticed that some actors speak Shakespeare's lines so self-consciously that the audience cannot understand the meaning the author was trying to convey—while others speak these difficult lines so casually and naturally that you are unaware you are listening to Elizabethan English?

Have you noticed that English actresses can make perfect English sound like "old home week" in a country devoted to slang? The secret lies in their natural and casual manner of speech. So many of us are apt to listen to ourselves when we use a nicely turned phrase—instead of using it merely for the greater degree of clarity and accuracy of our statements!

## 3. SHAKESPEARE AND THE BIBLE

The reading of Bible stories and Shakespeare will do more for your speech than almost any other two books. One way to cultivate a genuine liking for Shakespeare is first to read Lamb's "Tales from Shakespeare," thus becoming familiar with the plots of the plays. You will then have more interest in reading the originals.

## TWENTY GREAT SHORT STORIES OF THE BIBLE

1. Joseph. Genesis 37-48.
2. Balaam and Balak. Numbers 22-24.
3. The Capture of Jericho. Joshua 6.
4. The Wars of Gideon. Judges 6-8.
5. Jephthah's Daughter. Judges 11.
6. Samson. Judges 14-16.
7. Ruth. The whole book.
8. David and Goliath. I Samuel 17.
9. David and Jonathan. I Samuel 18-20.
10. Elijah and the Prophets of Baal. I Kings 18.
11. Naboth's Vineyard. I Kings 21.
12. The Ascension of Elijah. II Kings 2.
13. Esther. The whole book.
14. The Three Hebrew Children. Daniel 3.
15. Daniel in the Lion's Den. Daniel 6.
16. Jonah. The whole book.
17. The Good Samaritan. Luke 10:25-37.
18. The Prodigal Son. Luke 15:11-32.
19. The Lame Man of Bethesda. John 5:1-9.
20. The Shipwreck of Paul. Acts 27.

## WORDS TO WATCH

A word so often mispronounced is *hospitable*. It should be sounded *HOS-pi-tible* and not *hos-PIT-able*. If you have any difficulty in saying it properly, practice the syllables slowly, imagining an accent on the third syllable, thus: *HOS-pi-TIB-el*.

*Denouement* (the solution or outcome of a plot) is pronounced *d'NOO-mah.*

## Never Say

"in back of" for "behind"

"can't hardly" for "can hardly"

"some place" for "somewhere"

"somewheres" for "somewhere"

"good" for "well"

"funny" for "strange" or "odd"

"sure" for "surely"

"a healthy place" for "a healthful place"

"no where near ready" for "not nearly ready"

"providing that—" for "provided that—"

"she don't" for "she doesn't"

# CHAPTER TEN

## *Pin Your Faith on Emotional Effects*

This chapter will be full of last-minute instructions. Forgive me if I hop from subject to subject with little warning. I am eager to crowd into these last pages every helpful suggestion possible. We have discussed almost every phase of conversation, but there are points to be emphasized and ideas to become more clear and important.

Perhaps the greatest problem of any conversation is to make it *spontaneous* and *free from any labored effort.* It is even better to say some tactless thing occasionally, than to speak in too studied a manner.

Everyone's tongue sometimes blunders into tactlessness. The sensitive person is apt to suffer overmuch and to punish herself too much for her lapses along this line. Also, she may decide that she had better crawl back into her shell and keep still rather than to repeat her mistakes again. This attitude is not the courageous one and is not very helpful to herself or to society in general.

All of us owe the duty of expressiveness to the world! We must learn to "take it on the chin" for our mistakes but *never be vanquished.* There is a spirit within us that deserves and demands freedom through us.

It is cowardly to deny ourselves expression through the fear of a little personal hurt, wounded vanity. The person who is not willing to face a mistake is the vainest person in the world. He would like everyone to think him perfect! Is this not the height of vanity?

Hold your head up! Lift your heart up! Turn your face to the light within your own soul! Do not try to wear a mask of perfection! Be content to be a human being of glorious heritage, learning through mistakes but ever pressing onward.

*LET NOTHING THROW YOU BACK INTO SELF-CON-SCIOUS SILENCE.* The stream of awareness flows through your consciousness as the blood flows through your veins. *The source of your life is inexhaustible.* You can always draw upon your source for ideas, words, inspiration, help of all kinds at all times! You live in a beneficent universe and can have from it *anything* if you *approach it constructively.*

Do not make a god of any particular ambition. To do so will make you tense and blind you to the beauties of life.

Learn to *be independent of anything that can happen to you.* Learn to be independent of material things, and even of companionship. Naturally, we want all we can get of these blessings, but they should not take the place of the joy of inner spiritual self-realization. There should be within you a point of poise and peace that nothing of the outside world can touch to alter or shake.

What has this to do with conversation? Just this: Without this realization of your rightful place in the universe you cannot have the poise that keeps your head clear and gives you the *right word* in any emergency. The mind within will deliver up to you the proper response to any given situation if you will keep your channel of expression *clear, relaxed, free* of fear, envy, hatred, jealousies and malice—and give it tools to work with—tools such as truly friendly impulses, honest interest in other people, a respect for your language, and a decent vocabulary.

All of which can be had by any human being! How simple, yet how straight and narrow is the pathway to any *accomplishment!* Yet it leads us through its very demands into heights where our vision is *broadened* to include everybody and everything.

The truly cosmopolitan person feels himself akin to the entire universe. Buying airplane tickets and traveling over the face of the earth will not, alone, make a cosmopolite. We can stay at home in the tiniest village, and by flinging our souls out into largeness become as truly cosmopolitan as the most indefatigable globe-trotter. We can—but do we?

The radio is the greatest proof that, in truth, we are actually in touch with everywhere at all times. Time and space no longer exist for the scientist. A song sung in New York is heard *instantly* in Africa. And though millions may listen to it, there is no sharing, no division of the song.

Each listener may have all of it! If we will give up pettiness and negativeness, clear our minds of any sense of limitation or comparison, we could enjoy the fruits of *pure being* and have every experience necessary to our development right where we are.

When we, ourselves, are freed we are then in a position to free others, to help them toward a more complete self-expression. A hostess who is *sure enough of herself* to give attention to *bringing out the talents* and expressiveness of her guests, will rapidly attain a reputation for charm.

There is a way to make the quietest little person expressive and the clever hostess will find it. When you entertain you should promise yourself that no one will leave your house without feeling that within its walls there was *release and appreciation.*

If a third person has stood or sat silent while two people have an animated exchange of several sentences, some on-looker, or one of the two, should include this silent one by a direct question, "Miss Quiet, what do you think of all this?" Miss Quiet, if she has no ideas, can say, "I'm just soaking it all in, speechless before all this wit and wisdom. But, I would like to know one thing—where does all the enthusiasm come from?" This remark will draw out a further animated discussion even at the expense of joking remarks about her staid point of view.

Sometimes, however, a timid person, who may be otherwise intelligent, will be panic-stricken when asked what he thinks about something, thus his normally clear mind is halted in its operations.

*HERE IS A HINT FOR A HOSTESS* in bringing out such a person. Remember, that if you ask what someone *thinks,* you have really asked him to assume personal responsibility for an opinion and you have also demanded that he make an open avowal of that opinion. Many shy people shrink from such exposure. But, if you ask him what he *feels* about something there is naturally less restraint, for he feels less personal responsibility for a critical opinion. Also, it is much easier to describe what he feels than what he thinks.

*THE FEELING, EMOTIONAL POINT OF VIEW EVOKES
A RESPONSE.* This situation constantly arises in everyone's experience—so isn't it time that we analyzed it and smoothed it out? Another proof that we should approach every subject, in so far as is possible, from the *emotional* point of view, if we want to draw the interest of others along with us and make it easy for them to express themselves!

When asked, "What do you think?" the average person in answering truthfully would have to say, "I don't think!" I do not mean that you should never say, "What do you think?" I merely want you to *understand the effect of what you say.* Use your good judgment as to when to say which.

Remember the story of the girl who thought a young man was cagey and difficult to draw into talk. She failed because she bombarded him with direct and personal questions. The second girl thought the young man responsive and communicative because she involved him in a discussion of family resemblances, in which he used himself and his family as examples of his points, thus telling her a great deal about himself.

By this method it is quite possible to learn all you want to know of the background and family life of the person you have just met. This procedure is excellent practice in keeping away from the personal, but learning what you want to know just the same. The subject of family resemblances, inherited tendencies, "look alikes" and kindred subjects serve in this connection.

A charming man I know will seat himself beside a woman at a party and say, with just the right amount of lightness in his voice, "Are you as nice as you seem to be?" I heard him say this to a thoroughly cultured woman one day, and she answered him in pretended confidence, "No, it's all just a big bluff."

He was so engaged by her refreshing repartee that he almost forgot he was in love with someone else and was about to be married. In fact, there was considerable tension over his dynamic interest in the newcomer. It was only by the most strenuous interference of friends that the first romance was preserved. Such is the glamor of light, amusing and refreshing conversation!

There is no reason why a woman cannot say to a man or to another woman for that matter, "Are you as nice as you seem to be?" Naturally, one must be the type to "get away with" a touch of daring in order to say such a thing.

Everyone is stimulated and entertained by a touch of daring. Men, especially, enjoy a bit of impudence in a woman, if it isn't overdone. Daring, in homeopathic doses, clears the air of tenseness and brings the atmosphere back to human values.

At the house-warming of a somewhat overdone mansion in California, the nervousness of the hostess had communicated itself to the guests. Conversation, in whispered, anemic starts and stops, could not be heard above the muffled music of the orchestra. Newcomers stepped into the great entrance hall, reminiscent of the Grand Central Station, heard the whispering, icy groups and took on the chill themselves.

Finally, an amusing woman arrived. She gazed around at the somewhat out-of-place grandeur and said in a voice that everyone could hear, "Some tent!" Honest and unrestrained laughter burst forth from every corner and from then on the evening was a great success. Impudence can be well-placed. We have frequent occasion to be grateful to the one who can be amusingly natural.

ONE NEED NOT BE A GREAT WIT TO BE AMUSING. A very delightful woman I know, who seems always to be the center of a laughing group, never says anything witty. She seems to regard the world as a very amusing place and is always telling little incidents that in themselves are nothing, but with her gurgling enjoyment of life and ability to make ordinary experiences entertaining she always has an audience.

If she went around the corner to the stationer to buy pens she always returned with some little story of the expression on someone's face, some remark the newsboy had made, some particularly engaging little dog's antics, the banter of a truck-driver and a taxi-driver, or a description of the feel or appearance of the morning.

This woman has beauty and dignity, yet her attitude of being immensely entertained by every little experience in life makes her seem very young and alive. She is famous for her charm. With her appreciation of life and her ability to see the drama of commonplace incidents she makes even the dullest subject delightful. I remember her saying that a newsboy had said to her, "Hi, there, girlie," when he came at her call for a paper—and she finished laughingly with, "Wasn't that beautiful?" A surprising use of words can be just as amusing as a remark full of high wit.

*ANOTHER EXCELLENT SUBSTITUTE FOR WIT* is the use of quick contrast in talk because it is stimulating and surprising. For instance, at the zoo, a woman was watching the hippopotamus heave its enormous body along. Everyone within earshot laughed when she said, "How graceful!"

*SARCASM RULED OUT.* One would have to be very careful not to let the principle of amusing contrast descend into sarcasm. If you make a rule never to employ it about people, but use it only in connection with animals or inanimate objects or abstract ideas, you will be safe. Sarcasm is employed all too often as a substitute for real wit, but it usually reacts unfavorably, in the end, on its user.

*TAKE THE OPPOSITE SLANT.* When any extreme is being discussed and the talk seems to reach a dead end of superlatives and is about to topple grotesquely of its own weight, bring contrast in to save it and to start it on a new tack. For instance, if the talk is about grim and dreadful things, one can usually relieve the tension by saying, "How playful!"

If the talk has exhausted itself on the subject of the hottest things in the world, suddenly switch to the coldest things. If violent colors are being discussed, wait for a lull and speak of the poignant beauty of white—white flowers in white vases against white walls—white gardens, the white silence of the far north.

Then go to the smartness of black—how French women cling to it— other French characteristics as compared to those of the English, Italian or Norse peoples. Thus you will find yourself *at ease all over the world in talk.*

For conversational ability, train yourself to feel the dramatic sweep of the influences back of all the small happenings and appearances of life—and, on the other hand, train yourself to *see* the details so that you do not exhaust people by keeping them always in too windy a sweep in the high places of thought.

*TRAIN YOURSELF TO SENSE THE NEED FOR REST* occasionally in the near at hand, the familiar, the minutiæ of life. A nice balance between underlying causes, deeper motives and, on the other side, the smaller resulting experiences of these forces will make you a very delightful conversationalist.

It has been said that love and lovers need no words. Yet, often love unlocks an otherwise stubborn tongue. Since love clothes the ordinary with a glamorous aura and causes us to regard the world through rosy glasses, it seems to me that a woman in love is the most charming of talkers because her comments must contain inspiring and beautiful appreciation of the world in general.

As a matter of fact, a woman in love is absolutely at her best in all matters. So often a woman writes me saying that because she is in love she cannot be clever and is at a disadvantage. What a mistake! It is not love she feels—but a selfish desire to possess something she feels she is incapable of gaining or holding.

Her feelings of inadequacy that make her uncomfortable are concerned wholly with herself. *One does not suffer through self-consciousness unless the mind is on the self.* True love takes the attention to the beloved one and to the beautiful world in which he lives, moves and has his remarkable being!

There is no fear in love. Love does not plot things for effect. Love makes us honest, broad and un-self-conscious! Love is content to be itself and finds its joy in expressing itself—not in counting what returns may have been washed up on its shore. The beachcombers of love are but a little removed from the gold-diggers!

Let us not concern ourselves with what we will get out of love, but turn our attention rather to what we can get out of life—*life as a whole.* If we pour our best out into life, we will be enriched and love will have this richness to nourish it when it comes along. When we face life as a whole, when we turn our faces to the great universe in which we function, we can *know* that every experience necessary to our development will come to us *at the proper time and in the proper place.* You need envy no one. You need no wiles to get Mary's beau for your own. *Your own will come to you.*

See that your thoughts are fine and large. See that you are not fearful. Relax your nervousness in the presence of men. Do not let your age or tradition trick you into feeling that you have about fifteen minutes in which to trap a husband. Never mind what the *average* person does. There is no reason why you should walk up the aisle with some merely presentable man just because all the sheep of your acquaintance have done so and expect you to do so. Don't try to force your own life into such a narrow groove. Make your life well-rounded.

Be *real* yourself—and *know* that *real* things will come to you. Love cannot find you through the walls of fear, envy, pettiness, self-consciousness, the desire for self-aggrandizement, or as an escape. Do not put your trust in any particular person, but *trust the laws of life.*

Keep your wires clear of all negation and discord, or mere littleness, and you will find that pleasant things will begin to happen to you, that appreciation and tenderness will come to you. There are good enough and love enough and splendid things enough for everybody! Relax your nervous vigilance over petty hopes and fling your demand for *splendid reality* out into the universe.

It is your unconscious demand that is met. We cultivate the *unconscious demand through our daily thinking.* When your mind and heart are filled with confidence and faith in life, you will not feel suddenly devastated and empty when you want to be charming to your loved one. There will be no fear of inadequacy in your eyes but the glow of dreams and a happy assurance.

In such a beautiful frame of mind one's talents flourish, one's mind is exalted and as clear as a bell. The language of love is the language of beauty. Hardness and cynicism drop away and one is not ashamed to admit that life is beautiful. Lovers are never through talking because every little detail of life is magnified and made interesting. They see the relation between the personal and the impersonal and mix them in pleasing proportion. The desire to share their great happiness makes them graciously and delightfully *inclusive.*

The secret of charming talk with a lover (or anyone else, for that matter) is this same ability to slide gracefully from the personal to the impersonal and back again if you wish. Nothing is so endearing as to make someone feel that you are interested in his (or her) welfare —that you are appreciative of his abilities and amused by his wit. Be a splendid and satisfying audience for his dreams and accomplishments, but be sure you do not stay on these topics overlong. By transition of subject, which I am sure you have mastered by now, you should take the talk out into the world again, away from the personal.

For instance, after you have discussed John's talents, his hopes and chances, all of which you have applauded and appreciated, you might say, "There is a familiar strain, a common denominator that all wonderful men seem to share. It is a driving force, a relentless urge that compels them to stay at a task until it is done."

John might say, "My driving force, my urge, is you, Darling." And he will have spoken the truth.

Feminine admiration and the unconscious demand of women who expect men to be strong and accomplished is the sustaining factor back of nearly every great man. The *continuity* of simple faith in a man's ability binds him to a task as no amount of audible urging and nagging could do.

You will notice in this first remark that you assumed John was wonderful without actually saying so. Though there is no reason why you should not tell him he is wonderful so long as the compliment applies to some virtue you wish to nourish.

It is not a good policy to tell a young man, for no good reason, that he is wonderful. You should make him feel that he has *earned* your remark by some reaction to *you*. Often a harebrained young man may acquire the idea that he is wonderful and proceed to seek an ever varying audience on which to impress himself.

A man may be coaxed into better manners and higher performance at any point by your choosing the right moment to say, "Oh, John, you're such a thoroughbred." If he really is a thoroughbred, he will be reminded of living up to it. If he isn't a thoroughbred he will become fascinated by the idea.

Never overdo any of your suggestions. They will lack conviction if you repeat them too often. Make a rule, just for fun, to pay a man a compliment just once during an evening. Be sure it is not a simpering, petty compliment, but something that will make him feel manly and stimulated.

A girl I know once said to her dancing partner, "A dance is something more than a dance, the way you do it. You make it seem so natural—as if you were obeying something deeply fundamental."

Her remark was genuine. She felt it to be true. He was so impressed by her understanding of the workings of his nature that within a month he asked her to marry him.

Say to a man, "Read this book. You, of all people, will enjoy it." You have paid a compliment to his delicacy of understanding. How much better than to say, "One of the reasons I like you, John, is because you're so intelligent."

Another way to pay a compliment to a man's (or anyone's) understanding is to glance straight into his eyes with a look that says, "We understand this point together, don't we?"

The quickest way to get the "feel" of conversations with men in general and also for small talk of all kinds is to *read plays*. In almost any good play that concerns itself with polite people you can learn a great deal about conversational *style and facility*.

If I could recommend only one author, I would unhesitatingly say, "Oscar Wilde." He was a master of the trivial, the effete, the inconsequential. But, of such is good small talk composed! Dust off your copy of Oscar Wilde's writings and drink in an excellent technique.

Here is frothy repartee and pointed, perfumed persiflage. Here is that delicate handling of the feelings of others. Here is that polite enthusiasm that wanes to silence before crudeness or unpleasantness. Altogether, one must assume that Wilde had a sublime understanding of how men and women communicate their ideas in the most agreeable, stimulating way.

It has been my intent to inspire you to express *yourself—to bring out whatever you may feel lies within you* at any given time. An expression of your real self would be just as delightful as the person you may admire and secretly hope to be like. She is the Woman You Want to Be.

I hope deeply that you will be so *lifted by the vision of your own possibilities* that you will never again, so long as you live, compare yourself with anyone else. Imagine a rose's comparing itself with a lily! Or a sunset's envying a song! You are lovely in your own way.

If you should express what the Father of us all put you here to express, you would astonish yourself and delight the whole world perhaps. Naturally, you are different from every other person. In this difference lies your charm and interest for other people. As you become standardized you sacrifice this charm. For this reason, I dislike so heartily to give you set things to say, except as mere examples.

I want your *own free and charming spirit to bubble forth* in agreeable reaction to any contact of your life. You should not speak as anyone else speaks, at least, not deliberately. Say what you are moved to say—and say it as you are moved to say it.

As you find your speech released you will also find that your laughter is more spontaneous and more musical.

The most important point is that you feel no mental or physical restraint to cause you to be stilted or artificial. Bad as it is I would rather hear a loud laugh than the self-conscious simper of the woman who is afraid to laugh, or the hollow mockery of merriment in the voice of the woman with no mirth in her heart. Listen to the laughter of children, not when they are shouting their bravado, but when they are really amused. It is truly engaging.

Carry the muscles of your face in such a lifted position that it is easy to slide right into a laugh. It must be a great deal of work to laugh when the muscles must be brought up from their lowest possible droop.

The lightness and brightness of a gallant attitude is typical of the American woman. The attitude of being a good sport about life is part of our rich American heritage. Certainly we, as individuals, should never let ourselves sag into despondency, dishonoring the finest quality of character our ancestors forged from their own courage.

Whenever I am tempted to think that life is monotonous and burdensome I think of the miles of stone fences our ancestors built. How could they have had faith and vision and courage to stay at such long and difficult building?

We should be ashamed to complain or to let ourselves sink into weak despair. *Let us catch the vision of building something fine for the future* as well as for the present.

Let us, each in his own place, and to the extent of his ability, bring about a richer use of our wonderful language. Let each of us find beauty in strength and ruggedness as well as in delicacy. Let each of us send out into the national and the world personality such feelings and thoughts as will lift it eventually into a higher understanding, away from fear and brutality, and into the bright light of loving agreement.

Having this goal will loosen your tongue, for it will start a stream of force moving within you that can no more be held down in silence than steam can be held back. Here is a fountain of conversational material. Here is a wellspring of feeling that will make your impulses so strong and rich that their vibrations will add verve and importance to your presence. Then other people will listen to you eagerly.

The clear gaze of one who has a *spiritual goal* and is *calmly* on his way *holds the attention of others*. You need not trouble to explain all this to every person you meet. But you should *fill your own heart and mind with noble purpose and meaning,* so that you will never feel empty and inadequate at any time but will always have something on which to stand, something on which to draw when you meet unexpected demands.

Perhaps there is more to say on the subject of conversation, but my greatest service to you is so to inspire you to be sensitive to self-improvement that you will go *on and on and on* in your search for broader and grander self-expression.

It is an endless search, a fascinating and glorious one. As the Bible says, "It does not yet appear what ye shall be." But since we cannot progress beyond the present, unless we *fashion a ladder from within ourselves,* we should not depend upon any other source.

Gain knowledge, read, study, listen and learn, but make your new knowledge merely *fuel for the fires of your spirit* to consume and change into experience.

You have set your feet on the pathway of progress, on the trail of beauty, on the search for what is fine and enduring. Your heart tells you that *this way lies happiness.* Your mind tells you that *this way lies accomplishment.*

If you use your new knowledge for personal gain (and why shouldn't you?) be sure that your gain hurts no one else. Stolen spoils can be stolen again. *Live creatively—not competitively!* Then there is so much to talk about that there is no time to say it all.

But, no matter how pleased you may become with your own ability as it develops—remember "It takes two to bring any truth into the world—one to say it and one to hear it." Learn to listen and to wait, then you will have, at least, the appearance of poise.

Listen for life to happen, *expecting only the best,* counting all good *for something.* Listen with your ears, of course, but listen with your eyes, your breath, your hands, your body—most important—listen with your heart to the dreams and hopes of every human being who can be released sufficiently in your presence to tell you of them. Count them precious and guard the confidence that is given you.

Let your words cover the hurts and mistakes of others. Let your words *clear the vision of every person you talk with.* If the flame of your own idealism has been lighted or brightened, then hold it high so that its light may shine as far as possible.

*ILLUMINED MINDS AND HEARTS* kindled with the passion of helpfulness are the torch-bearers for the rest of humanity. You may have come toward the sun of knowledge for your own warmth, you may have taken up your torch to light your own way, but for whatever reason you took it up you cannot put it down.

*AS YOU POSSESS BEAUTY, IT POSSESSES YOU.* As you enter into largeness it enters into you. As you pour out your song, a greater song enters your heart. May the remainder of your life be blessed by greater and greater freedom of the divine flame within you into the fullest possible self-expression.

If you falter or the way seems to darken, fancy you hear me saying, "Go on!"

Fancy? That will not be fancy, for I shall always be saying it.

# Postscript

## *Adjusting Yourself to Today*

But how to live beautifully today—on less than usual? Faced with the shortages, priorities and allotments of consumer goods, we must make life and happiness for ourselves. No longer is it to be delivered on our doorstep wrapped in cellophane.

We have more to do—and less on which to do it. Yet down in our hearts we know that we have the skill, the courage, the ingenuity, the imagination *and* the all-important good-taste to make a very fair success of living with the materials at hand.

### REDISCOVER OLD PLEASURES

Take the subject of pleasure. It is entirely in what you think about it. For instance, haven't you often heard it said that if people had to work as hard for a living as they do at play that they would think themselves dreadfully persecuted? If you can't play golf, for instance, you still have your legs. And it is sheer wilful moaning that will keep you from taking the long walks that won't cost a penny, but will help to keep your figure in trim and your nerves and your liver in order.

Window shopping is probably a luxury you haven't indulged in for years. Try it—a whole evening of it. If you are married go window shopping together; the playful youthfulness of imagining someone you know or yourself or your house decked in the things you see—or imagining yourself creating lovely things—may possibly re-enchant your marriage. Remember how you and your young man used to window shop and dream? Rediscover the fun of planning. This way lies romance.

415

Consider all your inconveniences temporary—just for the duration of the war. Skip over them as you mentally would some obstacle that is going to be removed shortly. And keep your mind's eye on time to come.

Feel as noble as you care to about what your effort and your money are buying for yourself and the world—but keep it in mind as the most worthwhile objective ever given mankind.

## DON'T GO STALE—LEARN TO RELAX

I know you are not sparing yourself in gifts and work for the Red Cross, bond buying, local charities and civilian defense. But let me sound a warning about getting too grim about it. Athletes talk about "going stale," and those of us who put our shoulder to any wheel, especially at the beginning, are likely to be so intense, so prodigal of strength that we, too, go stale. It takes just a while to get into a rhythm of effort, to find one's second wind, to work to a regular stroke in which we can give only as much as is necessary of that inner essence. You must save some of it for recreation to keep you efficient. Instead of feeling that you are slighting the job when you stop for relaxation and fun, just know that only in this way can you keep yourself at your peak so that you can give your best.

## HOMEMADE HAPPINESS

We shall be using substitutes for many erstwhile luxuries before very long. (They tell us that some of our cosmetics and make-up aids will be curtailed because their ingredients are used as high explosives. Fancy men's just discovering that at this late date—when that's what we've been using them for all this time!) Some of us will test our skill in finding something homemade just as good. It's surprising how often we find the substitute no sacrifice at all.

It comes as a surprise to many of us that one game is about as engrossing as another. It is the sense of contest, of pitting luck and skill against that of the others that makes a game fun. So, parlor croquet, table-tennis, charades, twenty questions, rhyming contests, pitching horseshoes and potato races can be made just as amusing for sophisticates as many more expensive and less hilarious games.

Fashion, as well as necessity, decrees simplicity. And from this need we shall find many lost treasures. We shall pick up many forgotten enchantments in a slower tempo. We may even find that a little money well-spent can buy more than a great sum scattered too thirstily and greedily. We cannot buy happiness any more than we can buy scenery. We can only buy a ticket to it—and then try to catch it in its moods of glory.

Hospitality, good talk and gaiety are the stuff of social happiness. When you are really having a good time, it is not because Mrs. Hostess is laden with her famous gems, or because you are eating from priceless, heirloom Venetian glass. You are happy, if you are, because someone has managed to flash a light of warmth, appreciation, challenge or compliment your way. One of the most telling and touching scenes for me in *Gone with the Wind* was the picture of Melanie entertaining with gracious charm after the war in her bare little house with broken tea-cups without saucers—and no one but the feverishly grasping Scarlett noticed the lack.

We may or may not be reduced to similar straits, but even if we are, we shall do as Melanie did—with seeming detachment from all materialism—rising graciously above anything, spiritually whole and entirely ourselves.

It has never been considered the essence of elegance anyway to depend on luxurious appointments for hospitality. It's nice to have them —but a charming host or hostess can offer the merest cracker with a natural, gracious and unaffected warmth, with all the true elegance necessary for anybody's entertainment. I have noticed that people who had to depend upon fancy trappings for their fun seldom keep their friends or win secure positions.

## CHIC—KEEP IT FLYING

It is good to learn that we are shaped from within—not from without. It is truly surprising what meager materials can be turned to use with style, color, grace and fine effect. Along this line there comes to mind a conversation about the elements of chic—what really con-stitutes it. We agreed that two women can do exactly the same things, be dressed in exactly the same way, and one will have chic and the other will lack it—so we decided that chic was a quality of personality, an inner attitude. True, a lovely hat helped that inner attitude tre-mendously—but lacking the hat the attitude can still work wonders.

So do not be afraid of losing beauty, femininity or chic if you have it—and if you haven't it, this is a good chance to get it. Isadora Dun-can left a memory of beauty that the world will never forget. Her tools? A few yards of cheesecloth and a feeling of grace and womanly dignity.

But women don't look beautiful or graceful in their service uni-forms, I can hear you say. Well, it's their own fault if they don't. What demand or grind of effort can really compel a woman to be slumped, awkward, coarse and careless? Certainly a woman at a serious de-fense job can't be thinking of the figure she is cutting—but neither is it necessary for her to be studiedly unlovely as some of them are—and then blame it on her job.

A real lady can ride a horse all day and win honors in a hunt, and never once talk like a stable boy. The fact that some of them do is beside the point. There is no reason why a lady in a good-looking uni-form with a leather belt and boots should think it adds to her job for her to take on a leathery attitude and imagine she must act like Captain Flagg in *What Price Glory?* Women, like savages, are natural actors, and there is no doubt of the temptation to hitch up the leather belt and swear a bit—but if nobody notices them they forget it like naughty children bringing home talk they heard in the street.

## YOUR DUTIES TO THE MEN

In a real crisis, all comparison or criticism is off. There is only the stricken to help, the fire to put out—the job, whatever it is, to do. Anybody's opinion becomes superfluous. Yet every country, in the height of greatest war effort, has reported that the men wanted their women to stay as feminine as possible—and had voted thumbs down on having the girls wear their uniforms on dates. Men want their women soft and pretty even in short respites from bombardment!

For the duration, then, to be practical and at the same time hold up the flag of decorative femininity, make out a little plan of attire, of grooming and beauty care. As an absolute contrast to the severity of uniforms, have a blouse or so with a washable wide frill all around the neck and down the front—that is unless you weigh over a hundred and fifty. There's nothing so restful to the war-weary eye, the men tell me, as a starched frill. A couple of spring-fresh little seersucker dresses are the greatest comfort at any time—now doubly appreciated. If you can, have three—have one navy, one white—and the other a becoming print. They don't have to be ironed—just stretch them into shape over the shower pole, pat the cuffs in the way they should go—straighten the hem well—and put it on fresh next day. If you can't find the kind you want, then make them.

This war is going to bring about as much home-sewing as anything else. Sewing classes should be held (some of those poor Red Cross aprons I have seen!). And salvaging begins at home. Before you throw away that old blanket, bedspread or portière, see if you can't cut a good-looking cape out of it—and have your tailor, if he's still there, finish the seams for you. Capes have such a gallant swashbuckling look about them, and they are becoming to everybody—and fortunately don't have to be fitted.

One clever outfit I saw consisted of a basic dress of neutral color, with which was worn a cape. For evening the cape was put on as a skirt—full and swirling for dancing—and to the bodice had been added a wide frill of organza. With her hair brushed high, and her face fresh and eyes sparkling, the wearer of this magical outfit looked utterly delightful.

For the sake of your own morale and that of the men who will see you, have a lace dress. After weeks or months at a war grind, I should think a man would give a good deal to see a yard or so of lace. Lace packs well—will go without pressing better than any other material—and always lends its ethereal quality to the nearest woman.

And if you're dressing for the soldiers remember that men adore blue. They also like red and white. No patriotic pun intended. It's an actual fact.

## DON'T FORGET YOUR BODY

*FOR YOUR BEAUTY CARE*—and please care more than ever—reduce your gestures and paraphernalia as it suits you—but don't eliminate a complexion brush and cologne. Brushes are such an important part of grooming—good grooming is good brooming—a little case of them would be the wonderful gift one could give a woman trying to live in minutes and inches.

Don't forget that your hair and skin and eyes show strain long before your body feels it. So don't let your hair get tired—and your skin get weary. Brush them both up—with their own brushes of course. Rest your eyes often—rub cream or vaseline (or vegetable oil used for cooking) into your lashes every night and you will find they will seem to hold their own and even improve.

Incidentally this vegetable oil is very good for oil shampoos—to rub into the base of the finger nails to keep the cuticle in condition and to rub into your tired feet at times.

If your defense job keeps you out in the glaring sun and wind wear oil on your face all the time and let it shine smartly, wearing only lip-rouge besides—or else cover your face and neck with a good make-up base and powder—else you'll soon look like a forty-niner.

When you're so tired you can hardly move—and you feel feverish from head to foot—take a warm bath—drink two glasses of water—lie down—put cologne diluted with witch hazel on your scalp with an eye-dropper (it won't hurt your wave that way)—splash your body with a few drops of rubbing alcohol—put pads of cotton saturated with witch hazel over your eyes and lie without a pillow, breathing deeply for five to ten minutes. You will be wonderfully refreshed.

## DON'T LET LIVING GET DULL

If at any time, this is the time to make an extra effort to keep yourself, your home and your life brighter than ever. Don't let your house get rusty and dull. You may curtail expenses and still have an attractive place. Why not see, just for fun, what it would cost to have some refurbishing done? Even if you can't afford new furniture—but maybe you can—you can bring bright color in with a few pots of paint and a few yards of gay cloth.

Have your handsome things thoroughly cleaned, sprayed against moths and then cover them with some bright washable material. Think of chenille and seersucker for covers, draperies and bedspreads. They will look fresh and never need ironing.

## DON'T WASTE TIME

Your fingers can always be busy even when you are resting. Have a bit of sewing, or knitting, or crocheting always at hand. The minutes that might be wasted in idle talk can be made to count.

## DON'T FORGET TO SING

Singing is the soul's expression. It cleans out the corners of the heart and doesn't let stale emotions pile up. If you can't sing out loud for fear of disturbing someone or being conspicuous, then sing in your mind, thinking the actual words and tune. Do so going down the street and see what it does to your posture, your walk, your spirits. Sing new songs, old songs, hymns, national anthems, football songs, arias, swing, anything—but sing! Get the neighbors in and sing. Set aside a regular evening for a song-fest. A singing nation has heart!

## IF YOU HAVE LOST A LOVED ONE

I dare to enter your personal sorrow because I have helped so many people who were hurt. No one can really walk with us in our dark valleys of pain—and yet, down through the years we all have or will feel the grip of desolation. In war or peace our loved ones leave us—some day. War is but the more deliberate end. I know the clinging of the heart for even one more minute, one more hour, one more year—and the sharp agony of the loss. At such times my deepest pity is for those who have no sense of eternal pattern shaping itself from the fragmentary consciousness of life. Their loss is absolute, unmitigated. But these unfortunate ones are few.

Most of us can lay our bruised lives in the tender arms of infinite love and there find solace and healing. We have a faith, no, an inner *knowing,* that the great universe can lose nothing within itself—that whatever we are in essence, that we have always been and shall ever be. This little life may be but a day in eternity, where the soul dug deeper for its strength and went on finer than before. Ask yourself this question. Would you rather never to have known your dear one— in order to be spared this pain? You know you would not! Then count the days and years you had him—that is a long time to have held something fine—of your own. You have been a privileged person —one to be trusted with fineness, or life would not have given you the trust. As you were trusted then so are you trusted now—to fulfil the highest of yourself—to live with vision and fineness—to be proud of having been a vessel for life and love. You are trusted to know that whatever pattern is being worked out it is balanced and perfect as the universe is balanced and perfect. Your loved one's life was given for the ideal of human freedom—an ideal that comes ever nearer and swings wider every time we fight for it. The peace and grandeur of that fact will settle in your heart and soothe and lift you up. Your courage is sublime—but your faith—that is divine. Quiet joy will come again. Life will flow to you full and strong again. The sun, the spring, work to be done—what you can give to others, these will draw you again into the engrossing artistry of life well-lived. As a tribute to your loved one, make your life and yourself as lovely, as fine, as useful as ever you can.

## HOW WILL YOU STAND AFTER THE WAR?

Above all you do, don't drop out of normal social activities. Be determinedly hospitable. Get out the corn-popper. Have play readings —each of the neighbors reading a part. Reading aloud is being rediscovered today. Alexander Woollcott once said that almost every man has a poem in his vest pocket. And choose your own reading matter carefully. It can be an escape as well as entertainment and nourishment for the mind and soul.

An air-raid warden in London wrote that she reads mystery stories to take her mind entirely from the tragedies that occurred last night and those that may happen tonight. Another woman says that poetry helps her keep closer touch with sane beauty in the harsh duties that tire the body and weary the spirit. Still another devotes herself to historical novels packed with adventure.

The interesting thought was brought out that these tired workers hardly hear the booming of the great guns—one of them even referred to it as "a comfortingly loud barrage"—that they sleep through pandemonium and hear only the tinkle of the telephone bell that calls them to duty. Isn't this further evidence that we can train our sensibilities to register whatever we wish to register and *only* that?

Consider that at this moment you register only the impressions you wish to recognize. It is true!

Consider also that when the war is over you can have from all your experiences whatever you *choose* to bring with you from them. So choose now whether you are going to be embittered, drained, pessimistic and tired—or whether you are going to be disciplined, healthier, better adjusted to reality, more inspired and exalted, and full of plans for the future.

The courage and indomitable spirit of our men and women are going to win this war—and are going to leap into the aftertask of making this a better world in which to live. Not the least important of your contributions will be bringing to it *your* full measure of grace, beauty and *charm*.


**THE END**

*Books by Margery Wilson*

BELIEVE IN YOURSELF

HOW TO LIVE BEYOND YOUR MEANS

HOW TO MAKE THE MOST OF WIFE

THE NEW ETIQUETTE

THE WOMAN YOU WANT TO BE

MAKE UP YOUR MIND

CHARM

YOUR PERSONALITY AND GOD